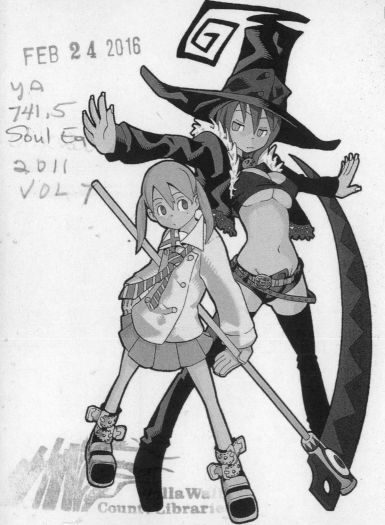

SOUL█EATER

7

ATSUSHI OHKUBO

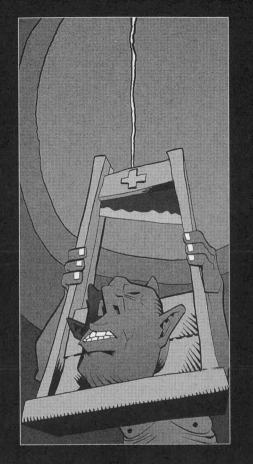

SOUL EATER

vol. 7
by ATSUSHI OHKUBO

SOUL EATER 7

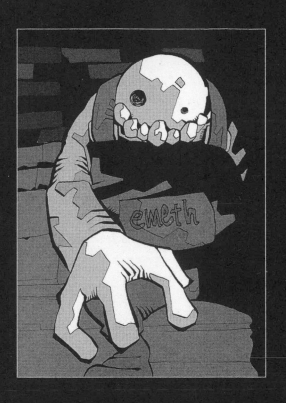

emeth

CONTENTS

Chapter 23: Normalcy 005

Chapter 24: The Trial Enrollment (Part 1) .. 041

Chapter 25: The Trial Enrollment (Part 2).. 081

Chapter 26: The Trial Enrollment (Part 3)...117

Chapter 27: The Bodyguard (Part 1)........159

Let our SOULS drive us

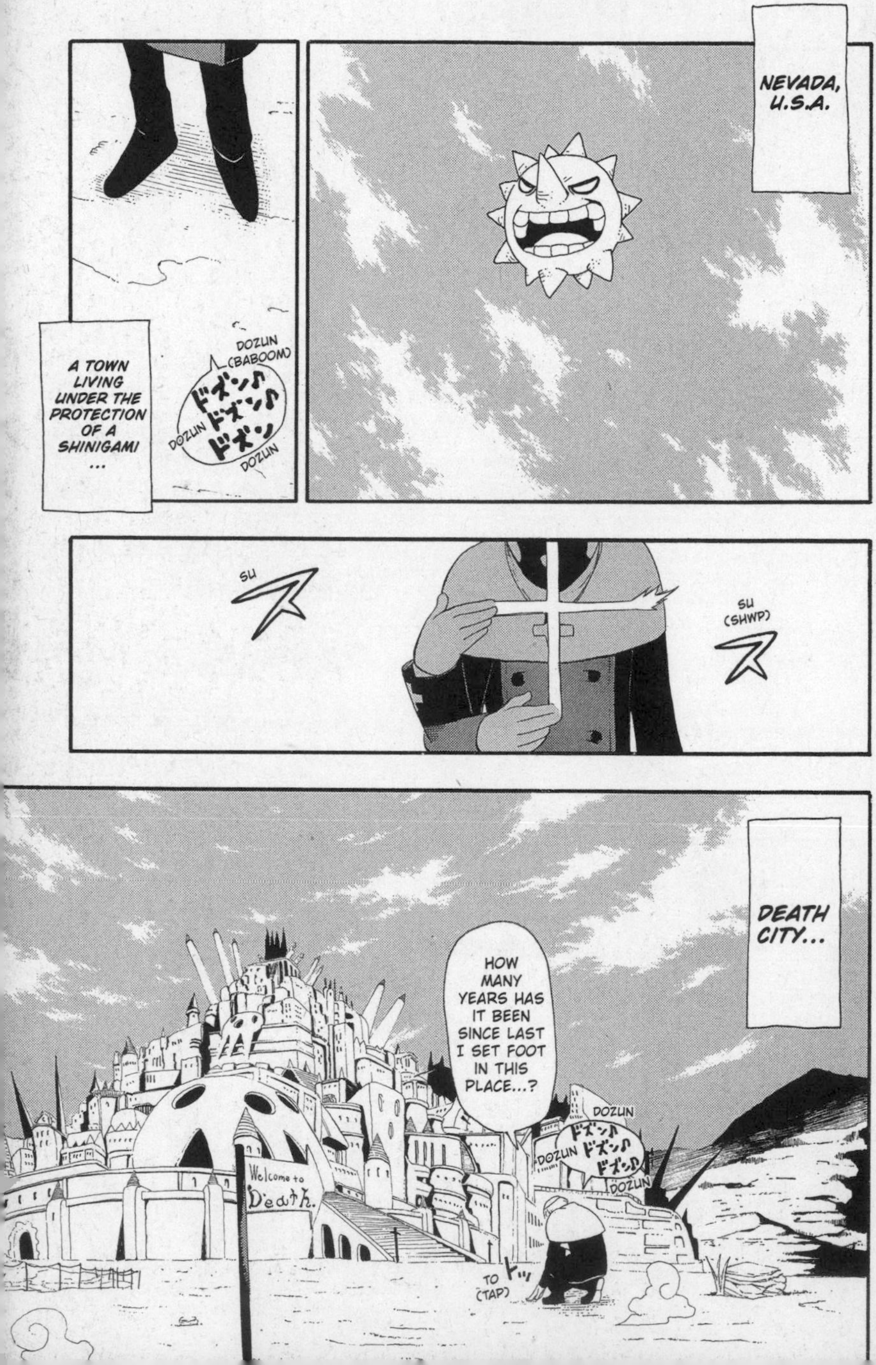
NEVADA, U.S.A.
A TOWN LIVING UNDER THE PROTECTION OF A SHINIGAMI ...
DOZUN (BABOOM) DOZUN DOZUN
ドズン♪ ドズン♪ ドズン
SU (SHWP)
ス
SU
ス
DEATH CITY...
HOW MANY YEARS HAS IT BEEN SINCE LAST I SET FOOT IN THIS PLACE...?
DOZUN DOZUN DOZUN
ドズン♪ ドズン♪ ドズン♪
Welcome to Death.
TO (TAP)
トッ

CHAPTER 23: NORMALCY

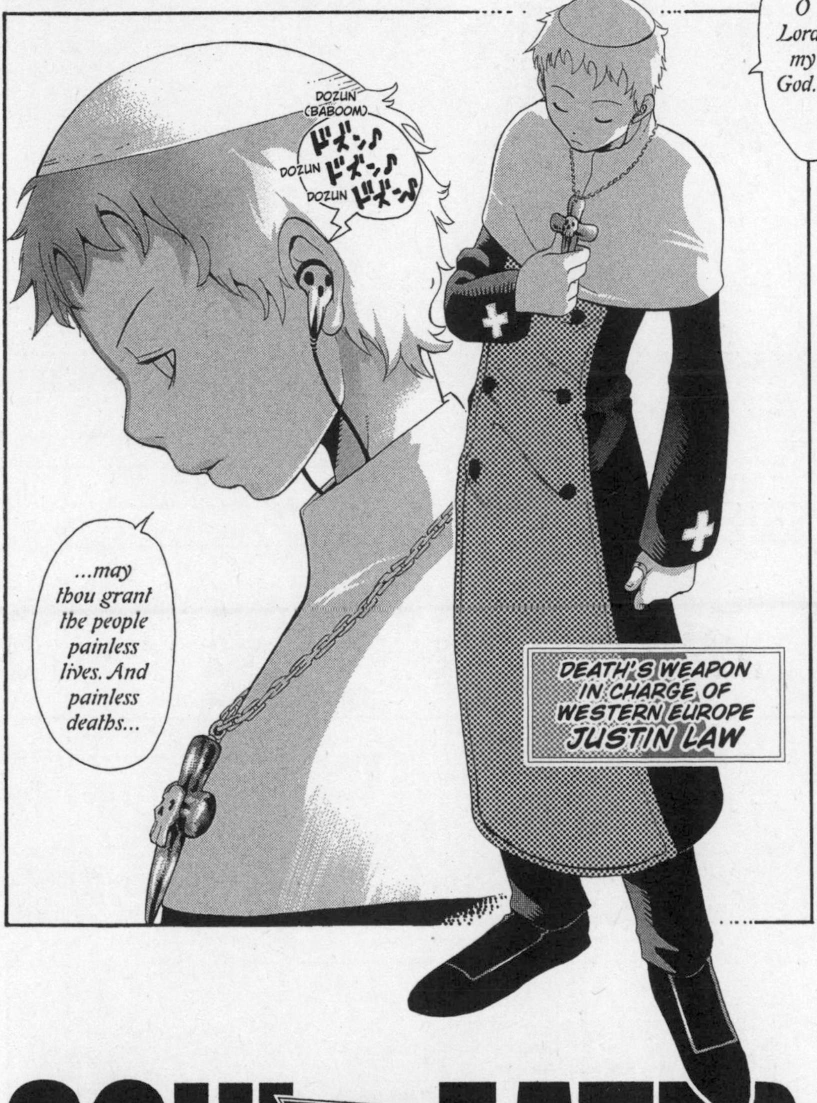

SOUL EATER

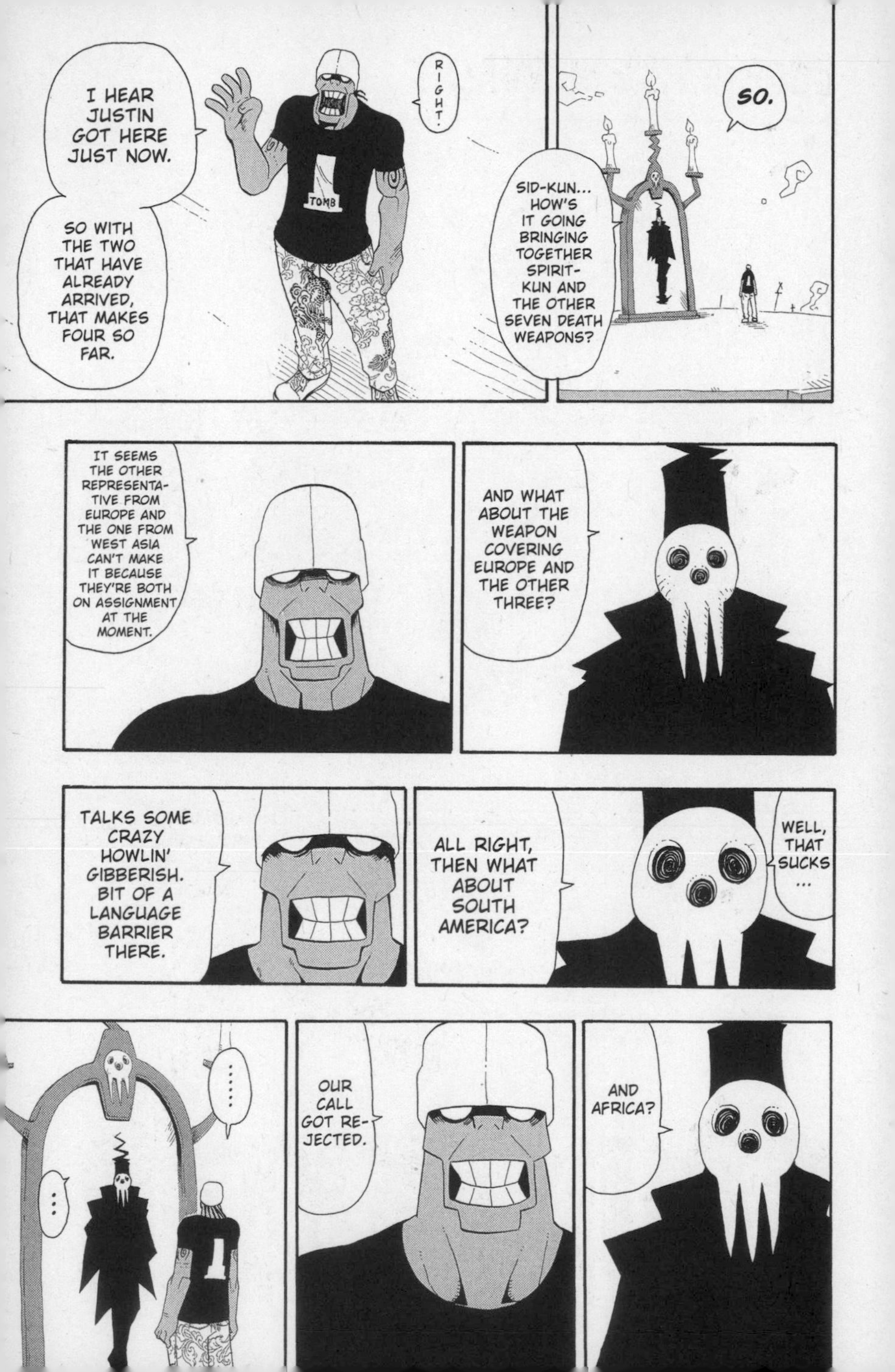
SO.
SID-KUN... HOW'S IT GOING BRINGING TOGETHER SPIRIT-KUN AND THE OTHER SEVEN DEATH WEAPONS?
RIGHT.
I HEAR JUSTIN GOT HERE JUST NOW.
SO WITH THE TWO THAT HAVE ALREADY ARRIVED, THAT MAKES FOUR SO FAR.
TOMB
AND WHAT ABOUT THE WEAPON COVERING EUROPE AND THE OTHER THREE?
IT SEEMS THE OTHER REPRESENTA-TIVE FROM EUROPE AND THE ONE FROM WEST ASIA CAN'T MAKE IT BECAUSE THEY'RE BOTH ON ASSIGNMENT AT THE MOMENT.
WELL, THAT SUCKS...
ALL RIGHT, THEN WHAT ABOUT SOUTH AMERICA?
TALKS SOME CRAZY HOWLIN' GIBBERISH. BIT OF A LANGUAGE BARRIER THERE.
AND AFRICA?
OUR CALL GOT RE-JECTED.
......
...

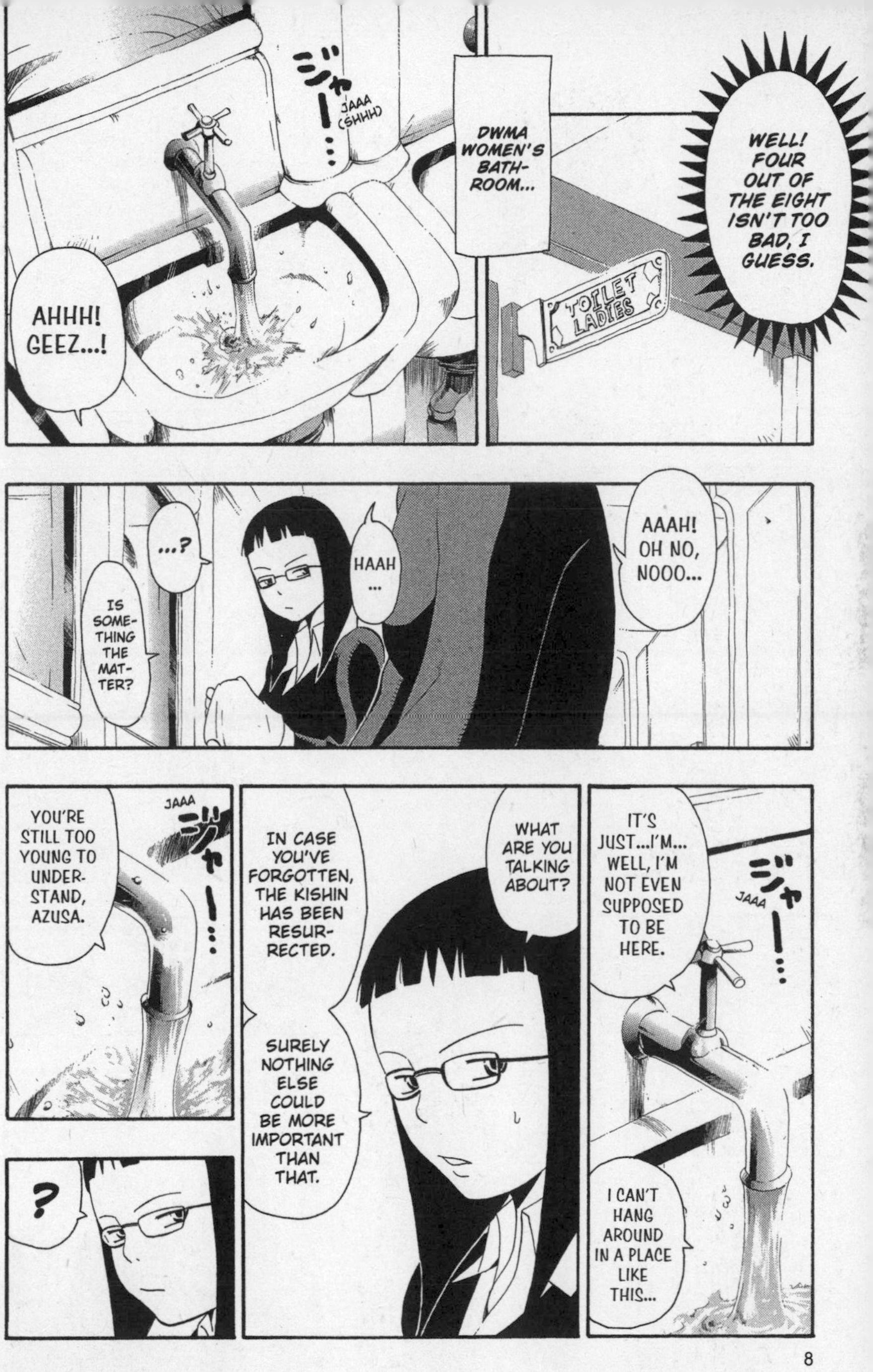
WELL! FOUR OUT OF THE EIGHT ISN'T TOO BAD, I GUESS.
DWMA WOMEN'S BATH-ROOM...
TOILET LADIES
ジャー…
JAAA (SHHH)
AHHH! GEEZ...!
AAAH! OH NO, NOOO...
HAAH ...
...?
IS SOME-THING THE MAT-TER?
IT'S JUST...I'M... WELL, I'M NOT EVEN SUPPOSED TO BE HERE.
ジャー…
JAAA
I CAN'T HANG AROUND IN A PLACE LIKE THIS...
WHAT ARE YOU TALKING ABOUT?
IN CASE YOU'VE FORGOTTEN, THE KISHIN HAS BEEN RESUR-RECTED.
SURELY NOTHING ELSE COULD BE MORE IMPORTANT THAN THAT.
JAAA
ジャー…
YOU'RE STILL TOO YOUNG TO UNDER-STAND, AZUSA.
?

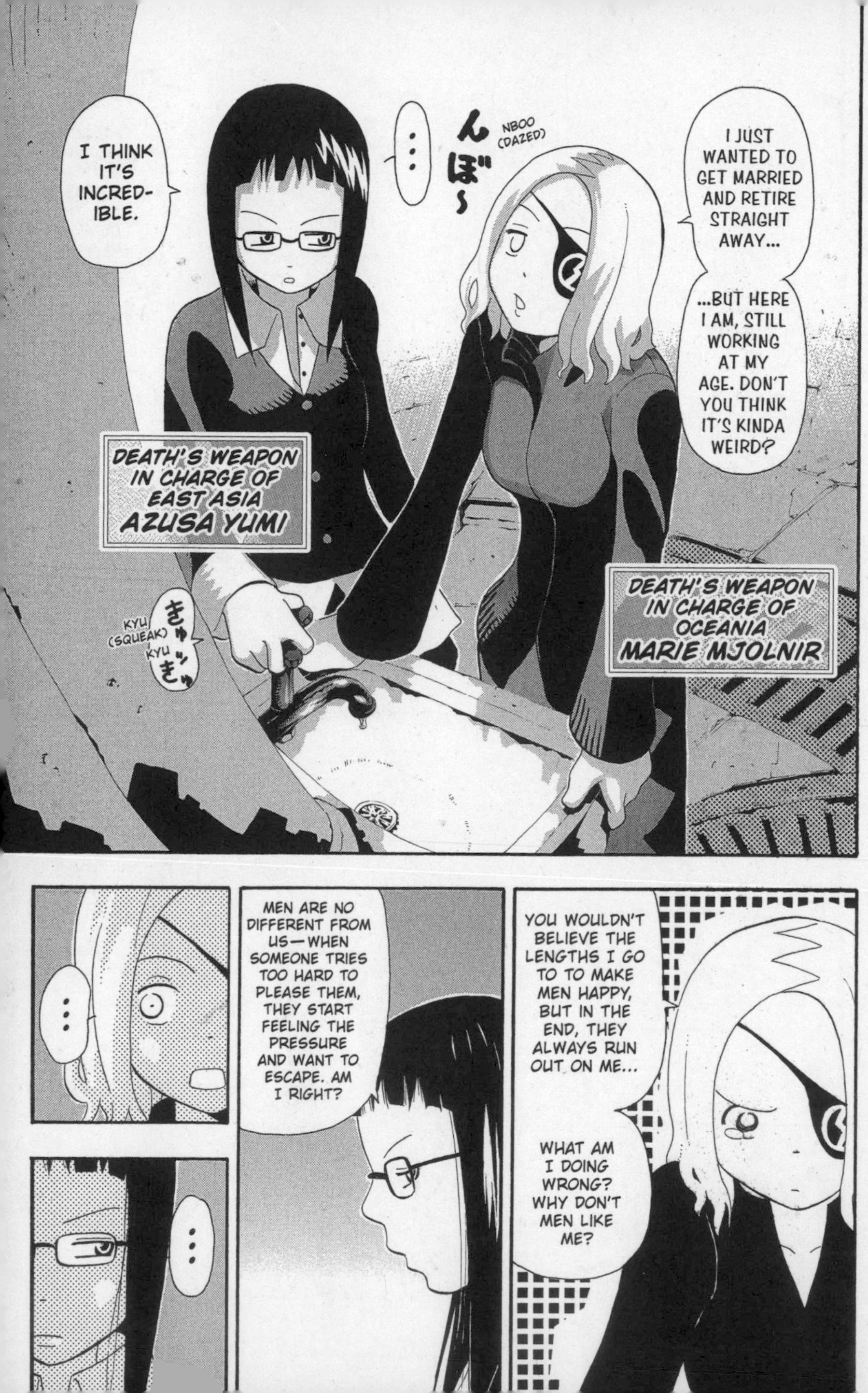
I JUST WANTED TO GET MARRIED AND RETIRE STRAIGHT AWAY...
...BUT HERE I AM, STILL WORKING AT MY AGE. DON'T YOU THINK IT'S KINDA WEIRD?
んぼ〜 NBOO (DAZED)
...
I THINK IT'S INCRED-IBLE.
DEATH'S WEAPON IN CHARGE OF OCEANIA MARIE MJOLNIR
DEATH'S WEAPON IN CHARGE OF EAST ASIA AZUSA YUMI
きゅッきゅ KYU (SQUEAK) KYU
YOU WOULDN'T BELIEVE THE LENGTHS I GO TO TO MAKE MEN HAPPY, BUT IN THE END, THEY ALWAYS RUN OUT ON ME...
WHAT AM I DOING WRONG? WHY DON'T MEN LIKE ME?
MEN ARE NO DIFFERENT FROM US—WHEN SOMEONE TRIES TOO HARD TO PLEASE THEM, THEY START FEELING THE PRESSURE AND WANT TO ESCAPE. AM I RIGHT?
...
...

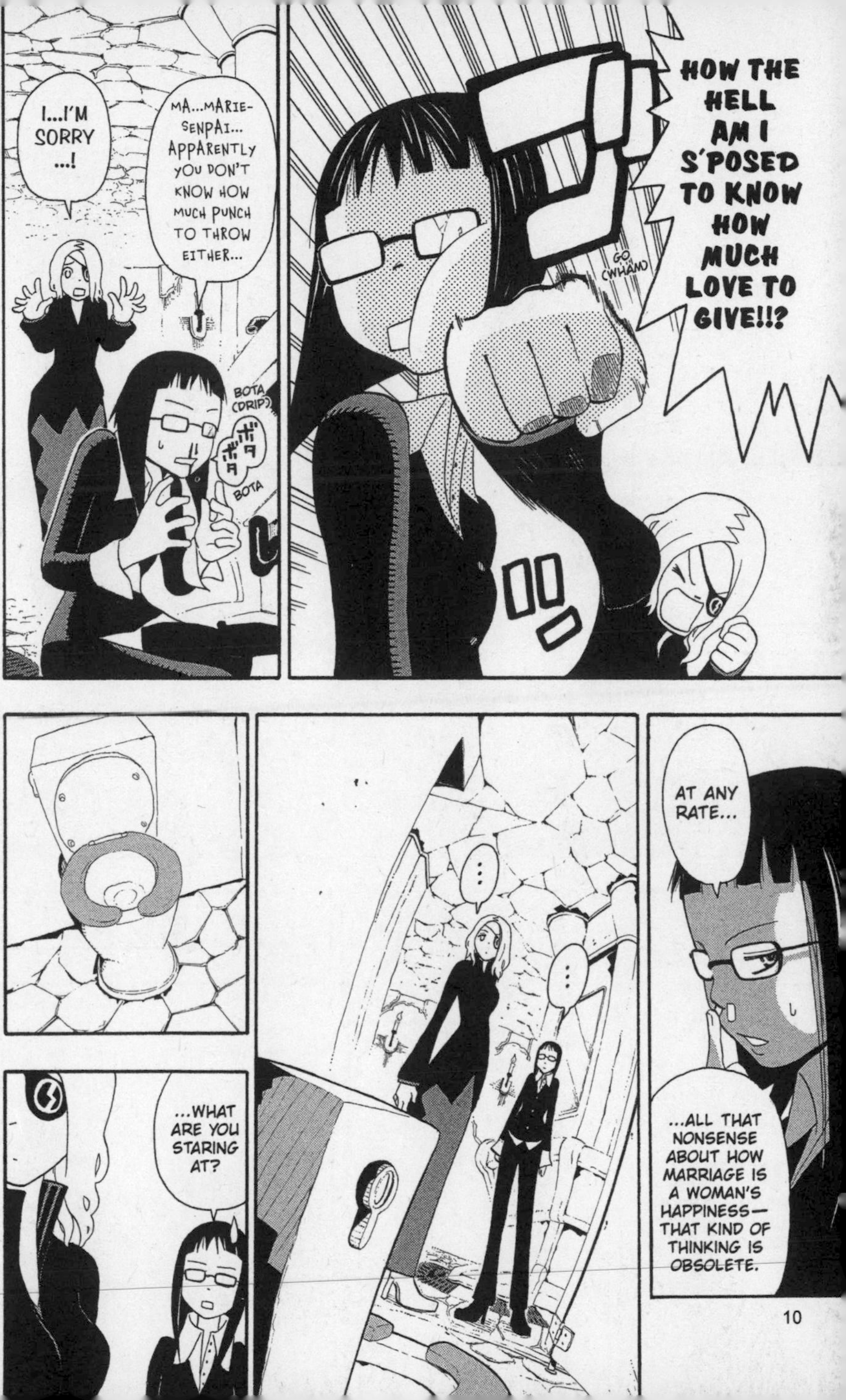
HOW THE HELL AM I S'POSED TO KNOW HOW MUCH LOVE TO GIVE!!?
GO (WHAM)
MA...MARIE-SENPAI... APPARENTLY YOU DON'T KNOW HOW MUCH PUNCH TO THROW EITHER...
I...I'M SORRY ...!
BOTA (DRIP)
ボタボタ
BOTA
AT ANY RATE...
...ALL THAT NONSENSE ABOUT HOW MARRIAGE IS A WOMAN'S HAPPINESS—THAT KIND OF THINKING IS OBSOLETE.
...
...
...WHAT ARE YOU STARING AT?

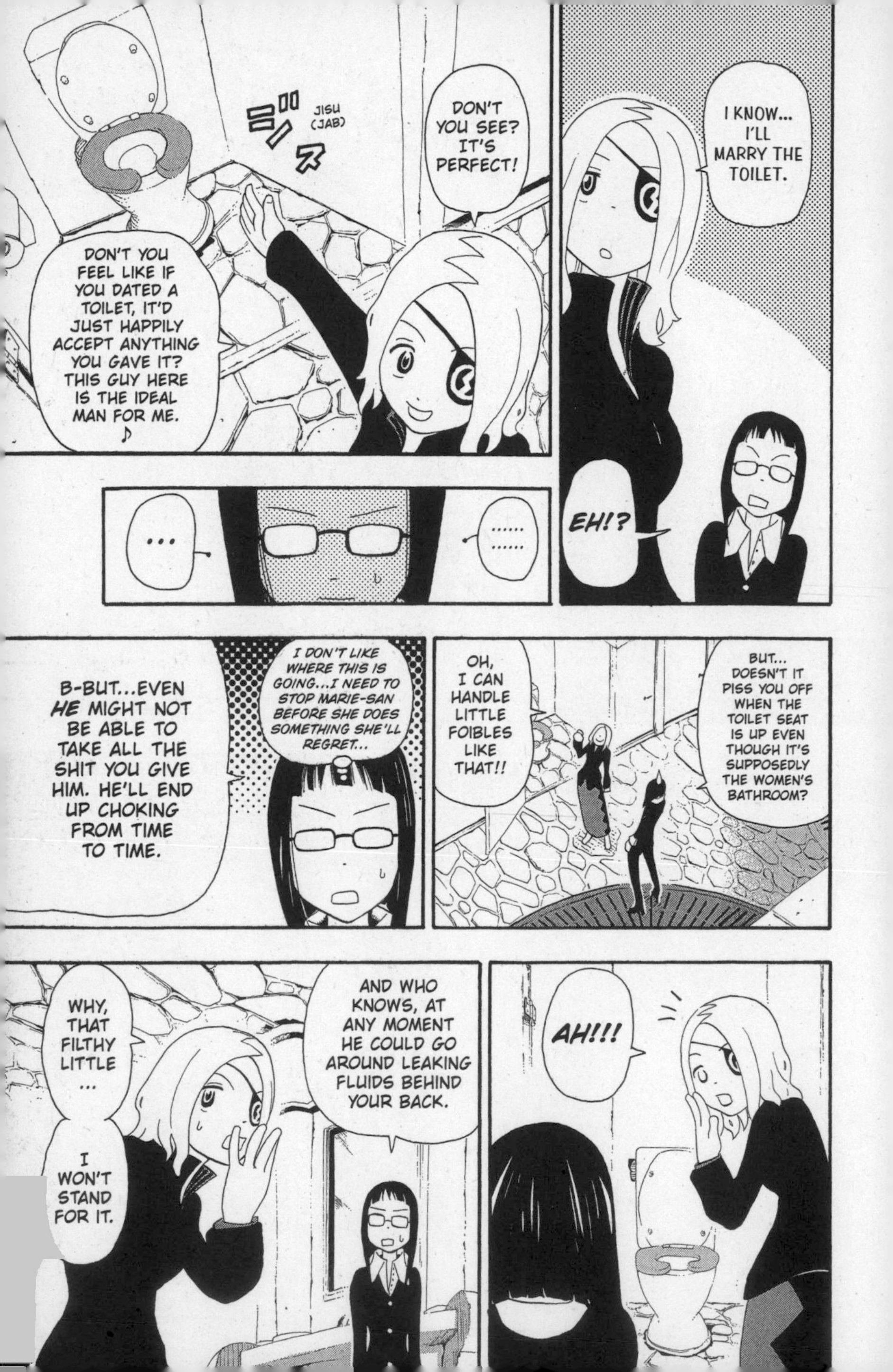
I KNOW... I'LL MARRY THE TOILET.
EH!?
DON'T YOU SEE? IT'S PERFECT!
JISU (JAB)
DON'T YOU FEEL LIKE IF YOU DATED A TOILET, IT'D JUST HAPPILY ACCEPT ANYTHING YOU GAVE IT? THIS GUY HERE IS THE IDEAL MAN FOR ME. ♪
......
......
...
BUT... DOESN'T IT PISS YOU OFF WHEN THE TOILET SEAT IS UP EVEN THOUGH IT'S SUPPOSEDLY THE WOMEN'S BATHROOM?
OH, I CAN HANDLE LITTLE FOIBLES LIKE THAT!!
I DON'T LIKE WHERE THIS IS GOING...I NEED TO STOP MARIE-SAN BEFORE SHE DOES SOMETHING SHE'LL REGRET...
B-BUT...EVEN *HE* MIGHT NOT BE ABLE TO TAKE ALL THE SHIT YOU GIVE HIM. HE'LL END UP CHOKING FROM TIME TO TIME.
AH!!!
AND WHO KNOWS, AT ANY MOMENT HE COULD GO AROUND LEAKING FLUIDS BEHIND YOUR BACK.
WHY, THAT FILTHY LITTLE ...
I WON'T STAND FOR IT.

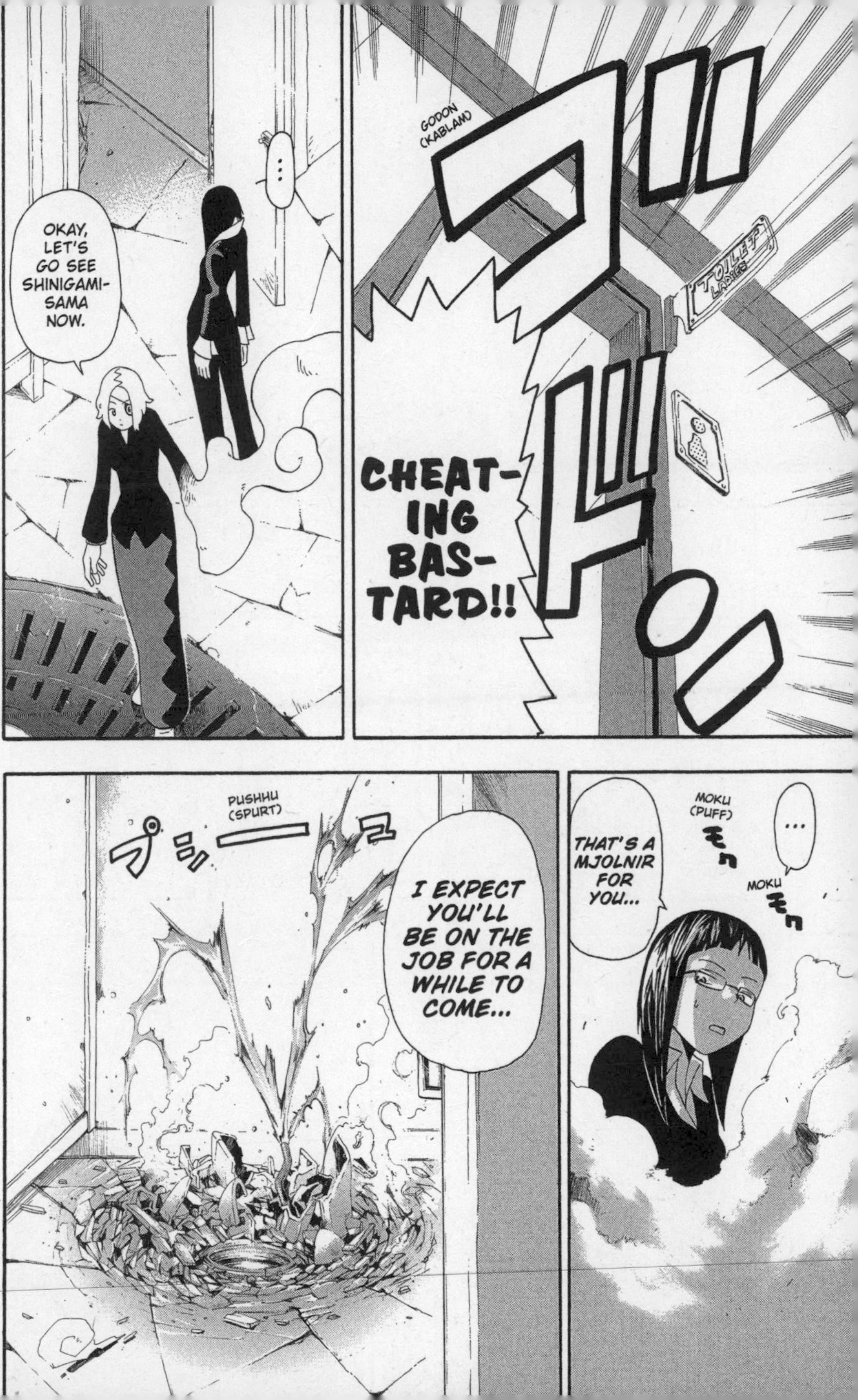
GODON (KABLAM)
CHEAT-ING BAS-TARD!!
...
OKAY, LET'S GO SEE SHINIGAMI-SAMA NOW.
...
MOKU (PUFF)
THAT'S A MJOLNIR FOR YOU...
MOKU
PUSHHU (SPURT)
I EXPECT YOU'LL BE ON THE JOB FOR A WHILE TO COME...

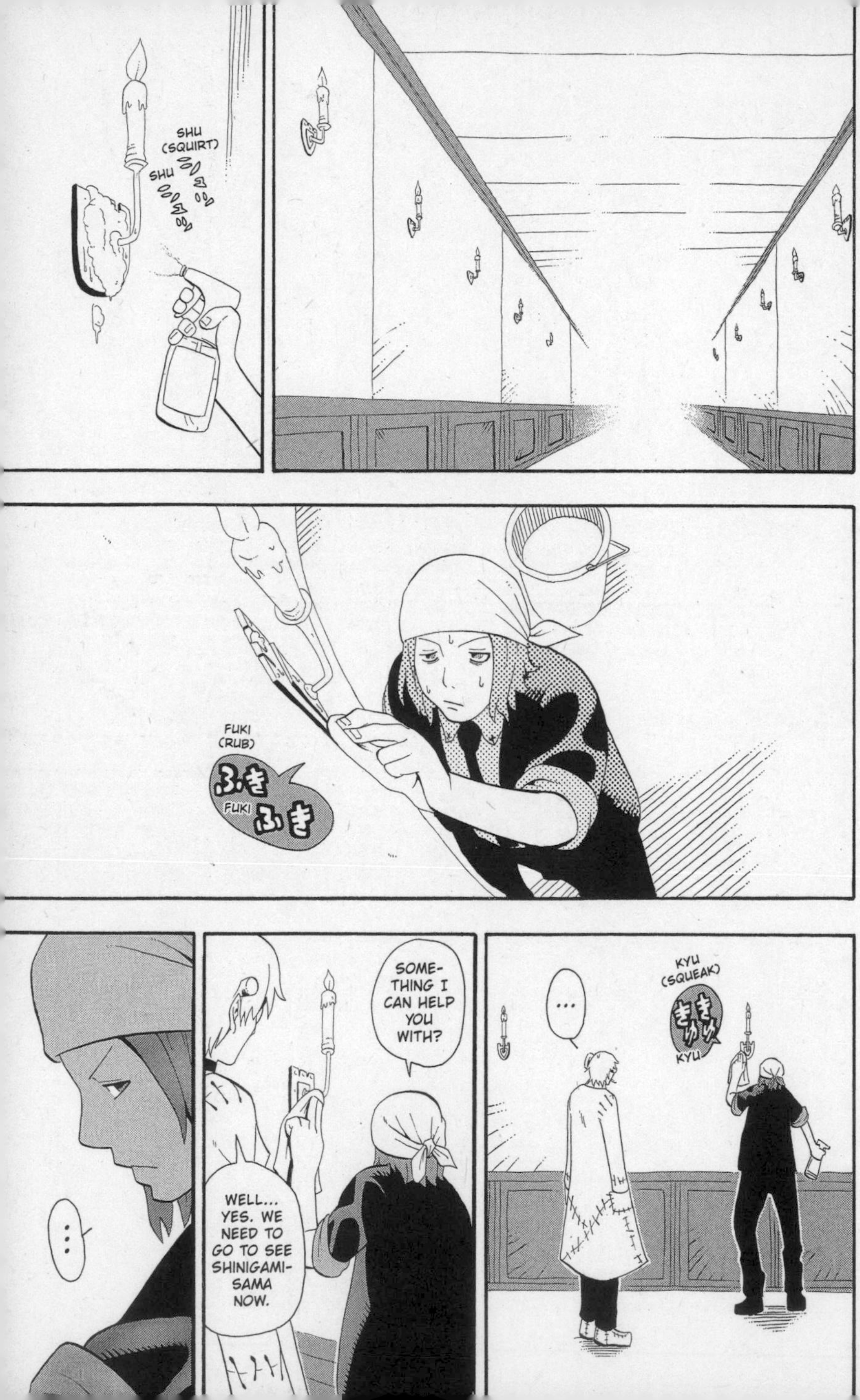
SHU (SQUIRT)
SHU
FUKI (RUB)
ふき FUKI ふき
...
KYU (SQUEAK)
KYU
SOME-THING I CAN HELP YOU WITH?
WELL... YES. WE NEED TO GO TO SEE SHINIGAMI-SAMA NOW.
...

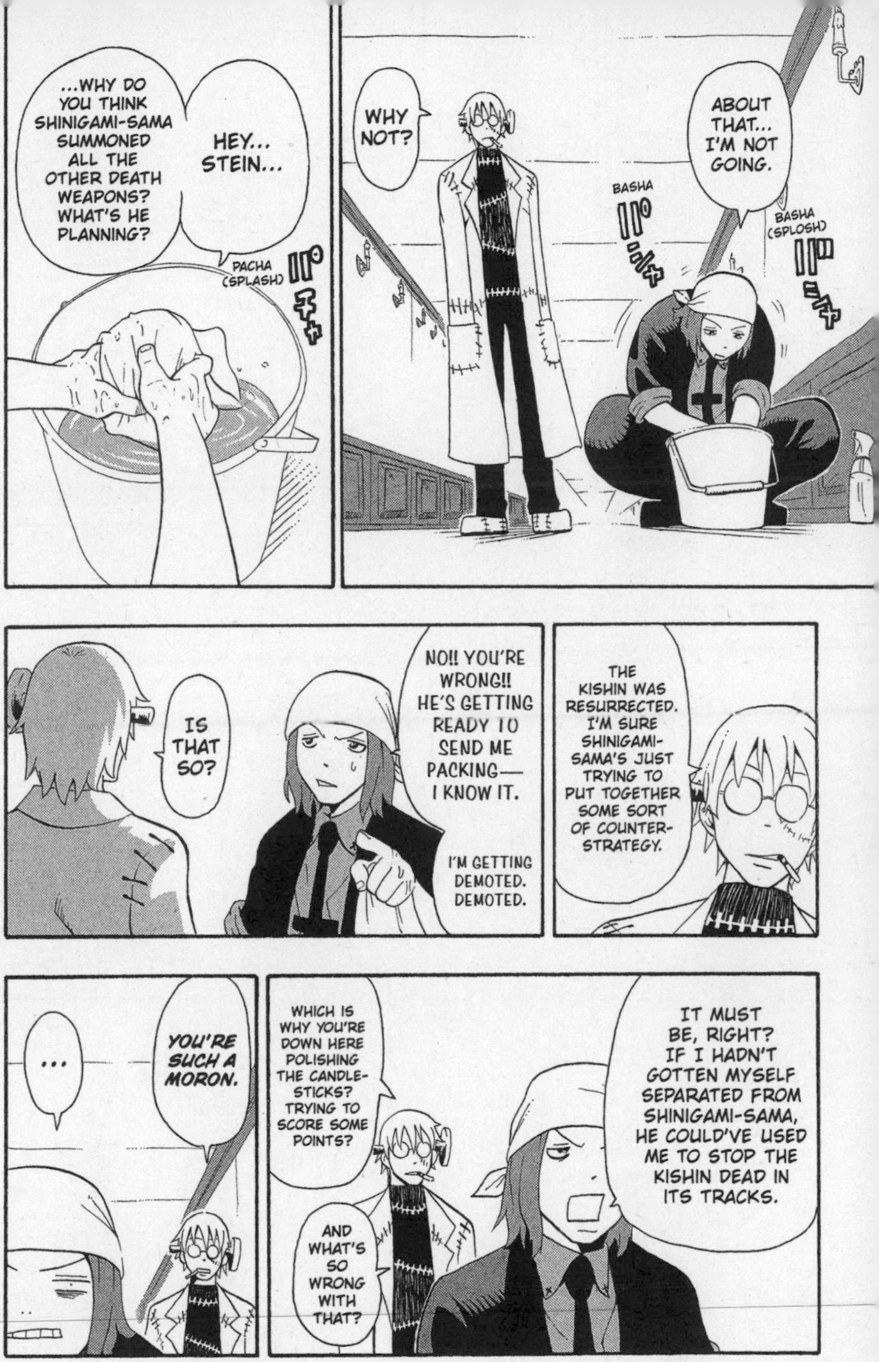
ABOUT THAT... I'M NOT GOING.
BASHA (SPLOSH)
BASHA
WHY NOT?
HEY... STEIN...
...WHY DO YOU THINK SHINIGAMI-SAMA SUMMONED ALL THE OTHER DEATH WEAPONS? WHAT'S HE PLANNING?
PACHA (SPLASH)
THE KISHIN WAS RESURRECTED. I'M SURE SHINIGAMI-SAMA'S JUST TRYING TO PUT TOGETHER SOME SORT OF COUNTER-STRATEGY.
NO!! YOU'RE WRONG!! HE'S GETTING READY TO SEND ME PACKING— I KNOW IT.
I'M GETTING DEMOTED. DEMOTED.
IS THAT SO?
IT MUST BE, RIGHT? IF I HADN'T GOTTEN MYSELF SEPARATED FROM SHINIGAMI-SAMA, HE COULD'VE USED ME TO STOP THE KISHIN DEAD IN ITS TRACKS.
WHICH IS WHY YOU'RE DOWN HERE POLISHING THE CANDLE-STICKS? TRYING TO SCORE SOME POINTS?
AND WHAT'S SO WRONG WITH THAT?
YOU'RE SUCH A MORON.
...

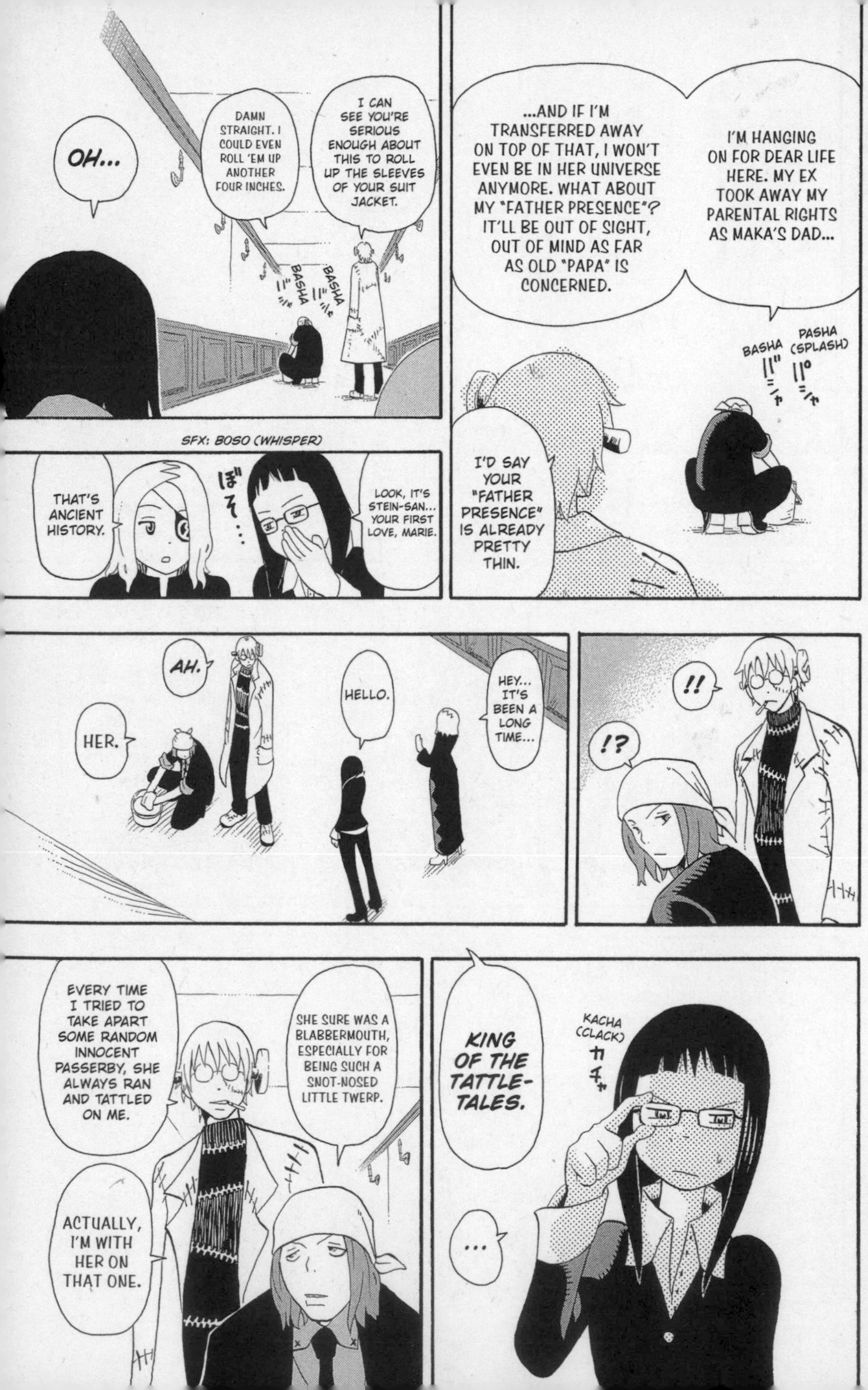
I'M HANGING ON FOR DEAR LIFE HERE. MY EX TOOK AWAY MY PARENTAL RIGHTS AS MAKA'S DAD...
...AND IF I'M TRANSFERRED AWAY ON TOP OF THAT, I WON'T EVEN BE IN HER UNIVERSE ANYMORE. WHAT ABOUT MY "FATHER PRESENCE"? IT'LL BE OUT OF SIGHT, OUT OF MIND AS FAR AS OLD "PAPA" IS CONCERNED.
PASHA (SPLASH)
BASHA
I'D SAY YOUR "FATHER PRESENCE" IS ALREADY PRETTY THIN.
I CAN SEE YOU'RE SERIOUS ENOUGH ABOUT THIS TO ROLL UP THE SLEEVES OF YOUR SUIT JACKET.
DAMN STRAIGHT. I COULD EVEN ROLL 'EM UP ANOTHER FOUR INCHES.
BASHA
BASHA
OH...
SFX: BOSO (WHISPER)
LOOK, IT'S STEIN-SAN... YOUR FIRST LOVE, MARIE.
THAT'S ANCIENT HISTORY.
!!
!?
HEY... IT'S BEEN A LONG TIME...
HELLO.
AH.
HER.
KACHA (CLACK)
KING OF THE TATTLE-TALES.
...
SHE SURE WAS A BLABBERMOUTH, ESPECIALLY FOR BEING SUCH A SNOT-NOSED LITTLE TWERP.
EVERY TIME I TRIED TO TAKE APART SOME RANDOM INNOCENT PASSERBY, SHE ALWAYS RAN AND TATTLED ON ME.
ACTUALLY, I'M WITH HER ON THAT ONE.

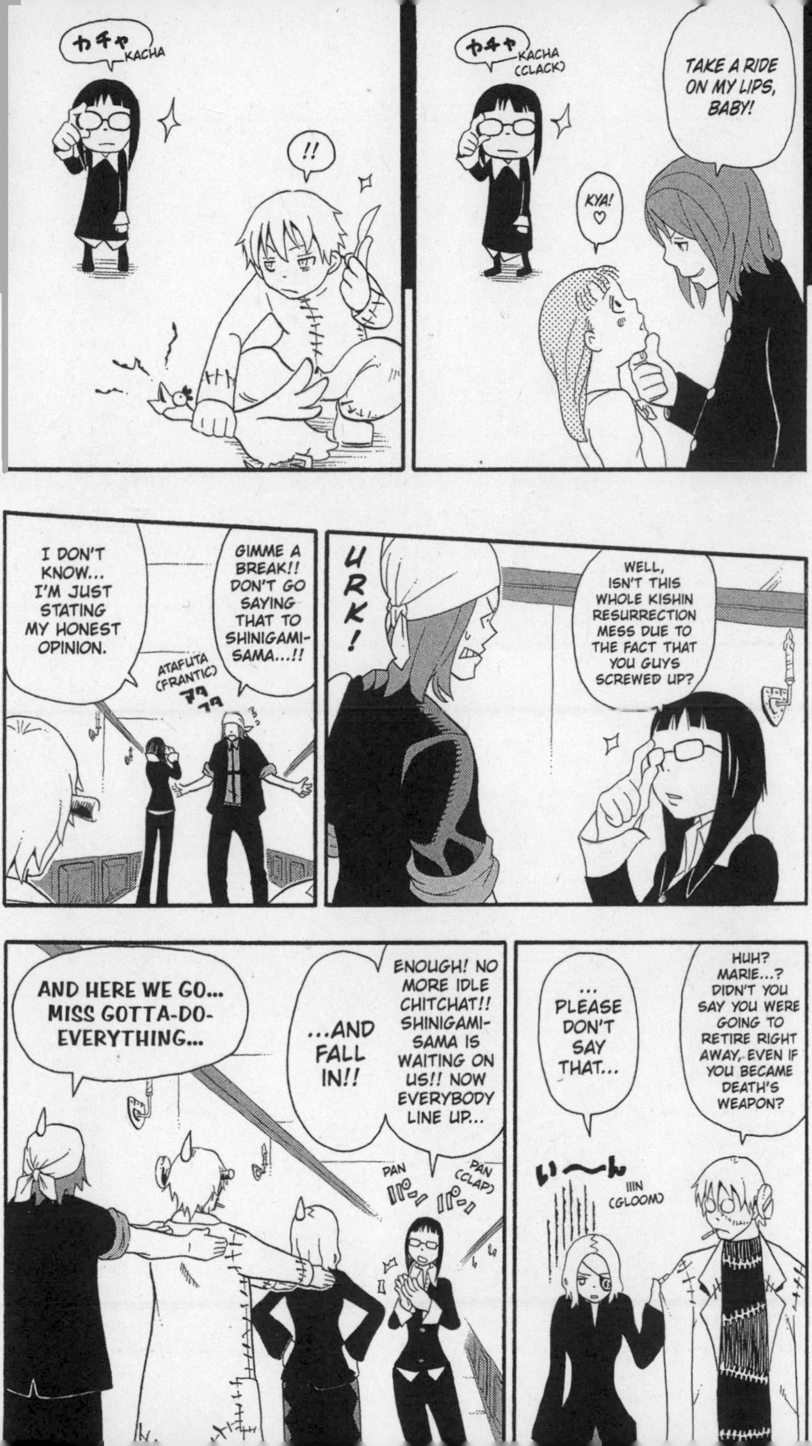
カチャ KACHA (CLACK)
TAKE A RIDE ON MY LIPS, BABY!
KYA! ♡
カチャ KACHA
!!
URK!
WELL, ISN'T THIS WHOLE KISHIN RESURRECTION MESS DUE TO THE FACT THAT YOU GUYS SCREWED UP?
GIMME A BREAK!! DON'T GO SAYING THAT TO SHINIGAMI-SAMA...!!
ATAFUTA (FRANTIC)
I DON'T KNOW... I'M JUST STATING MY HONEST OPINION.
HUH? MARIE...? DIDN'T YOU SAY YOU WERE GOING TO RETIRE RIGHT AWAY, EVEN IF YOU BECAME DEATH'S WEAPON?
... PLEASE DON'T SAY THAT...
IIIN (GLOOM)
ENOUGH! NO MORE IDLE CHITCHAT!! SHINIGAMI-SAMA IS WAITING ON US!! NOW EVERYBODY LINE UP...
PAN (CLAP)
PAN
...AND FALL IN!!
AND HERE WE GO... MISS GOTTA-DO-EVERYTHING...

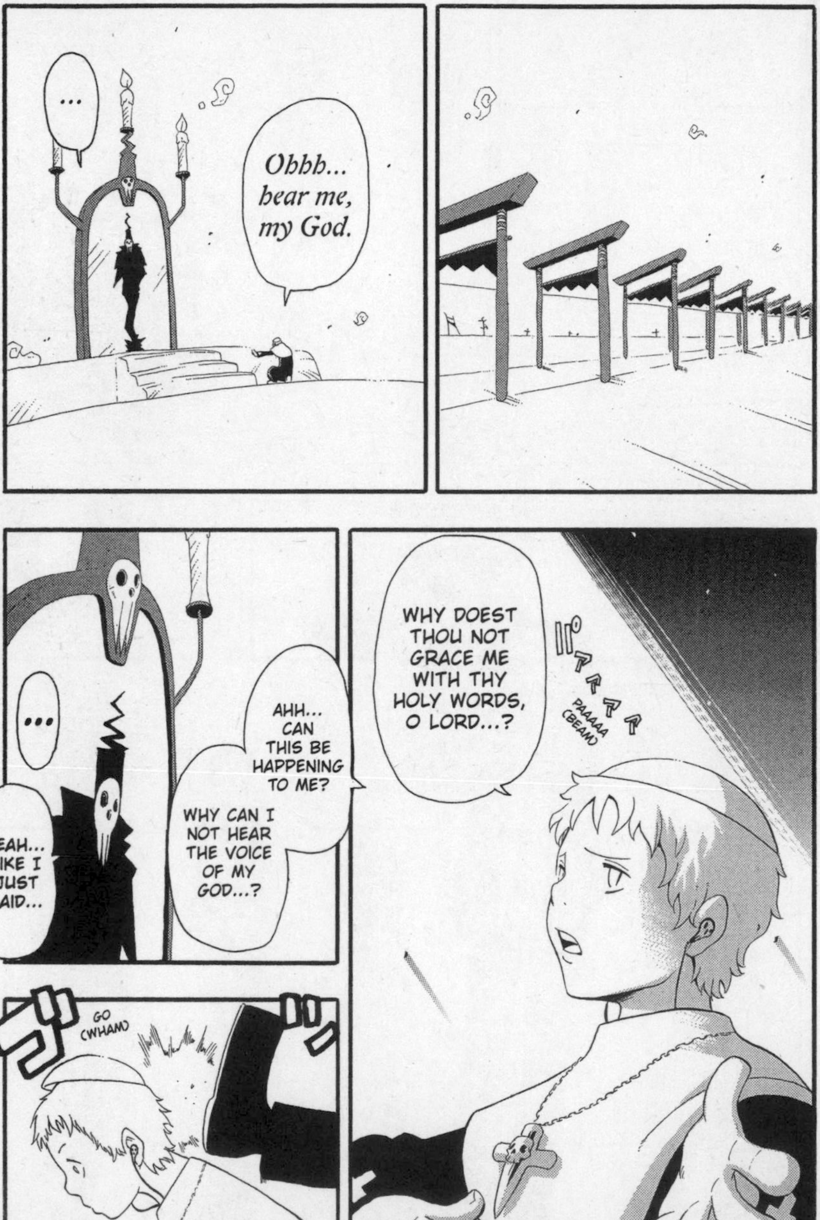
Ohhh... hear me, my God.
...
WHY DOEST THOU NOT GRACE ME WITH THY HOLY WORDS, O LORD...?
PAAAAA (BEAM)
AHH... CAN THIS BE HAPPENING TO ME?
WHY CAN I NOT HEAR THE VOICE OF MY GOD...?
...
YEAH... LIKE I JUST SAID...
GO (WHAM)

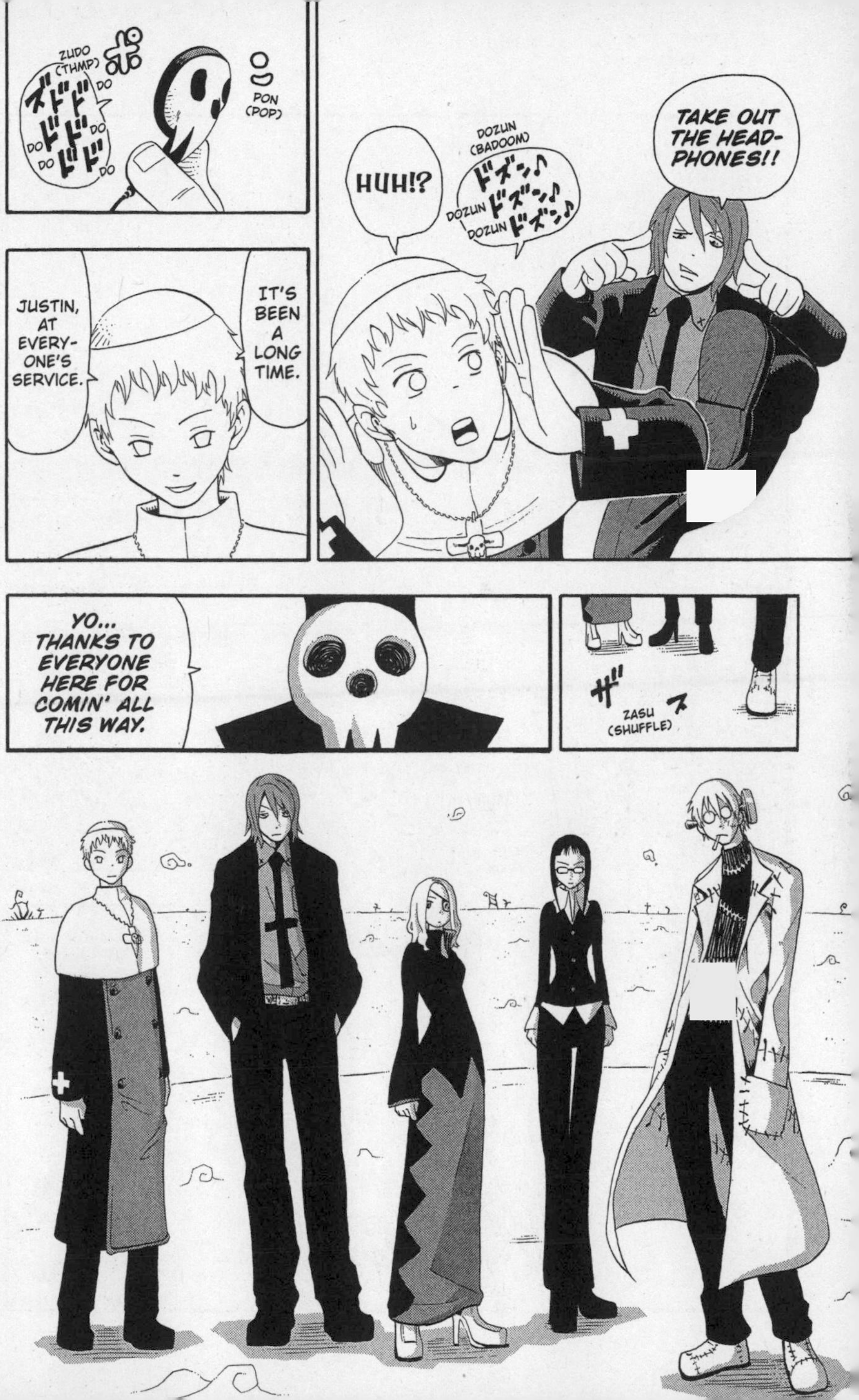
TAKE OUT THE HEAD-PHONES!!
DOZUN (BADOOM)
ドズン♪ DOZUN ドズン♪ DOZUN ドズン♪
HUH!?
PON (POP)
ポ
ZUDO (THMP)
ズドド DO DO ドド DO DO ドド DO
IT'S BEEN A LONG TIME.
JUSTIN, AT EVERY-ONE'S SERVICE.
ザ ス
ZASU (SHUFFLE)
YO... THANKS TO EVERYONE HERE FOR COMIN' ALL THIS WAY.

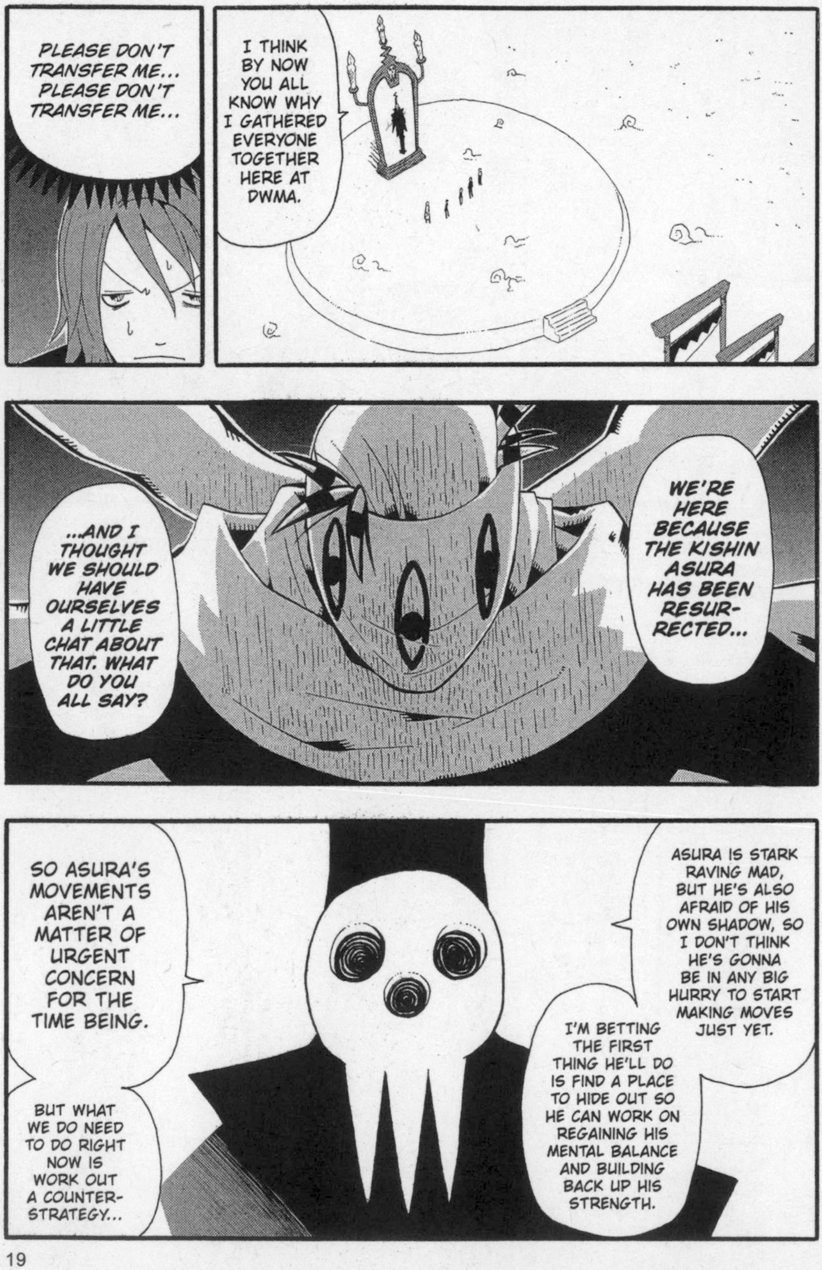
I THINK BY NOW YOU ALL KNOW WHY I GATHERED EVERYONE TOGETHER HERE AT DWMA.
PLEASE DON'T TRANSFER ME... PLEASE DON'T TRANSFER ME...
WE'RE HERE BECAUSE THE KISHIN ASURA HAS BEEN RESUR-RECTED...
...AND I THOUGHT WE SHOULD HAVE OURSELVES A LITTLE CHAT ABOUT THAT. WHAT DO YOU ALL SAY?
ASURA IS STARK RAVING MAD, BUT HE'S ALSO AFRAID OF HIS OWN SHADOW, SO I DON'T THINK HE'S GONNA BE IN ANY BIG HURRY TO START MAKING MOVES JUST YET.
I'M BETTING THE FIRST THING HE'LL DO IS FIND A PLACE TO HIDE OUT SO HE CAN WORK ON REGAINING HIS MENTAL BALANCE AND BUILDING BACK UP HIS STRENGTH.
SO ASURA'S MOVEMENTS AREN'T A MATTER OF URGENT CONCERN FOR THE TIME BEING.
BUT WHAT WE DO NEED TO DO RIGHT NOW IS WORK OUT A COUNTER-STRATEGY...

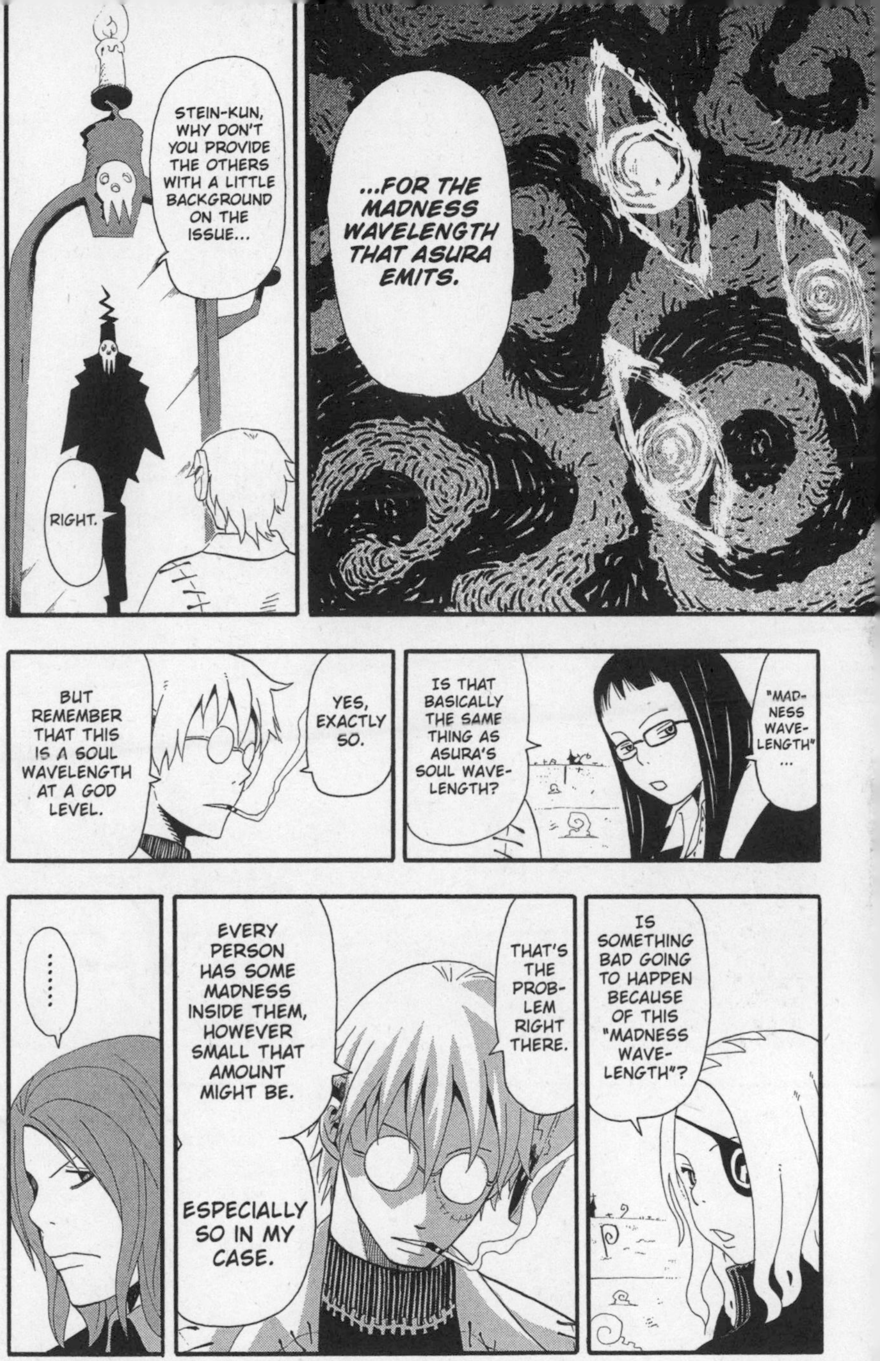
...FOR THE MADNESS WAVELENGTH THAT ASURA EMITS.
STEIN-KUN, WHY DON'T YOU PROVIDE THE OTHERS WITH A LITTLE BACKGROUND ON THE ISSUE...
RIGHT.
"MADNESS WAVELENGTH"...
IS THAT BASICALLY THE SAME THING AS ASURA'S SOUL WAVELENGTH?
YES, EXACTLY SO.
BUT REMEMBER THAT THIS IS A SOUL WAVELENGTH AT A GOD LEVEL.
IS SOMETHING BAD GOING TO HAPPEN BECAUSE OF THIS "MADNESS WAVELENGTH"?
THAT'S THE PROBLEM RIGHT THERE.
EVERY PERSON HAS SOME MADNESS INSIDE THEM, HOWEVER SMALL THAT AMOUNT MIGHT BE.
ESPECIALLY SO IN MY CASE.
......

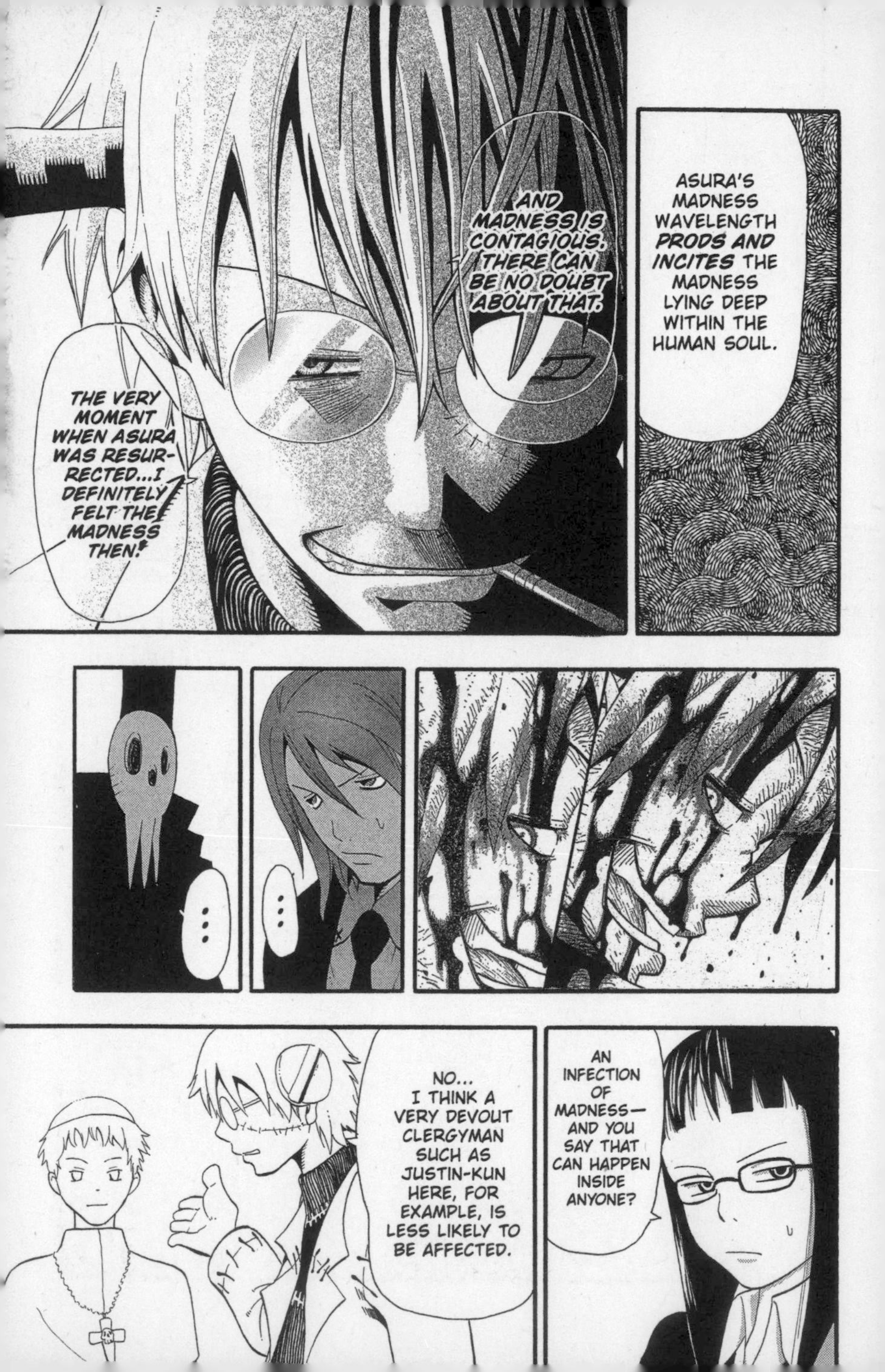
ASURA'S MADNESS WAVELENGTH PRODS AND INCITES THE MADNESS LYING DEEP WITHIN THE HUMAN SOUL.
AND MADNESS IS CONTAGIOUS. THERE CAN BE NO DOUBT ABOUT THAT.
THE VERY MOMENT WHEN ASURA WAS RESURRECTED...I DEFINITELY FELT THE MADNESS THEN!
...
...
AN INFECTION OF MADNESS—AND YOU SAY THAT CAN HAPPEN INSIDE ANYONE?
NO... I THINK A VERY DEVOUT CLERGYMAN SUCH AS JUSTIN-KUN HERE, FOR EXAMPLE, IS LESS LIKELY TO BE AFFECTED.

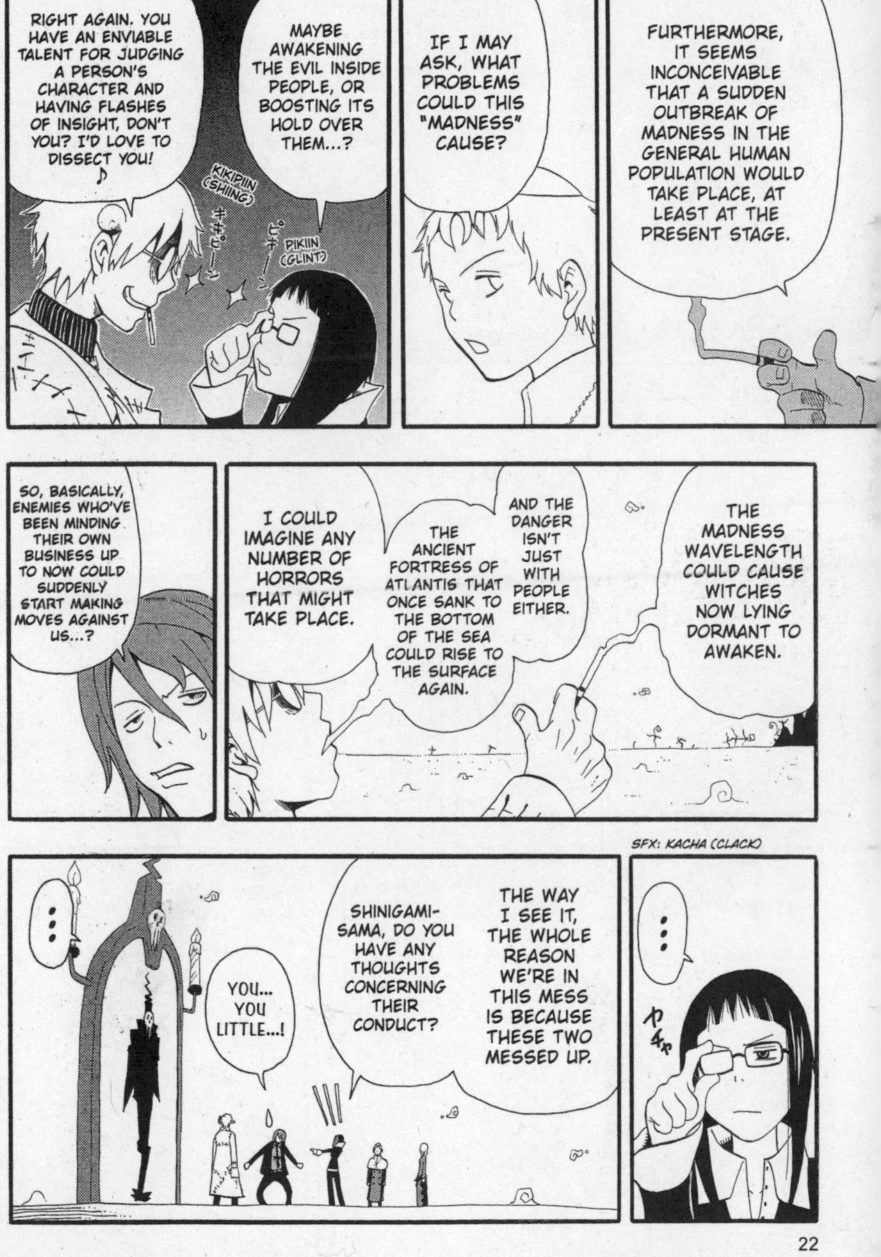
FURTHERMORE, IT SEEMS INCONCEIVABLE THAT A SUDDEN OUTBREAK OF MADNESS IN THE GENERAL HUMAN POPULATION WOULD TAKE PLACE, AT LEAST AT THE PRESENT STAGE.
IF I MAY ASK, WHAT PROBLEMS COULD THIS "MADNESS" CAUSE?
MAYBE AWAKENING THE EVIL INSIDE PEOPLE, OR BOOSTING ITS HOLD OVER THEM...?
PIKIIN (GLINT)
KIKIPIIN (SHIING)
RIGHT AGAIN. YOU HAVE AN ENVIABLE TALENT FOR JUDGING A PERSON'S CHARACTER AND HAVING FLASHES OF INSIGHT, DON'T YOU? I'D LOVE TO DISSECT YOU! ♪
THE MADNESS WAVELENGTH COULD CAUSE WITCHES NOW LYING DORMANT TO AWAKEN.
AND THE DANGER ISN'T JUST WITH PEOPLE EITHER.
THE ANCIENT FORTRESS OF ATLANTIS THAT ONCE SANK TO THE BOTTOM OF THE SEA COULD RISE TO THE SURFACE AGAIN.
I COULD IMAGINE ANY NUMBER OF HORRORS THAT MIGHT TAKE PLACE.
SO, BASICALLY, ENEMIES WHO'VE BEEN MINDING THEIR OWN BUSINESS UP TO NOW COULD SUDDENLY START MAKING MOVES AGAINST US...?
SFX: KACHA (CLACK)
...
THE WAY I SEE IT, THE WHOLE REASON WE'RE IN THIS MESS IS BECAUSE THESE TWO MESSED UP.
SHINIGAMI-SAMA, DO YOU HAVE ANY THOUGHTS CONCERNING THEIR CONDUCT?
YOU... YOU LITTLE...!
...

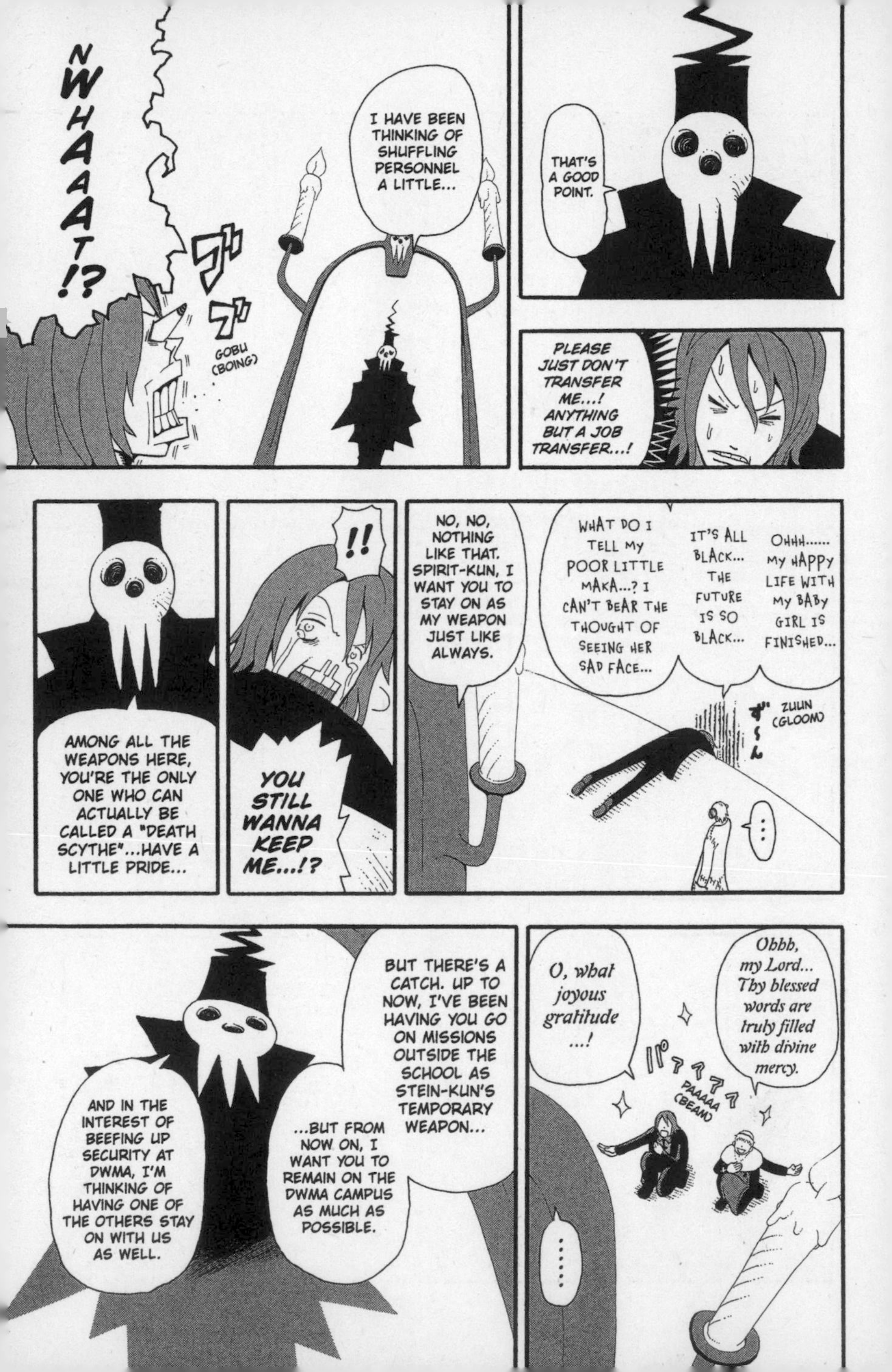
THAT'S A GOOD POINT.
PLEASE JUST DON'T TRANSFER ME...! ANYTHING BUT A JOB TRANSFER...!
I HAVE BEEN THINKING OF SHUFFLING PERSONNEL A LITTLE...
NWHAAAAT!?
ゴブ
GOBU (BOING)
OHHH...... MY HAPPY LIFE WITH MY BABY GIRL IS FINISHED...
IT'S ALL BLACK... THE FUTURE IS SO BLACK...
WHAT DO I TELL MY POOR LITTLE MAKA...? I CAN'T BEAR THE THOUGHT OF SEEING HER SAD FACE...
NO, NO, NOTHING LIKE THAT. SPIRIT-KUN, I WANT YOU TO STAY ON AS MY WEAPON JUST LIKE ALWAYS.
ずーん
ZUUN (GLOOM)
...
!!
YOU STILL WANNA KEEP ME...!?
AMONG ALL THE WEAPONS HERE, YOU'RE THE ONLY ONE WHO CAN ACTUALLY BE CALLED A "DEATH SCYTHE"...HAVE A LITTLE PRIDE...
Ohhh, my Lord... Thy blessed words are truly filled with divine mercy.
O, what joyous gratitude...!
パァァァァ
PAAAAA (BEAM)
......
BUT THERE'S A CATCH. UP TO NOW, I'VE BEEN HAVING YOU GO ON MISSIONS OUTSIDE THE SCHOOL AS STEIN-KUN'S TEMPORARY WEAPON...
...BUT FROM NOW ON, I WANT YOU TO REMAIN ON THE DWMA CAMPUS AS MUCH AS POSSIBLE.
AND IN THE INTEREST OF BEEFING UP SECURITY AT DWMA, I'M THINKING OF HAVING ONE OF THE OTHERS STAY ON WITH US AS WELL.

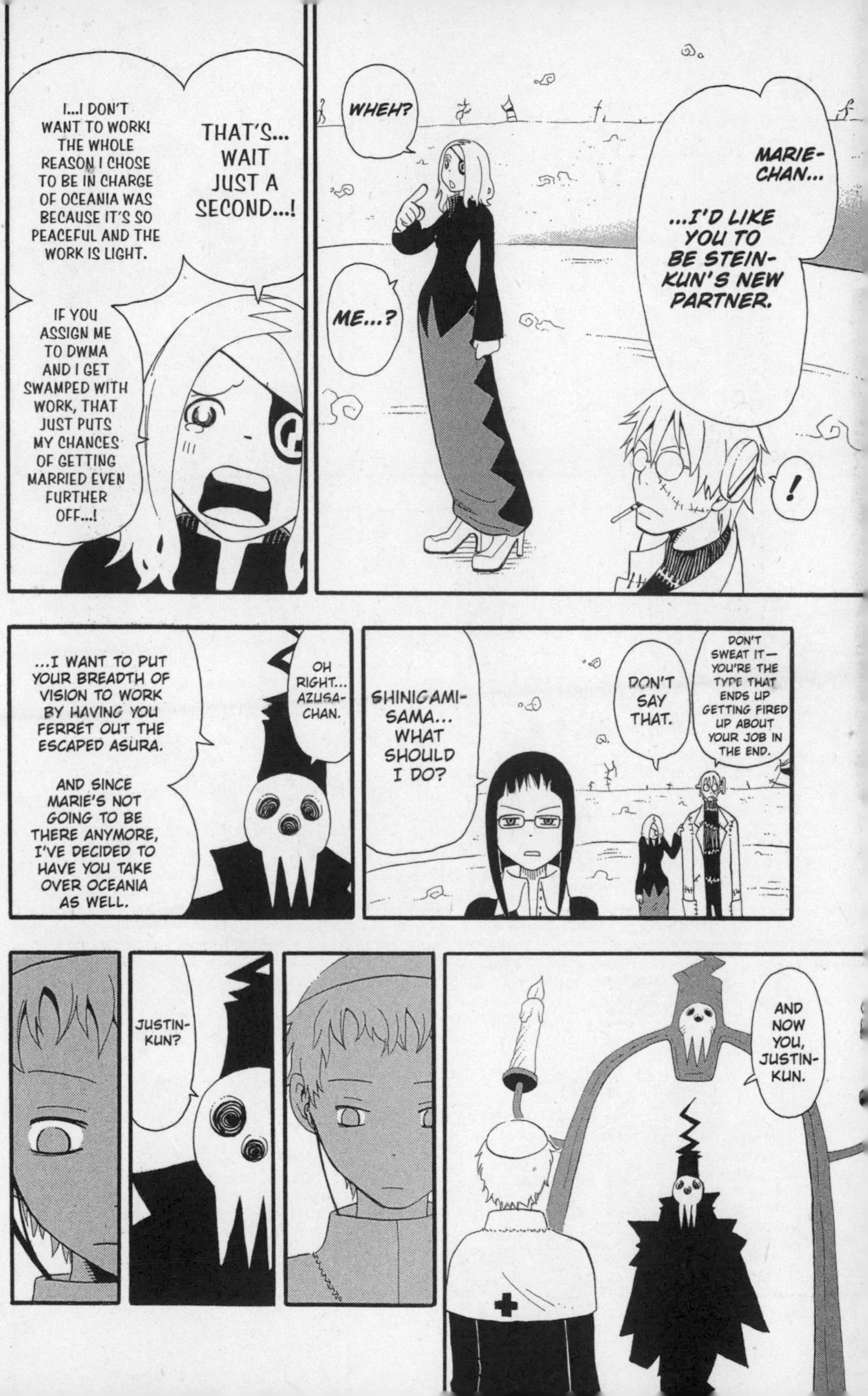
MARIE-CHAN...
...I'D LIKE YOU TO BE STEIN-KUN'S NEW PARTNER.
!
WHEH?
ME...?
THAT'S... WAIT JUST A SECOND...!
I...I DON'T WANT TO WORK! THE WHOLE REASON I CHOSE TO BE IN CHARGE OF OCEANIA WAS BECAUSE IT'S SO PEACEFUL AND THE WORK IS LIGHT.
IF YOU ASSIGN ME TO DWMA AND I GET SWAMPED WITH WORK, THAT JUST PUTS MY CHANCES OF GETTING MARRIED EVEN FURTHER OFF...!
DON'T SWEAT IT— YOU'RE THE TYPE THAT ENDS UP GETTING FIRED UP ABOUT YOUR JOB IN THE END.
DON'T SAY THAT.
SHINIGAMI-SAMA... WHAT SHOULD I DO?
OH RIGHT... AZUSA-CHAN.
...I WANT TO PUT YOUR BREADTH OF VISION TO WORK BY HAVING YOU FERRET OUT THE ESCAPED ASURA.
AND SINCE MARIE'S NOT GOING TO BE THERE ANYMORE, I'VE DECIDED TO HAVE YOU TAKE OVER OCEANIA AS WELL.
AND NOW YOU, JUSTIN-KUN.
JUSTIN-KUN?

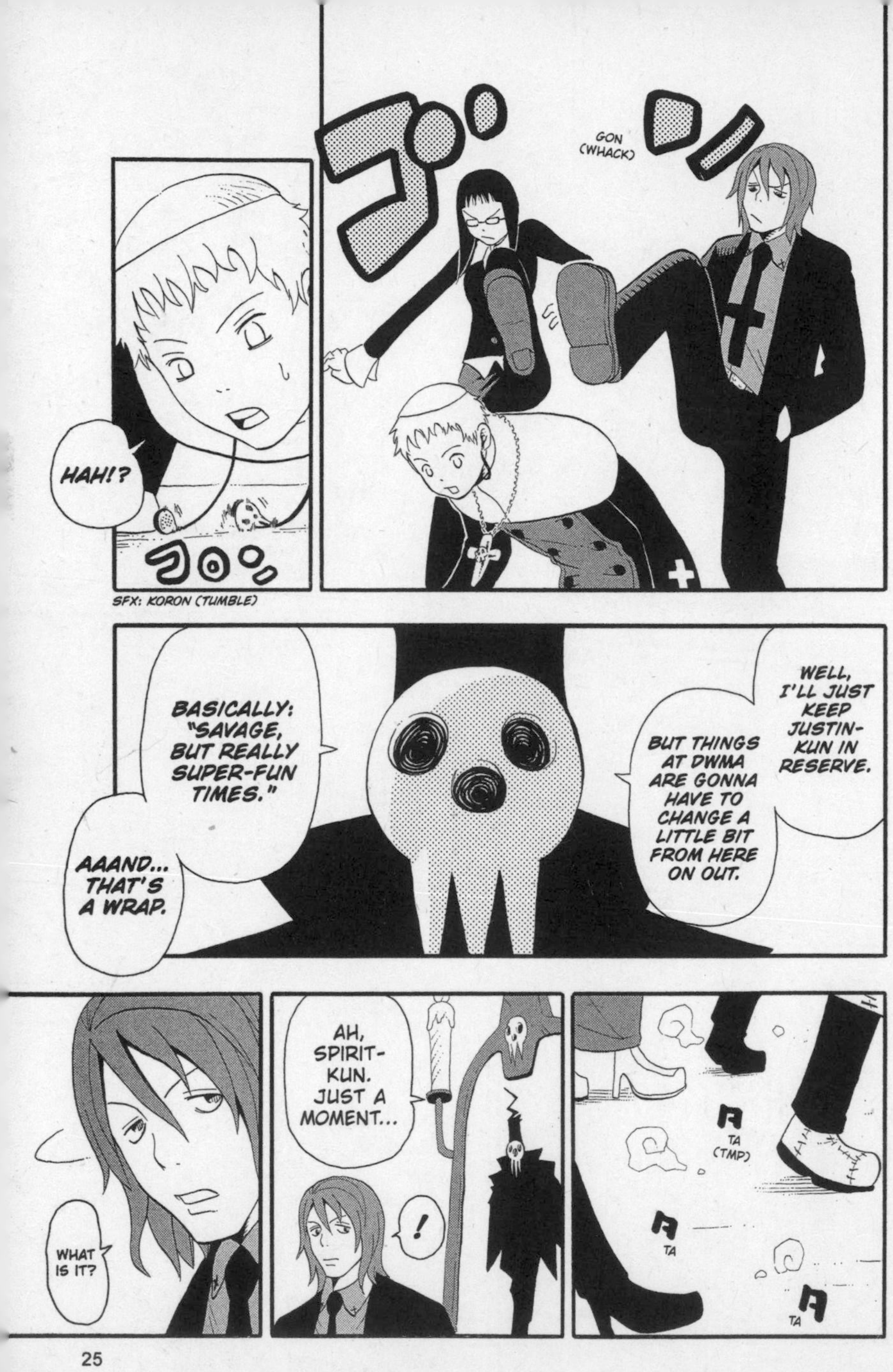
GON (WHACK)
HAH!?
SFX: KORON (TUMBLE)
WELL, I'LL JUST KEEP JUSTIN-KUN IN RESERVE.
BUT THINGS AT DWMA ARE GONNA HAVE TO CHANGE A LITTLE BIT FROM HERE ON OUT.
BASICALLY: "SAVAGE, BUT REALLY SUPER-FUN TIMES."
AAAND... THAT'S A WRAP.
TA (TMP)
TA
TA
AH, SPIRIT-KUN. JUST A MOMENT...
!
WHAT IS IT?

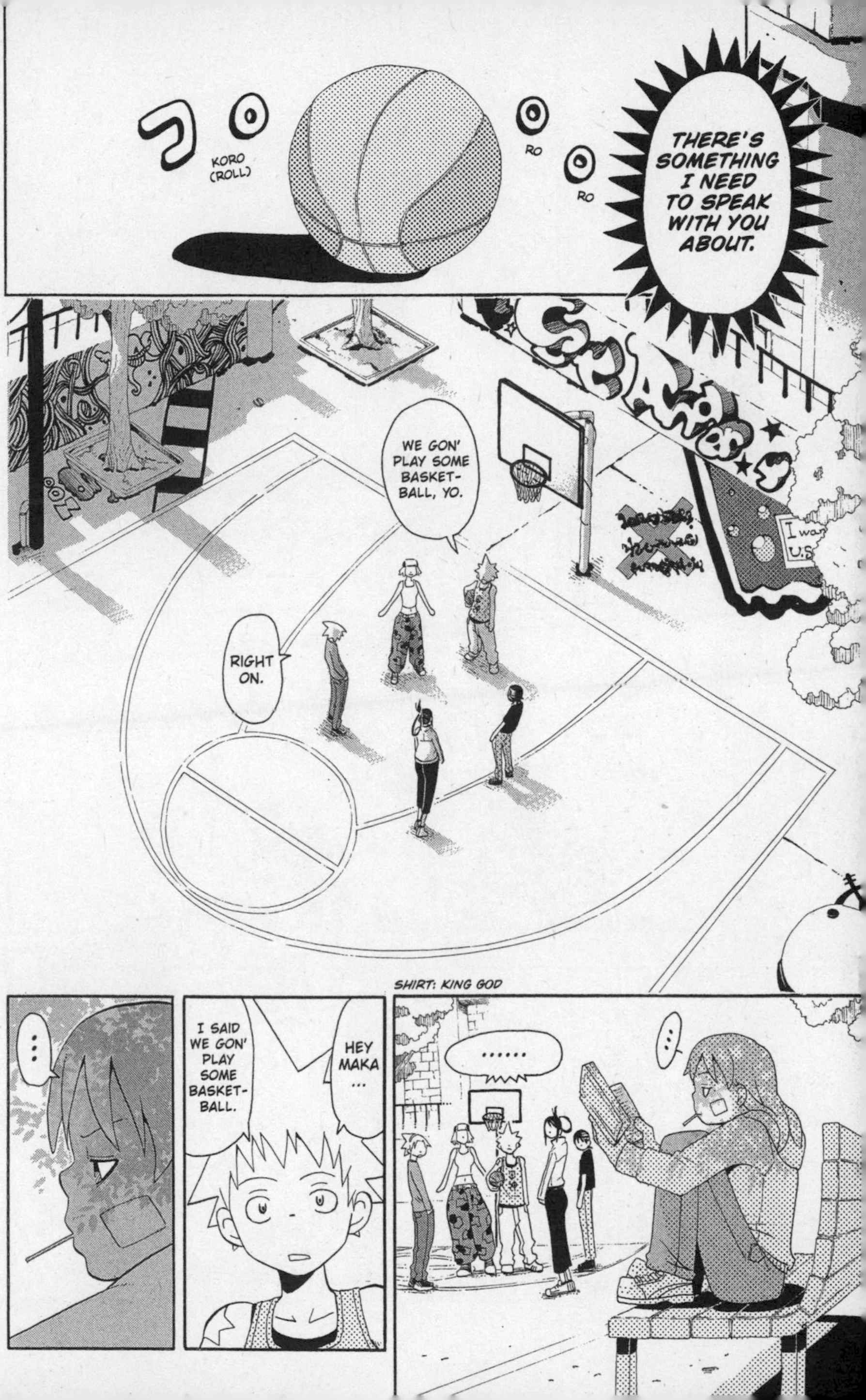
THERE'S SOMETHING I NEED TO SPEAK WITH YOU ABOUT.
KORO (ROLL)
RO
RO
WE GON' PLAY SOME BASKET-BALL, YO.
RIGHT ON.
SHIRT: KING GOD
...
......
HEY MAKA ...
I SAID WE GON' PLAY SOME BASKET-BALL.
...

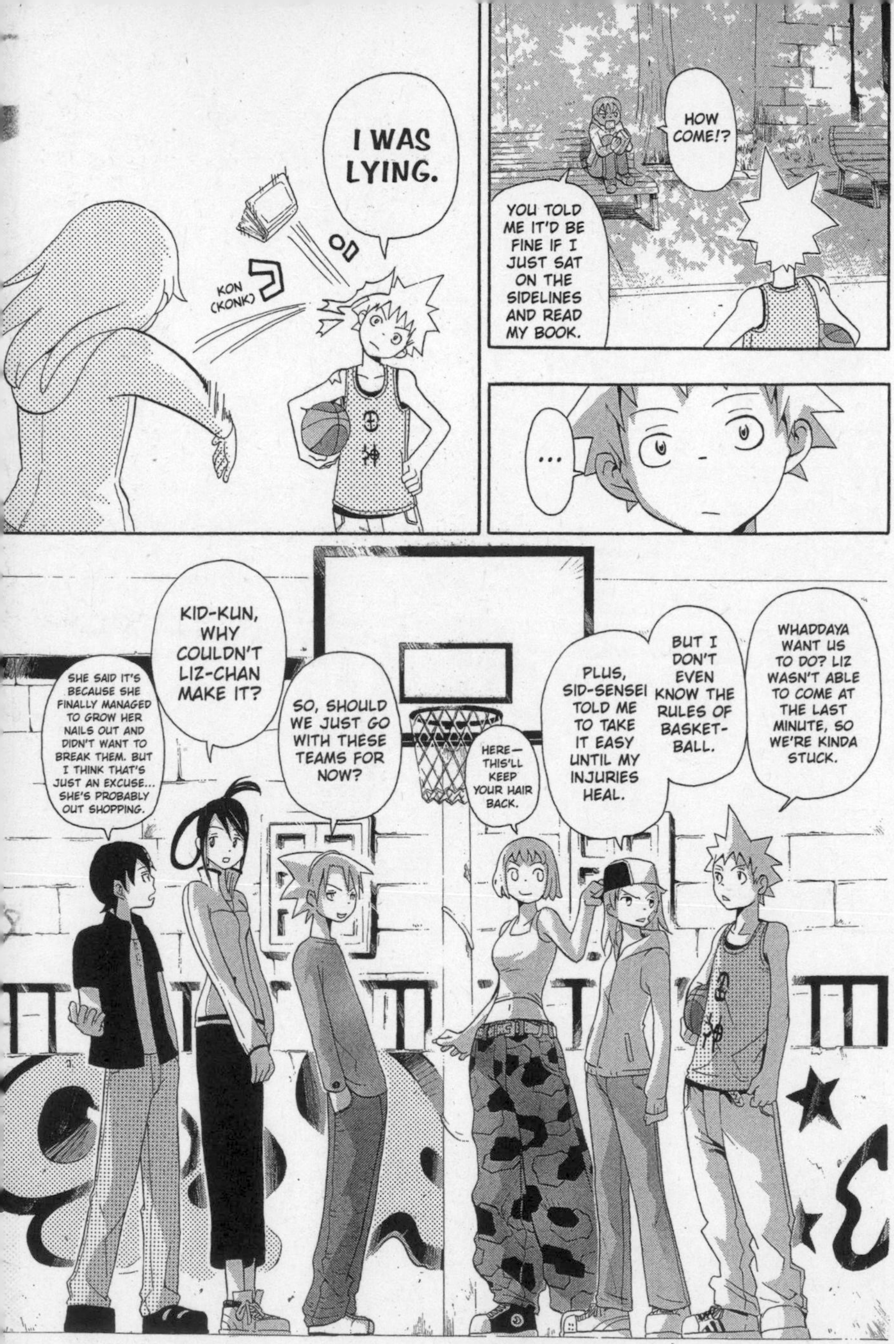
HOW COME!?
YOU TOLD ME IT'D BE FINE IF I JUST SAT ON THE SIDELINES AND READ MY BOOK.
...
I WAS LYING.
KON (KONK)
WHADDAYA WANT US TO DO? LIZ WASN'T ABLE TO COME AT THE LAST MINUTE, SO WE'RE KINDA STUCK.
BUT I DON'T EVEN KNOW THE RULES OF BASKET-BALL.
PLUS, SID-SENSEI TOLD ME TO TAKE IT EASY UNTIL MY INJURIES HEAL.
HERE— THIS'LL KEEP YOUR HAIR BACK.
SO, SHOULD WE JUST GO WITH THESE TEAMS FOR NOW?
KID-KUN, WHY COULDN'T LIZ-CHAN MAKE IT?
SHE SAID IT'S BECAUSE SHE FINALLY MANAGED TO GROW HER NAILS OUT AND DIDN'T WANT TO BREAK THEM. BUT I THINK THAT'S JUST AN EXCUSE... SHE'S PROBABLY OUT SHOPPING.

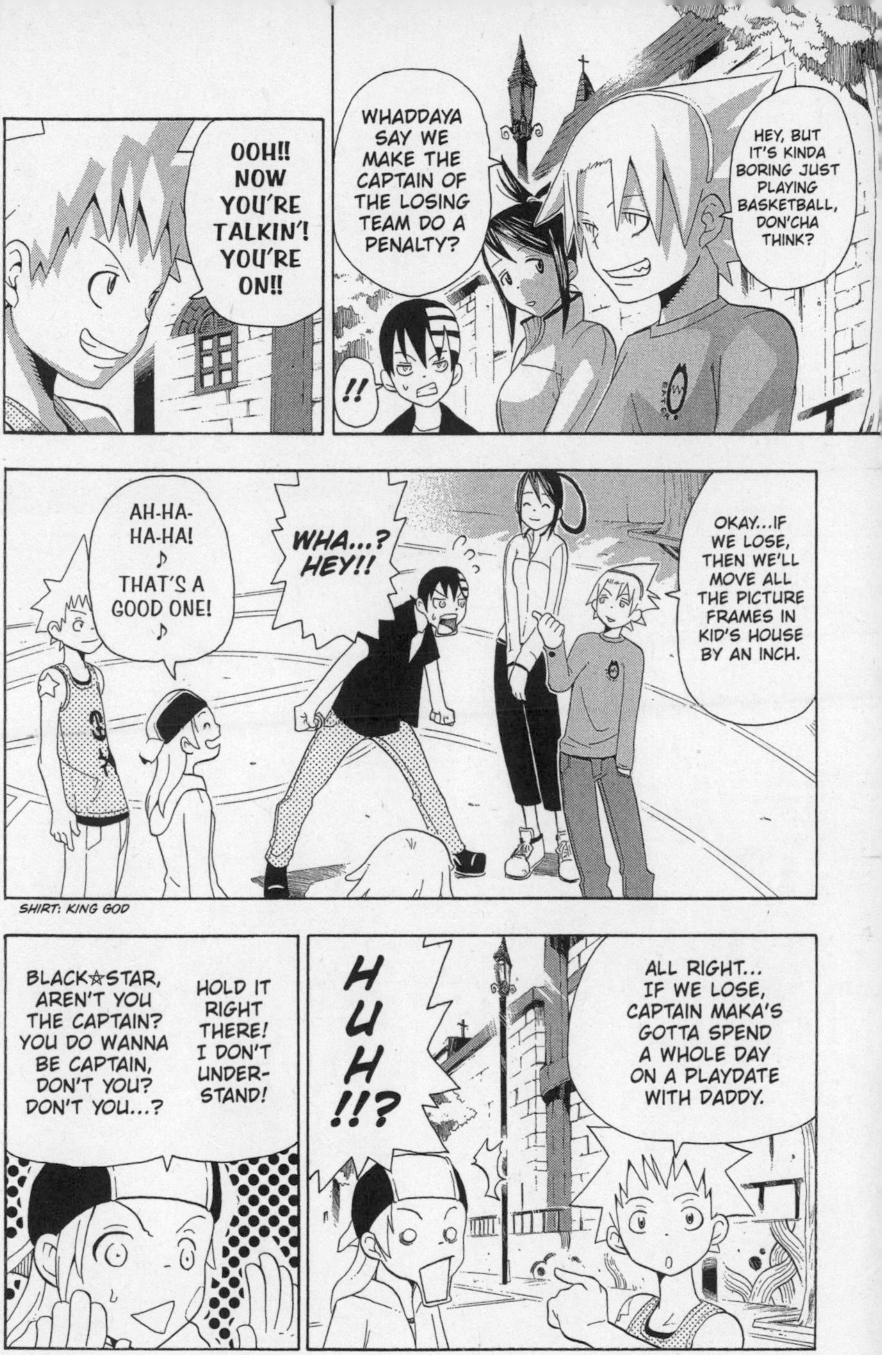
HEY, BUT IT'S KINDA BORING JUST PLAYING BASKETBALL, DON'CHA THINK?
WHADDAYA SAY WE MAKE THE CAPTAIN OF THE LOSING TEAM DO A PENALTY?
!!
OOH!! NOW YOU'RE TALKIN'! YOU'RE ON!!
OKAY...IF WE LOSE, THEN WE'LL MOVE ALL THE PICTURE FRAMES IN KID'S HOUSE BY AN INCH.
WHA...? HEY!!
AH-HA-HA-HA! ♪ THAT'S A GOOD ONE! ♪
SHIRT: KING GOD
ALL RIGHT... IF WE LOSE, CAPTAIN MAKA'S GOTTA SPEND A WHOLE DAY ON A PLAYDATE WITH DADDY.
HUH!!?
HOLD IT RIGHT THERE! I DON'T UNDER-STAND!
BLACK☆STAR, AREN'T YOU THE CAPTAIN? YOU DO WANNA BE CAPTAIN, DON'T YOU? DON'T YOU...?

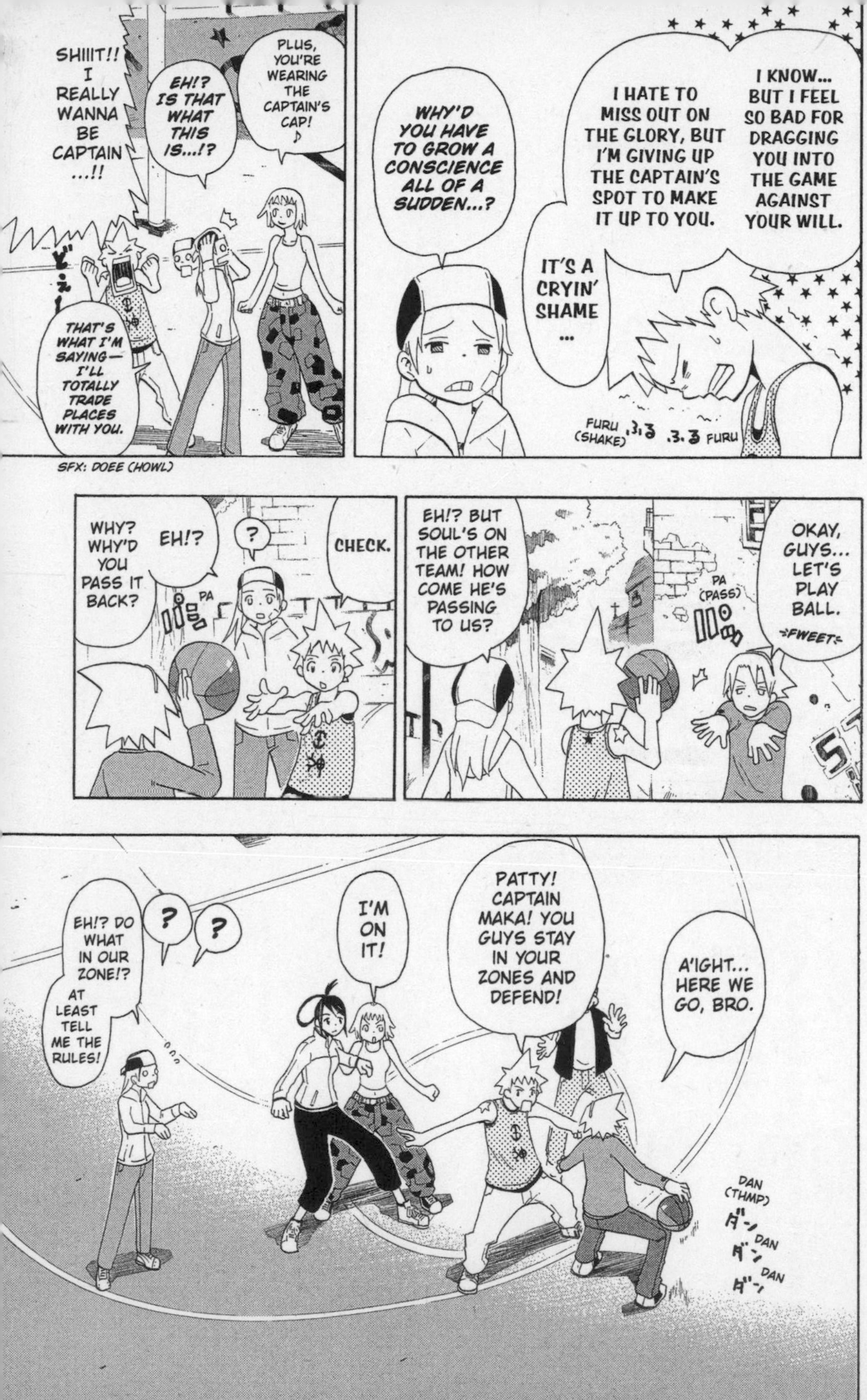
I KNOW... BUT I FEEL SO BAD FOR DRAGGING YOU INTO THE GAME AGAINST YOUR WILL.
I HATE TO MISS OUT ON THE GLORY, BUT I'M GIVING UP THE CAPTAIN'S SPOT TO MAKE IT UP TO YOU.
WHY'D YOU HAVE TO GROW A CONSCIENCE ALL OF A SUDDEN...?
IT'S A CRYIN' SHAME...
FURU (SHAKE) FURU
PLUS, YOU'RE WEARING THE CAPTAIN'S CAP! ♪
EH!? IS THAT WHAT THIS IS...!?
SHIIIT!! I REALLY WANNA BE CAPTAIN...!!
THAT'S WHAT I'M SAYING—I'LL TOTALLY TRADE PLACES WITH YOU.
SFX: DOEE (HOWL)
OKAY, GUYS... LET'S PLAY BALL.
FWEET
PA (PASS)
EH!? BUT SOUL'S ON THE OTHER TEAM! HOW COME HE'S PASSING TO US?
CHECK.
?
EH!?
WHY? WHY'D YOU PASS IT BACK?
PA
A'IGHT... HERE WE GO, BRO.
PATTY! CAPTAIN MAKA! YOU GUYS STAY IN YOUR ZONES AND DEFEND!
I'M ON IT!
?
?
EH!? DO WHAT IN OUR ZONE!?
AT LEAST TELL ME THE RULES!
DAN (THMP)
DAN
DAN

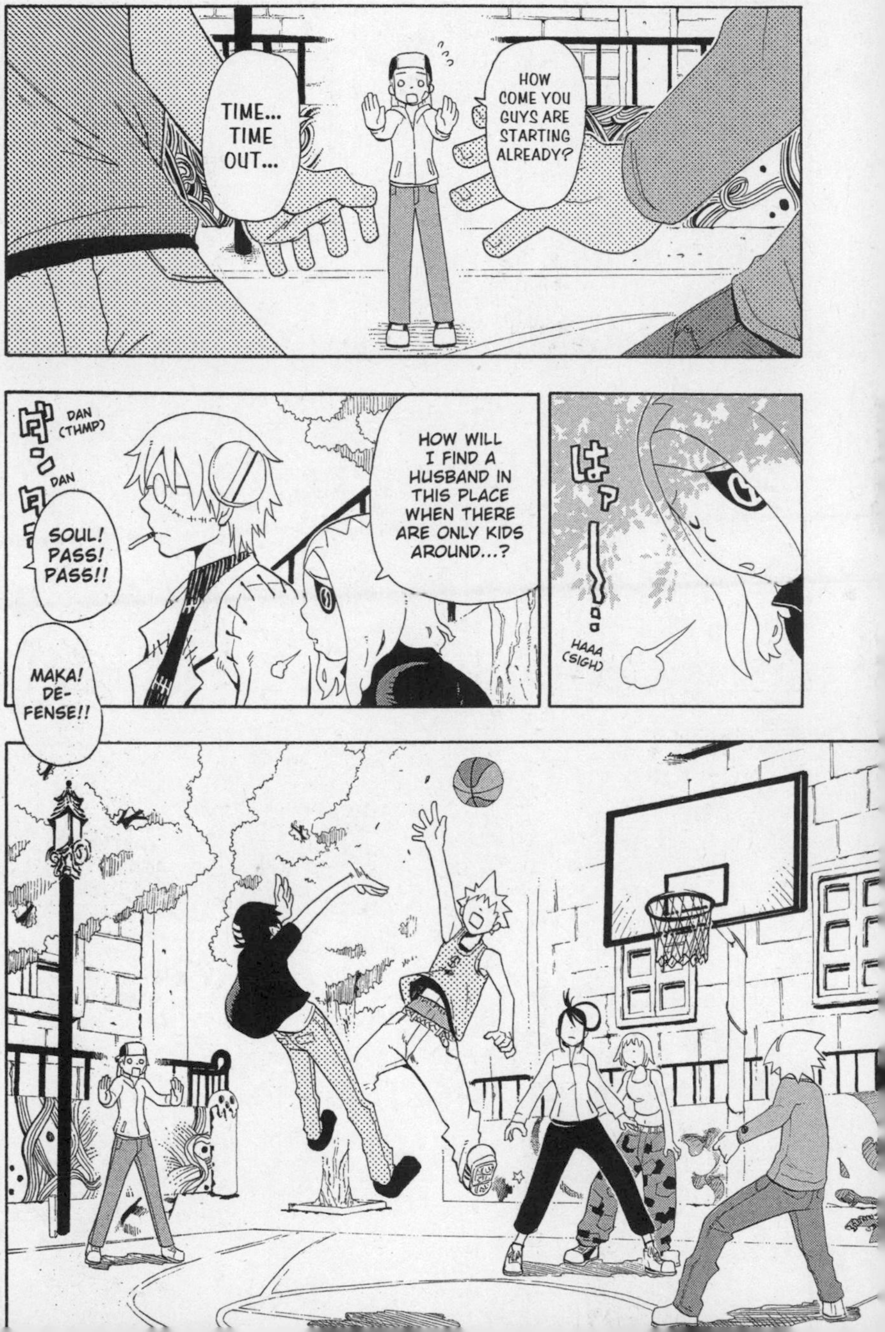
HOW COME YOU GUYS ARE STARTING ALREADY?
TIME... TIME OUT...
HAAA (SIGH)
HOW WILL I FIND A HUSBAND IN THIS PLACE WHEN THERE ARE ONLY KIDS AROUND...?
DAN (THMP)
DAN
SOUL! PASS! PASS!!
MAKA! DE-FENSE!!

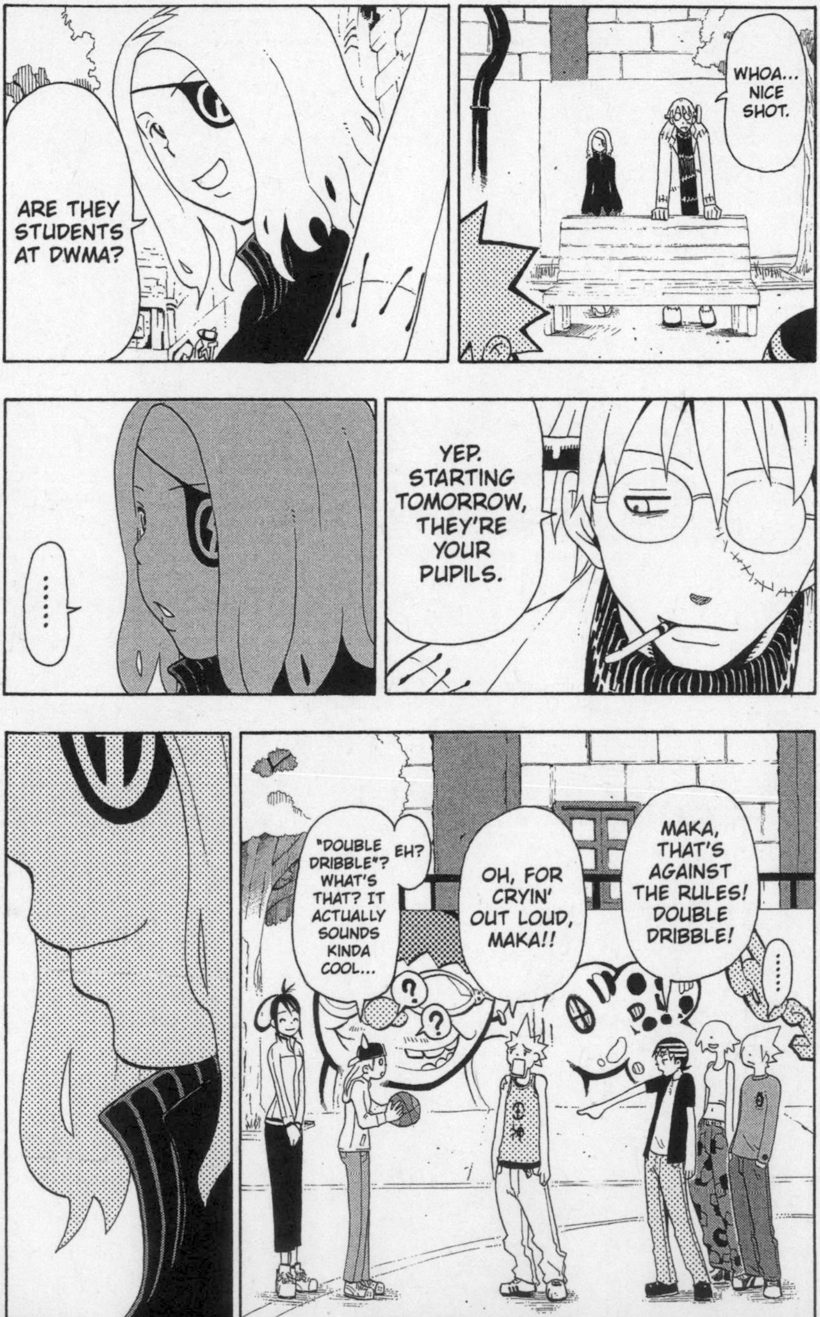
WHOA... NICE SHOT.
ARE THEY STUDENTS AT DWMA?
YEP. STARTING TOMORROW, THEY'RE YOUR PUPILS.
......
MAKA, THAT'S AGAINST THE RULES! DOUBLE DRIBBLE!
......
OH, FOR CRYIN' OUT LOUD, MAKA!!
EH?
"DOUBLE DRIBBLE"? WHAT'S THAT? IT ACTUALLY SOUNDS KINDA COOL...

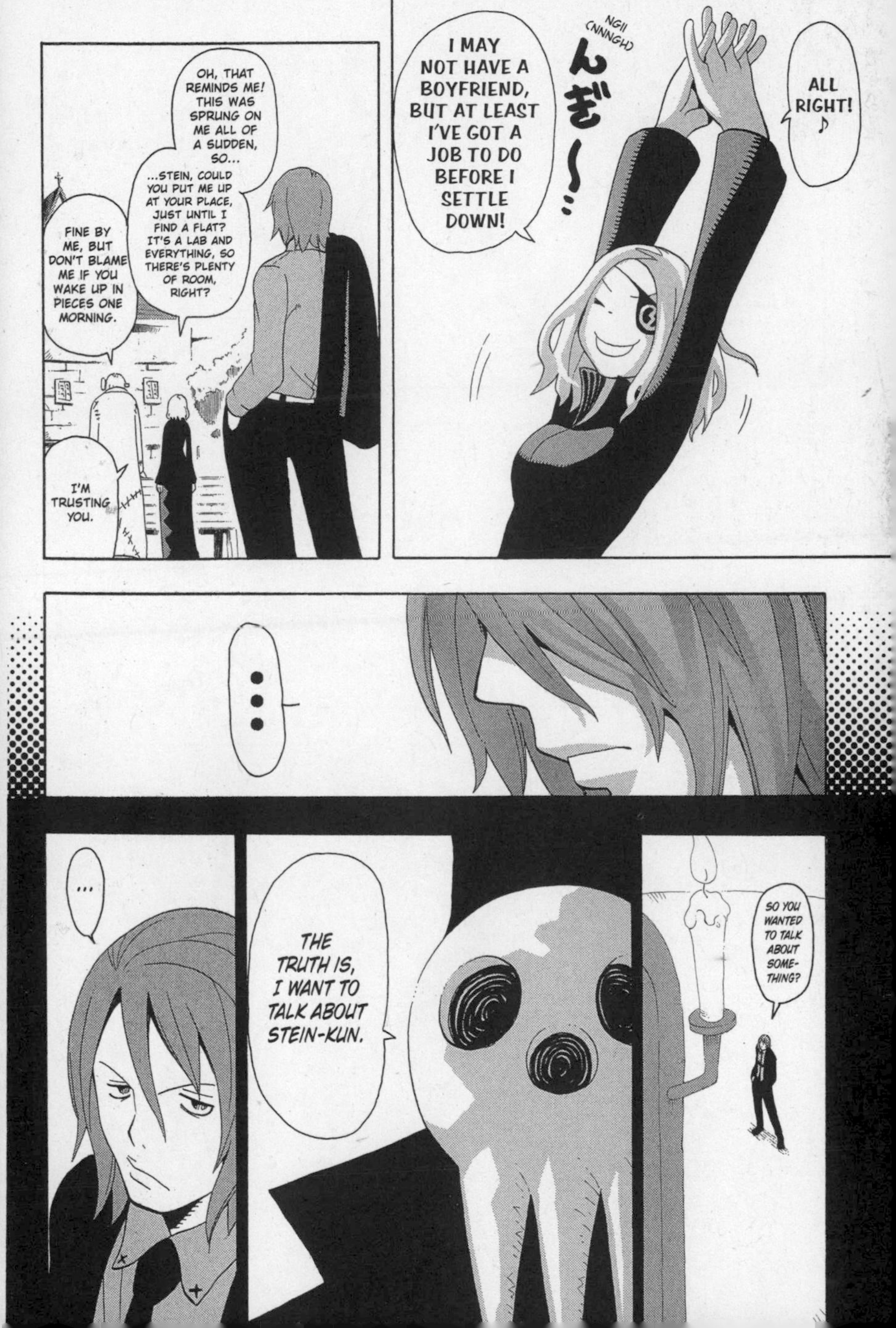
ALL RIGHT! ♪
NGII (NNNGH)
んぎ〜っ
I MAY NOT HAVE A BOYFRIEND, BUT AT LEAST I'VE GOT A JOB TO DO BEFORE I SETTLE DOWN!
OH, THAT REMINDS ME! THIS WAS SPRUNG ON ME ALL OF A SUDDEN, SO...
...STEIN, COULD YOU PUT ME UP AT YOUR PLACE, JUST UNTIL I FIND A FLAT? IT'S A LAB AND EVERYTHING, SO THERE'S PLENTY OF ROOM, RIGHT?
FINE BY ME, BUT DON'T BLAME ME IF YOU WAKE UP IN PIECES ONE MORNING.
I'M TRUSTING YOU.
•••
SO YOU WANTED TO TALK ABOUT SOME-THING?
THE TRUTH IS, I WANT TO TALK ABOUT STEIN-KUN.
...

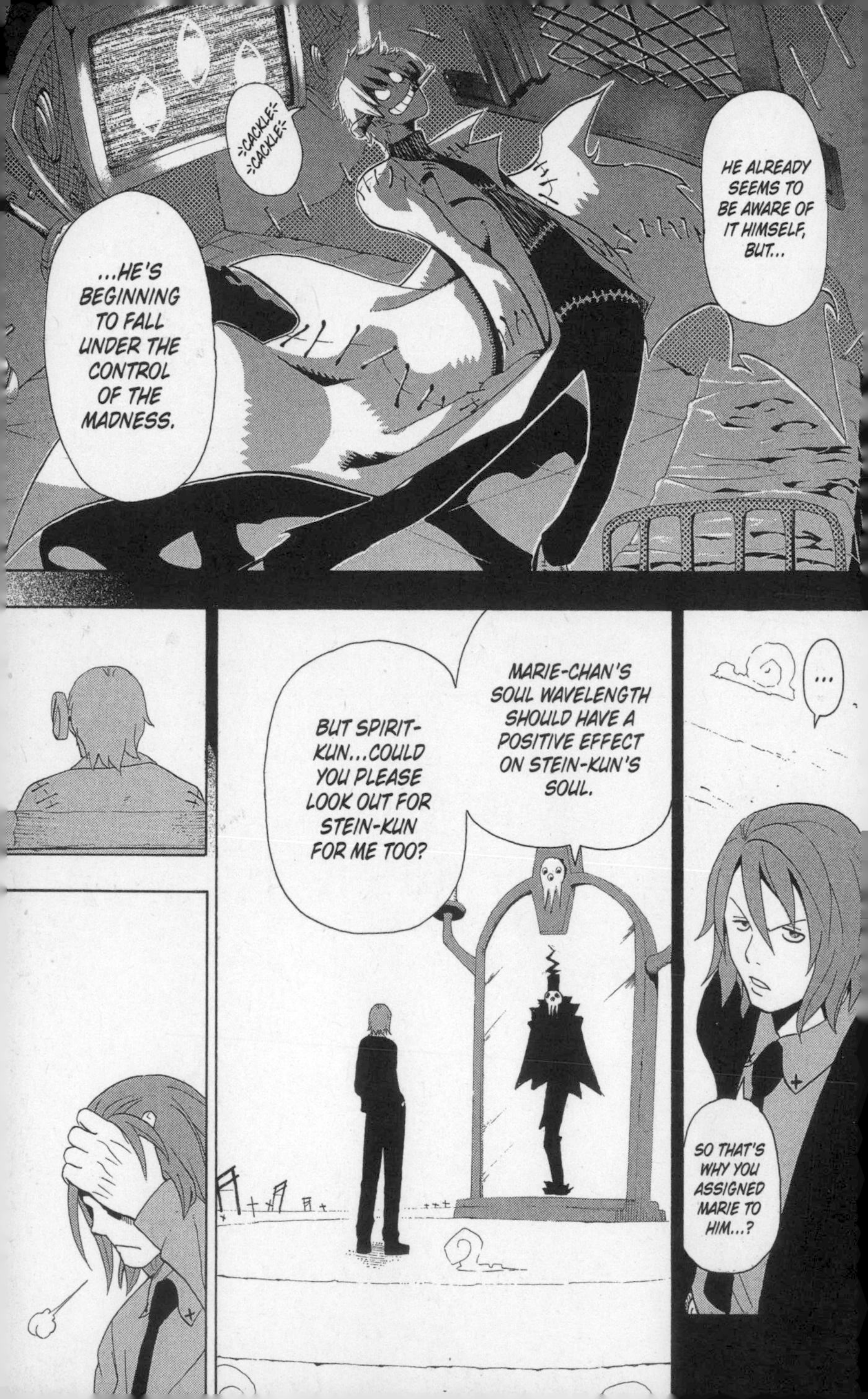
HE ALREADY SEEMS TO BE AWARE OF IT HIMSELF, BUT...
CACKLE CACKLE
...HE'S BEGINNING TO FALL UNDER THE CONTROL OF THE MADNESS.
...
SO THAT'S WHY YOU ASSIGNED MARIE TO HIM...?
MARIE-CHAN'S SOUL WAVELENGTH SHOULD HAVE A POSITIVE EFFECT ON STEIN-KUN'S SOUL.
BUT SPIRIT-KUN...COULD YOU PLEASE LOOK OUT FOR STEIN-KUN FOR ME TOO?

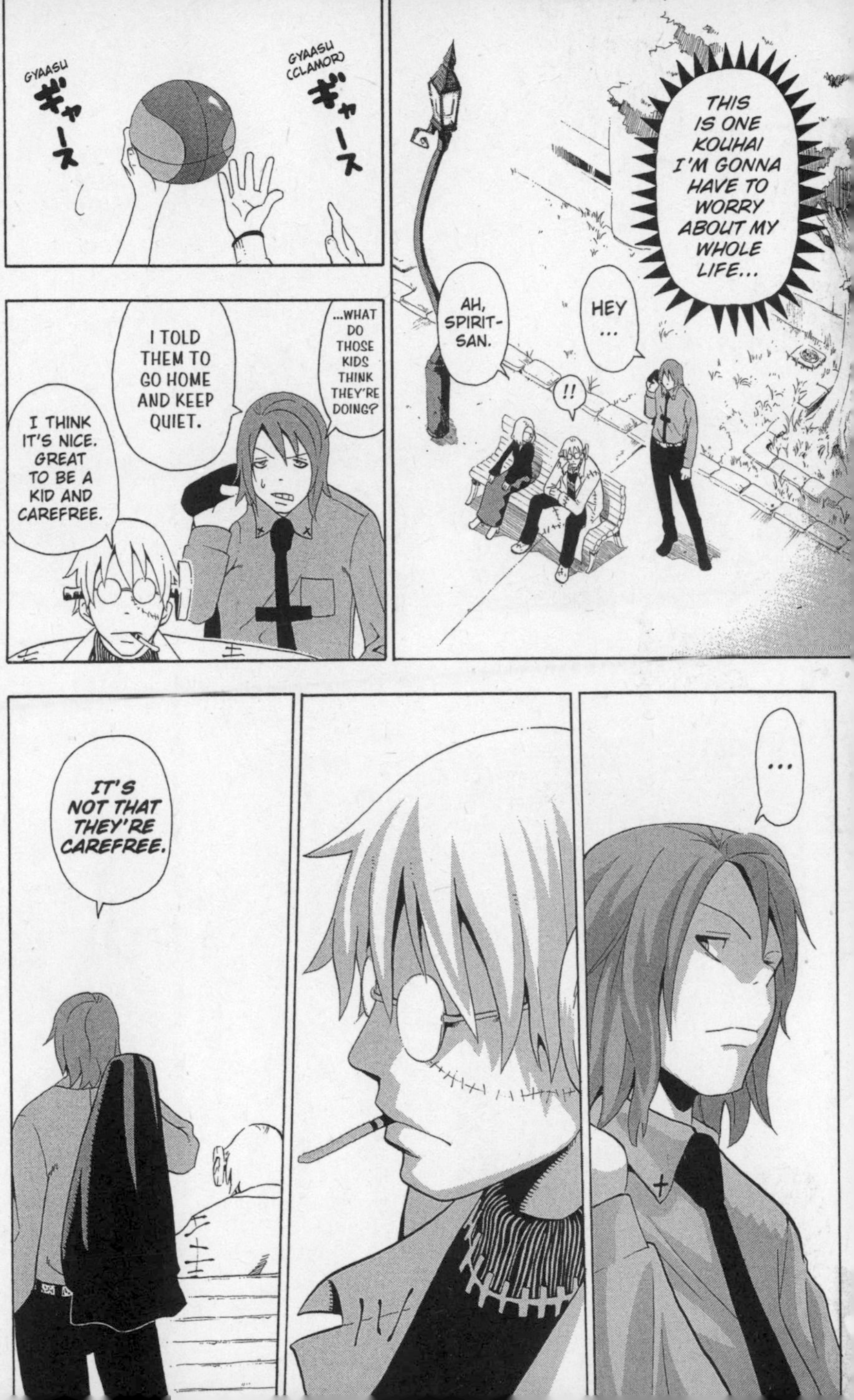
THIS IS ONE KOUHAI I'M GONNA HAVE TO WORRY ABOUT MY WHOLE LIFE...
HEY ...
AH, SPIRIT-SAN.
!!
GYAASU (CLAMOR)
ギャース
GYAASU
ギャース
...WHAT DO THOSE KIDS THINK THEY'RE DOING?
I TOLD THEM TO GO HOME AND KEEP QUIET.
I THINK IT'S NICE. GREAT TO BE A KID AND CAREFREE.
...
IT'S NOT THAT THEY'RE CAREFREE.

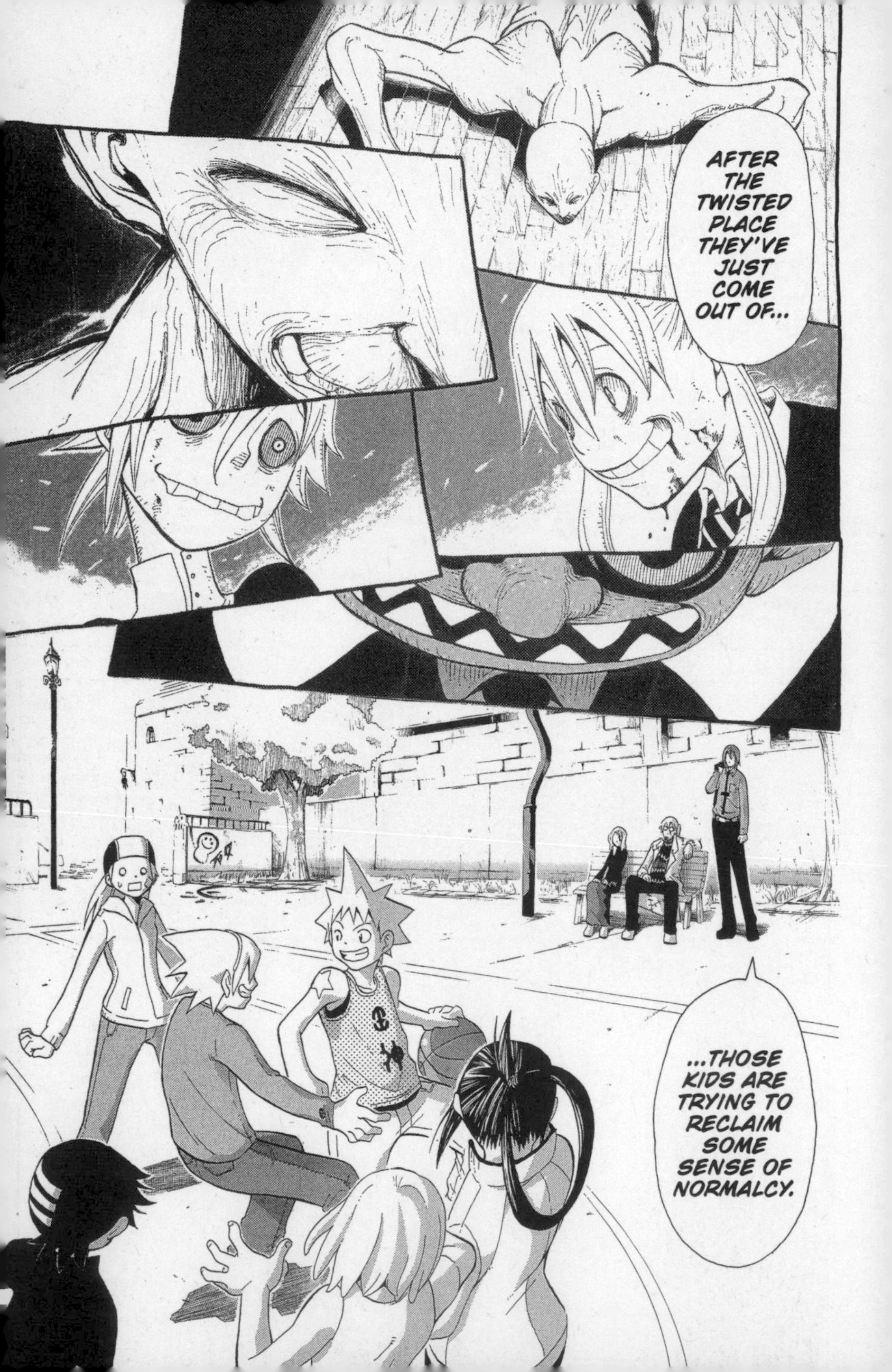
AFTER THE TWISTED PLACE THEY'VE JUST COME OUT OF...
...THOSE KIDS ARE TRYING TO RECLAIM SOME SENSE OF NORMALCY.

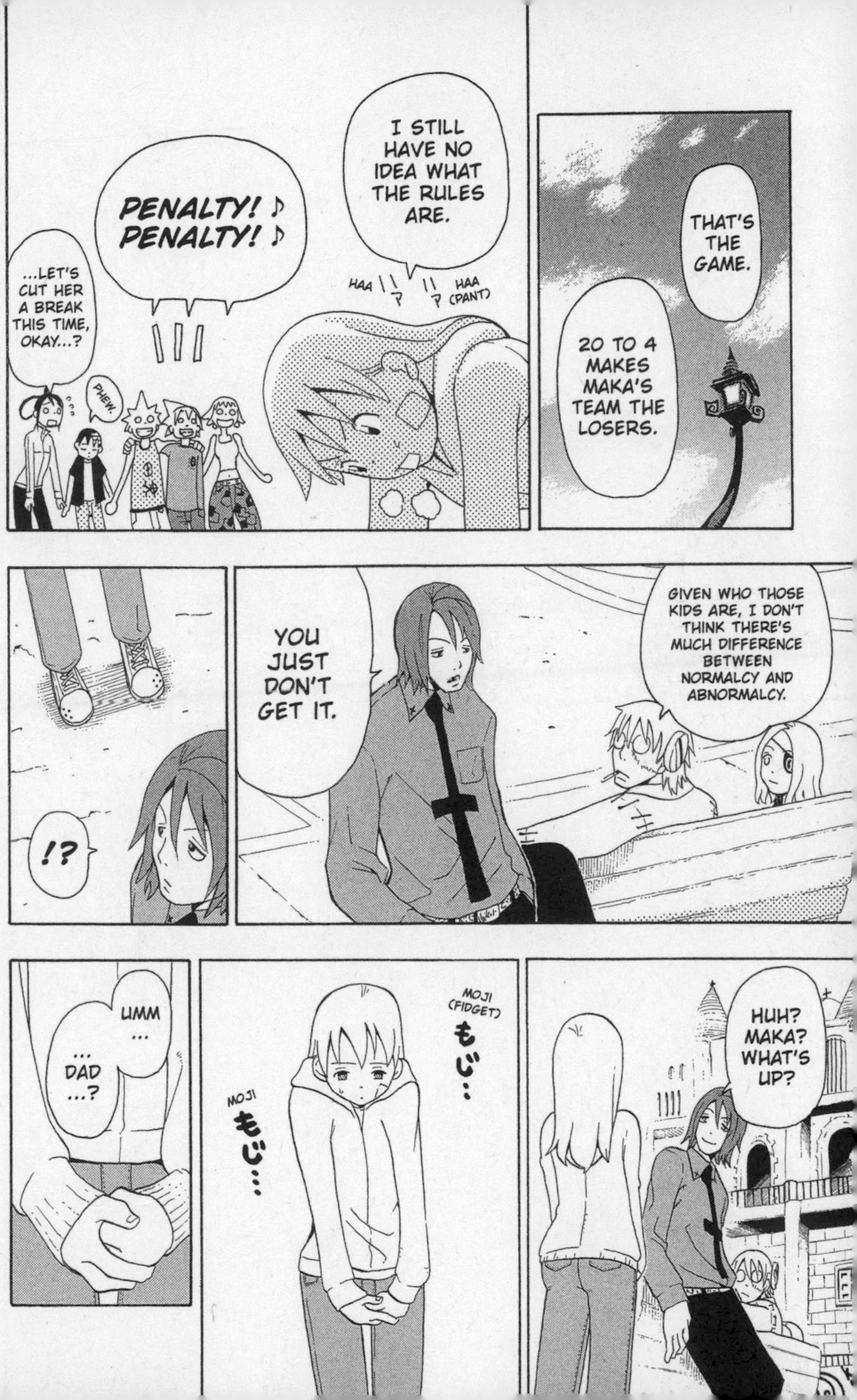
THAT'S THE GAME.
20 TO 4 MAKES MAKA'S TEAM THE LOSERS.
I STILL HAVE NO IDEA WHAT THE RULES ARE.
HAA HAA (PANT)
PENALTY! ♪ PENALTY! ♪
...LET'S CUT HER A BREAK THIS TIME, OKAY...?
PHEW.
GIVEN WHO THOSE KIDS ARE, I DON'T THINK THERE'S MUCH DIFFERENCE BETWEEN NORMALCY AND ABNORMALCY.
YOU JUST DON'T GET IT.
!?
HUH? MAKA? WHAT'S UP?
MOJI (FIDGET)
もじ‥
MOJI
もじ‥
UMM ...
... DAD ...?

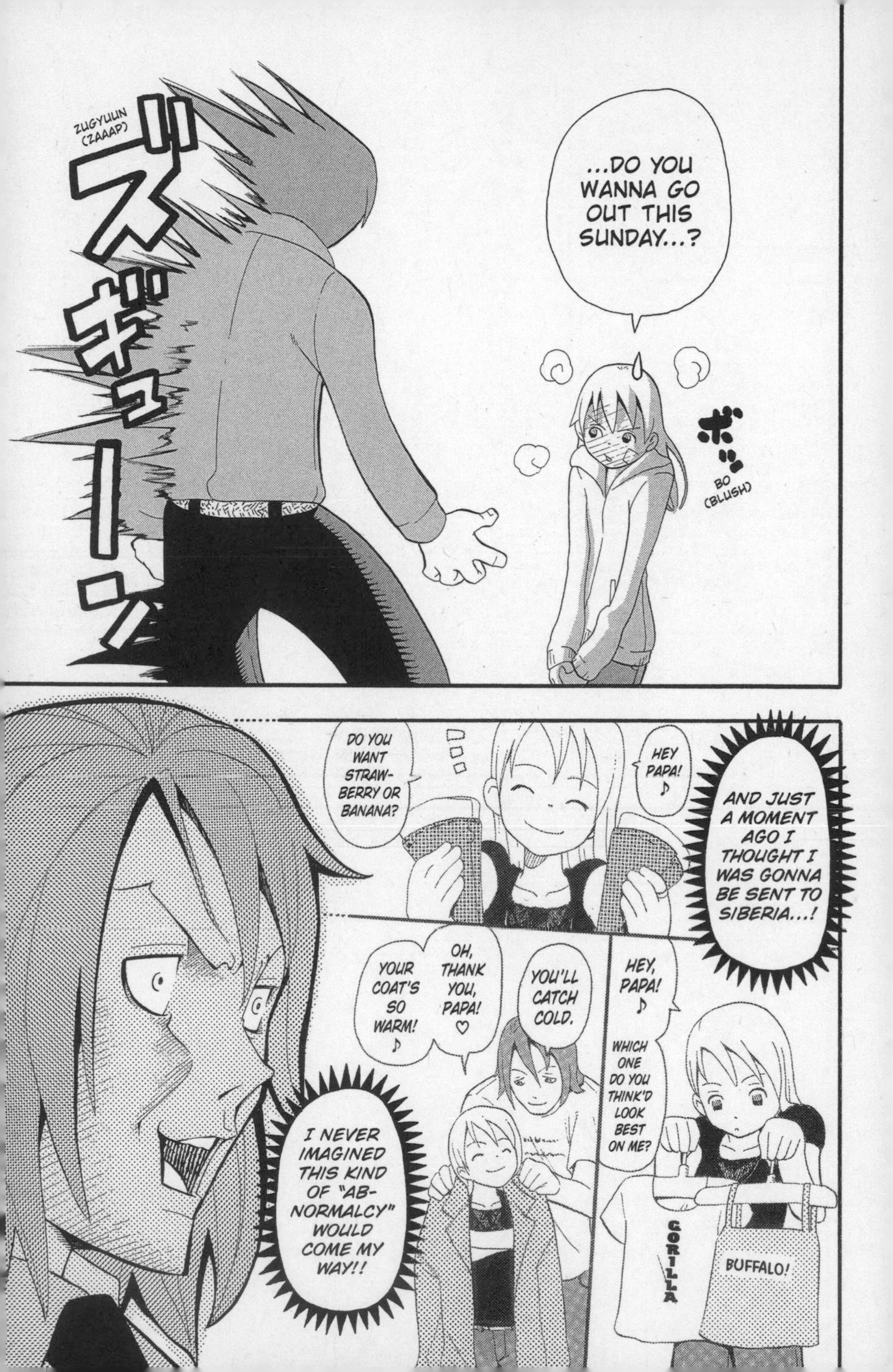
...DO YOU WANNA GO OUT THIS SUNDAY...?
ボッ
BO (BLUSH)
ズギューーーッ
ZUGYUUN (ZAAAP)
HEY PAPA! ♪
DO YOU WANT STRAWBERRY OR BANANA?
AND JUST A MOMENT AGO I THOUGHT I WAS GONNA BE SENT TO SIBERIA...!
HEY, PAPA! ♪
WHICH ONE DO YOU THINK'D LOOK BEST ON ME?
BUFFALO!
GORILLA
YOU'LL CATCH COLD.
OH, THANK YOU, PAPA! ♡
YOUR COAT'S SO WARM! ♪
I NEVER IMAGINED THIS KIND OF "AB-NORMALCY" WOULD COME MY WAY!!

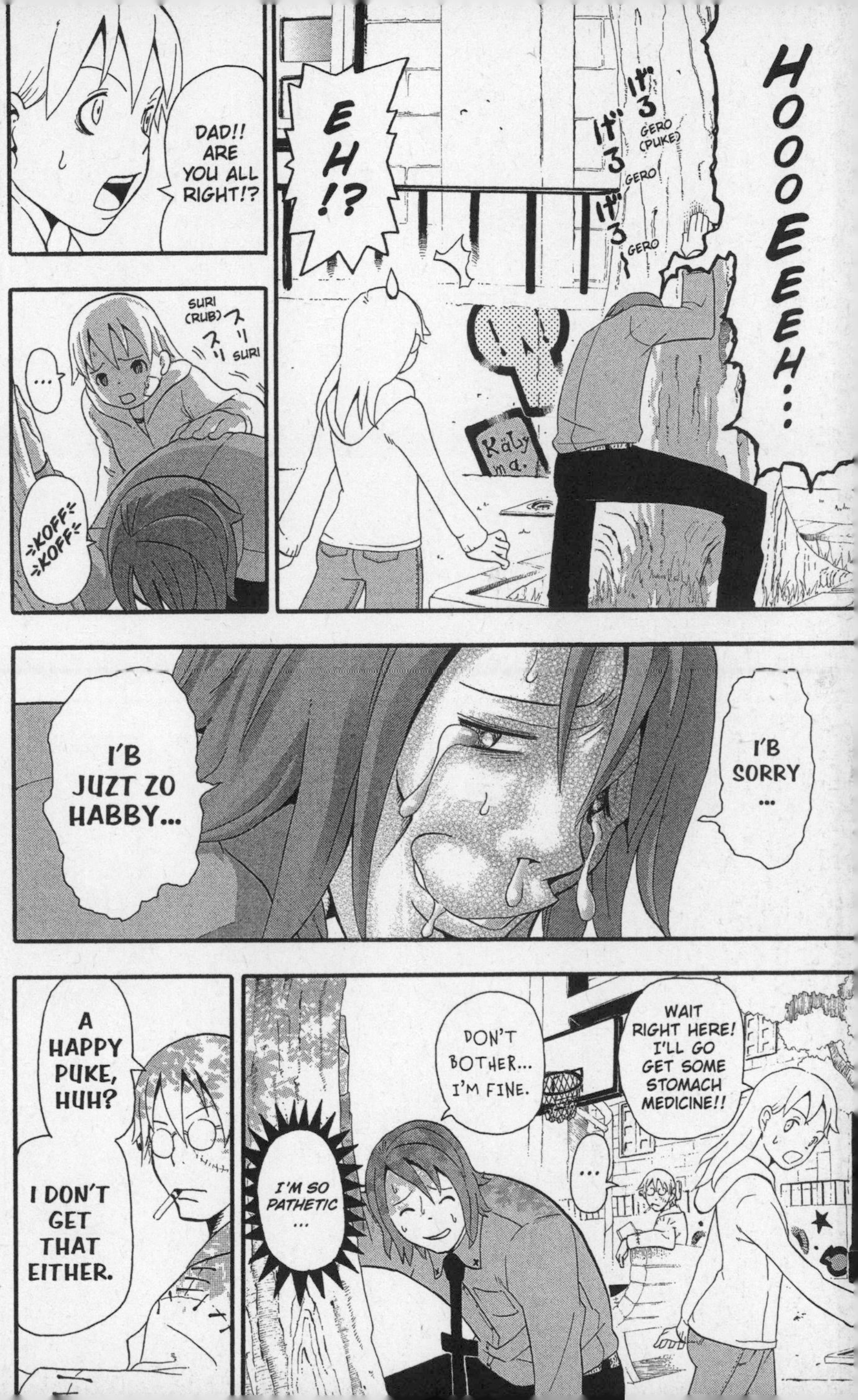
HOOOEEEH...
げろ
GERO (PUKE)
げろ
GERO
げろ
GERO
EH!?
DAD!! ARE YOU ALL RIGHT!?
スリスリ
SURI (RUB) SURI
...
KOFF KOFF
I'B SORRY...
I'B JUZT ZO HABBY...
WAIT RIGHT HERE! I'LL GO GET SOME STOMACH MEDICINE!!
DON'T BOTHER... I'M FINE.
...
I'M SO PATHETIC...
A HAPPY PUKE, HUH?
I DON'T GET THAT EITHER.

SOUL EATER

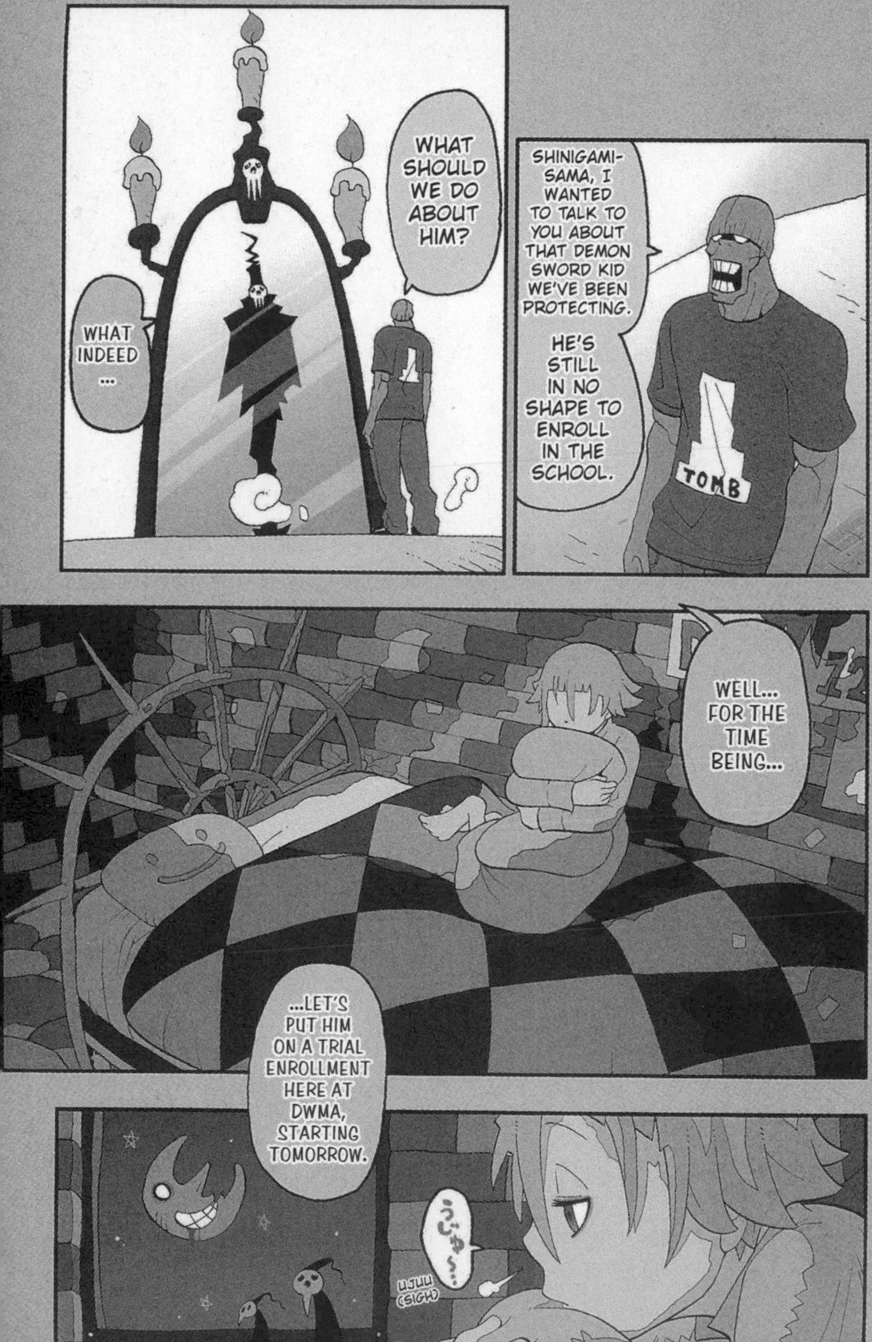
SHINIGAMI-SAMA, I WANTED TO TALK TO YOU ABOUT THAT DEMON SWORD KID WE'VE BEEN PROTECTING.
HE'S STILL IN NO SHAPE TO ENROLL IN THE SCHOOL.
TOMB
WHAT SHOULD WE DO ABOUT HIM?
WHAT INDEED ...
WELL... FOR THE TIME BEING...
...LET'S PUT HIM ON A TRIAL ENROLLMENT HERE AT DWMA, STARTING TOMORROW.
うじゅ～...
UJUU (SIGH)

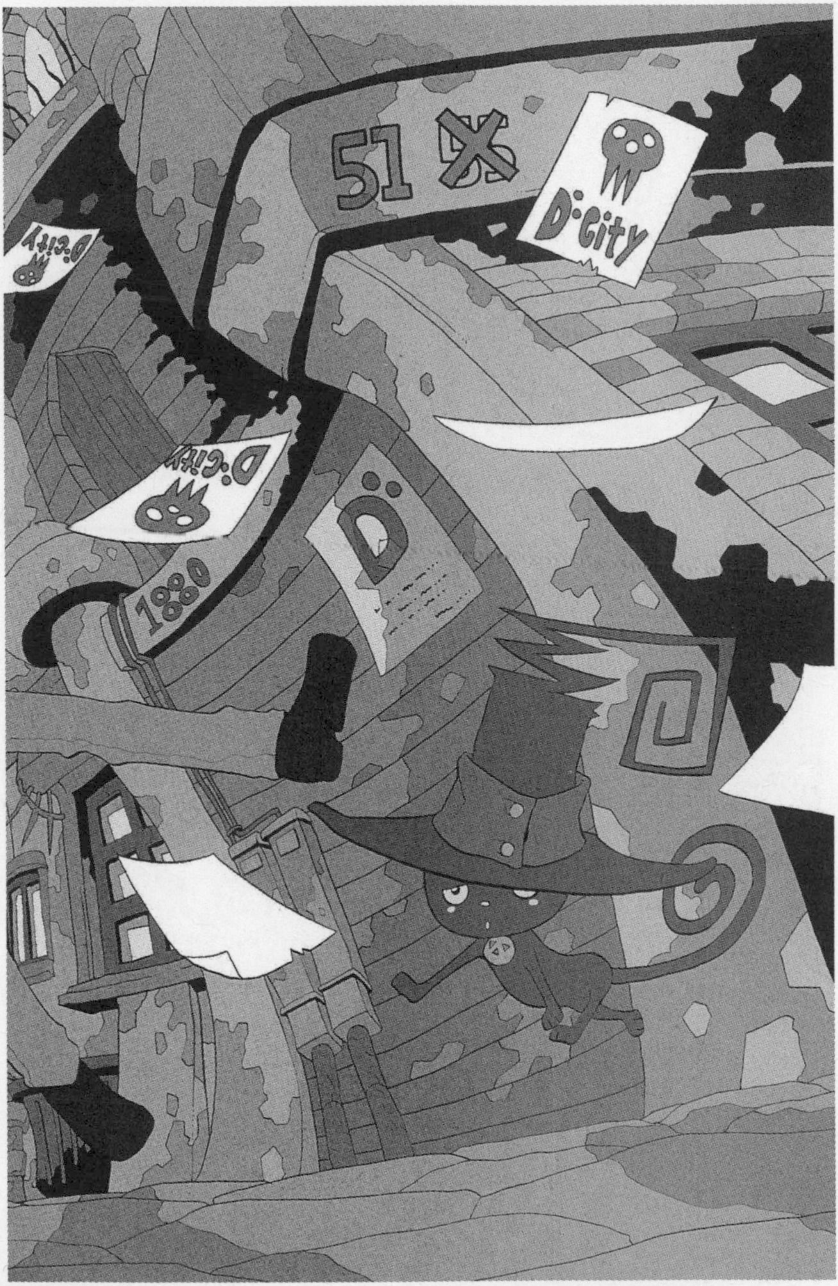
51
D·City

CHAPTER 24: THE TRIAL ENROLLMENT (PART 1)

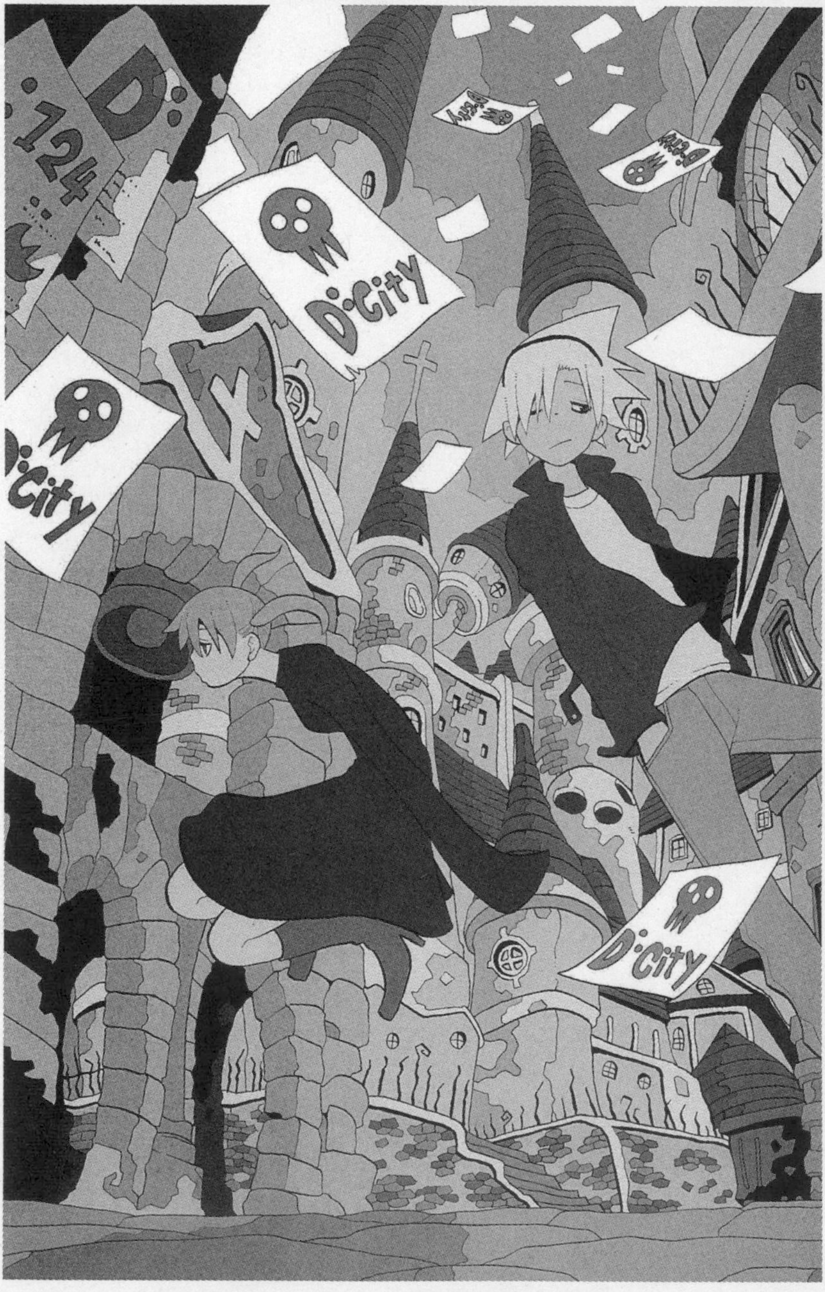
D
124
D·City
D·City
D·City
D·City

SOUL EATER

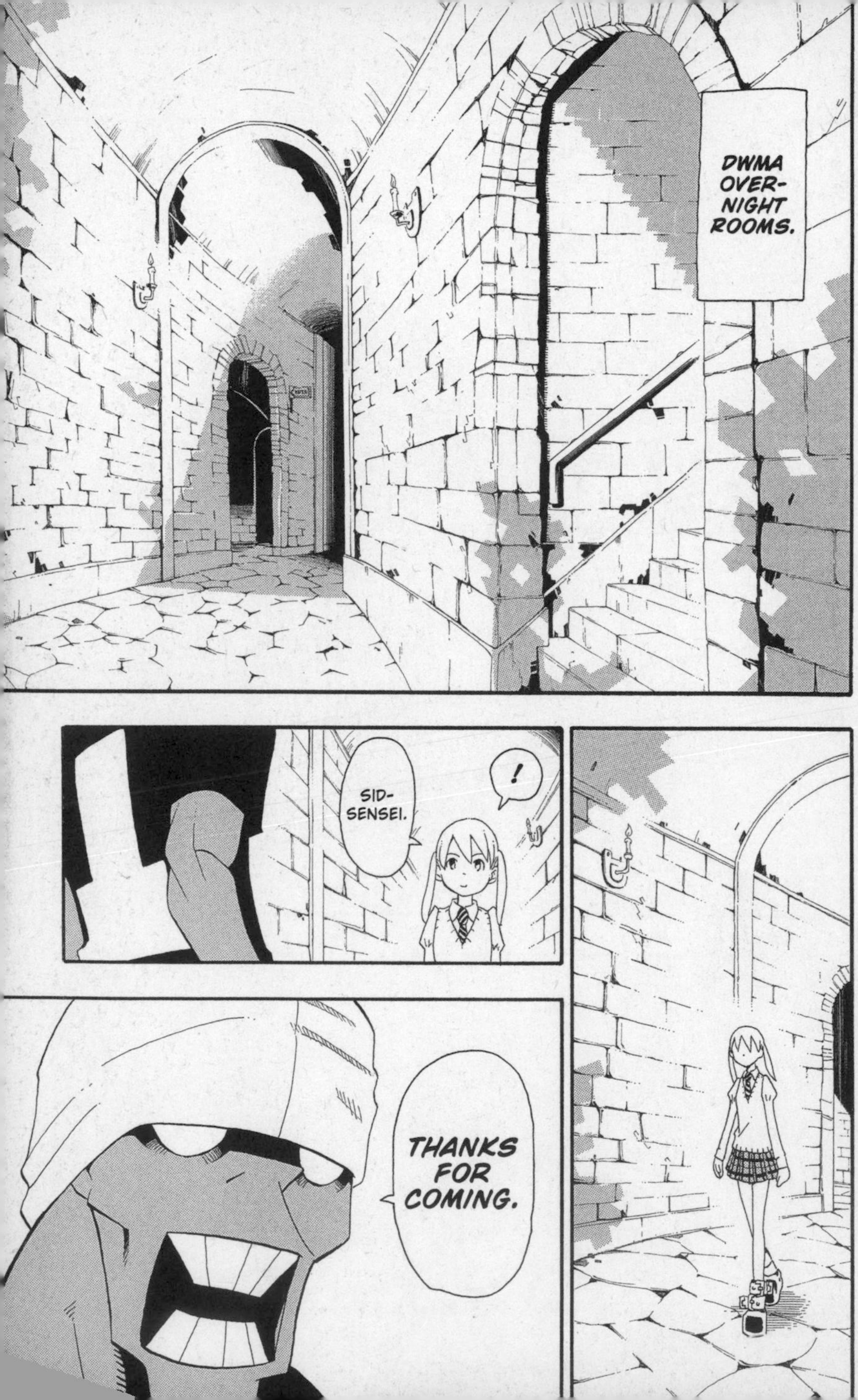
DWMA OVER-NIGHT ROOMS.
!
SID-SENSEI.
THANKS FOR COMING.

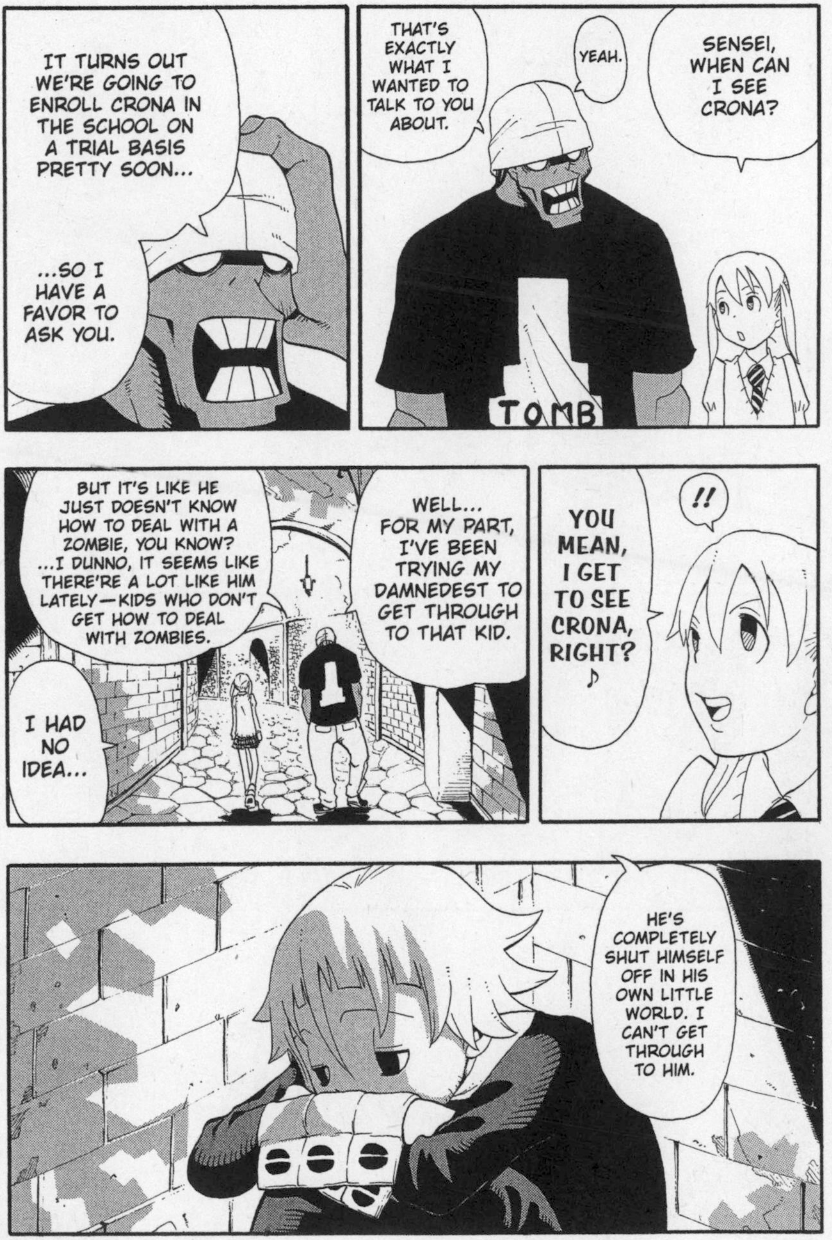
SENSEI, WHEN CAN I SEE CRONA?
YEAH.
THAT'S EXACTLY WHAT I WANTED TO TALK TO YOU ABOUT.
TOMB
IT TURNS OUT WE'RE GOING TO ENROLL CRONA IN THE SCHOOL ON A TRIAL BASIS PRETTY SOON...
...SO I HAVE A FAVOR TO ASK YOU.
!!
YOU MEAN, I GET TO SEE CRONA, RIGHT? ♪
WELL... FOR MY PART, I'VE BEEN TRYING MY DAMNEDEST TO GET THROUGH TO THAT KID.
BUT IT'S LIKE HE JUST DOESN'T KNOW HOW TO DEAL WITH A ZOMBIE, YOU KNOW? ...I DUNNO, IT SEEMS LIKE THERE'RE A LOT LIKE HIM LATELY—KIDS WHO DON'T GET HOW TO DEAL WITH ZOMBIES.
I HAD NO IDEA...
HE'S COMPLETELY SHUT HIMSELF OFF IN HIS OWN LITTLE WORLD. I CAN'T GET THROUGH TO HIM.

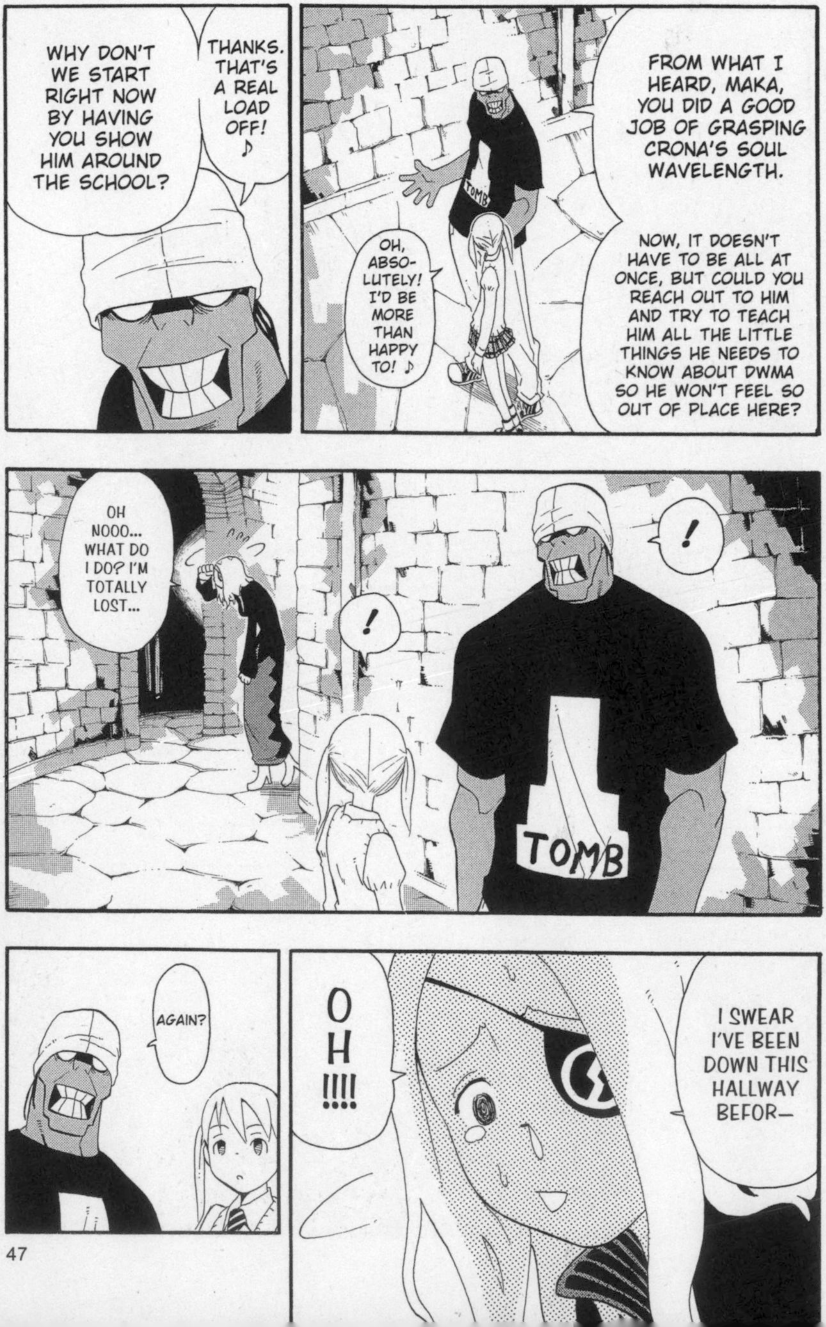

FROM WHAT I HEARD, MAKA, YOU DID A GOOD JOB OF GRASPING CRONA'S SOUL WAVELENGTH.
NOW, IT DOESN'T HAVE TO BE ALL AT ONCE, BUT COULD YOU REACH OUT TO HIM AND TRY TO TEACH HIM ALL THE LITTLE THINGS HE NEEDS TO KNOW ABOUT DWMA SO HE WON'T FEEL SO OUT OF PLACE HERE?
OH, ABSO-LUTELY! I'D BE MORE THAN HAPPY TO! ♪
TOMB
WHY DON'T WE START RIGHT NOW BY HAVING YOU SHOW HIM AROUND THE SCHOOL?
THANKS. THAT'S A REAL LOAD OFF! ♪
!
!
TOMB
OH NOOO... WHAT DO I DO? I'M TOTALLY LOST...
I SWEAR I'VE BEEN DOWN THIS HALLWAY BEFOR—
OH !!!!
AGAIN?

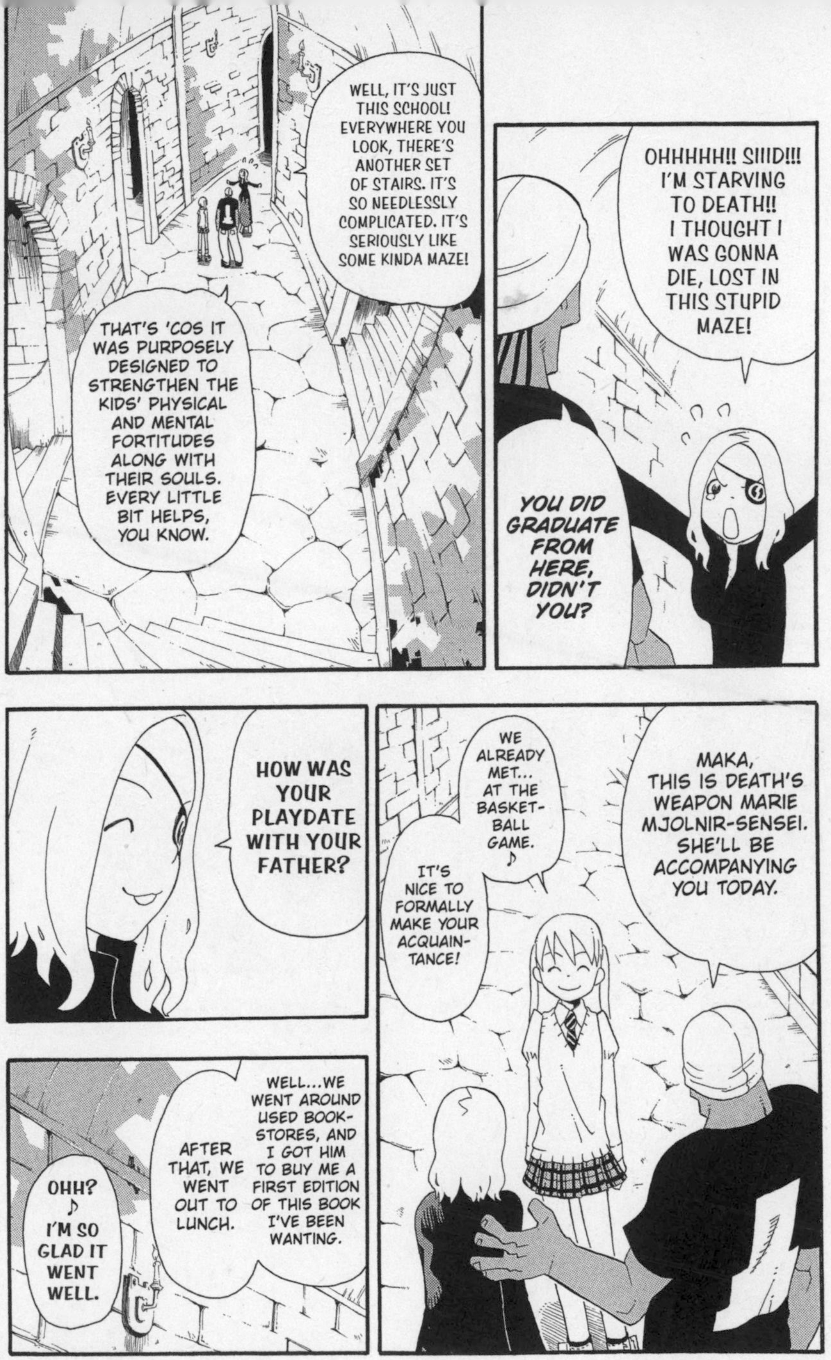
OHHHHH!! SIIID!!! I'M STARVING TO DEATH!! I THOUGHT I WAS GONNA DIE, LOST IN THIS STUPID MAZE!
YOU DID GRADUATE FROM HERE, DIDN'T YOU?
WELL, IT'S JUST THIS SCHOOL! EVERYWHERE YOU LOOK, THERE'S ANOTHER SET OF STAIRS. IT'S SO NEEDLESSLY COMPLICATED. IT'S SERIOUSLY LIKE SOME KINDA MAZE!
THAT'S 'COS IT WAS PURPOSELY DESIGNED TO STRENGTHEN THE KIDS' PHYSICAL AND MENTAL FORTITUDES ALONG WITH THEIR SOULS. EVERY LITTLE BIT HELPS, YOU KNOW.
MAKA, THIS IS DEATH'S WEAPON MARIE MJOLNIR-SENSEI. SHE'LL BE ACCOMPANYING YOU TODAY.
WE ALREADY MET... AT THE BASKET-BALL GAME. ♪
IT'S NICE TO FORMALLY MAKE YOUR ACQUAIN-TANCE!
HOW WAS YOUR PLAYDATE WITH YOUR FATHER?
WELL...WE WENT AROUND USED BOOK-STORES, AND I GOT HIM TO BUY ME A FIRST EDITION OF THIS BOOK I'VE BEEN WANTING.
AFTER THAT, WE WENT OUT TO LUNCH.
OHH? ♪ I'M SO GLAD IT WENT WELL.

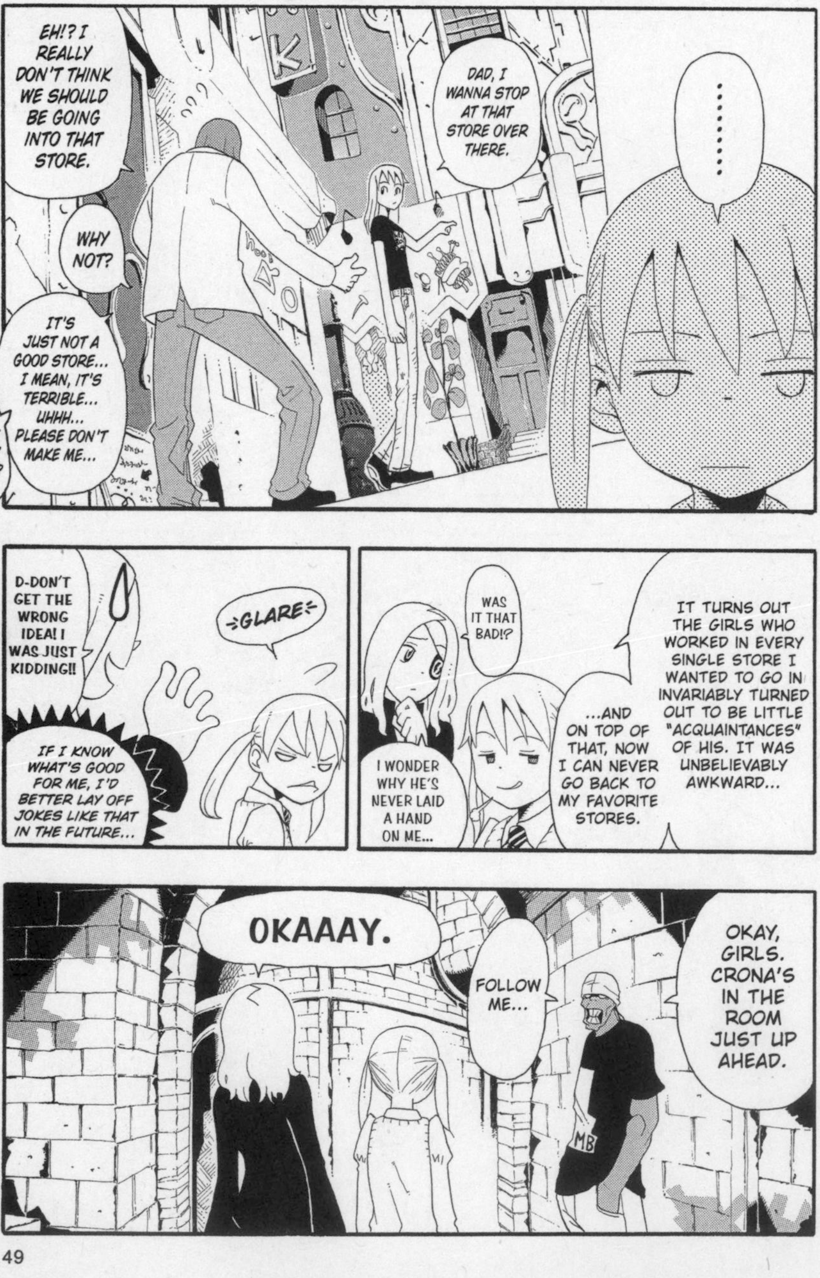
......
DAD, I WANNA STOP AT THAT STORE OVER THERE.
EH!? I REALLY DON'T THINK WE SHOULD BE GOING INTO THAT STORE.
WHY NOT?
IT'S JUST NOT A GOOD STORE... I MEAN, IT'S TERRIBLE... UHHH... PLEASE DON'T MAKE ME...
BUT WHY NOT?
IT TURNS OUT THE GIRLS WHO WORKED IN EVERY SINGLE STORE I WANTED TO GO IN INVARIABLY TURNED OUT TO BE LITTLE "ACQUAINTANCES" OF HIS. IT WAS UNBELIEVABLY AWKWARD...
...AND ON TOP OF THAT, NOW I CAN NEVER GO BACK TO MY FAVORITE STORES.
WAS IT THAT BAD!?
I WONDER WHY HE'S NEVER LAID A HAND ON ME...
-GLARE-
D-DON'T GET THE WRONG IDEA! I WAS JUST KIDDING!!
IF I KNOW WHAT'S GOOD FOR ME, I'D BETTER LAY OFF JOKES LIKE THAT IN THE FUTURE...
OKAY, GIRLS. CRONA'S IN THE ROOM JUST UP AHEAD.
FOLLOW ME...
OKAAAY.

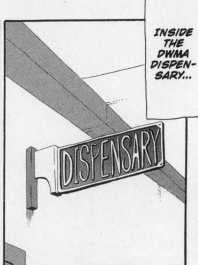

INSIDE THE DWMA DISPENSARY...

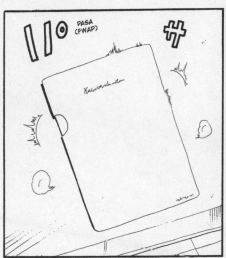

PASA
(FWAP)

GI
(CREAK)

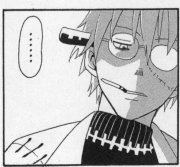

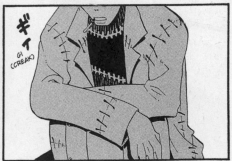

THE DEMON SWORD...

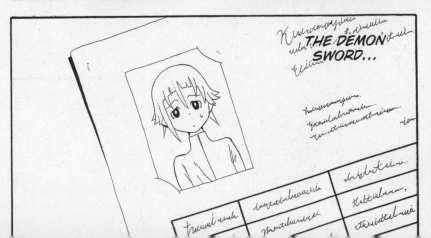

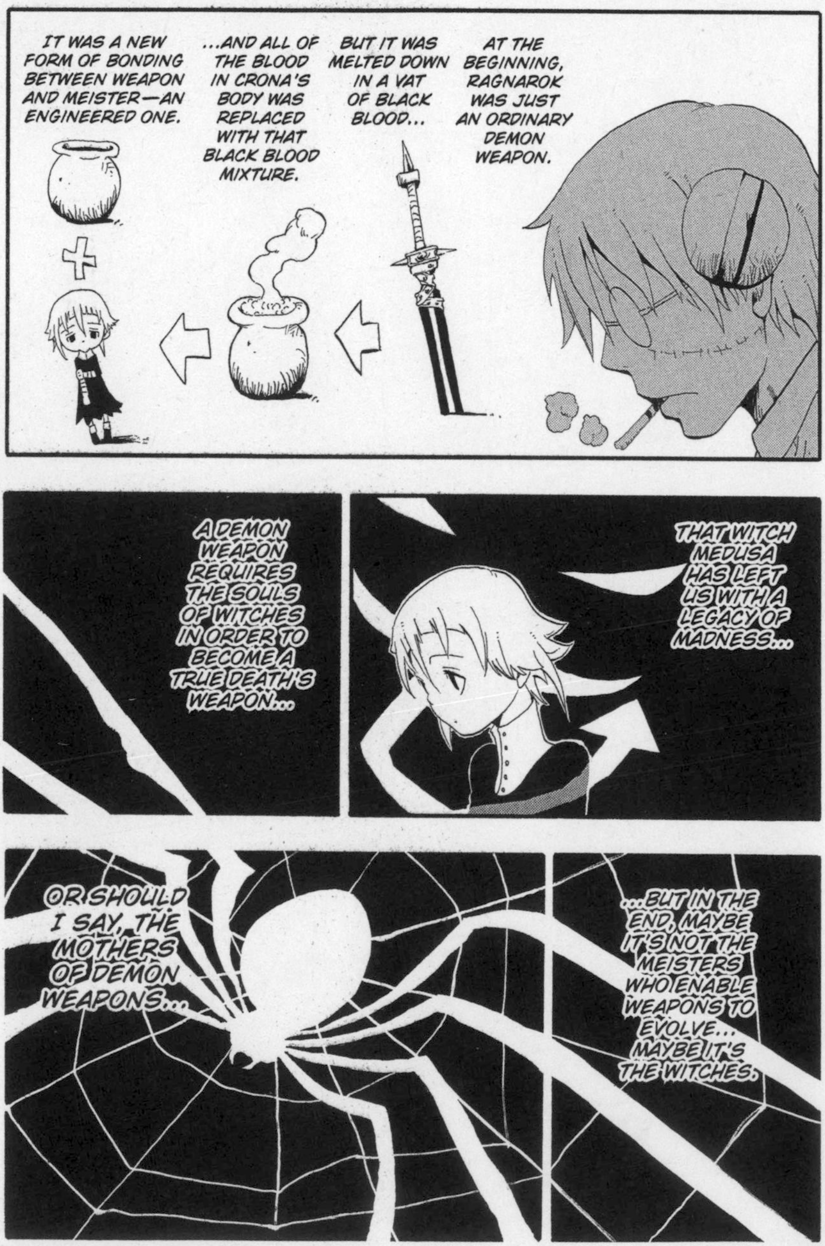
AT THE BEGINNING, RAGNAROK WAS JUST AN ORDINARY DEMON WEAPON.
BUT IT WAS MELTED DOWN IN A VAT OF BLACK BLOOD...
...AND ALL OF THE BLOOD IN CRONA'S BODY WAS REPLACED WITH THAT BLACK BLOOD MIXTURE.
IT WAS A NEW FORM OF BONDING BETWEEN WEAPON AND MEISTER—AN ENGINEERED ONE.
THAT WITCH MEDUSA HAS LEFT US WITH A LEGACY OF MADNESS...
A DEMON WEAPON REQUIRES THE SOULS OF WITCHES IN ORDER TO BECOME A TRUE DEATH'S WEAPON...
...BUT IN THE END, MAYBE IT'S NOT THE MEISTERS WHO ENABLE WEAPONS TO EVOLVE... MAYBE IT'S THE WITCHES.
OR SHOULD I SAY, THE MOTHERS OF DEMON WEAPONS...

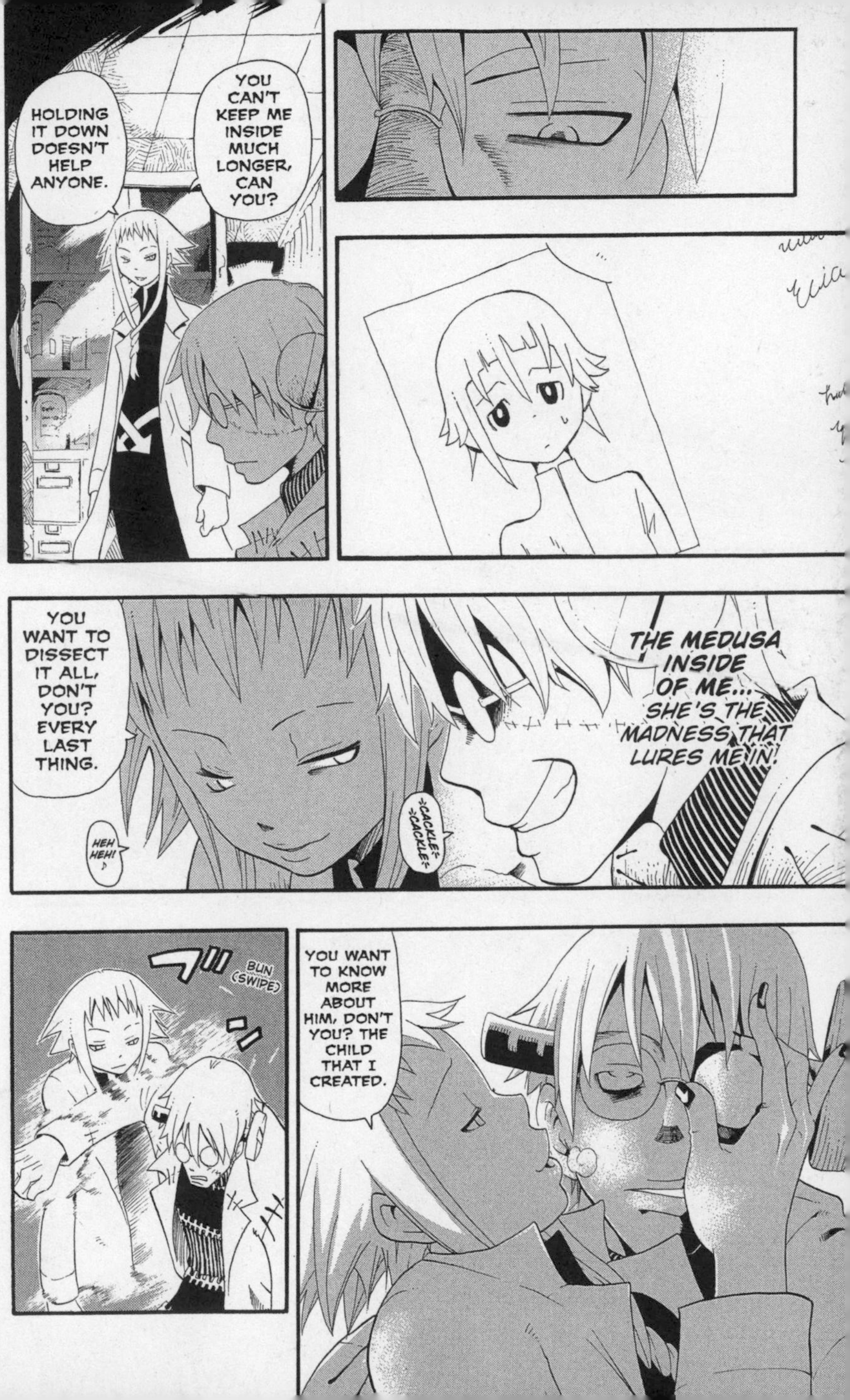
YOU CAN'T KEEP ME INSIDE MUCH LONGER, CAN YOU?
HOLDING IT DOWN DOESN'T HELP ANYONE.
THE MEDUSA INSIDE OF ME... SHE'S THE MADNESS THAT LURES ME IN!
CACKLE CACKLE
YOU WANT TO DISSECT IT ALL, DON'T YOU? EVERY LAST THING.
HEH HEH! ♪
YOU WANT TO KNOW MORE ABOUT HIM, DON'T YOU? THE CHILD THAT I CREATED.
BUN (SWIPE)

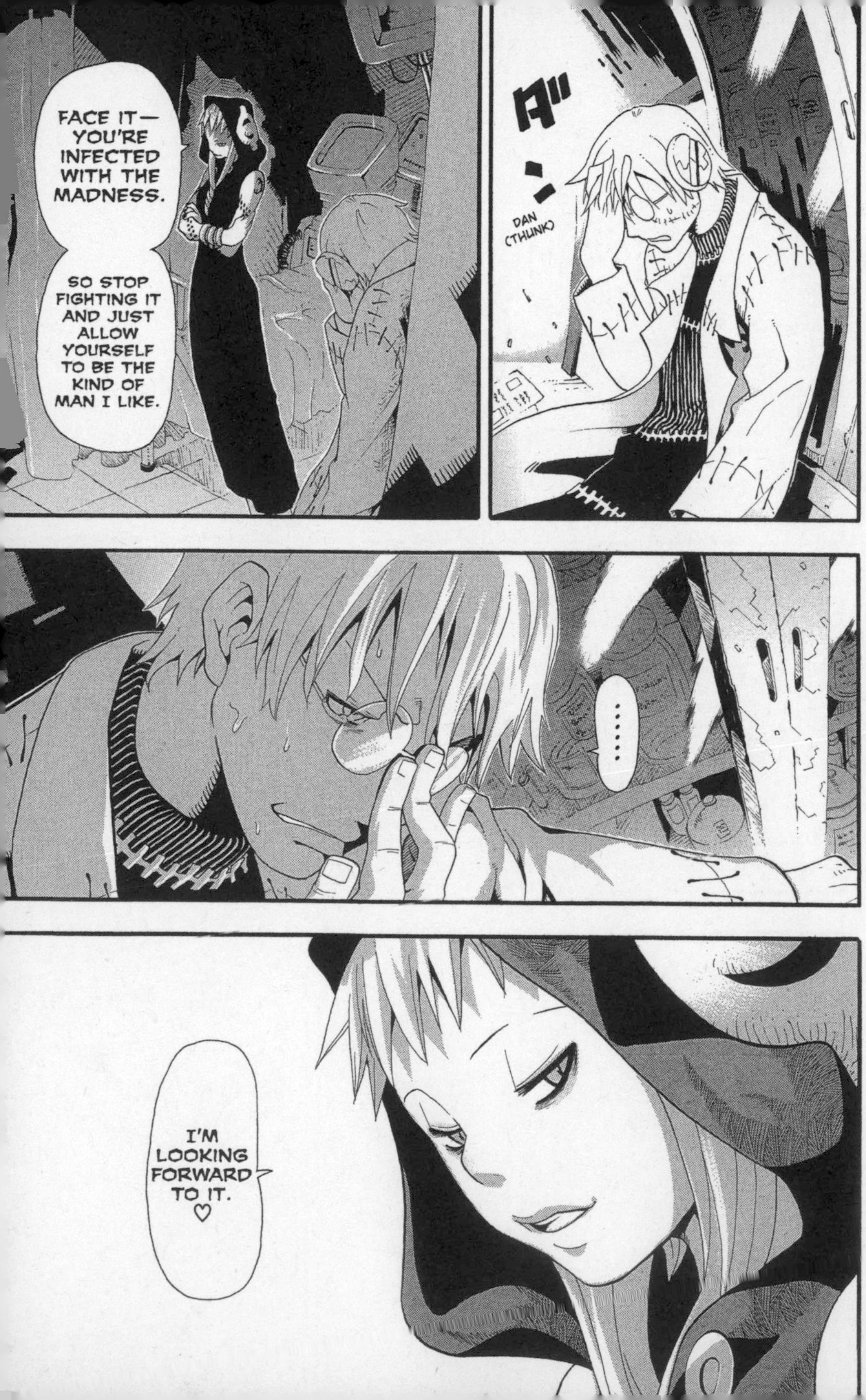
ダン
DAN (THUNK)
FACE IT—YOU'RE INFECTED WITH THE MADNESS.
SO STOP FIGHTING IT AND JUST ALLOW YOURSELF TO BE THE KIND OF MAN I LIKE.
......
I'M LOOKING FORWARD TO IT. ♡

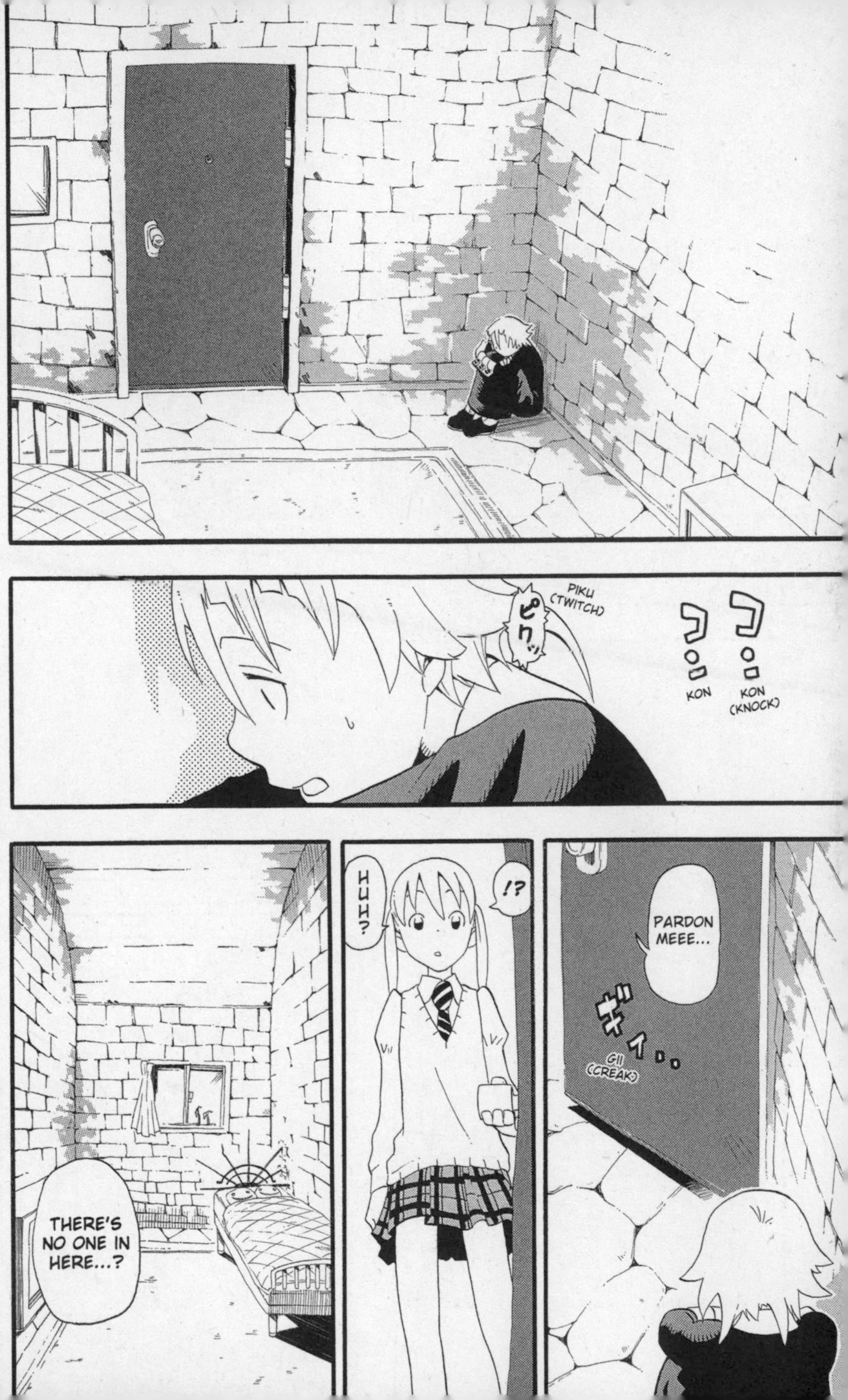
コン
KON
(KNOCK)
コン
KON
ピクッ
PIKU
(TWITCH)
PARDON MEEE...
ギィ
GII
(CREAK)
!?
HUH?
THERE'S NO ONE IN HERE...?

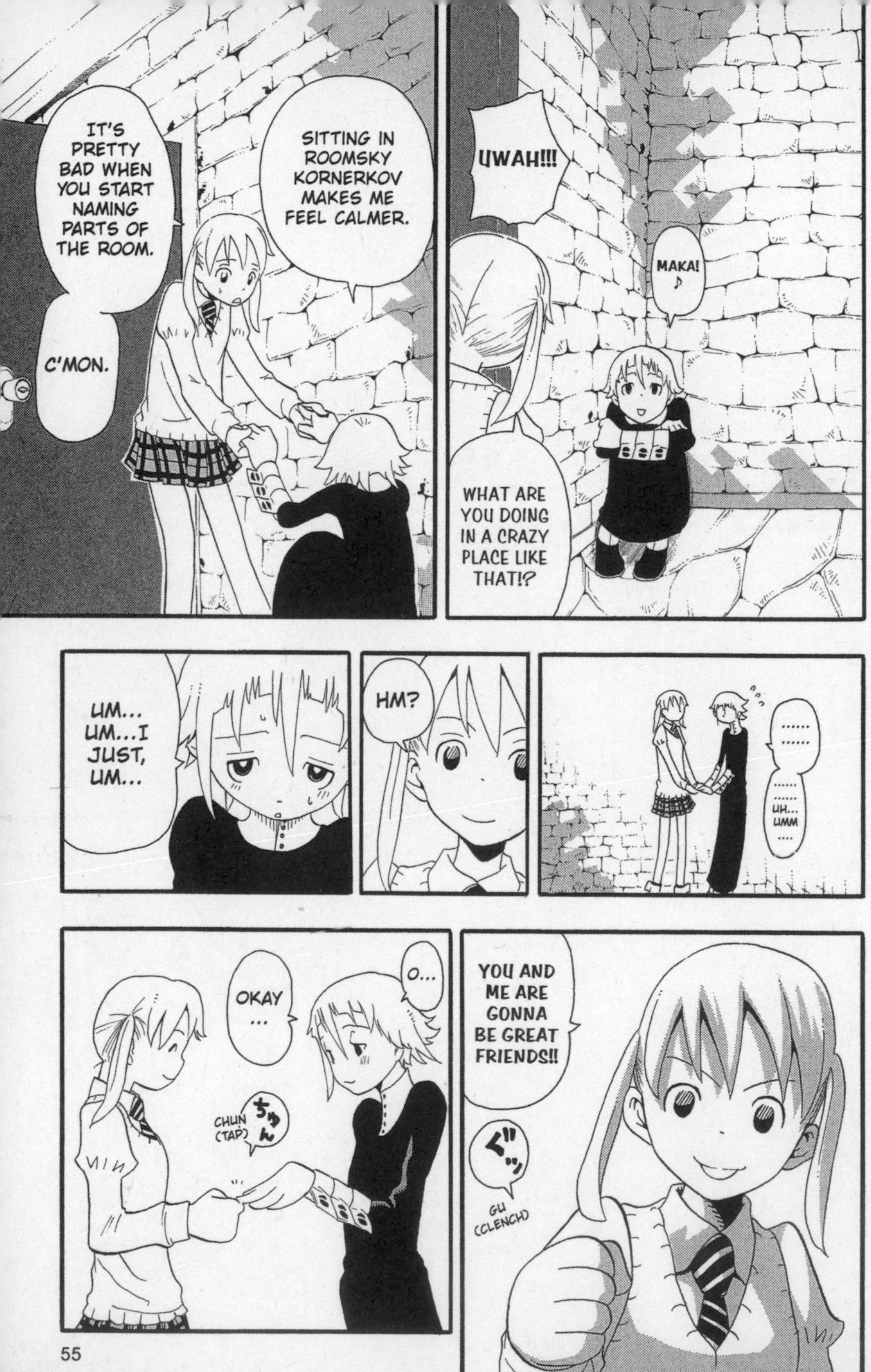

UWAH!!!
MAKA! ♪
WHAT ARE YOU DOING IN A CRAZY PLACE LIKE THAT!?
SITTING IN ROOMSKY KORNERKOV MAKES ME FEEL CALMER.
IT'S PRETTY BAD WHEN YOU START NAMING PARTS OF THE ROOM.
C'MON.
....
.... UH... UMM ....
HM?
UM... UM...I JUST, UM...
YOU AND ME ARE GONNA BE GREAT FRIENDS!!
ぐッ
GU (CLENCH)
O...
OKAY ...
ちゅん
CHUN (TAP)

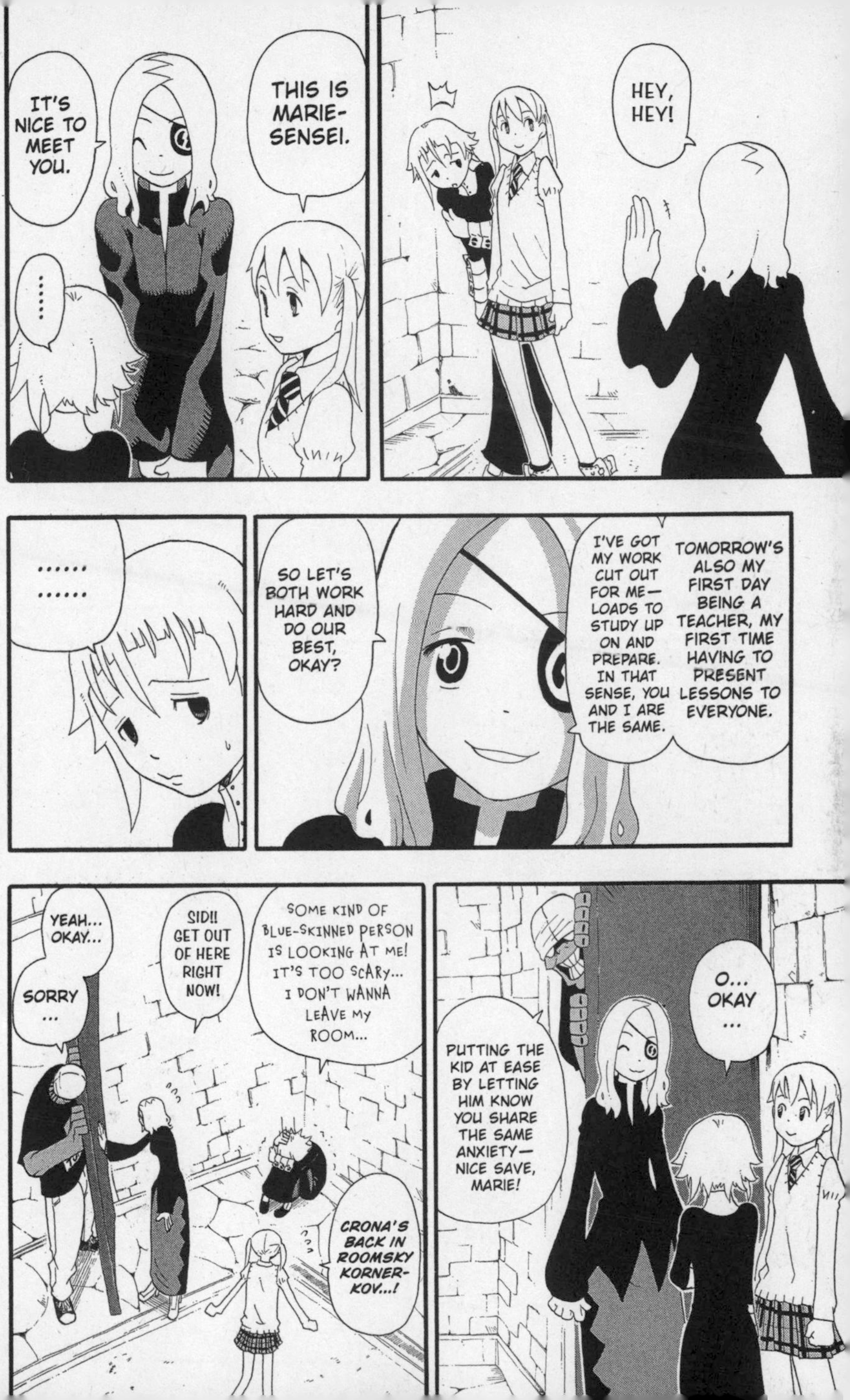
HEY, HEY!
THIS IS MARIE-SENSEI.
IT'S NICE TO MEET YOU.
......
TOMORROW'S ALSO MY FIRST DAY BEING A TEACHER, MY FIRST TIME HAVING TO PRESENT LESSONS TO EVERYONE.
I'VE GOT MY WORK CUT OUT FOR ME— LOADS TO STUDY UP ON AND PREPARE. IN THAT SENSE, YOU AND I ARE THE SAME.
SO LET'S BOTH WORK HARD AND DO OUR BEST, OKAY?
....
O... OKAY...
PUTTING THE KID AT EASE BY LETTING HIM KNOW YOU SHARE THE SAME ANXIETY— NICE SAVE, MARIE!
SOME KIND OF BLUE-SKINNED PERSON IS LOOKING AT ME! IT'S TOO SCARY... I DON'T WANNA LEAVE MY ROOM...
SID!! GET OUT OF HERE RIGHT NOW!
YEAH... OKAY...
SORRY...
CRONA'S BACK IN ROOMSKY KORNER-KOV...!

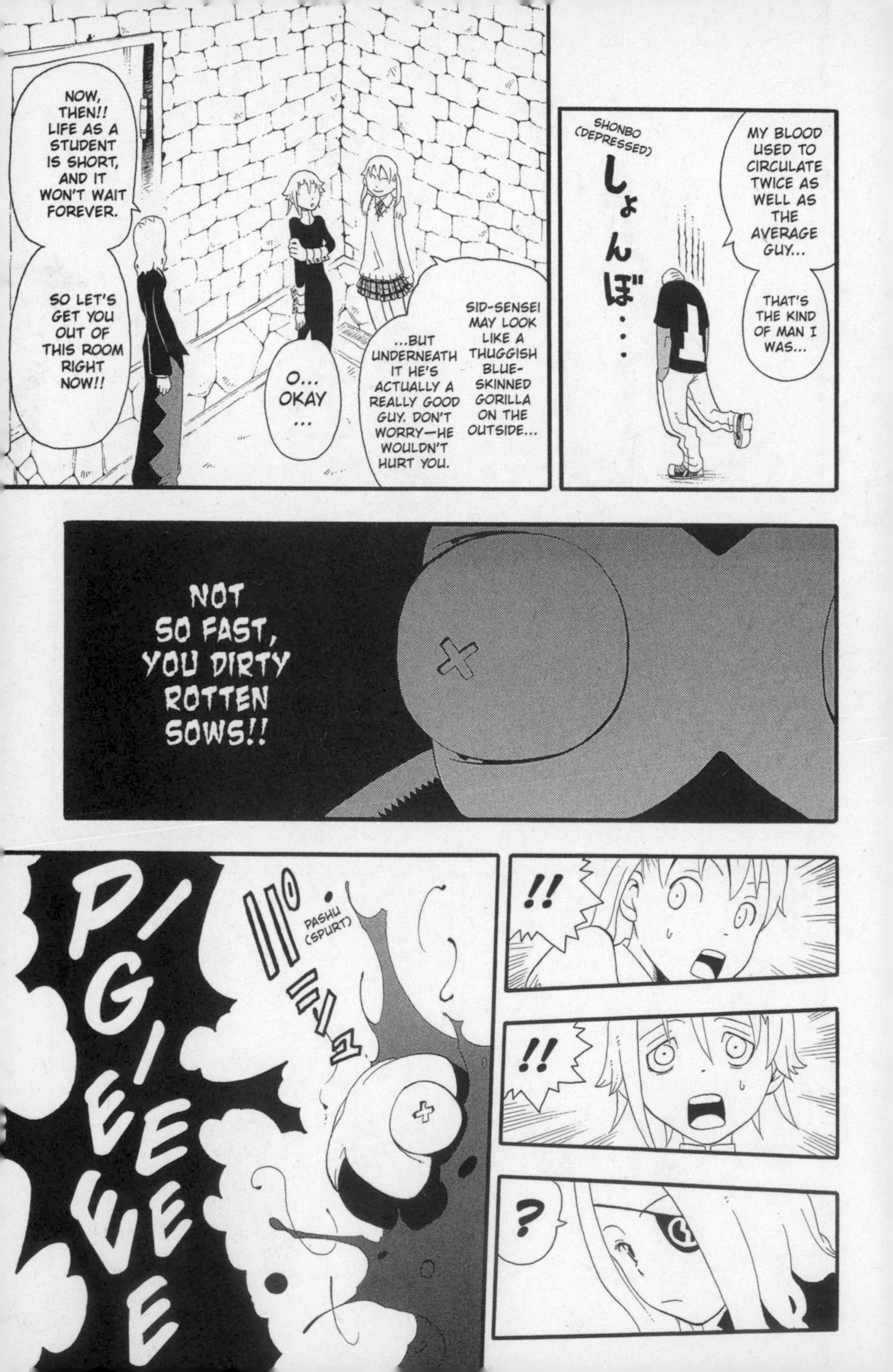
MY BLOOD USED TO CIRCULATE TWICE AS WELL AS THE AVERAGE GUY...
THAT'S THE KIND OF MAN I WAS...
しょんぼ・・・
SHONBO (DEPRESSED)
SID-SENSEI MAY LOOK LIKE A THUGGISH BLUE-SKINNED GORILLA ON THE OUTSIDE...
...BUT UNDERNEATH IT HE'S ACTUALLY A REALLY GOOD GUY. DON'T WORRY—HE WOULDN'T HURT YOU.
NOW, THEN!! LIFE AS A STUDENT IS SHORT, AND IT WON'T WAIT FOREVER.
SO LET'S GET YOU OUT OF THIS ROOM RIGHT NOW!!
O... OKAY ...
NOT SO FAST, YOU DIRTY ROTTEN SOWS!!
!!
!!
?
パシュ
PASHU (SPURT)
PIGIEEEEE

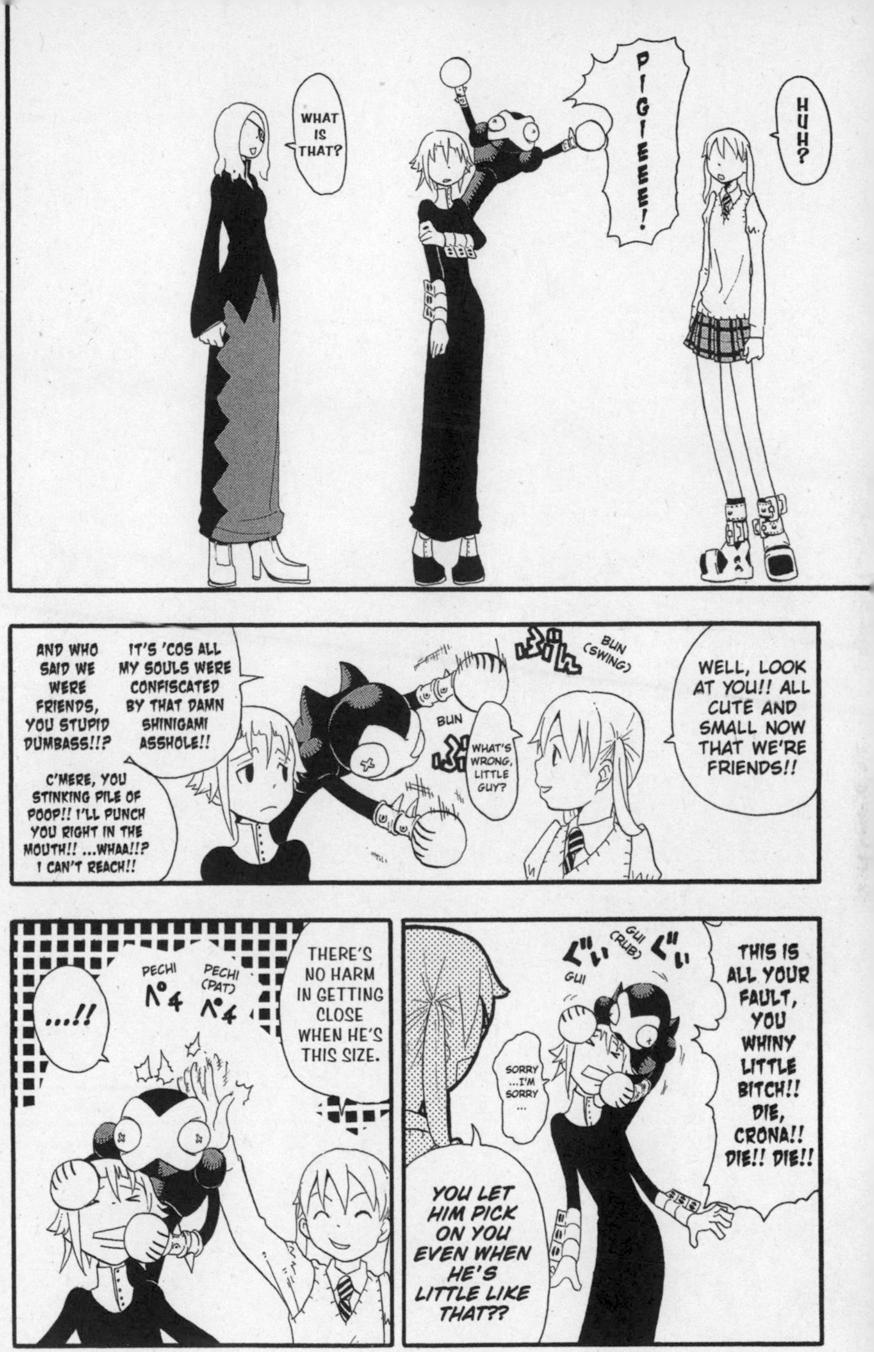
HUH?
PIGIEEE!
WHAT IS THAT?
WELL, LOOK AT YOU!! ALL CUTE AND SMALL NOW THAT WE'RE FRIENDS!!
BUN (SWING)
WHAT'S WRONG, LITTLE GUY?
BUN
IT'S 'COS ALL MY SOULS WERE CONFISCATED BY THAT DAMN SHINIGAMI ASSHOLE!!
AND WHO SAID WE WERE FRIENDS, YOU STUPID DUMBASS!!?
C'MERE, YOU STINKING PILE OF POOP!! I'LL PUNCH YOU RIGHT IN THE MOUTH!! ...WHAA!!? I CAN'T REACH!!
THIS IS ALL YOUR FAULT, YOU WHINY LITTLE BITCH!! DIE, CRONA!! DIE!! DIE!!
GUI (RUB)
GUI
SORRY ...I'M SORRY ...
YOU LET HIM PICK ON YOU EVEN WHEN HE'S LITTLE LIKE THAT??
THERE'S NO HARM IN GETTING CLOSE WHEN HE'S THIS SIZE.
PECHI (PAT)
PECHI
...!!

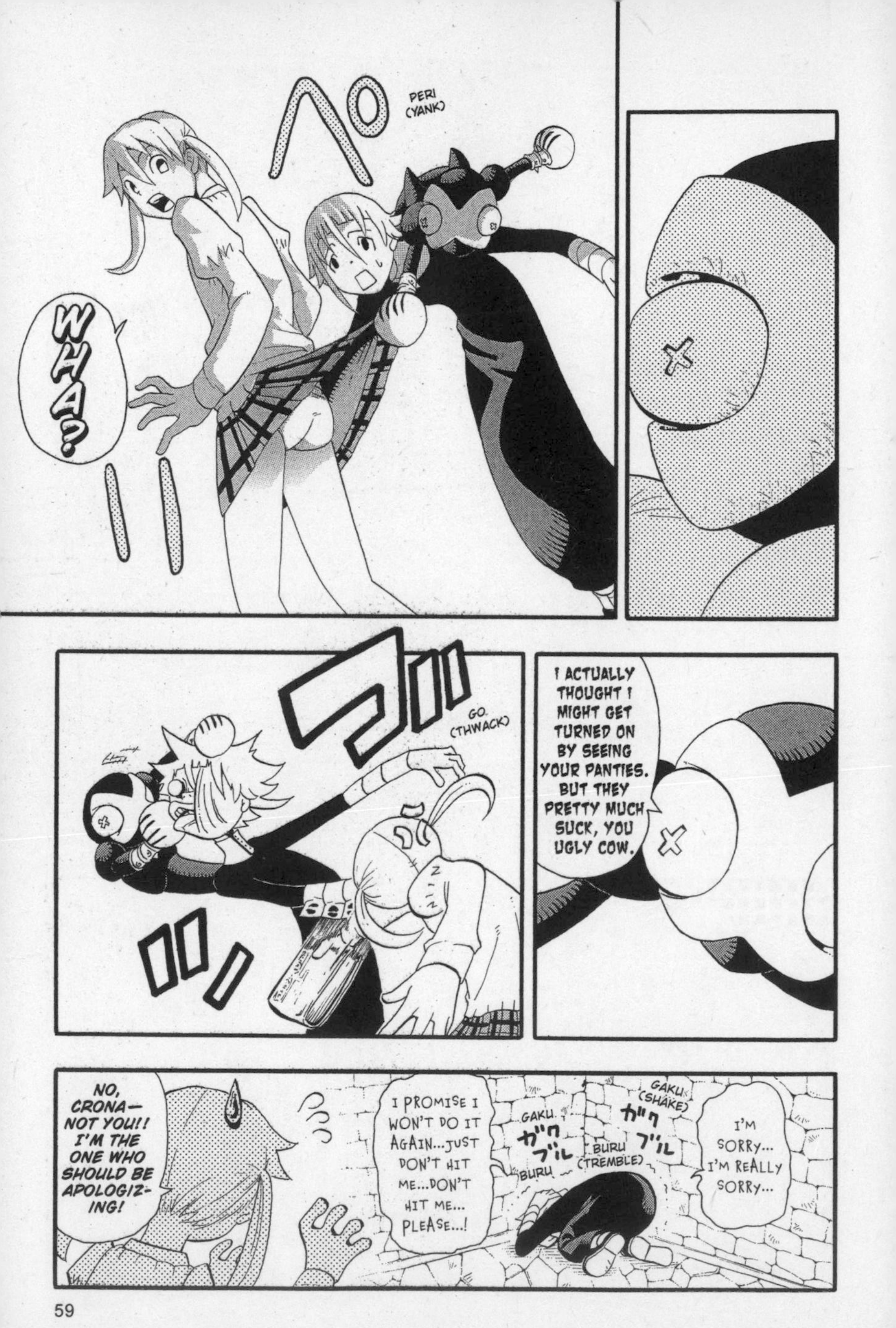

PERI (YANK)
WHA?
I ACTUALLY THOUGHT I MIGHT GET TURNED ON BY SEEING YOUR PANTIES. BUT THEY PRETTY MUCH SUCK, YOU UGLY COW.
GO. (THWACK)
I'M SORRY... I'M REALLY SORRY...
GAKU (SHAKE)
BURU (TREMBLE)
GAKU
BURU
I PROMISE I WON'T DO IT AGAIN...JUST DON'T HIT ME...DON'T HIT ME... PLEASE...!
NO, CRONA— NOT YOU!! I'M THE ONE WHO SHOULD BE APOLOGIZING!

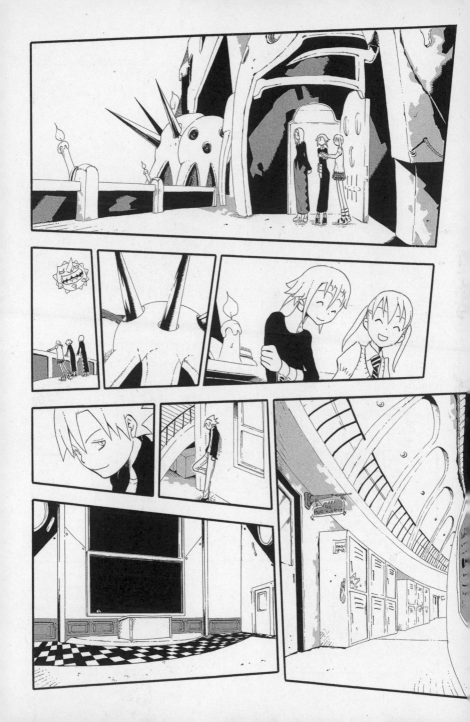

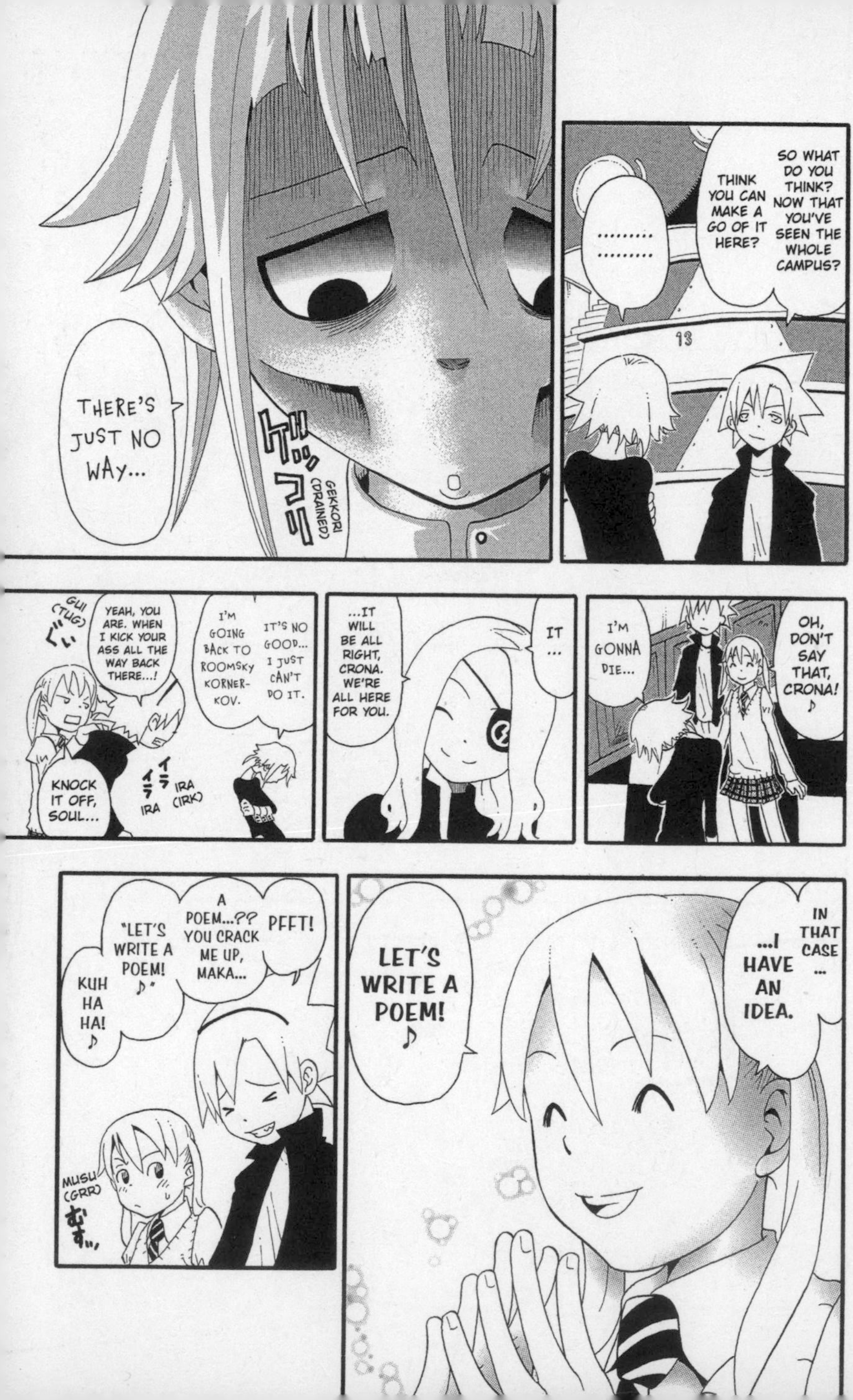
SO WHAT DO YOU THINK? NOW THAT YOU'VE SEEN THE WHOLE CAMPUS?
THINK YOU CAN MAKE A GO OF IT HERE?
....
....
THERE'S JUST NO WAY...
GEKKORI (DRAINED)
OH, DON'T SAY THAT, CRONA! ♪
I'M GONNA DIE...
IT ...
...IT WILL BE ALL RIGHT, CRONA. WE'RE ALL HERE FOR YOU.
IT'S NO GOOD... I JUST CAN'T DO IT.
I'M GOING BACK TO ROOMSKY KORNER-KOV.
YEAH, YOU ARE. WHEN I KICK YOUR ASS ALL THE WAY BACK THERE...!
GUI (TUG)
IRA IRA (IRK)
KNOCK IT OFF, SOUL...
IN THAT CASE ...
...I HAVE AN IDEA.
LET'S WRITE A POEM! ♪
PFFT!
A POEM...?? YOU CRACK ME UP, MAKA...
"LET'S WRITE A POEM! ♪"
KUH HA HA! ♪
MUSU (GRR)

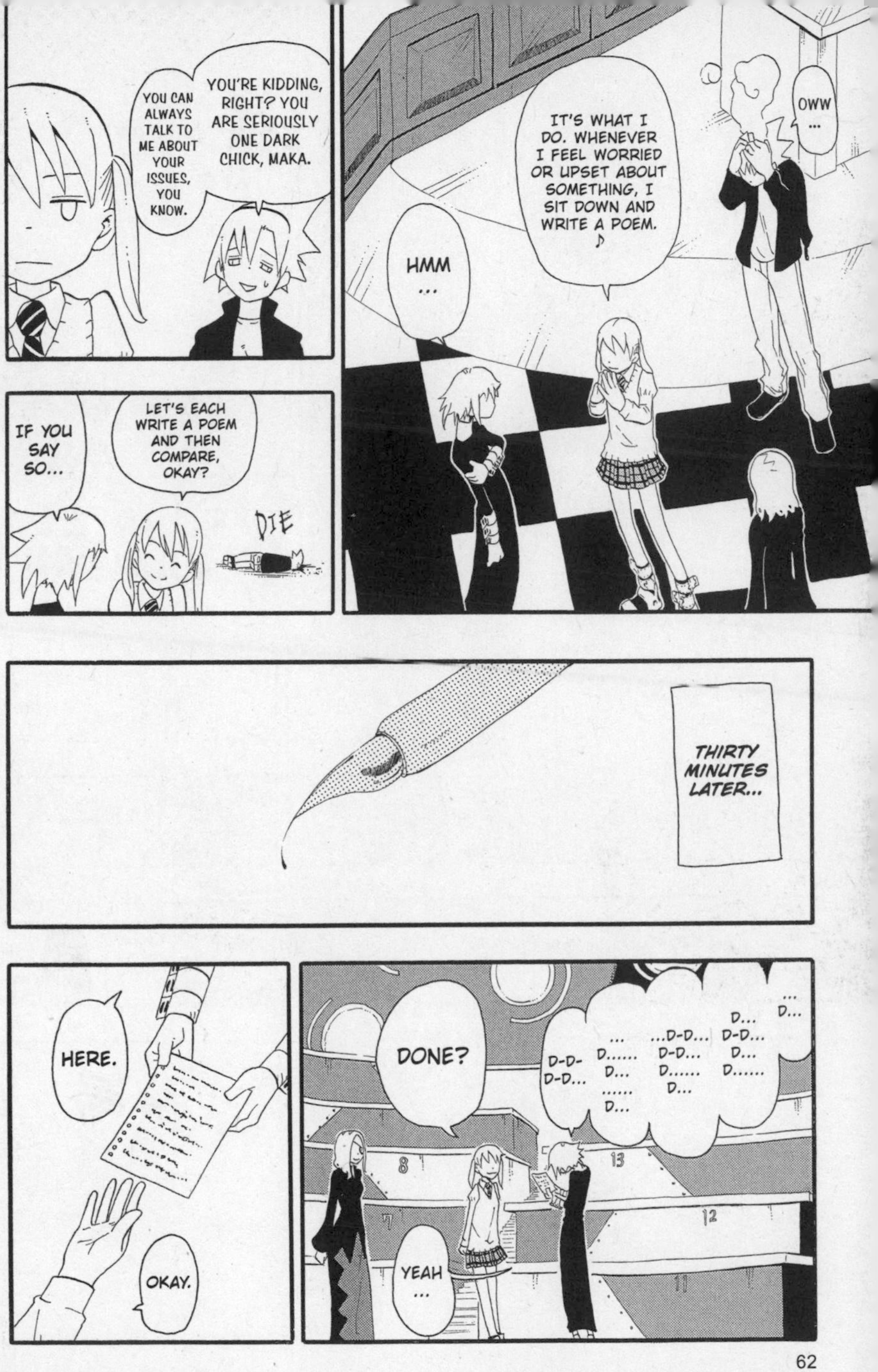
OWW ...
IT'S WHAT I DO. WHENEVER I FEEL WORRIED OR UPSET ABOUT SOMETHING, I SIT DOWN AND WRITE A POEM. ♪
HMM ...
YOU'RE KIDDING, RIGHT? YOU ARE SERIOUSLY ONE DARK CHICK, MAKA.
YOU CAN ALWAYS TALK TO ME ABOUT YOUR ISSUES, YOU KNOW.
LET'S EACH WRITE A POEM AND THEN COMPARE, OKAY?
IF YOU SAY SO...
DIE
THIRTY MINUTES LATER...
... D... D... D-D... D... D...... ...D-D... D-D... D...... D... ... D...... D-D- D-D... D... ...... D...
DONE?
YEAH ...
HERE.
OKAY.

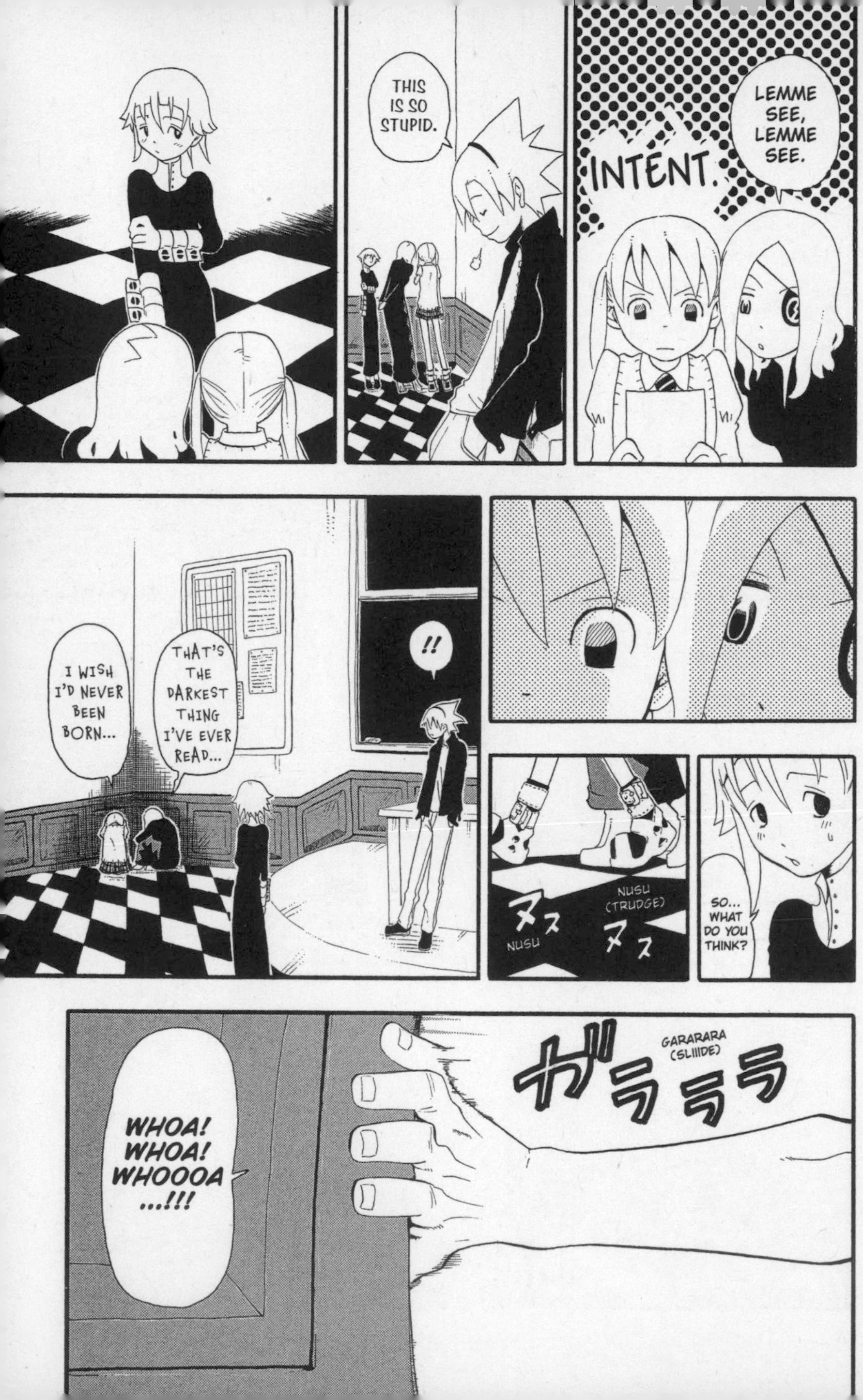
LEMME SEE, LEMME SEE.
INTENT.
THIS IS SO STUPID.
SO... WHAT DO YOU THINK?
NUSU (TRUDGE)
ヌス
NUSU
ヌス
!!
THAT'S THE DARKEST THING I'VE EVER READ...
I WISH I'D NEVER BEEN BORN...
GARARARA (SLIIIDE)
ガラララ
WHOA! WHOA! WHOOOA ...!!!

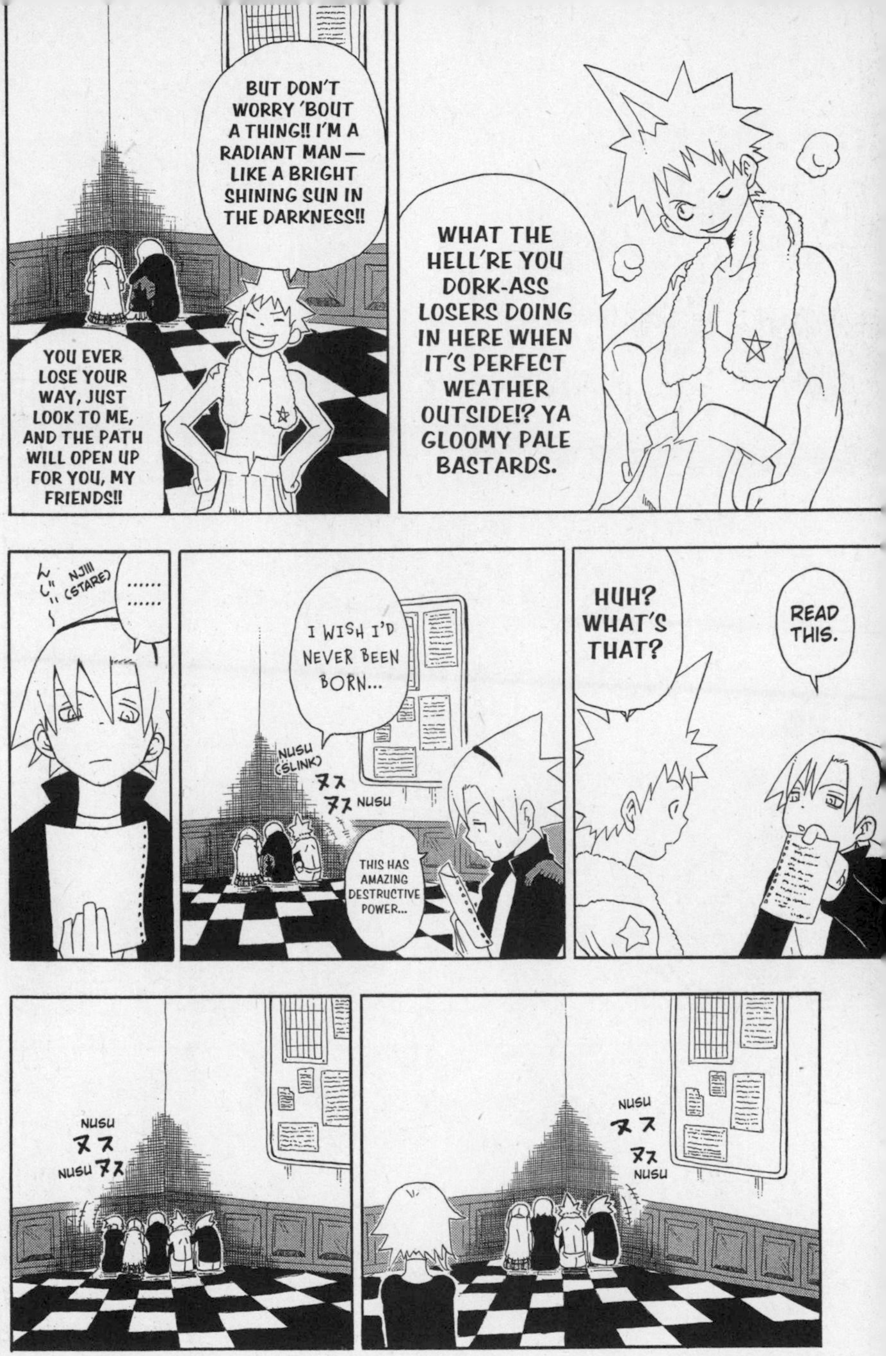
WHAT THE HELL'RE YOU DORK-ASS LOSERS DOING IN HERE WHEN IT'S PERFECT WEATHER OUTSIDE!? YA GLOOMY PALE BASTARDS.
BUT DON'T WORRY 'BOUT A THING!! I'M A RADIANT MAN—LIKE A BRIGHT SHINING SUN IN THE DARKNESS!!
YOU EVER LOSE YOUR WAY, JUST LOOK TO ME, AND THE PATH WILL OPEN UP FOR YOU, MY FRIENDS!!
READ THIS.
HUH? WHAT'S THAT?
I WISH I'D NEVER BEEN BORN...
NUSU (SLINK) ヌス
ヌス NUSU
THIS HAS AMAZING DESTRUCTIVE POWER...
んじー NJIII (STARE)
......
......
NUSU ヌス
ヌス NUSU
NUSU ヌス
NUSU ヌス

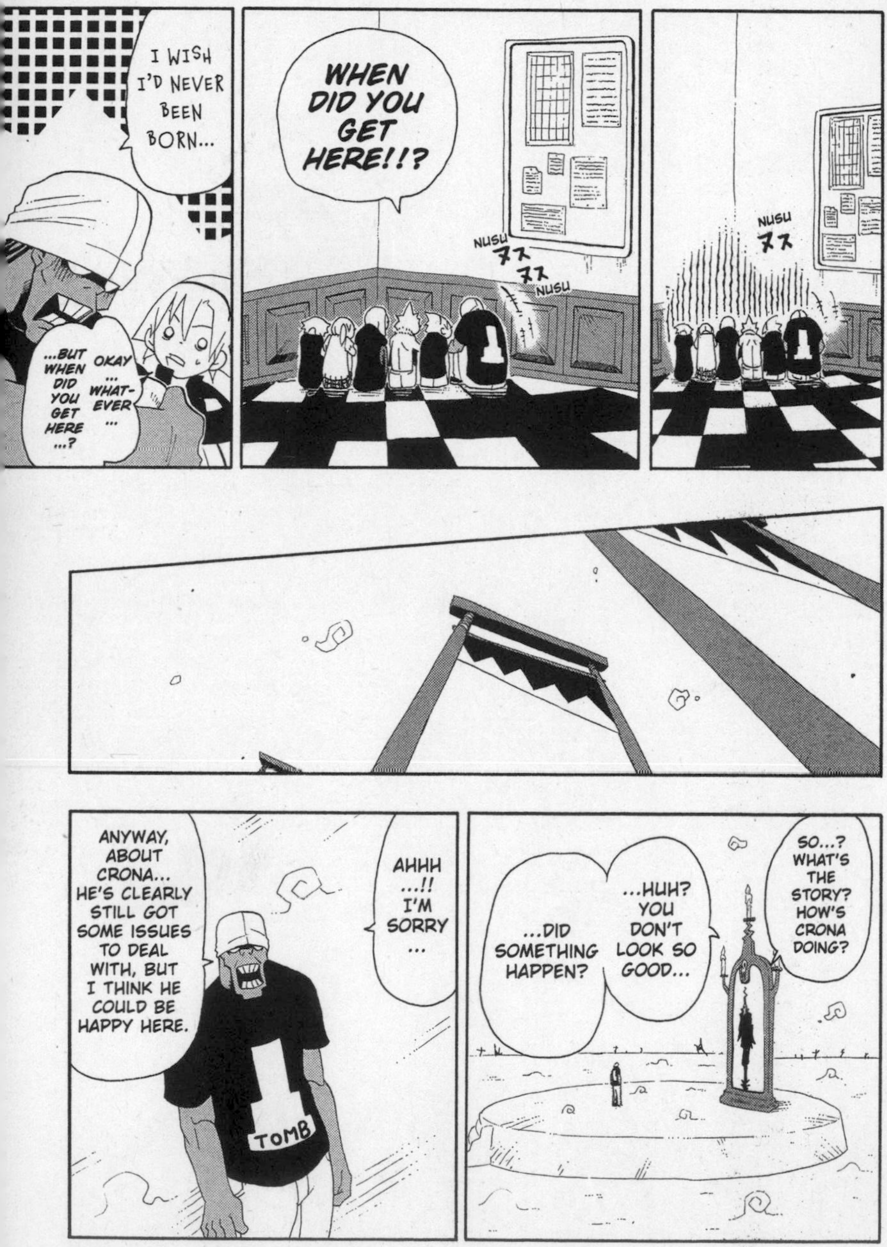
NUSU
ヌス
WHEN DID YOU GET HERE!!?
NUSU
ヌス
ヌス
NUSU
I WISH I'D NEVER BEEN BORN...
OKAY... WHATEVER...
...BUT WHEN DID YOU GET HERE...?
SO...? WHAT'S THE STORY? HOW'S CRONA DOING?
...HUH? YOU DON'T LOOK SO GOOD...
...DID SOMETHING HAPPEN?
AHHH...!! I'M SORRY...
ANYWAY, ABOUT CRONA... HE'S CLEARLY STILL GOT SOME ISSUES TO DEAL WITH, BUT I THINK HE COULD BE HAPPY HERE.
TOMB

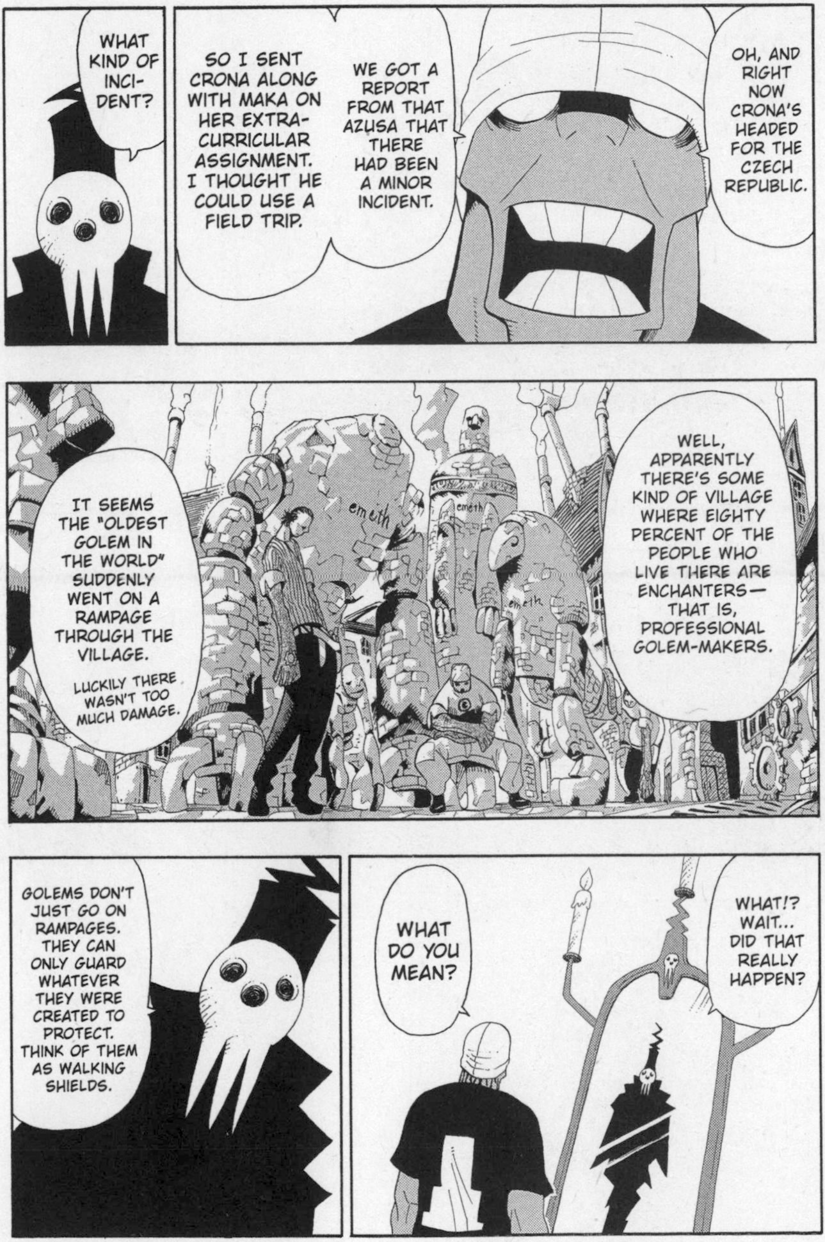
OH, AND RIGHT NOW CRONA'S HEADED FOR THE CZECH REPUBLIC.
SO I SENT CRONA ALONG WITH MAKA ON HER EXTRA-CURRICULAR ASSIGNMENT. I THOUGHT HE COULD USE A FIELD TRIP.
WE GOT A REPORT FROM THAT AZUSA THAT THERE HAD BEEN A MINOR INCIDENT.
WHAT KIND OF INCI-DENT?
WELL, APPARENTLY THERE'S SOME KIND OF VILLAGE WHERE EIGHTY PERCENT OF THE PEOPLE WHO LIVE THERE ARE ENCHANTERS— THAT IS, PROFESSIONAL GOLEM-MAKERS.
IT SEEMS THE "OLDEST GOLEM IN THE WORLD" SUDDENLY WENT ON A RAMPAGE THROUGH THE VILLAGE.
LUCKILY THERE WASN'T TOO MUCH DAMAGE.
emeth
emeth
emeth
WHAT!? WAIT... DID THAT REALLY HAPPEN?
WHAT DO YOU MEAN?
GOLEMS DON'T JUST GO ON RAMPAGES. THEY CAN ONLY GUARD WHATEVER THEY WERE CREATED TO PROTECT. THINK OF THEM AS WALKING SHIELDS.

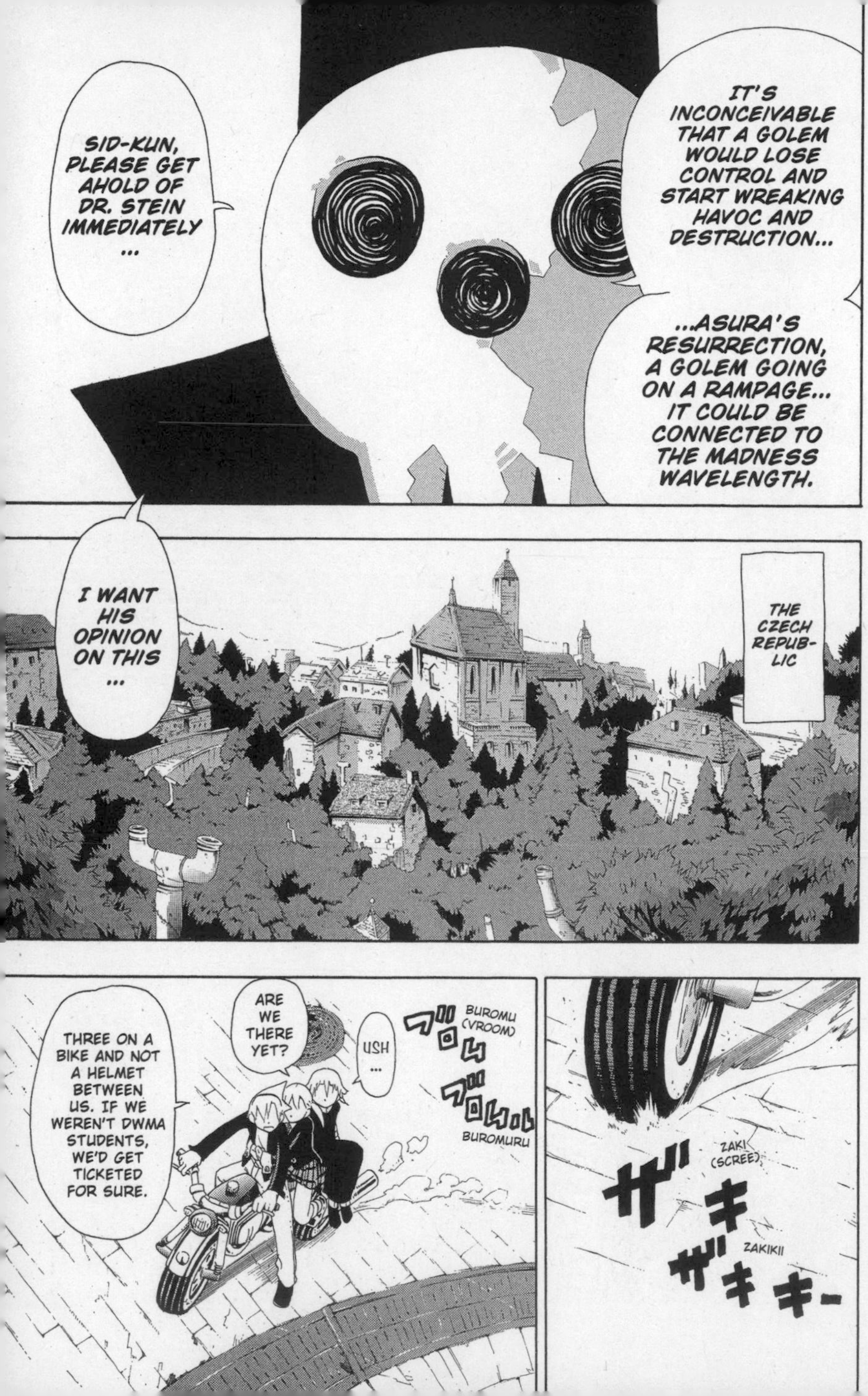
IT'S INCONCEIVABLE THAT A GOLEM WOULD LOSE CONTROL AND START WREAKING HAVOC AND DESTRUCTION...
...ASURA'S RESURRECTION, A GOLEM GOING ON A RAMPAGE... IT COULD BE CONNECTED TO THE MADNESS WAVELENGTH.
SID-KUN, PLEASE GET AHOLD OF DR. STEIN IMMEDIATELY ...
THE CZECH REPUB-LIC
I WANT HIS OPINION ON THIS ...
ザキ
ZAKI (SCREE)
ザキキー
ZAKIKII
ブロロ
BUROMU (VROOM)
ブロルルル
BUROMURU
USH ...
ARE WE THERE YET?
THREE ON A BIKE AND NOT A HELMET BETWEEN US. IF WE WEREN'T DWMA STUDENTS, WE'D GET TICKETED FOR SURE.

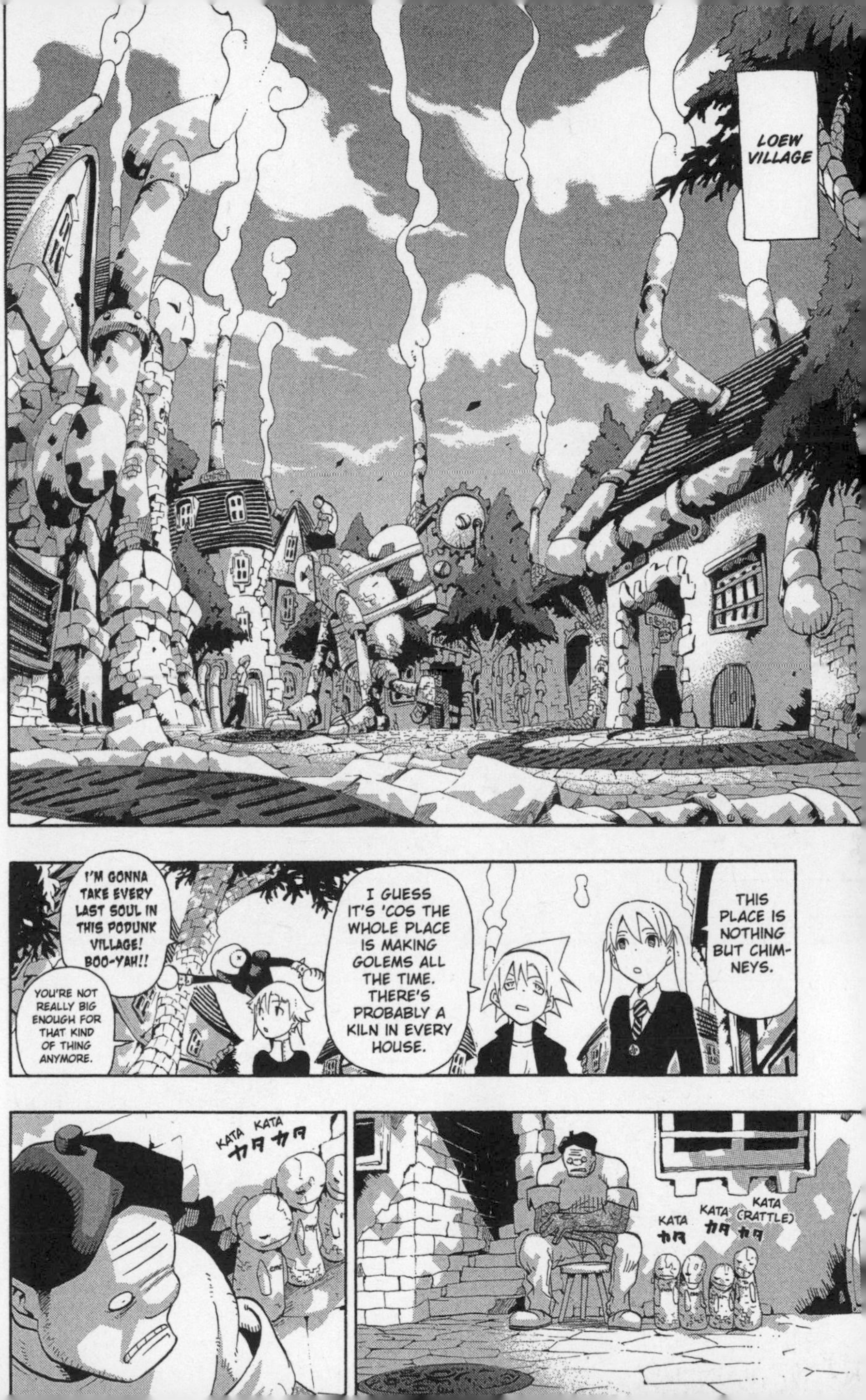
LOEW VILLAGE
THIS PLACE IS NOTHING BUT CHIMNEYS.
I GUESS IT'S 'COS THE WHOLE PLACE IS MAKING GOLEMS ALL THE TIME. THERE'S PROBABLY A KILN IN EVERY HOUSE.
I'M GONNA TAKE EVERY LAST SOUL IN THIS PODUNK VILLAGE! BOO-YAH!!
YOU'RE NOT REALLY BIG ENOUGH FOR THAT KIND OF THING ANYMORE.
KATA (RATTLE) カタ
KATA カタ
KATA カタ
KATA KATA カタカタ

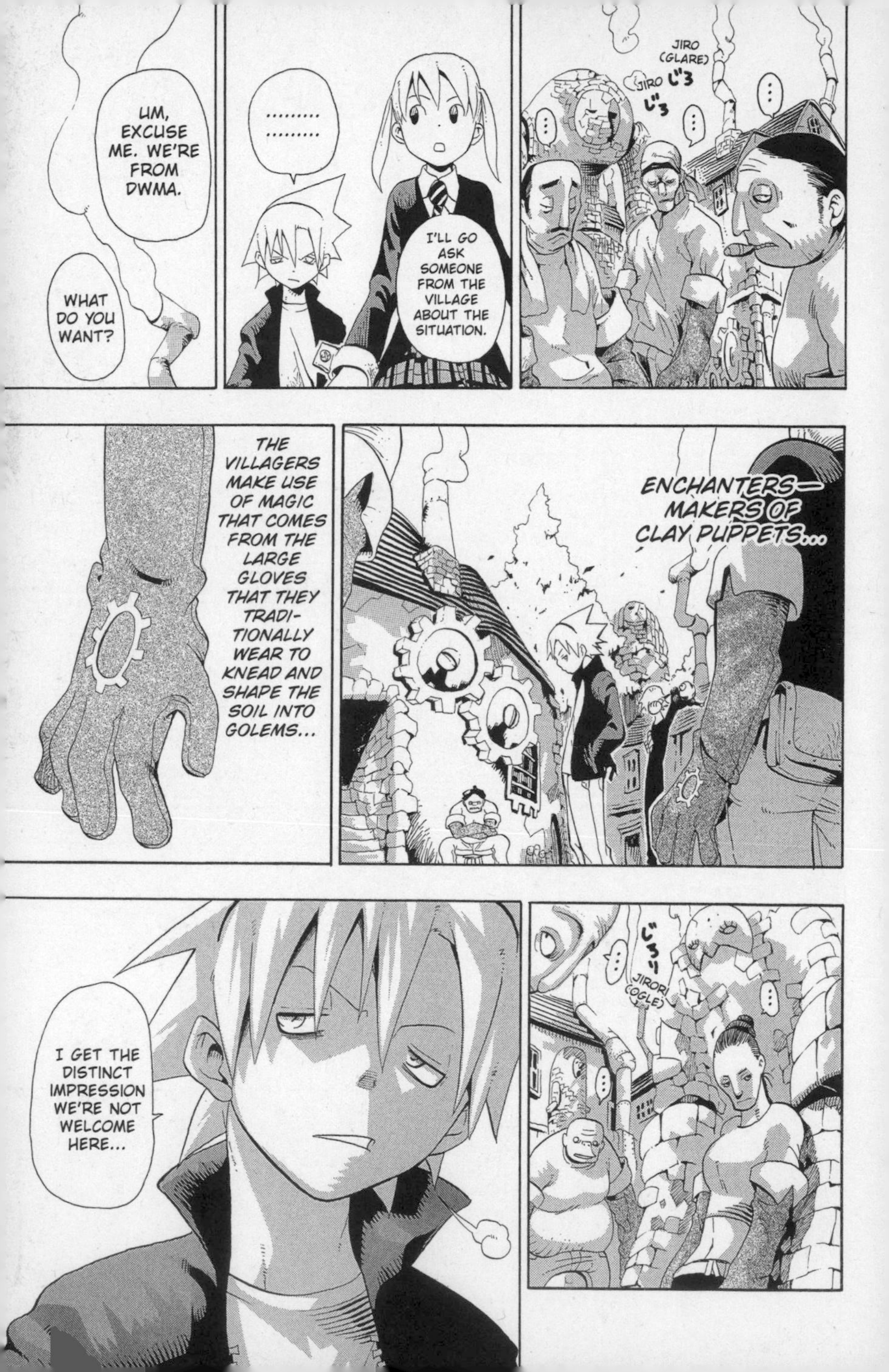
JIRO (GLARE)
JIRO
じろ
じろ
...
...
...
...
....
....
I'LL GO ASK SOMEONE FROM THE VILLAGE ABOUT THE SITUATION.
UM, EXCUSE ME. WE'RE FROM DWMA.
WHAT DO YOU WANT?
ENCHANTERS— MAKERS OF CLAY PUPPETS...
THE VILLAGERS MAKE USE OF MAGIC THAT COMES FROM THE LARGE GLOVES THAT THEY TRADITIONALLY WEAR TO KNEAD AND SHAPE THE SOIL INTO GOLEMS...
じろり
JIRORI (OGLE)
...
...
...
I GET THE DISTINCT IMPRESSION WE'RE NOT WELCOME HERE...

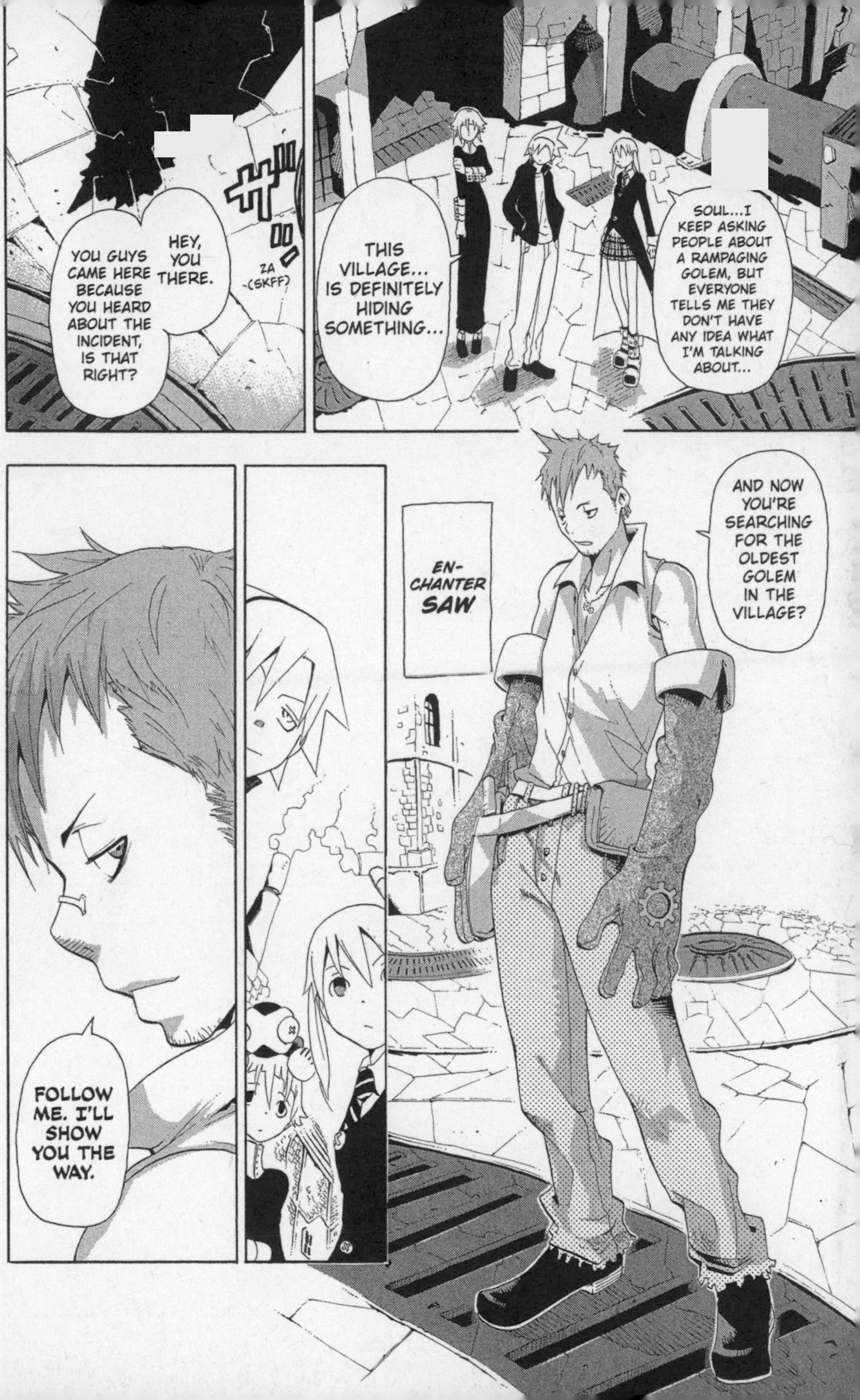
SOUL...I KEEP ASKING PEOPLE ABOUT A RAMPAGING GOLEM, BUT EVERYONE TELLS ME THEY DON'T HAVE ANY IDEA WHAT I'M TALKING ABOUT...
THIS VILLAGE... IS DEFINITELY HIDING SOMETHING...
ZA -(SKFF)
HEY, YOU THERE.
YOU GUYS CAME HERE BECAUSE YOU HEARD ABOUT THE INCIDENT, IS THAT RIGHT?
AND NOW YOU'RE SEARCHING FOR THE OLDEST GOLEM IN THE VILLAGE?
EN-CHANTER SAW
FOLLOW ME. I'LL SHOW YOU THE WAY.

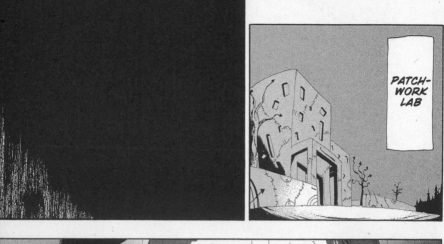

PATCH-
WORK
LAB

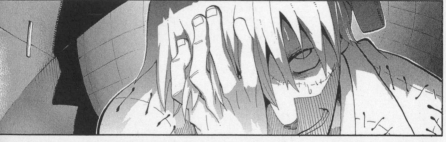

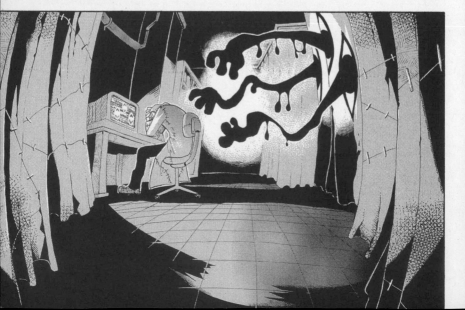

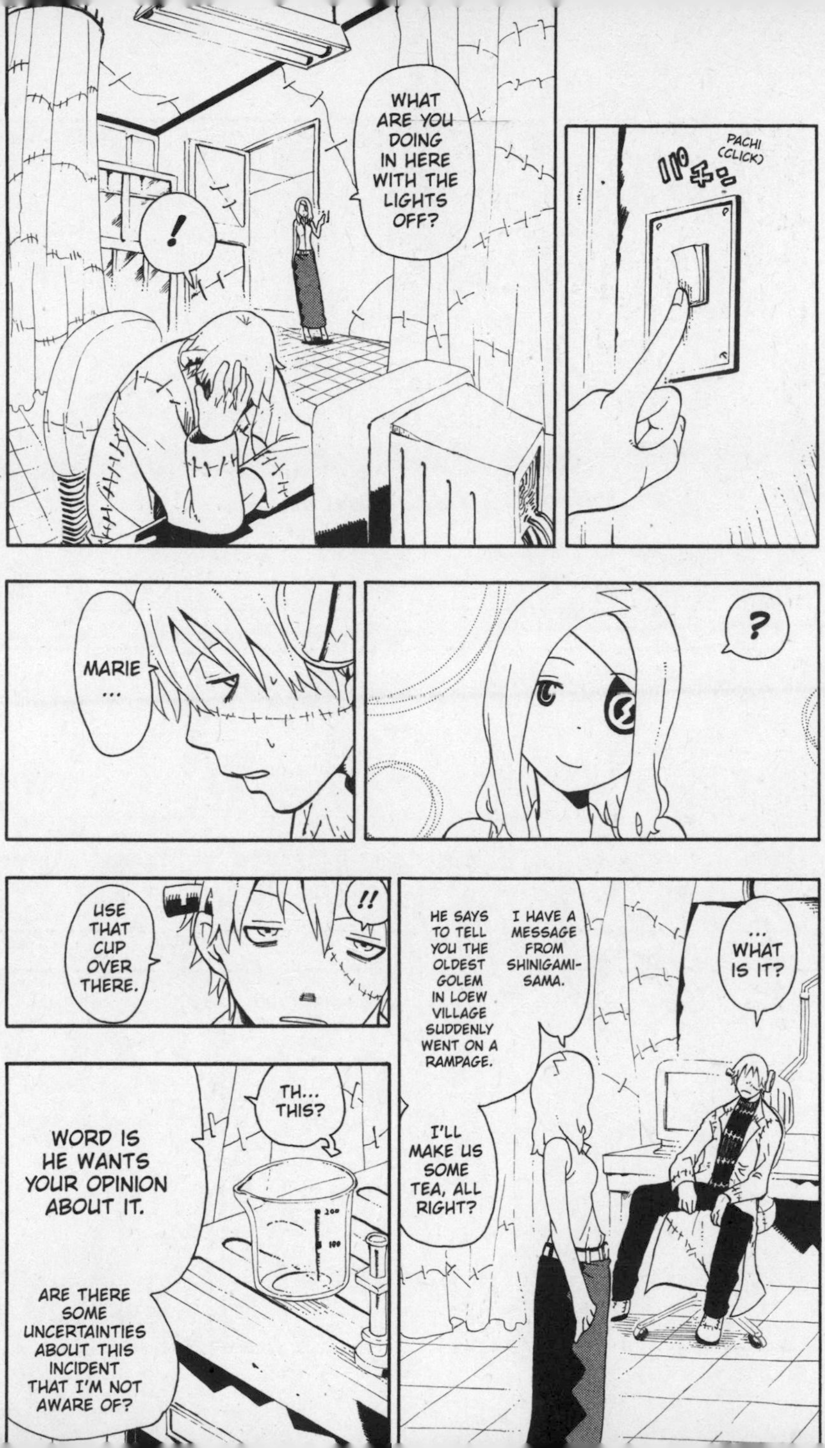
PACHI (CLICK)
WHAT ARE YOU DOING IN HERE WITH THE LIGHTS OFF?
!
?
MARIE ...
... WHAT IS IT?
I HAVE A MESSAGE FROM SHINIGAMI-SAMA.
HE SAYS TO TELL YOU THE OLDEST GOLEM IN LOEW VILLAGE SUDDENLY WENT ON A RAMPAGE.
I'LL MAKE US SOME TEA, ALL RIGHT?
!!
USE THAT CUP OVER THERE.
TH... THIS?
WORD IS HE WANTS YOUR OPINION ABOUT IT.
ARE THERE SOME UNCERTAINTIES ABOUT THIS INCIDENT THAT I'M NOT AWARE OF?

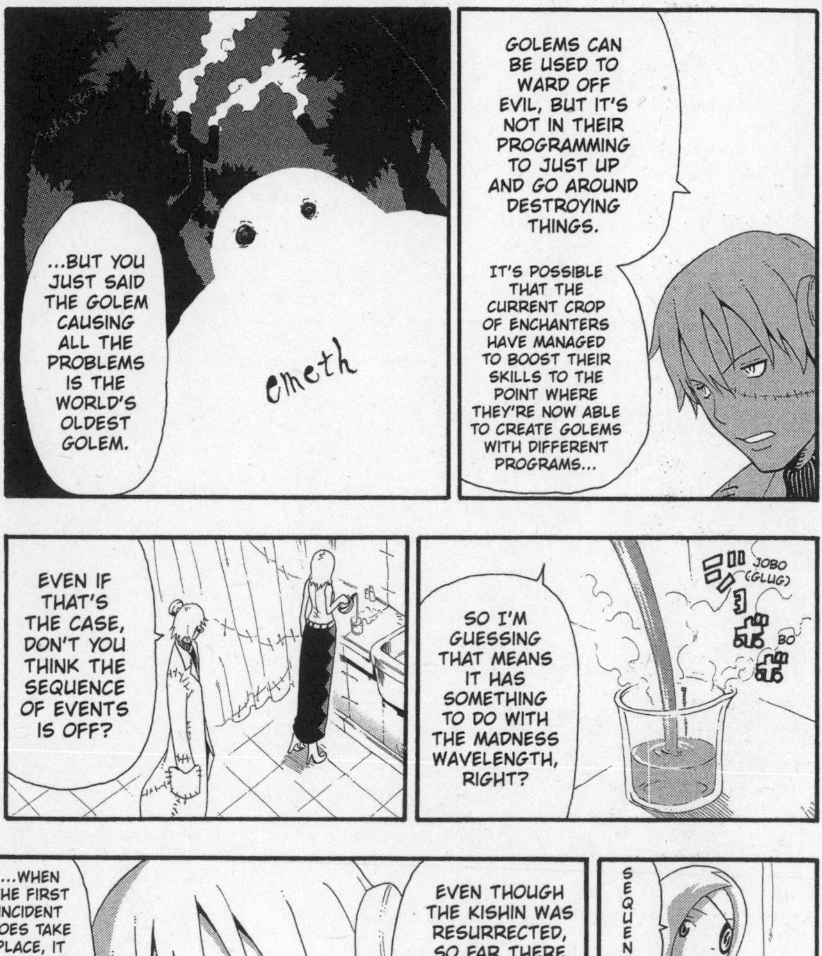
GOLEMS CAN BE USED TO WARD OFF EVIL, BUT IT'S NOT IN THEIR PROGRAMMING TO JUST UP AND GO AROUND DESTROYING THINGS.
IT'S POSSIBLE THAT THE CURRENT CROP OF ENCHANTERS HAVE MANAGED TO BOOST THEIR SKILLS TO THE POINT WHERE THEY'RE NOW ABLE TO CREATE GOLEMS WITH DIFFERENT PROGRAMS...
...BUT YOU JUST SAID THE GOLEM CAUSING ALL THE PROBLEMS IS THE WORLD'S OLDEST GOLEM.
emeth
JOBO (GLUG)
BO
SO I'M GUESSING THAT MEANS IT HAS SOMETHING TO DO WITH THE MADNESS WAVELENGTH, RIGHT?
EVEN IF THAT'S THE CASE, DON'T YOU THINK THE SEQUENCE OF EVENTS IS OFF?
SEQUENCE?
EVEN THOUGH THE KISHIN WAS RESURRECTED, SO FAR THERE HASN'T BEEN A SINGLE INCIDENT RELATED TO THE MADNESS WAVELENGTH. NOW, THAT'S A GOOD THING, BUT...
...WHEN THE FIRST INCIDENT DOES TAKE PLACE, IT TURNS OUT TO BE SOME "RAMPAGING GOLEM" THAT DOESN'T EVEN HAVE A SOUL TO BEGIN WITH. THAT DOESN'T MAKE ANY SENSE TO ME...

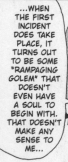

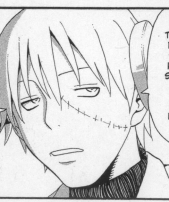

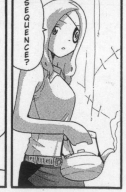

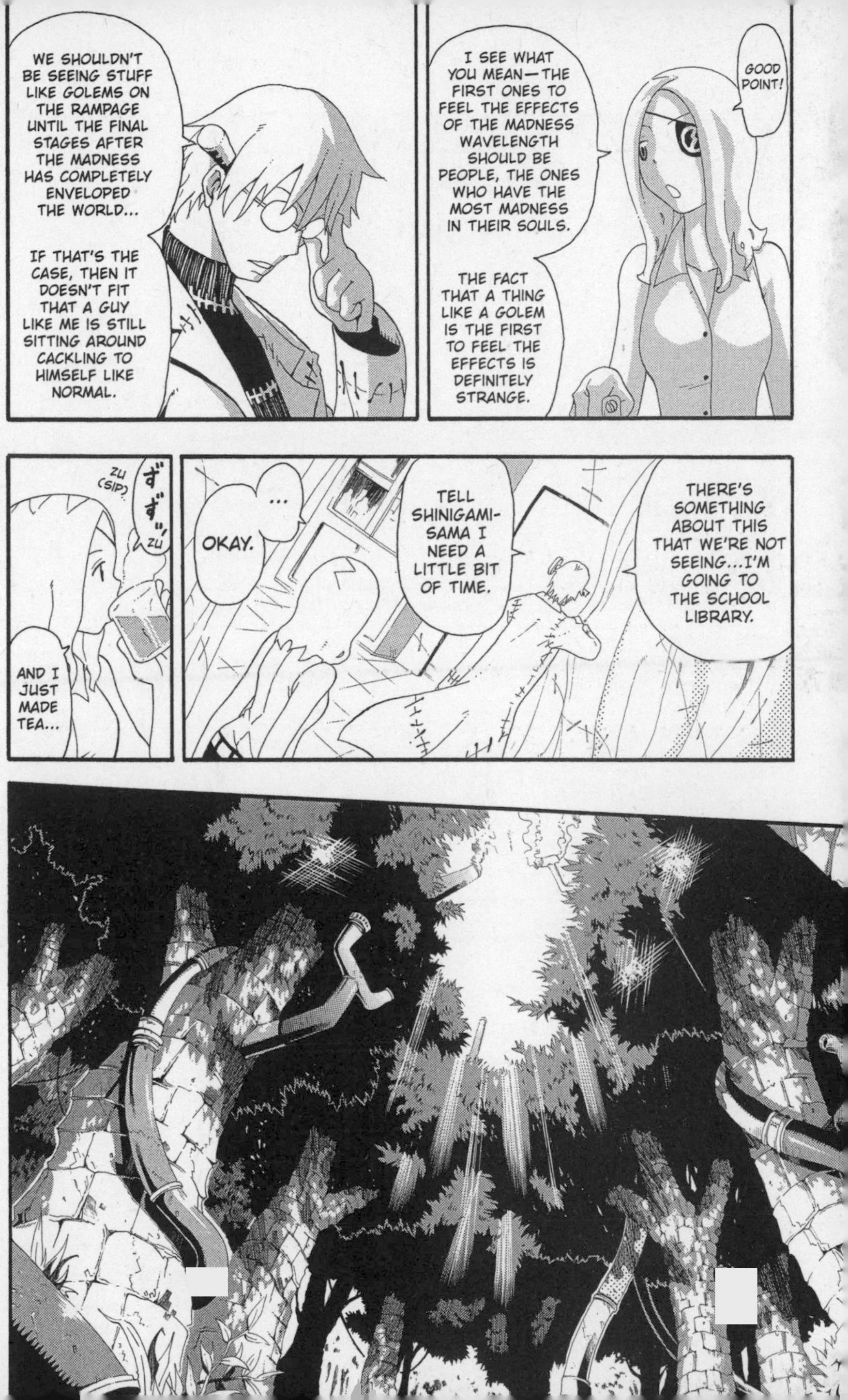
GOOD POINT!
I SEE WHAT YOU MEAN—THE FIRST ONES TO FEEL THE EFFECTS OF THE MADNESS WAVELENGTH SHOULD BE PEOPLE, THE ONES WHO HAVE THE MOST MADNESS IN THEIR SOULS.
THE FACT THAT A THING LIKE A GOLEM IS THE FIRST TO FEEL THE EFFECTS IS DEFINITELY STRANGE.
WE SHOULDN'T BE SEEING STUFF LIKE GOLEMS ON THE RAMPAGE UNTIL THE FINAL STAGES AFTER THE MADNESS HAS COMPLETELY ENVELOPED THE WORLD...
IF THAT'S THE CASE, THEN IT DOESN'T FIT THAT A GUY LIKE ME IS STILL SITTING AROUND CACKLING TO HIMSELF LIKE NORMAL.
THERE'S SOMETHING ABOUT THIS THAT WE'RE NOT SEEING...I'M GOING TO THE SCHOOL LIBRARY.
TELL SHINIGAMI-SAMA I NEED A LITTLE BIT OF TIME.
...
OKAY.
ずずッ
ZU (SIP) ZU
AND I JUST MADE TEA...

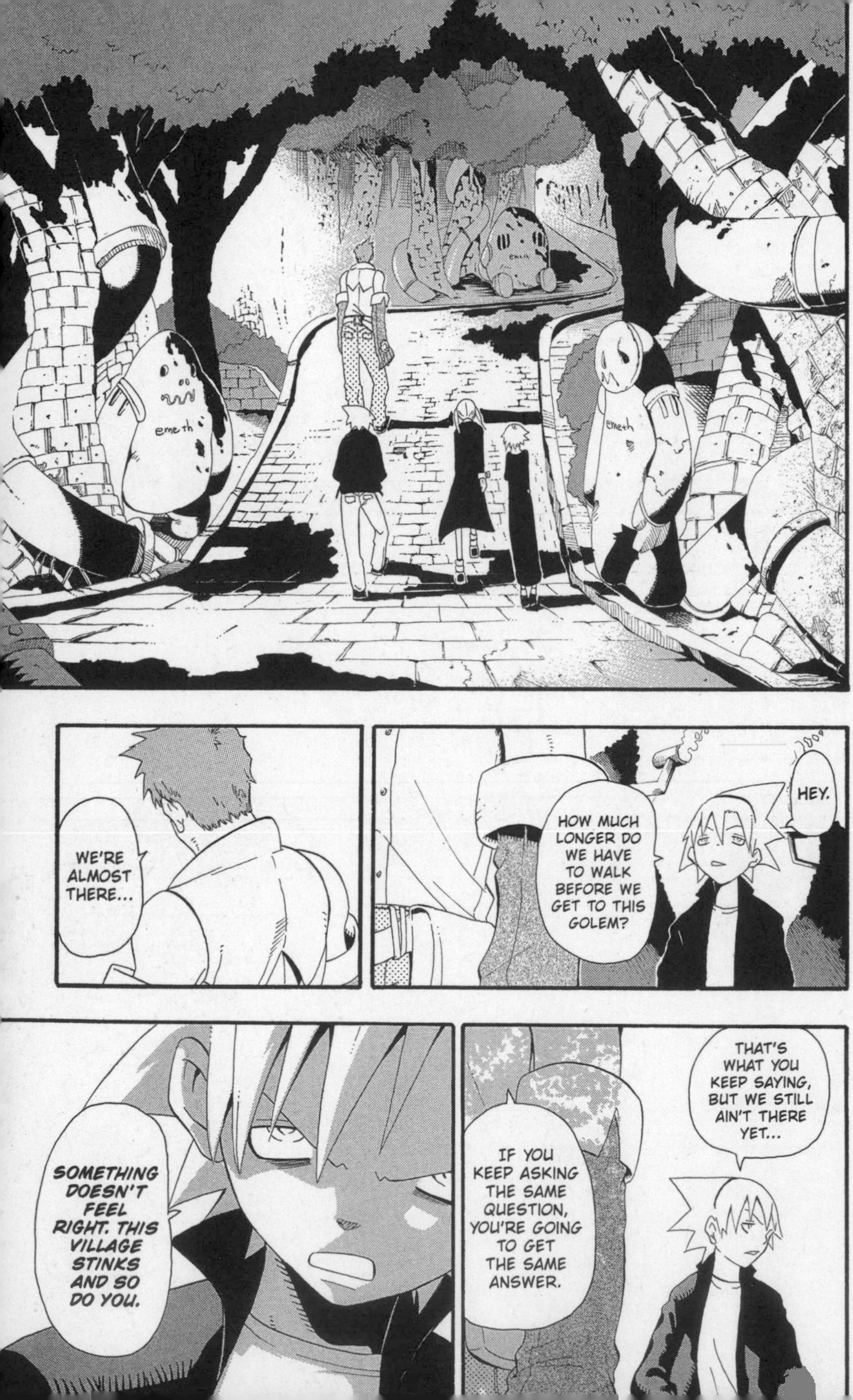
emeth
emeth
HEY.
HOW MUCH LONGER DO WE HAVE TO WALK BEFORE WE GET TO THIS GOLEM?
WE'RE ALMOST THERE...
THAT'S WHAT YOU KEEP SAYING, BUT WE STILL AIN'T THERE YET...
IF YOU KEEP ASKING THE SAME QUESTION, YOU'RE GOING TO GET THE SAME ANSWER.
SOMETHING DOESN'T FEEL RIGHT. THIS VILLAGE STINKS AND SO DO YOU.

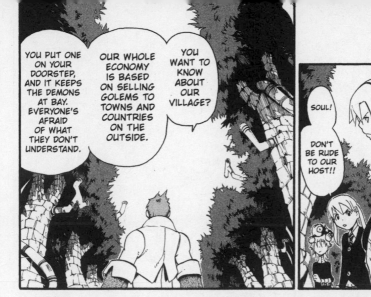

SOUL!
DON'T BE RUDE TO OUR HOST!!
YOU WANT TO KNOW ABOUT OUR VILLAGE?
OUR WHOLE ECONOMY IS BASED ON SELLING GOLEMS TO TOWNS AND COUNTRIES ON THE OUTSIDE.
YOU PUT ONE ON YOUR DOORSTEP, AND IT KEEPS THE DEMONS AT BAY. EVERYONE'S AFRAID OF WHAT THEY DON'T UNDERSTAND.
SO WHAT'RE YOU TRYING TO SAY, THAT WE'RE THE "DEMONS" IN THIS SCENARIO?
THAT'S NOT WHAT HE SAID, SOUL.
HOW COME YOU'RE SO QUICK TO JUMP ON HIM?
THAT'S EXACTLY WHAT THIS GUY'S SAYING! NOW SHUT IT.
EVERYONE JUST WANTS TO LIVE IN PEACE AND QUIET WITHOUT ANYONE COMING AROUND TO BOTHER THEM. JUST PEACE AND QUIET, WITHOUT ANY PROBLEMS.
THERE'S BEEN NO CONFLICT AMONG US... WE'VE BEEN AS STILL AS THE GOLEMS WE MAKE.
...
BUT IT'S THE SAME WITH PEOPLE, ISN'T IT? IT'S ALWAYS THE ONES WHO SEEM THE NICEST, THE ONES WHO NEVER RAISE A FUSS...

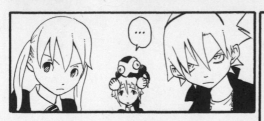

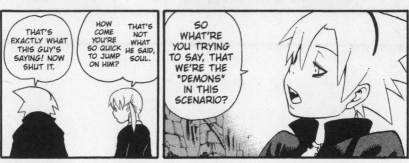

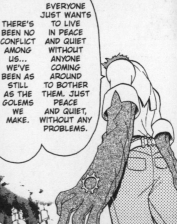

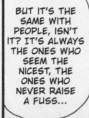

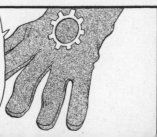

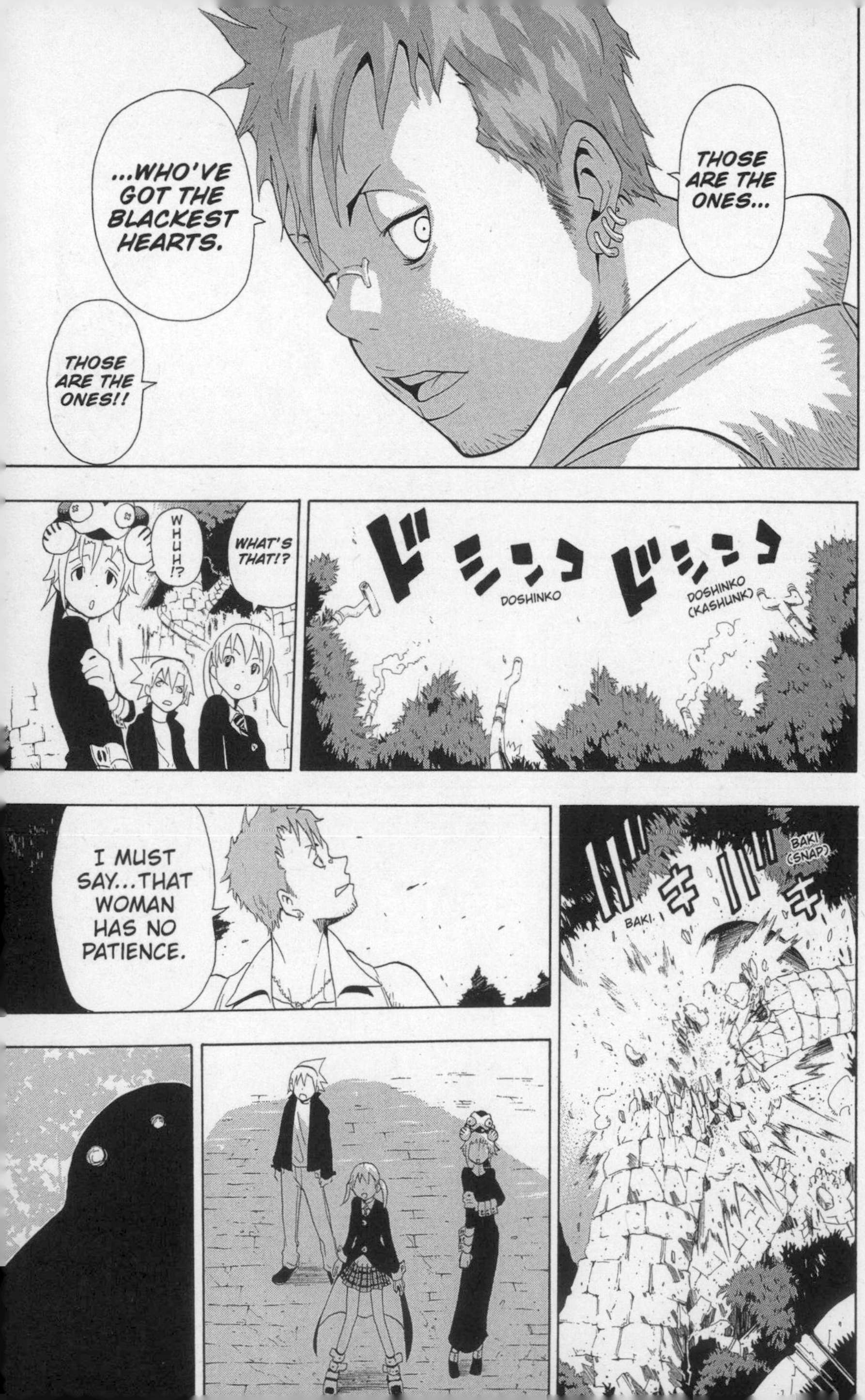
THOSE ARE THE ONES...
...WHO'VE GOT THE BLACKEST HEARTS.
THOSE ARE THE ONES!!
ドシンコ
DOSHINKO (KASHUNK)
ドシンコ
DOSHINKO
WHAT'S THAT!?
WHUH!?
バキ
BAKI (SNAP)
バキ
BAKI
I MUST SAY...THAT WOMAN HAS NO PATIENCE.

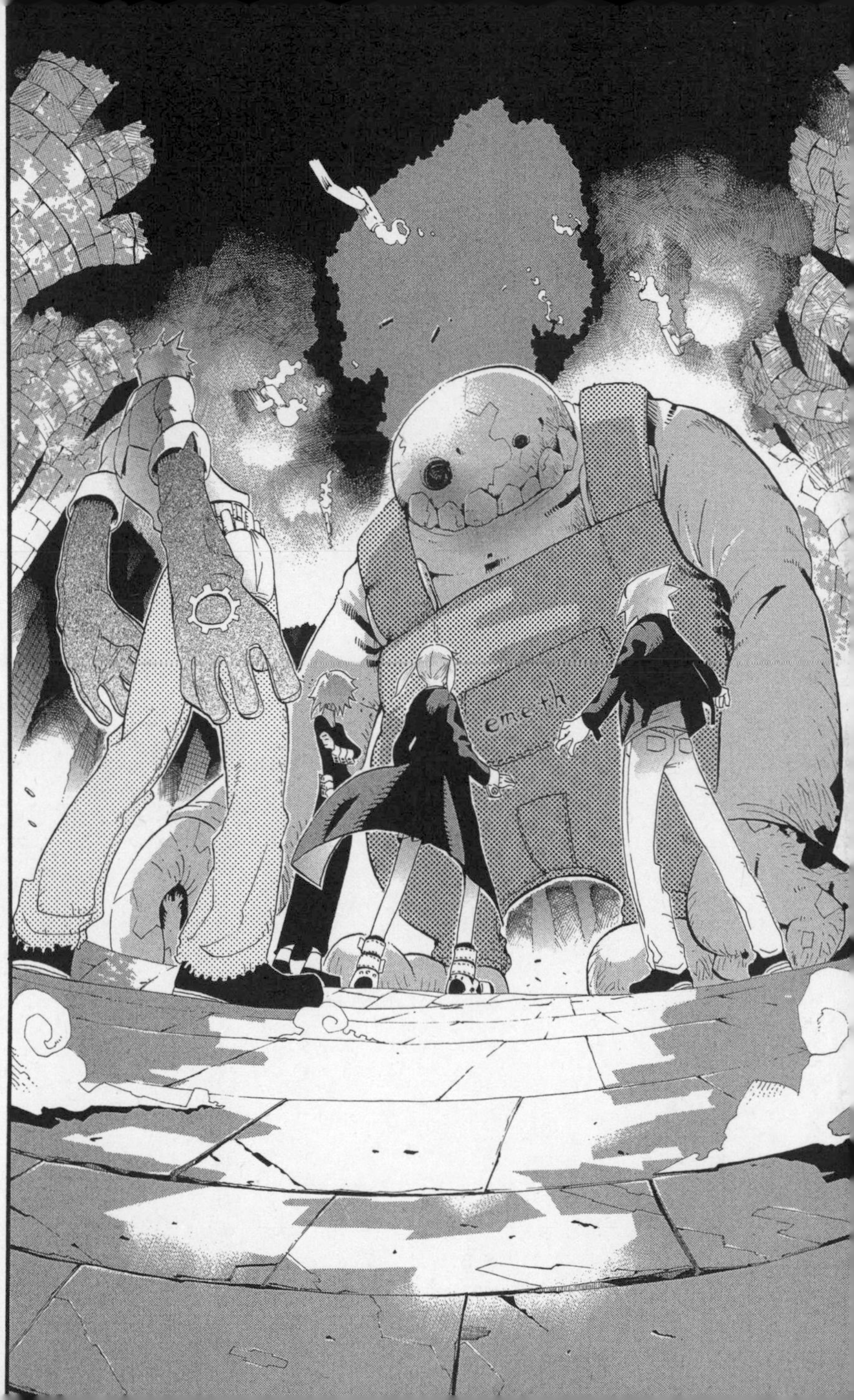
emeth

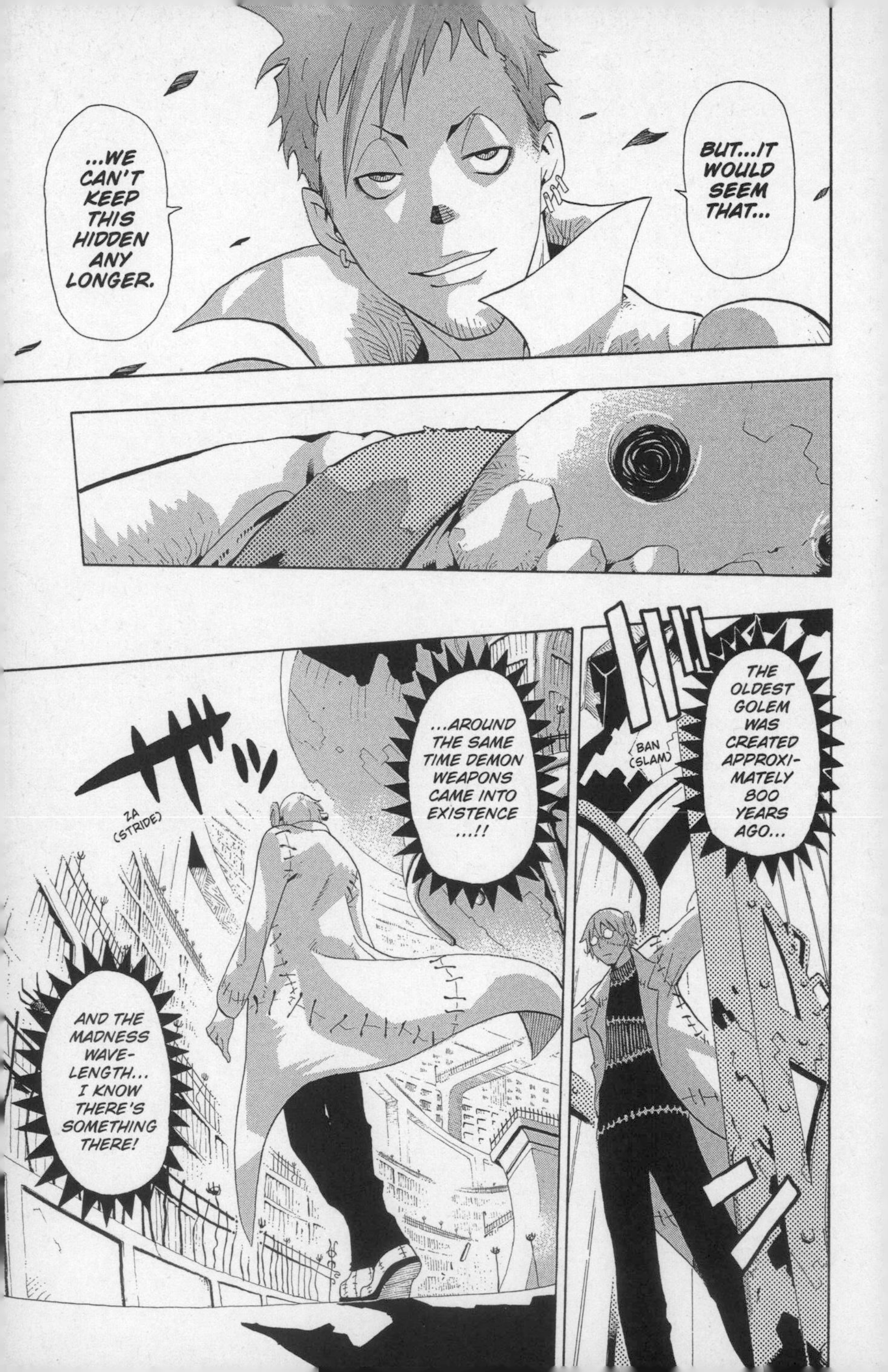
BUT...IT WOULD SEEM THAT...
...WE CAN'T KEEP THIS HIDDEN ANY LONGER.
BAN (SLAM)
THE OLDEST GOLEM WAS CREATED APPROXI-MATELY 800 YEARS AGO...
...AROUND THE SAME TIME DEMON WEAPONS CAME INTO EXISTENCE ...!!
ZA (STRIDE)
AND THE MADNESS WAVE-LENGTH... I KNOW THERE'S SOMETHING THERE!

SOUL EATER

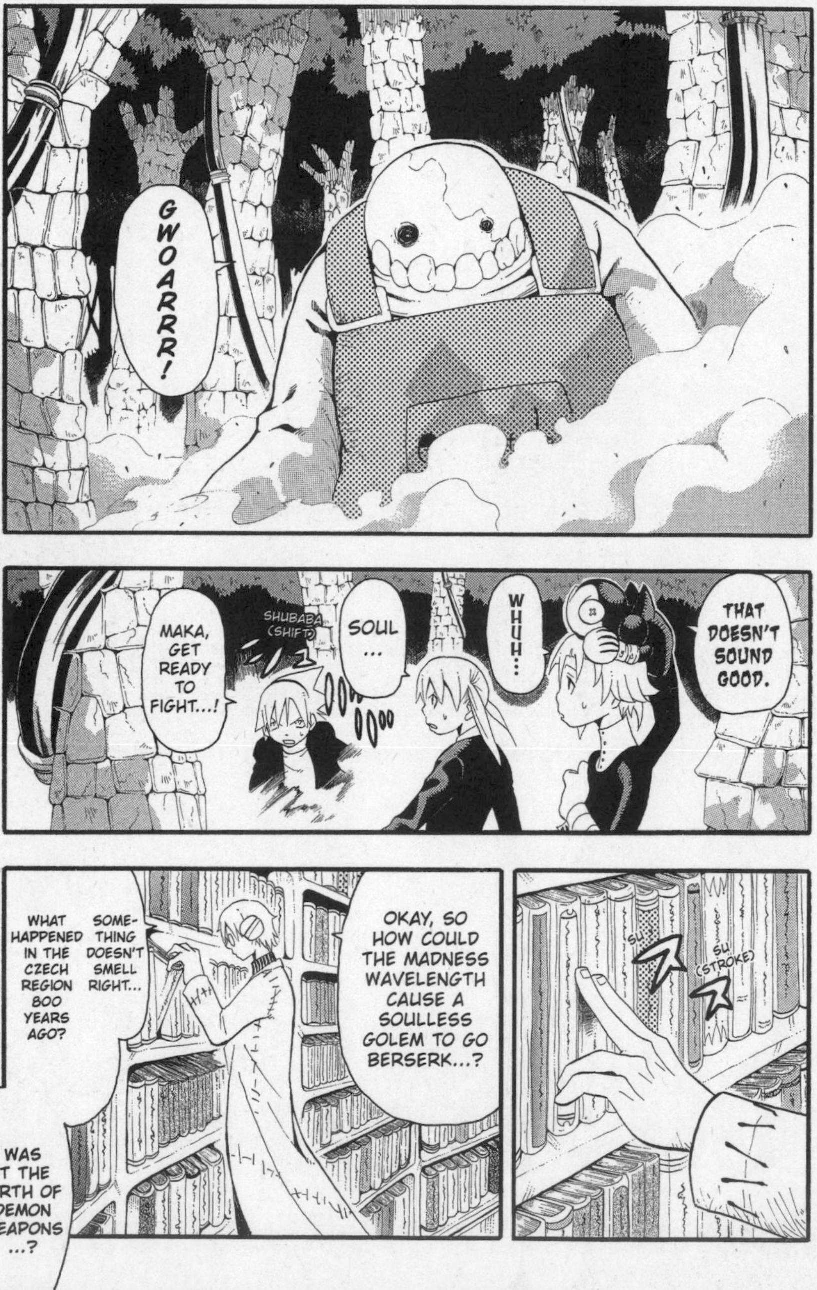
GWOARRR!
THAT DOESN'T SOUND GOOD.
WHUH...
SOUL...
SHUBABA (SHIFT)
MAKA, GET READY TO FIGHT...!
SU (STROKE)
SU
OKAY, SO HOW COULD THE MADNESS WAVELENGTH CAUSE A SOULLESS GOLEM TO GO BERSERK...?
SOMETHING DOESN'T SMELL RIGHT...
WHAT HAPPENED IN THE CZECH REGION 800 YEARS AGO?
WAS IT THE BIRTH OF DEMON WEAPONS...?

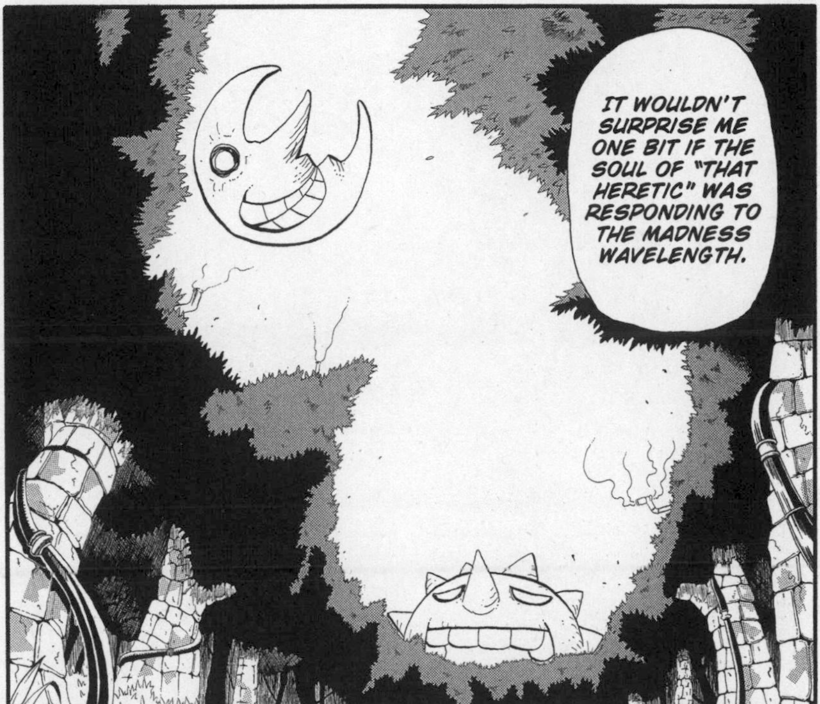
IT WOULDN'T SURPRISE ME ONE BIT IF THE SOUL OF "THAT HERETIC" WAS RESPONDING TO THE MADNESS WAVELENGTH.

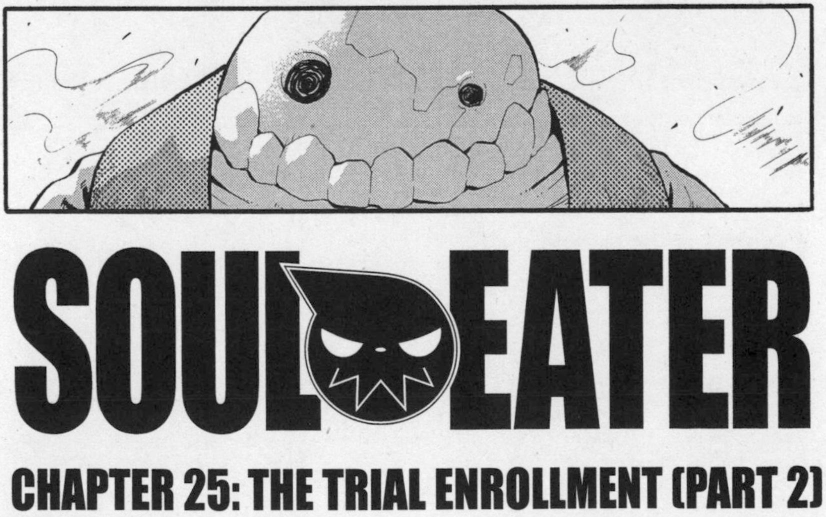

SOUL EATER

CHAPTER 25: THE TRIAL ENROLLMENT (PART 2)

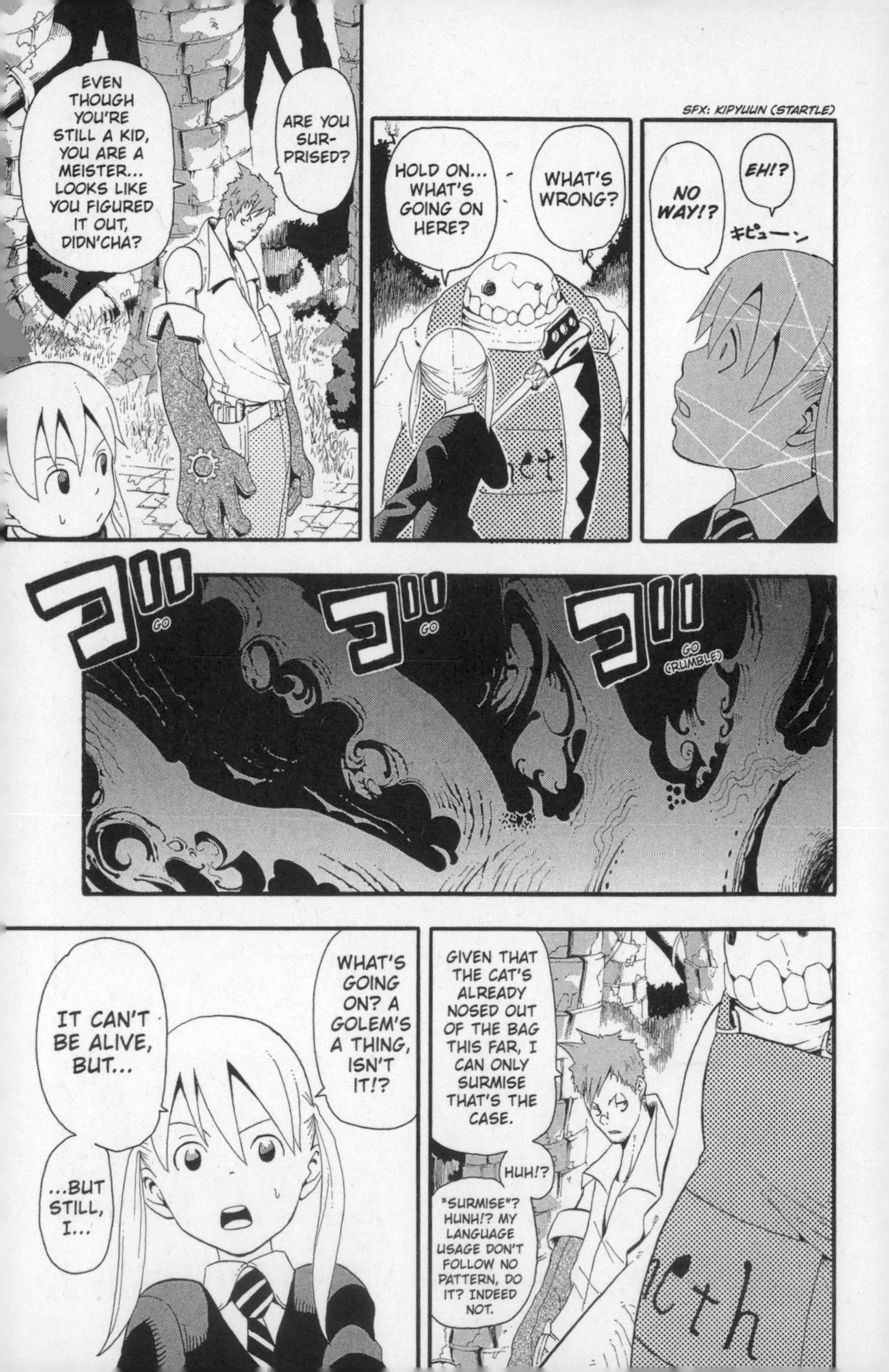
SFX: KIPYUUN (STARTLE)
EH!?
NO WAY!?
キピューン
WHAT'S WRONG?
HOLD ON... WHAT'S GOING ON HERE?
ARE YOU SUR-PRISED?
EVEN THOUGH YOU'RE STILL A KID, YOU ARE A MEISTER... LOOKS LIKE YOU FIGURED IT OUT, DIDN'CHA?
ゴ GO (RUMBLE)
ゴ GO
ゴ GO
GIVEN THAT THE CAT'S ALREADY NOSED OUT OF THE BAG THIS FAR, I CAN ONLY SURMISE THAT'S THE CASE.
HUH!?
"SURMISE"? HUNH!? MY LANGUAGE USAGE DON'T FOLLOW NO PATTERN, DO IT? INDEED NOT.
WHAT'S GOING ON? A GOLEM'S A THING, ISN'T IT!?
IT CAN'T BE ALIVE, BUT...
...BUT STILL, I...

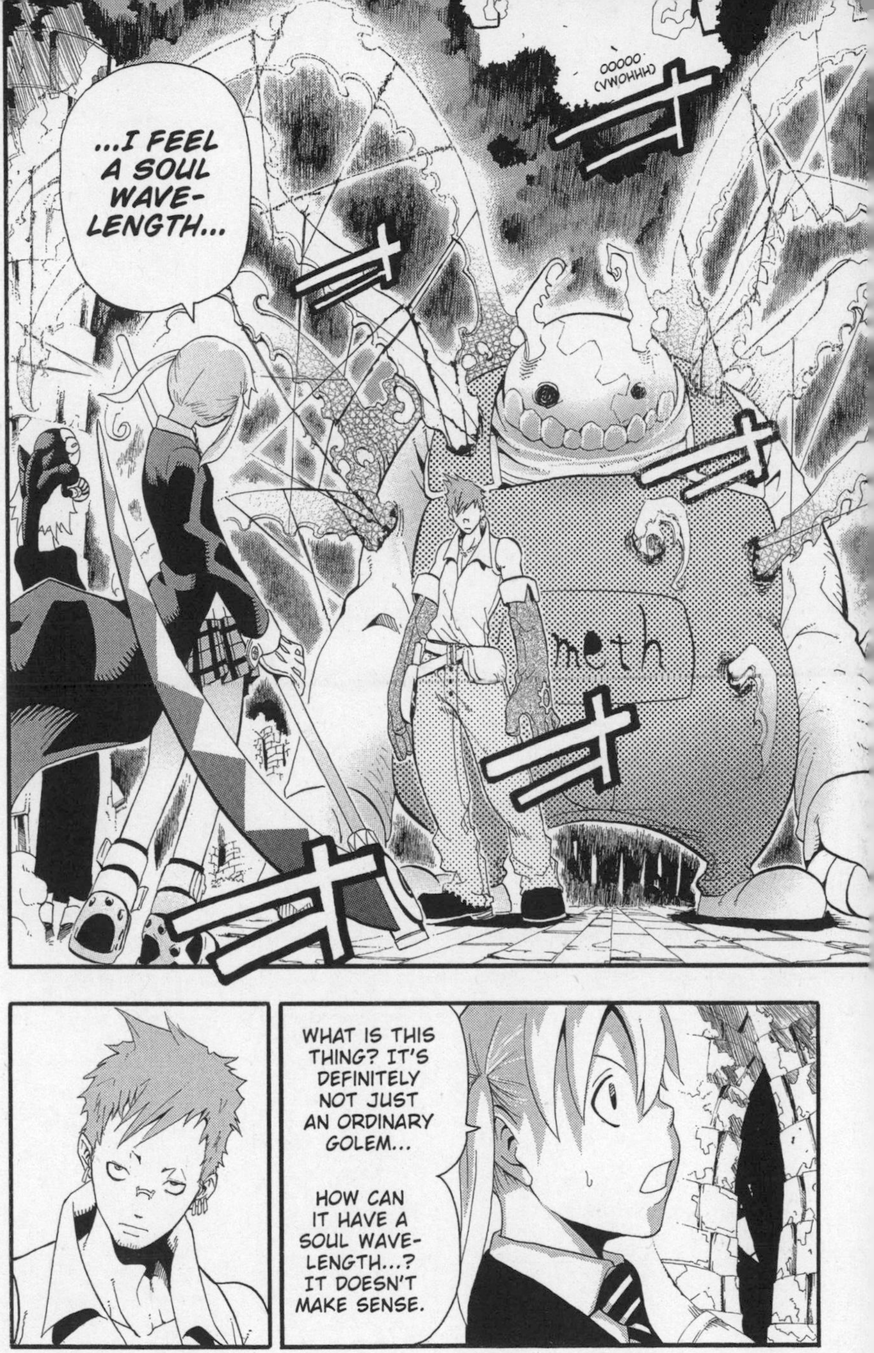
OOOOO (VWOHHH)
...I FEEL A SOUL WAVE-LENGTH...
WHAT IS THIS THING? IT'S DEFINITELY NOT JUST AN ORDINARY GOLEM...
HOW CAN IT HAVE A SOUL WAVE-LENGTH...? IT DOESN'T MAKE SENSE.

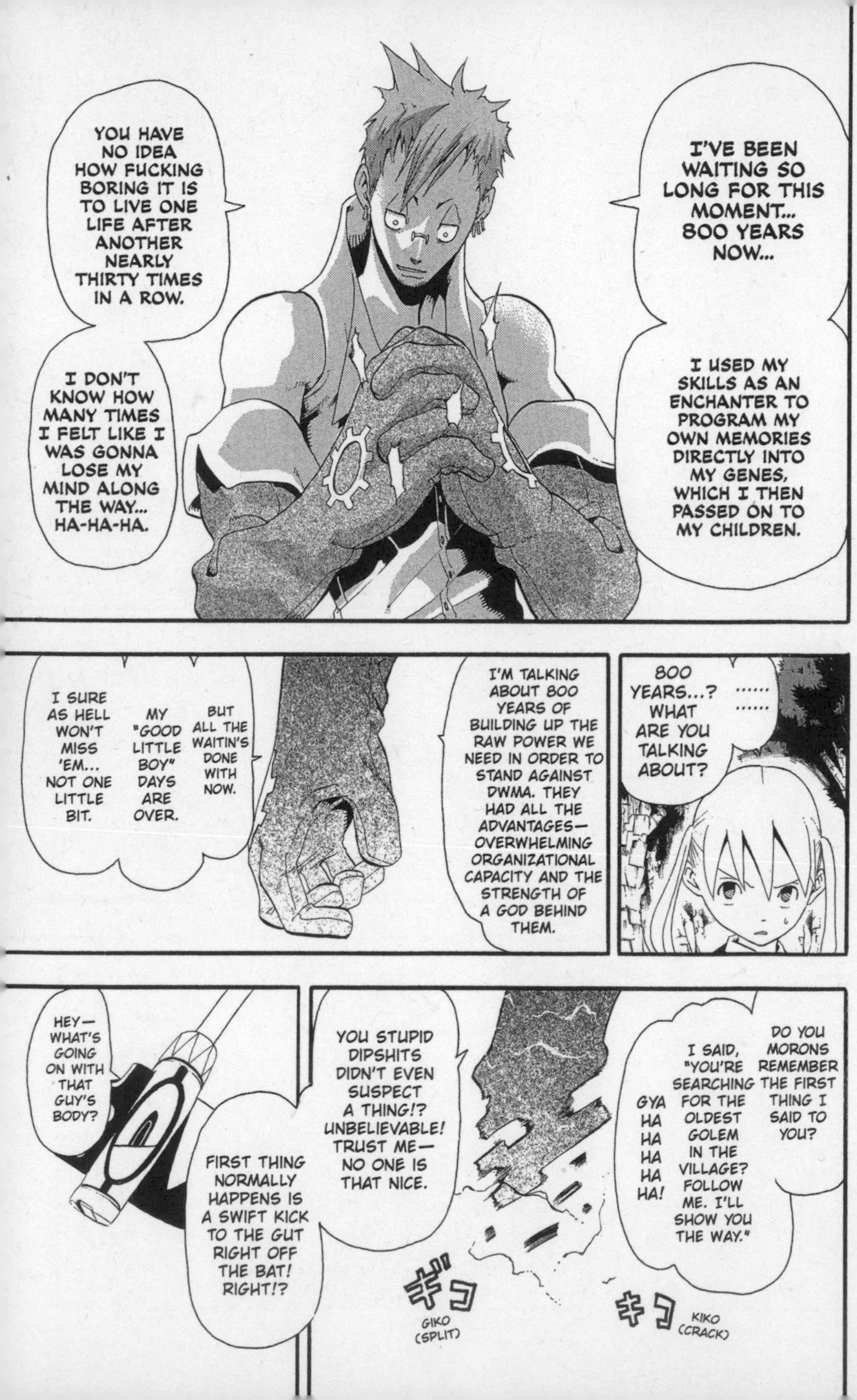
I'VE BEEN WAITING SO LONG FOR THIS MOMENT... 800 YEARS NOW...
I USED MY SKILLS AS AN ENCHANTER TO PROGRAM MY OWN MEMORIES DIRECTLY INTO MY GENES, WHICH I THEN PASSED ON TO MY CHILDREN.
YOU HAVE NO IDEA HOW FUCKING BORING IT IS TO LIVE ONE LIFE AFTER ANOTHER NEARLY THIRTY TIMES IN A ROW.
I DON'T KNOW HOW MANY TIMES I FELT LIKE I WAS GONNA LOSE MY MIND ALONG THE WAY... HA-HA-HA.
....
800 YEARS...? WHAT ARE YOU TALKING ABOUT?
I'M TALKING ABOUT 800 YEARS OF BUILDING UP THE RAW POWER WE NEED IN ORDER TO STAND AGAINST DWMA. THEY HAD ALL THE ADVANTAGES—OVERWHELMING ORGANIZATIONAL CAPACITY AND THE STRENGTH OF A GOD BEHIND THEM.
BUT ALL THE WAITIN'S DONE WITH NOW.
MY "GOOD LITTLE BOY" DAYS ARE OVER.
I SURE AS HELL WON'T MISS 'EM... NOT ONE LITTLE BIT.
DO YOU MORONS REMEMBER THE FIRST THING I SAID TO YOU?
I SAID, "YOU'RE SEARCHING FOR THE OLDEST GOLEM IN THE VILLAGE? FOLLOW ME. I'LL SHOW YOU THE WAY."
GYA HA HA HA HA HA!
YOU STUPID DIPSHITS DIDN'T EVEN SUSPECT A THING!? UNBELIEVABLE! TRUST ME—NO ONE IS THAT NICE.
FIRST THING NORMALLY HAPPENS IS A SWIFT KICK TO THE GUT RIGHT OFF THE BAT! RIGHT!?
キコ
KIKO (CRACK)
ギコ
GIKO (SPLIT)
HEY—WHAT'S GOING ON WITH THAT GUY'S BODY?

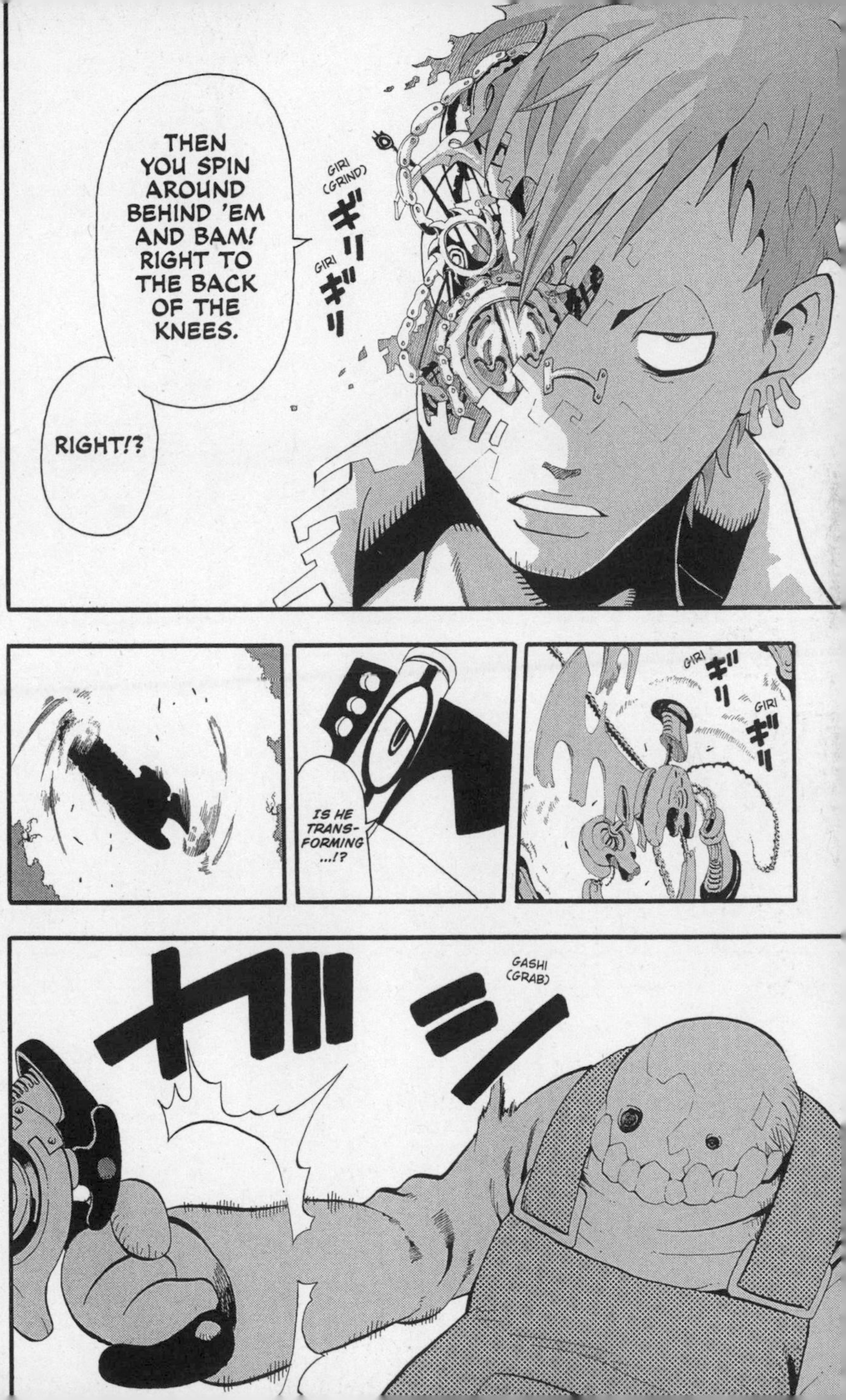
THEN YOU SPIN AROUND BEHIND 'EM AND BAM! RIGHT TO THE BACK OF THE KNEES.
RIGHT!?
GIRI (GRIND)
ギリ
GIRI
ギリ
GIRI
ギリ
GIRI
ギリ
IS HE TRANS-FORMING ...!?
GASHI (GRAB)

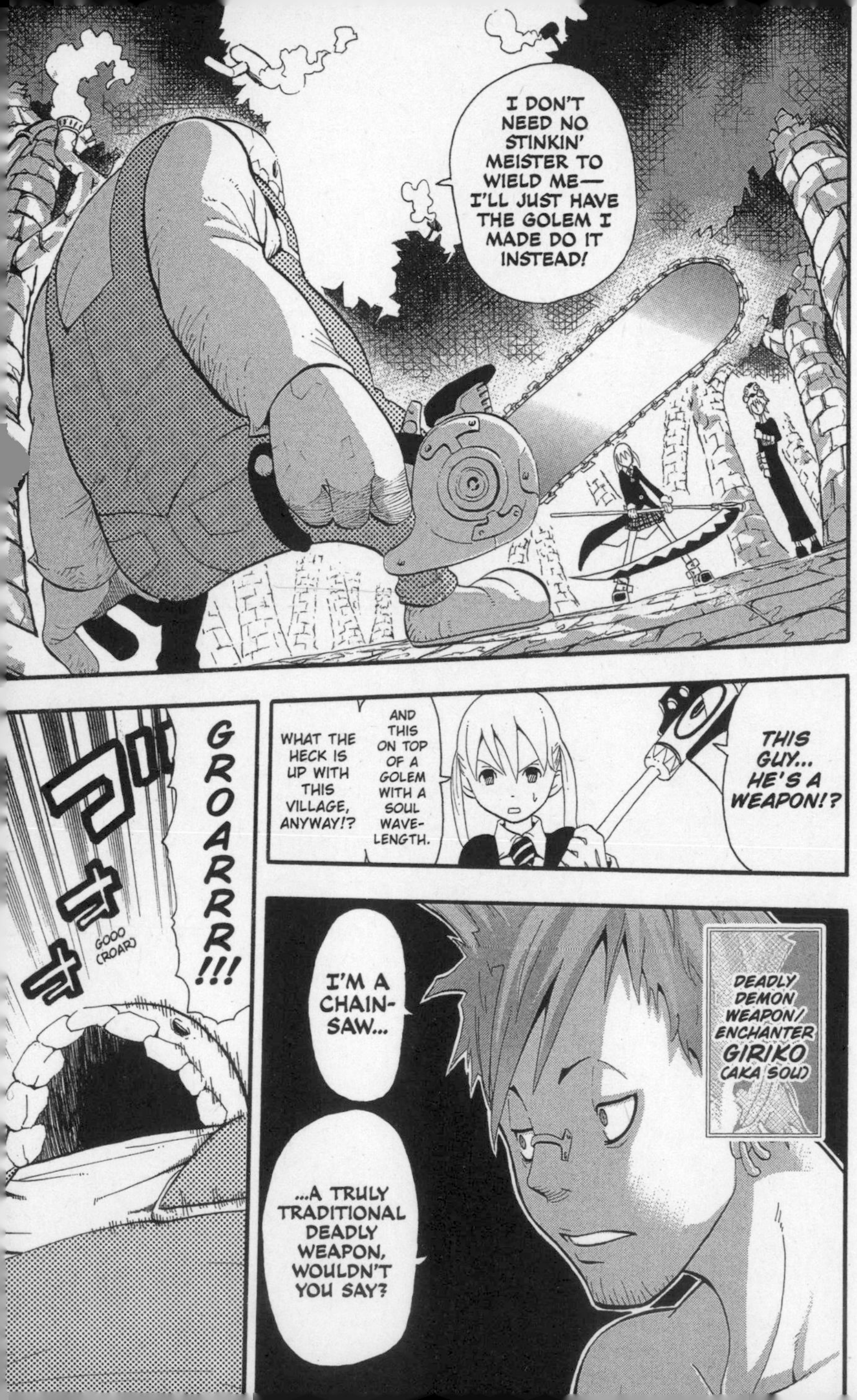
I DON'T NEED NO STINKIN' MEISTER TO WIELD ME—I'LL JUST HAVE THE GOLEM I MADE DO IT INSTEAD!
THIS GUY... HE'S A WEAPON!?
AND THIS ON TOP OF A GOLEM WITH A SOUL WAVE-LENGTH.
WHAT THE HECK IS UP WITH THIS VILLAGE, ANYWAY!?
DEADLY DEMON WEAPON/ENCHANTER GIRIKO (AKA SOU)
I'M A CHAIN-SAW...
...A TRULY TRADITIONAL DEADLY WEAPON, WOULDN'T YOU SAY?
GROARRR!!!
GOOO (ROAR)

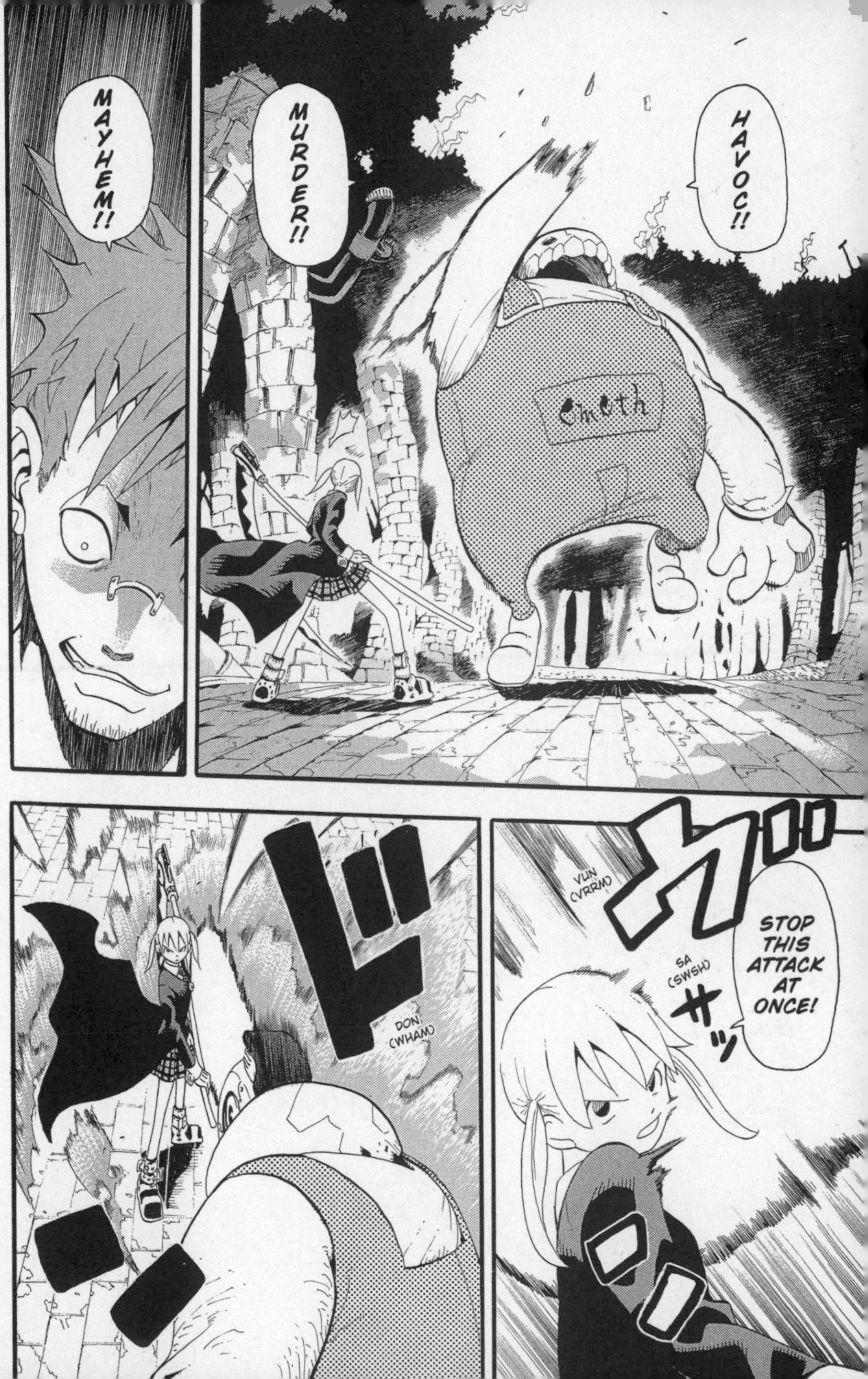
HAVOC!!
Emeth
MURDER!!
MAYHEM!!
VUN (VRRM)
STOP THIS ATTACK AT ONCE!
SA (SWSH)
DON (WHAM)

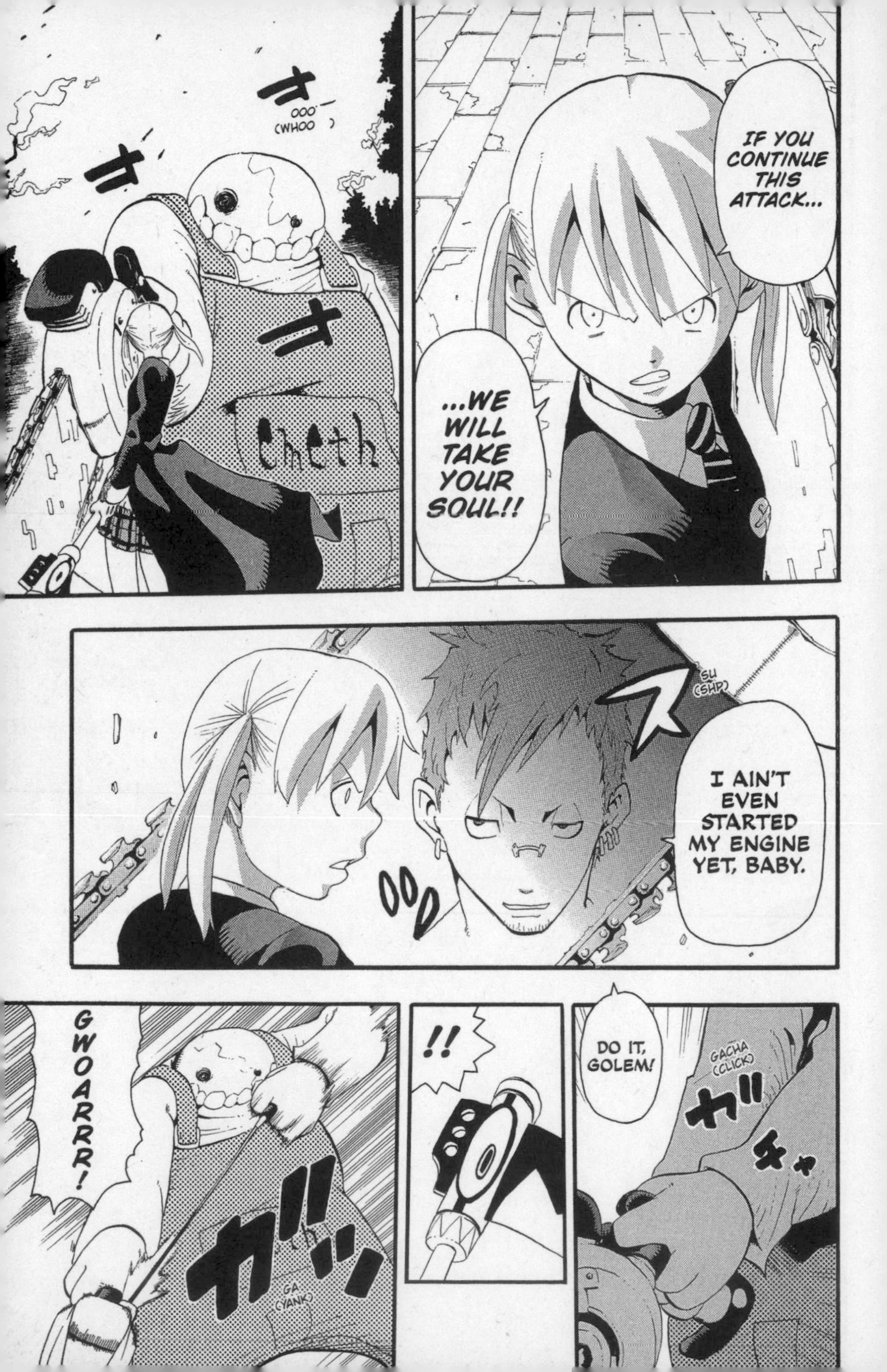

IF YOU CONTINUE THIS ATTACK...
...WE WILL TAKE YOUR SOUL!!
OOO (WHOO)
SU (SHP)
I AIN'T EVEN STARTED MY ENGINE YET, BABY.
DO IT, GOLEM!
GACHA (CLICK)
!!
GWOARRR!
GA (YANK)

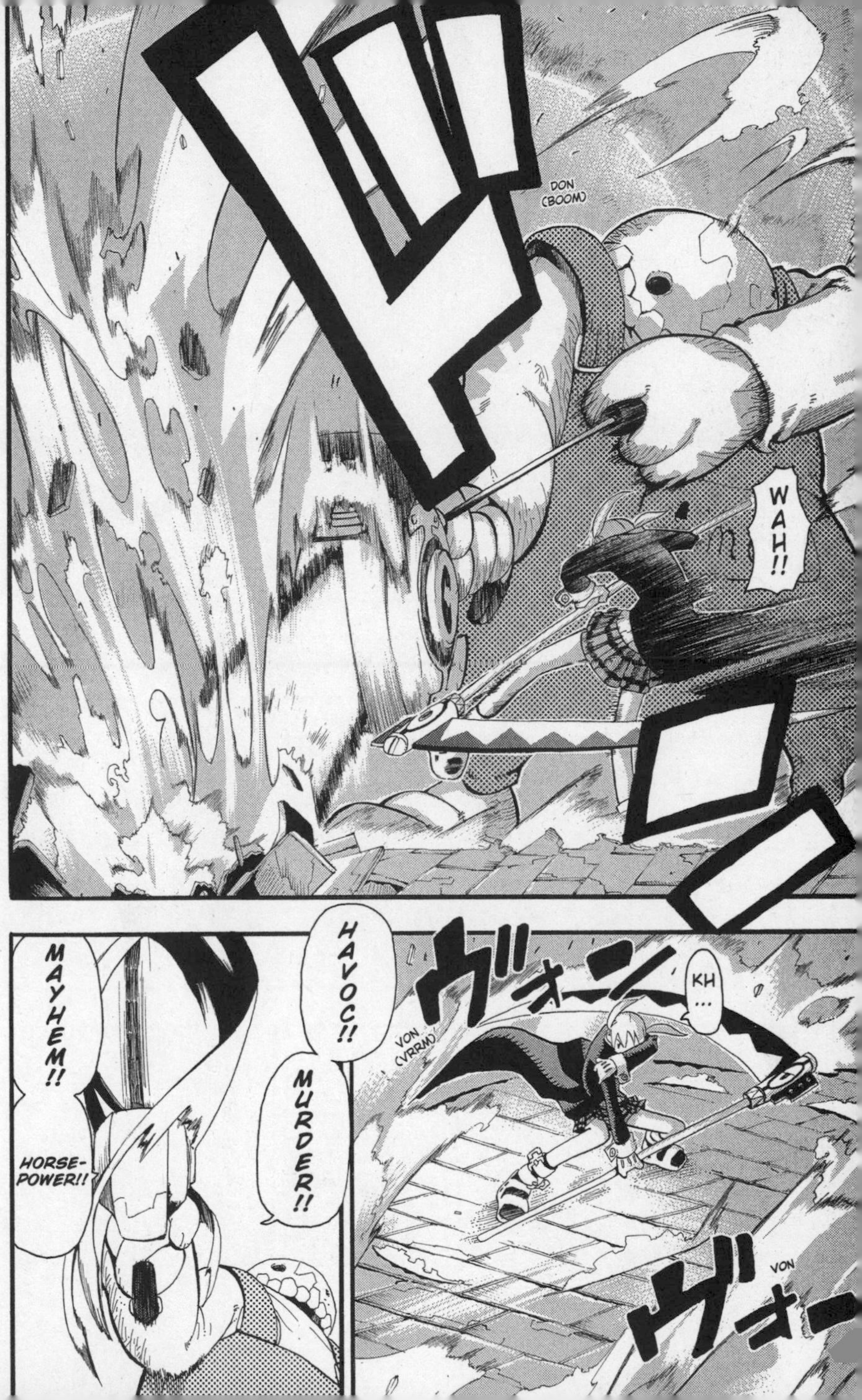
DON
(BOOM)
WAH!!
KH ...
VON
(VRRM)
VON
HAVOC!!
MURDER!!
MAYHEM!!
HORSE-POWER!!

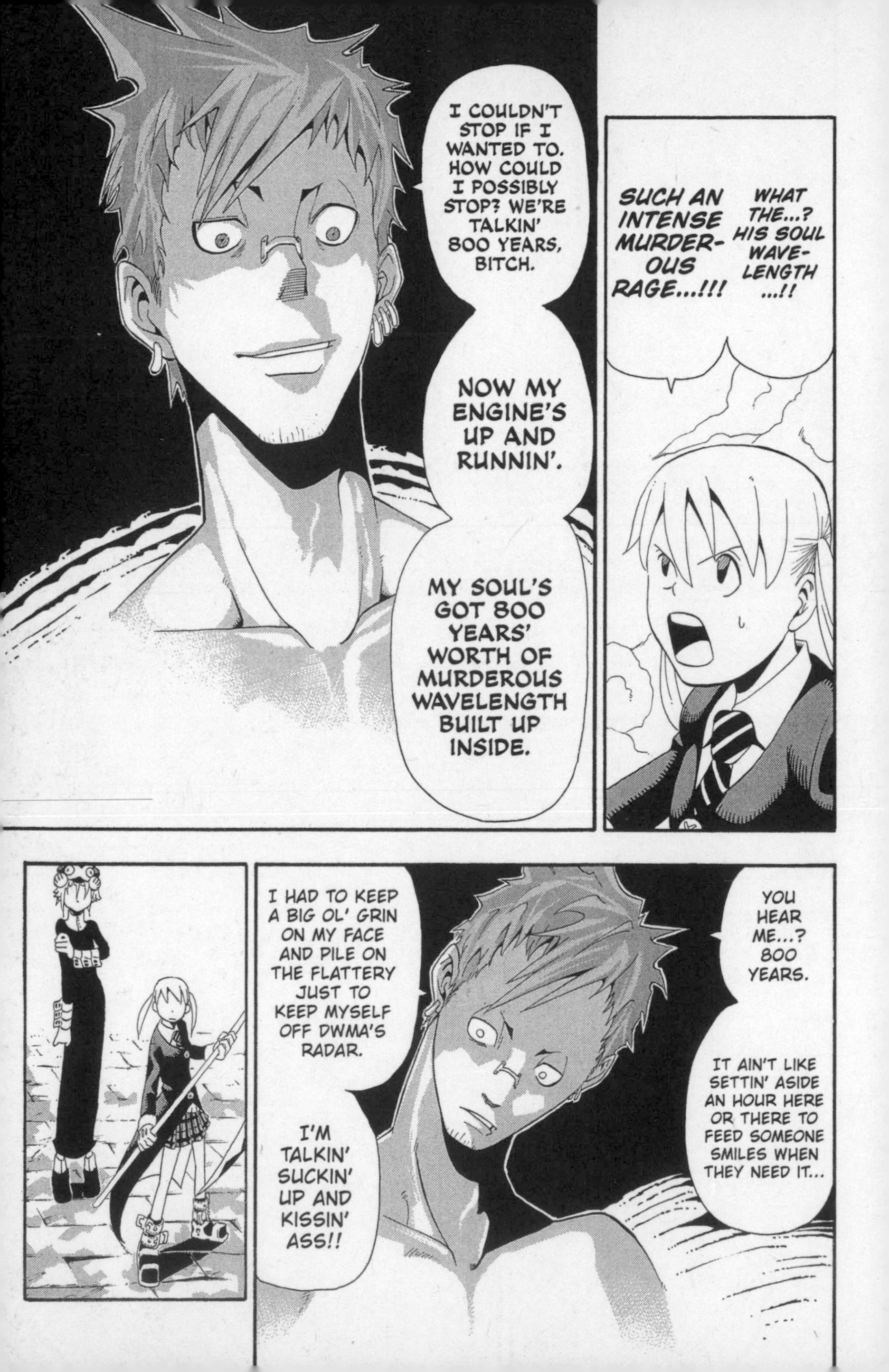
WHAT THE...? HIS SOUL WAVE-LENGTH ...!!
SUCH AN INTENSE MURDER-OUS RAGE...!!!
I COULDN'T STOP IF I WANTED TO. HOW COULD I POSSIBLY STOP? WE'RE TALKIN' 800 YEARS, BITCH.
NOW MY ENGINE'S UP AND RUNNIN'.
MY SOUL'S GOT 800 YEARS' WORTH OF MURDEROUS WAVELENGTH BUILT UP INSIDE.
YOU HEAR ME...? 800 YEARS.
IT AIN'T LIKE SETTIN' ASIDE AN HOUR HERE OR THERE TO FEED SOMEONE SMILES WHEN THEY NEED IT...
I HAD TO KEEP A BIG OL' GRIN ON MY FACE AND PILE ON THE FLATTERY JUST TO KEEP MYSELF OFF DWMA'S RADAR.
I'M TALKIN' SUCKIN' UP AND KISSIN' ASS!!

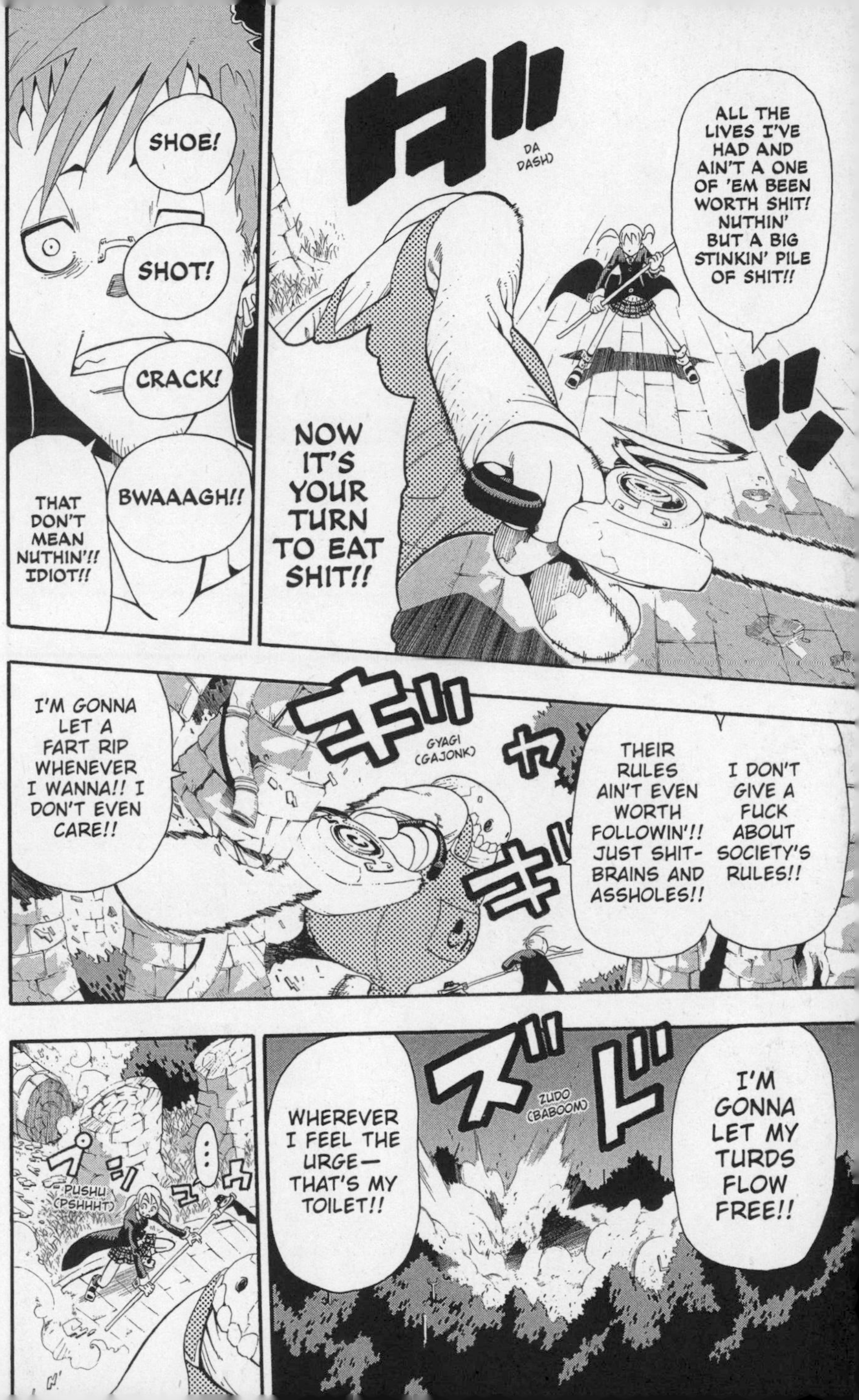
DA DASH)
ALL THE LIVES I'VE HAD AND AIN'T A ONE OF 'EM BEEN WORTH SHIT! NUTHIN' BUT A BIG STINKIN' PILE OF SHIT!!
NOW IT'S YOUR TURN TO EAT SHIT!!
SHOE!
SHOT!
CRACK!
BWAAAGH!!
THAT DON'T MEAN NUTHIN'!! IDIOT!!
I DON'T GIVE A FUCK ABOUT SOCIETY'S RULES!!
THEIR RULES AIN'T EVEN WORTH FOLLOWIN'!! JUST SHIT-BRAINS AND ASSHOLES!!
GYAGI (GAJONK)
I'M GONNA LET A FART RIP WHENEVER I WANNA!! I DON'T EVEN CARE!!
I'M GONNA LET MY TURDS FLOW FREE!!
ZUDO (BABOOM)
WHEREVER I FEEL THE URGE— THAT'S MY TOILET!!
PUSHU (PSHHHT)

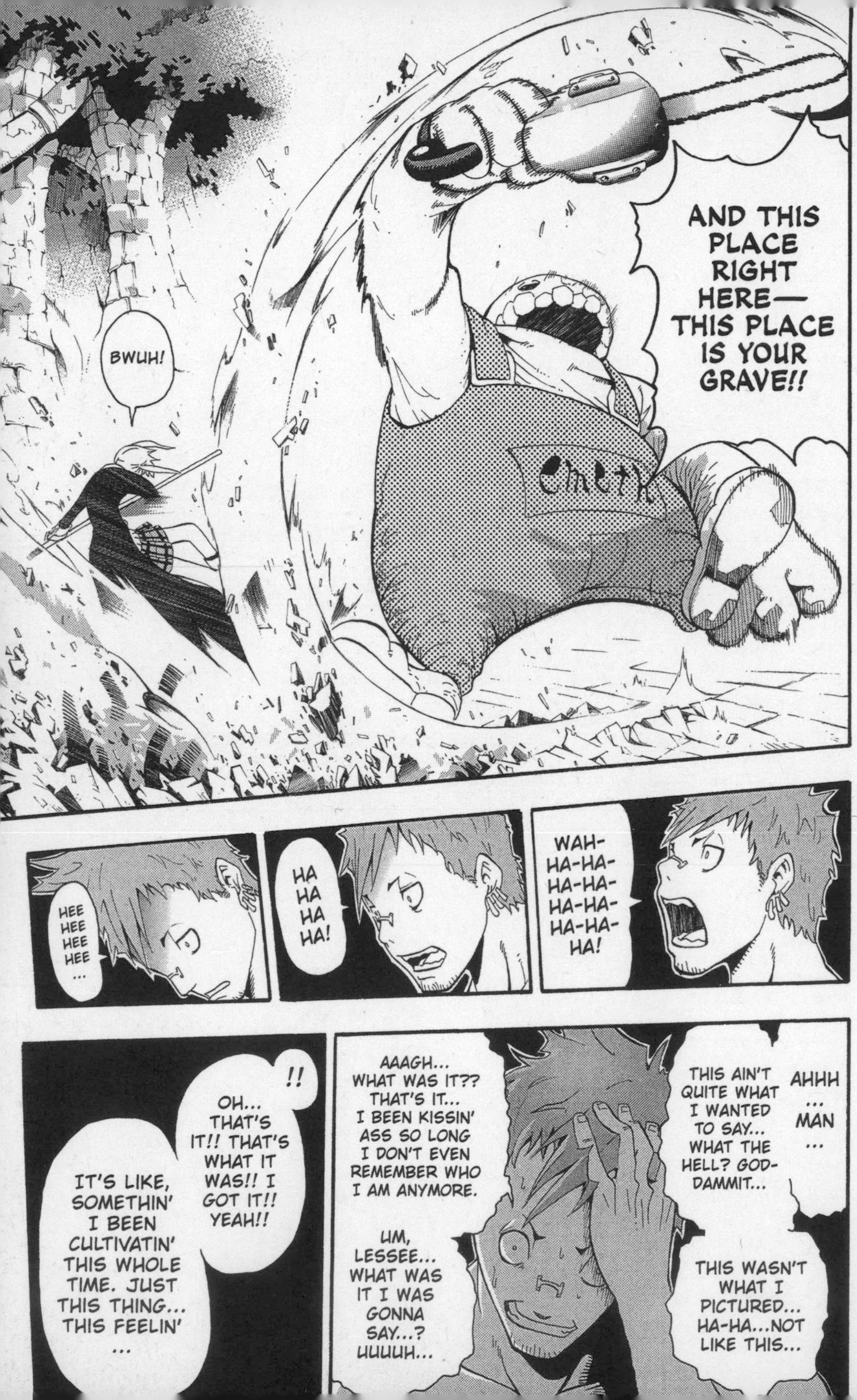
AND THIS PLACE RIGHT HERE— THIS PLACE IS YOUR GRAVE!!
BWUH!
WAH-HA-HA-HA-HA-HA-HA-HA-HA-HA!
HA HA HA HA!
HEE HEE HEE HEE ...
AHHH ... MAN ...
THIS AIN'T QUITE WHAT I WANTED TO SAY... WHAT THE HELL? GOD-DAMMIT...
AAAGH... WHAT WAS IT?? THAT'S IT... I BEEN KISSIN' ASS SO LONG I DON'T EVEN REMEMBER WHO I AM ANYMORE.
THIS WASN'T WHAT I PICTURED... HA-HA...NOT LIKE THIS...
UM, LESSEE... WHAT WAS IT I WAS GONNA SAY...? UUUUH...
!!
OH... THAT'S IT!! THAT'S WHAT IT WAS!! I GOT IT!! YEAH!!
IT'S LIKE, SOMETHIN' I BEEN CULTIVATIN' THIS WHOLE TIME. JUST THIS THING... THIS FEELIN' ...

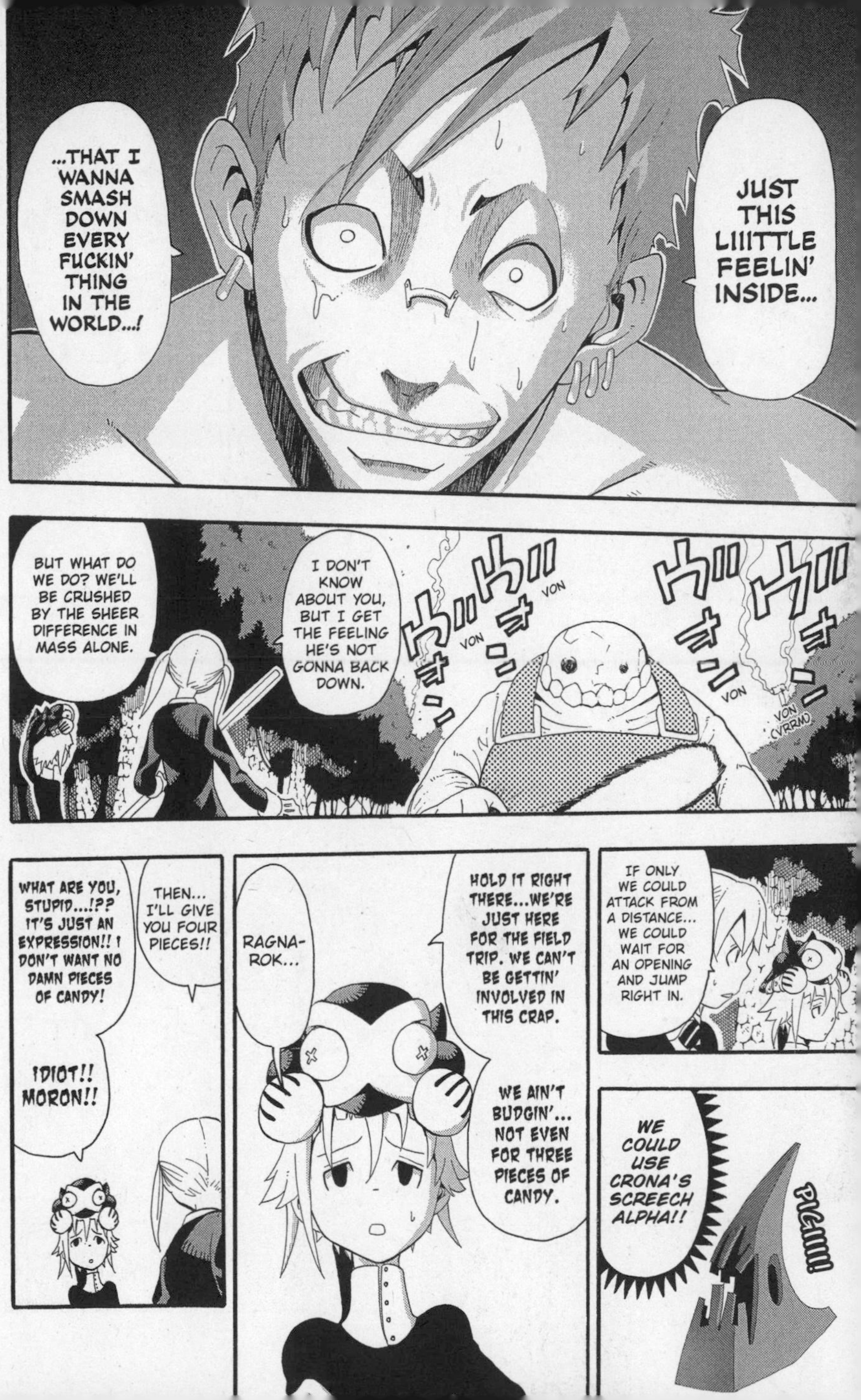

JUST THIS LIIITTLE FEELIN' INSIDE...
...THAT I WANNA SMASH DOWN EVERY FUCKIN' THING IN THE WORLD...!
ヴォン
VON
ヴォン
VON (VRRMO)
I DON'T KNOW ABOUT YOU, BUT I GET THE FEELING HE'S NOT GONNA BACK DOWN.
ヴォン
VON
ヴォン
VON
BUT WHAT DO WE DO? WE'LL BE CRUSHED BY THE SHEER DIFFERENCE IN MASS ALONE.
IF ONLY WE COULD ATTACK FROM A DISTANCE... WE COULD WAIT FOR AN OPENING AND JUMP RIGHT IN.
WE COULD USE CRONA'S SCREECH ALPHA!!
PIGIIII!
HOLD IT RIGHT THERE...WE'RE JUST HERE FOR THE FIELD TRIP. WE CAN'T BE GETTIN' INVOLVED IN THIS CRAP.
RAGNA-ROK...
WE AIN'T BUDGIN'... NOT EVEN FOR THREE PIECES OF CANDY.
THEN... I'LL GIVE YOU FOUR PIECES!!
WHAT ARE YOU, STUPID...!?? IT'S JUST AN EXPRESSION!! I DON'T WANT NO DAMN PIECES OF CANDY!
IDIOT!! MORON!!

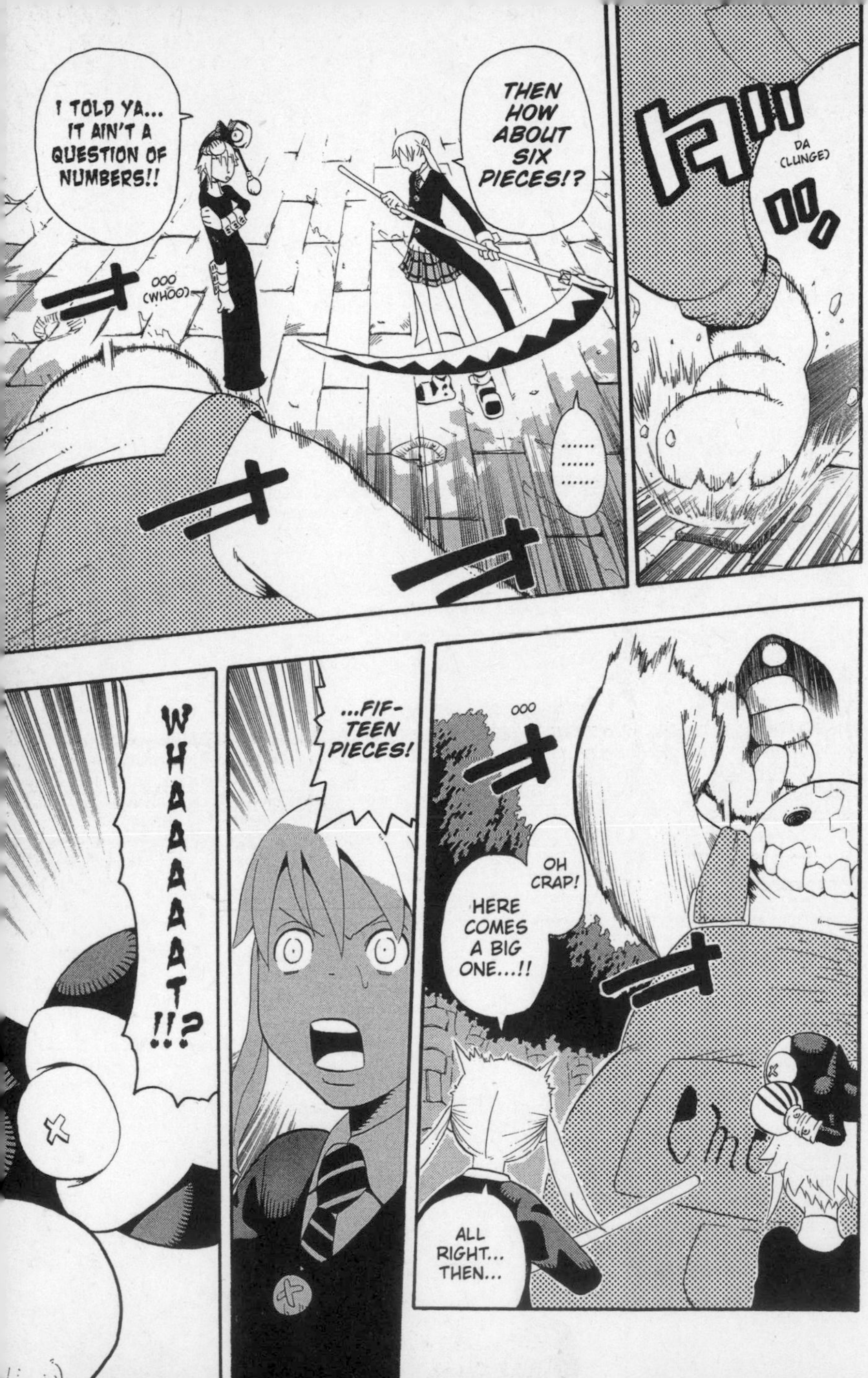
DA (LUNGE)
THEN HOW ABOUT SIX PIECES!?
I TOLD YA... IT AIN'T A QUESTION OF NUMBERS!!
OOO (WHOO)
......
......
......
OOO
OH CRAP!
HERE COMES A BIG ONE...!!
ALL RIGHT... THEN...
...FIF-TEEN PIECES!
WHAAAAAAT!!?

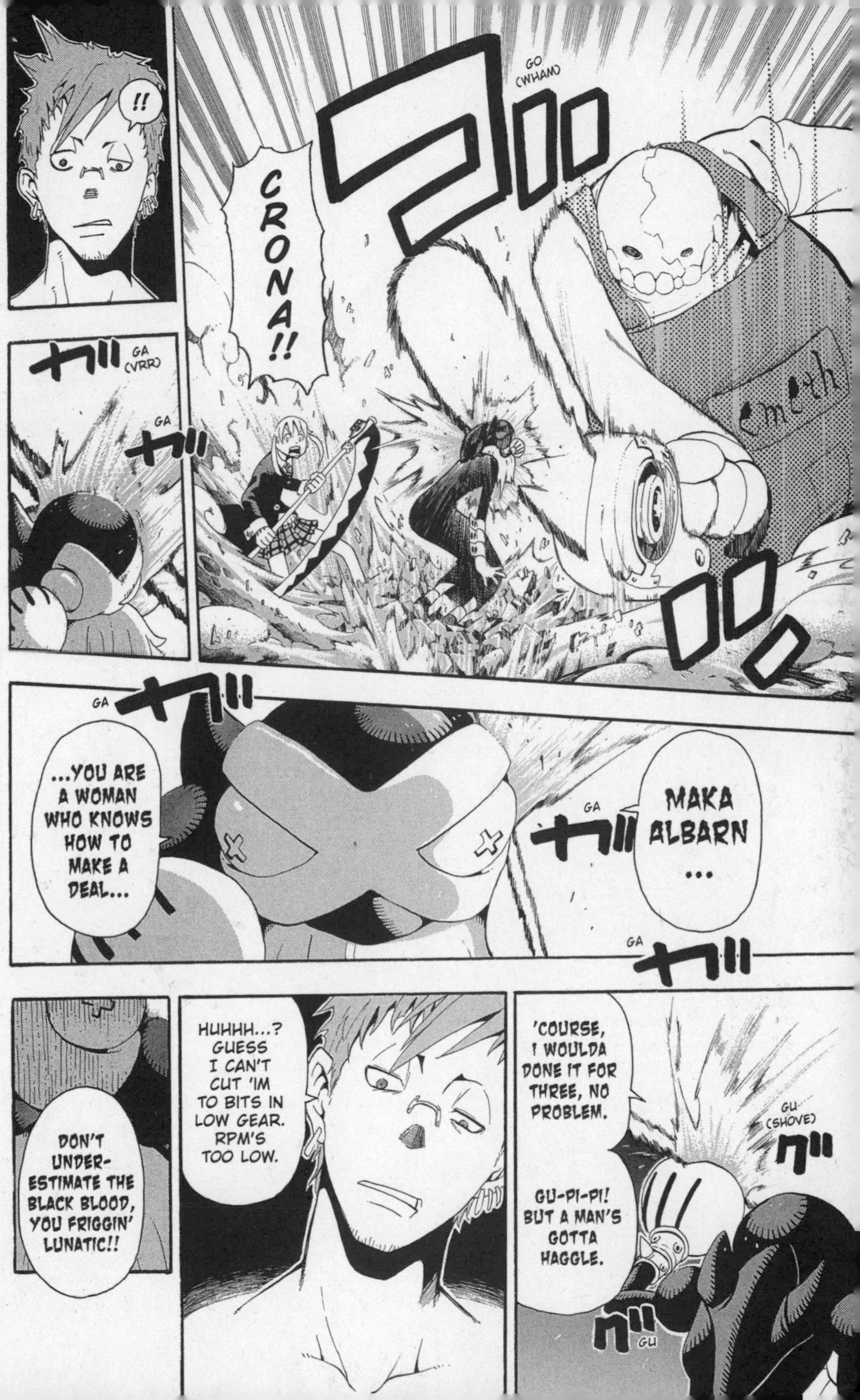
GO (WHAM)
CRONA!!
!!
GA (VRR)
GA
GA
MAKA ALBARN ...
...YOU ARE A WOMAN WHO KNOWS HOW TO MAKE A DEAL...
GA
'COURSE, I WOULDA DONE IT FOR THREE, NO PROBLEM.
GU (SHOVE)
GU-PI-PI! BUT A MAN'S GOTTA HAGGLE.
GU
HUHHH...? GUESS I CAN'T CUT 'IM TO BITS IN LOW GEAR. RPM'S TOO LOW.
DON'T UNDER-ESTIMATE THE BLACK BLOOD, YOU FRIGGIN' LUNATIC!!

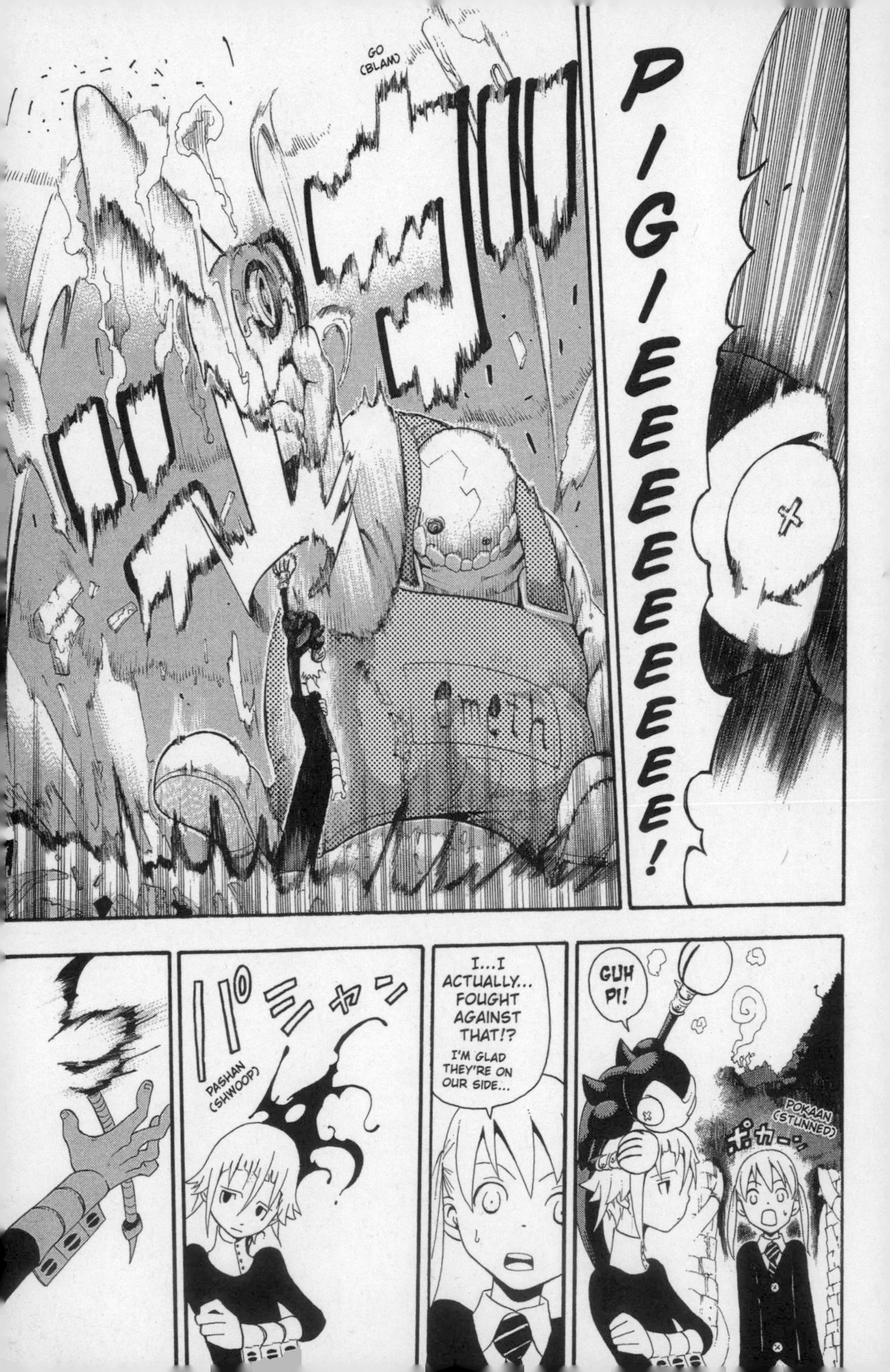
PIGIEEEEEEEEEE!
GO (BLAM)
GUH PI!
POKAAN (STUNNED)
I...I ACTUALLY... FOUGHT AGAINST THAT!?
I'M GLAD THEY'RE ON OUR SIDE...
PASHAN (SHWOOP)

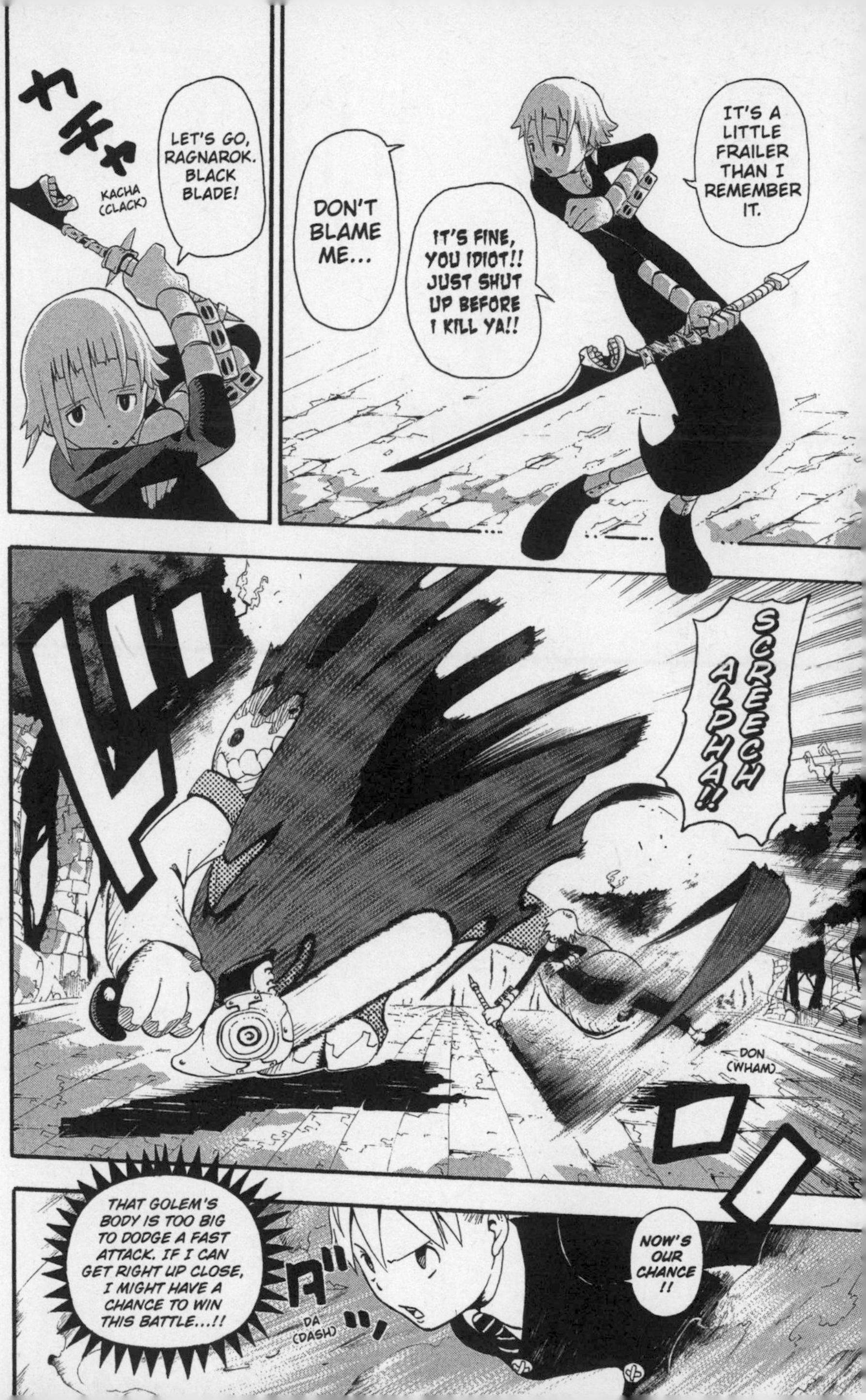
IT'S A LITTLE FRAILER THAN I REMEMBER IT.
IT'S FINE, YOU IDIOT!! JUST SHUT UP BEFORE I KILL YA!!
DON'T BLAME ME...
LET'S GO, RAGNAROK. BLACK BLADE!
KACHA (CLACK)
SCREECH ALPHA!!
DON (WHAM)
NOW'S OUR CHANCE!!
THAT GOLEM'S BODY IS TOO BIG TO DODGE A FAST ATTACK. IF I CAN GET RIGHT UP CLOSE, I MIGHT HAVE A CHANCE TO WIN THIS BATTLE...!!
DA (DASH)

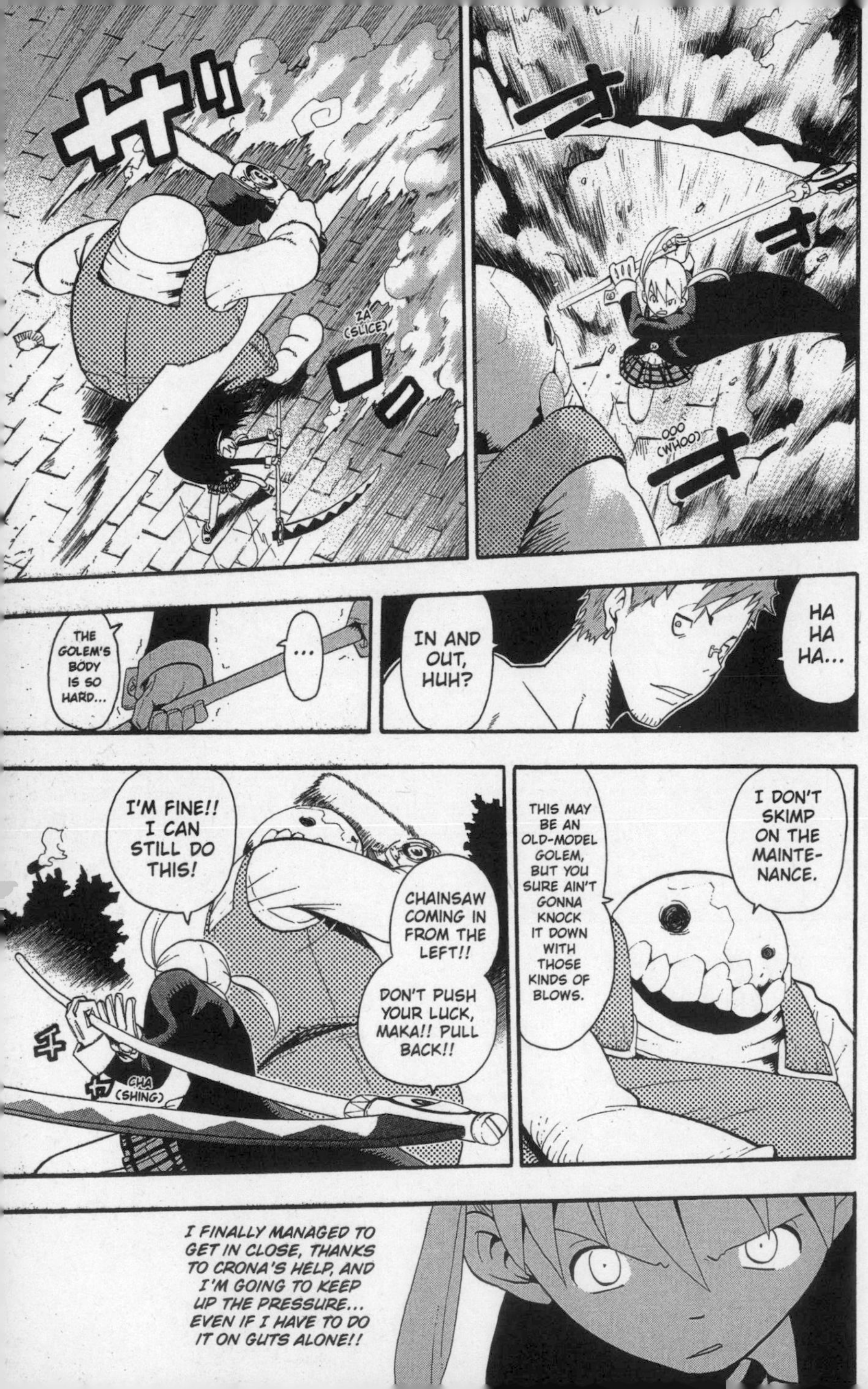
OOO
(WHOO)
ZA
(SLICE)
HA HA HA...
IN AND OUT, HUH?
...
THE GOLEM'S BODY IS SO HARD...
I DON'T SKIMP ON THE MAINTE-NANCE.
THIS MAY BE AN OLD-MODEL GOLEM, BUT YOU SURE AIN'T GONNA KNOCK IT DOWN WITH THOSE KINDS OF BLOWS.
CHAINSAW COMING IN FROM THE LEFT!!
DON'T PUSH YOUR LUCK, MAKA!! PULL BACK!!
I'M FINE!! I CAN STILL DO THIS!
CHA
(SHING)
I FINALLY MANAGED TO GET IN CLOSE, THANKS TO CRONA'S HELP, AND I'M GOING TO KEEP UP THE PRESSURE... EVEN IF I HAVE TO DO IT ON GUTS ALONE!!

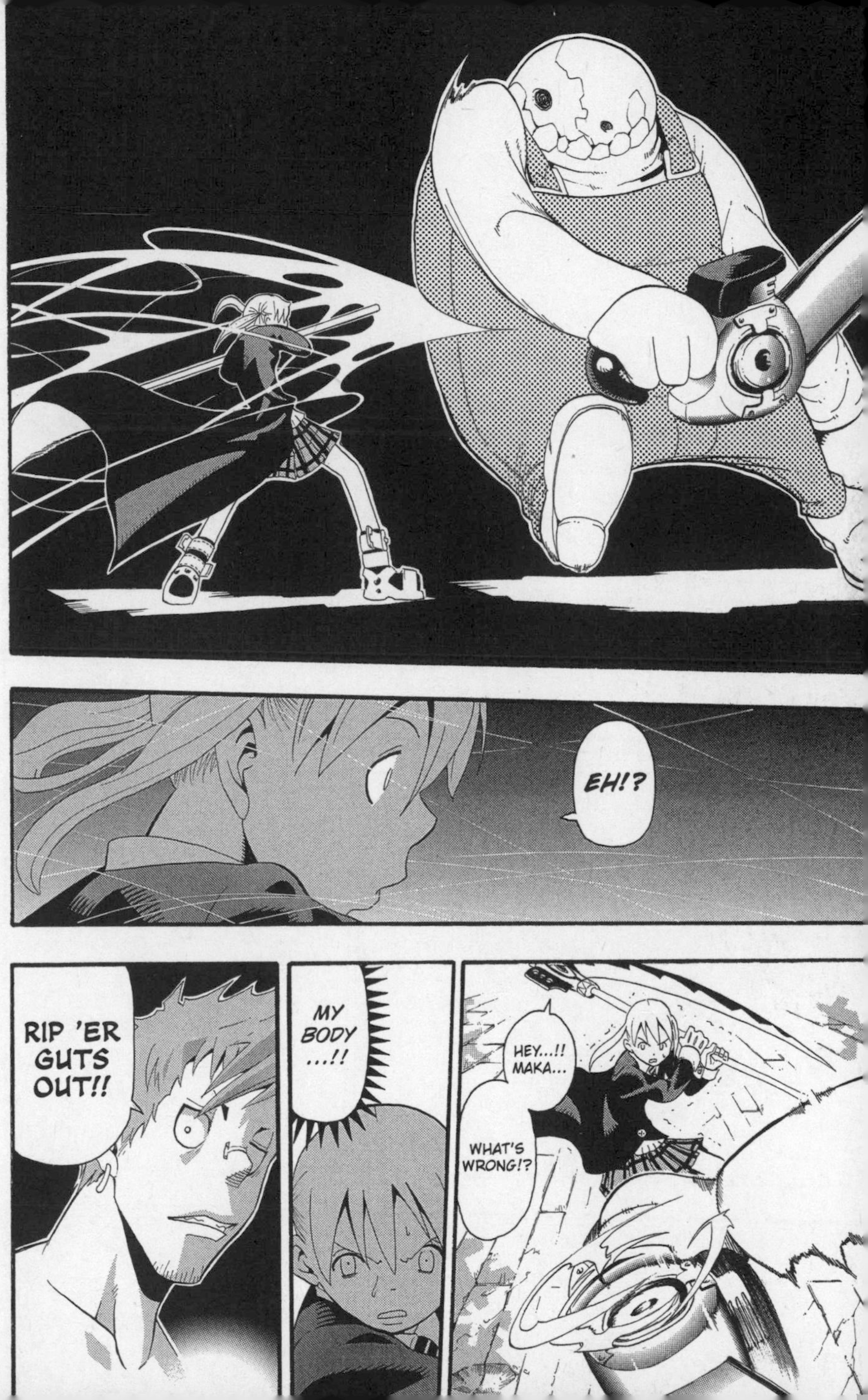
EH!?
HEY...!! MAKA...
WHAT'S WRONG!?
MY BODY ...!!
RIP 'ER GUTS OUT!!

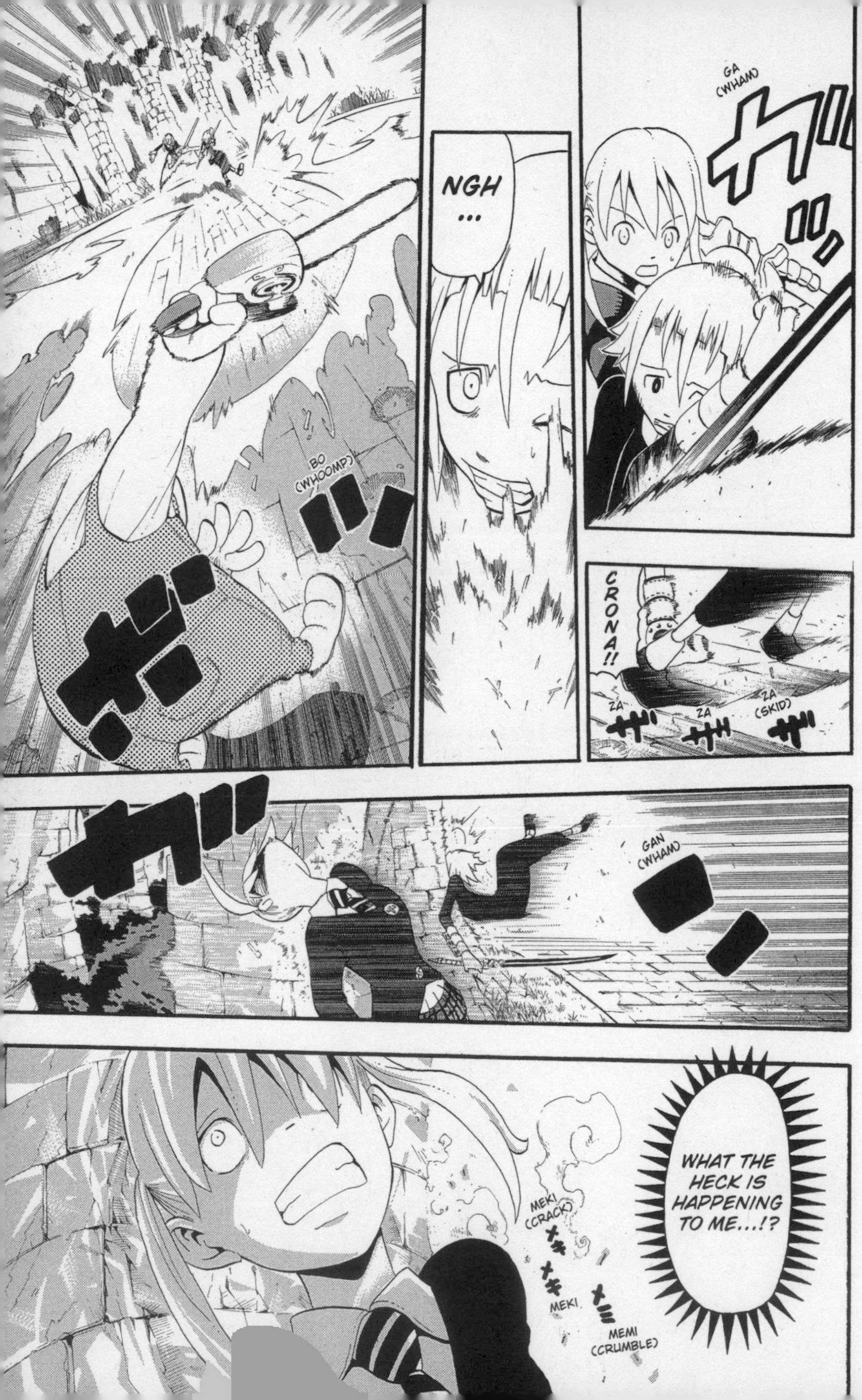
GA (WHAM)
CRONA!!
ZA
ZA
ZA (SKID)
NGH ...
BO (WHOOMP)
GAN (WHAM)
WHAT THE HECK IS HAPPENING TO ME...!?
MEKI (CRACK)
MEKI
MEMI (CRUMBLE)

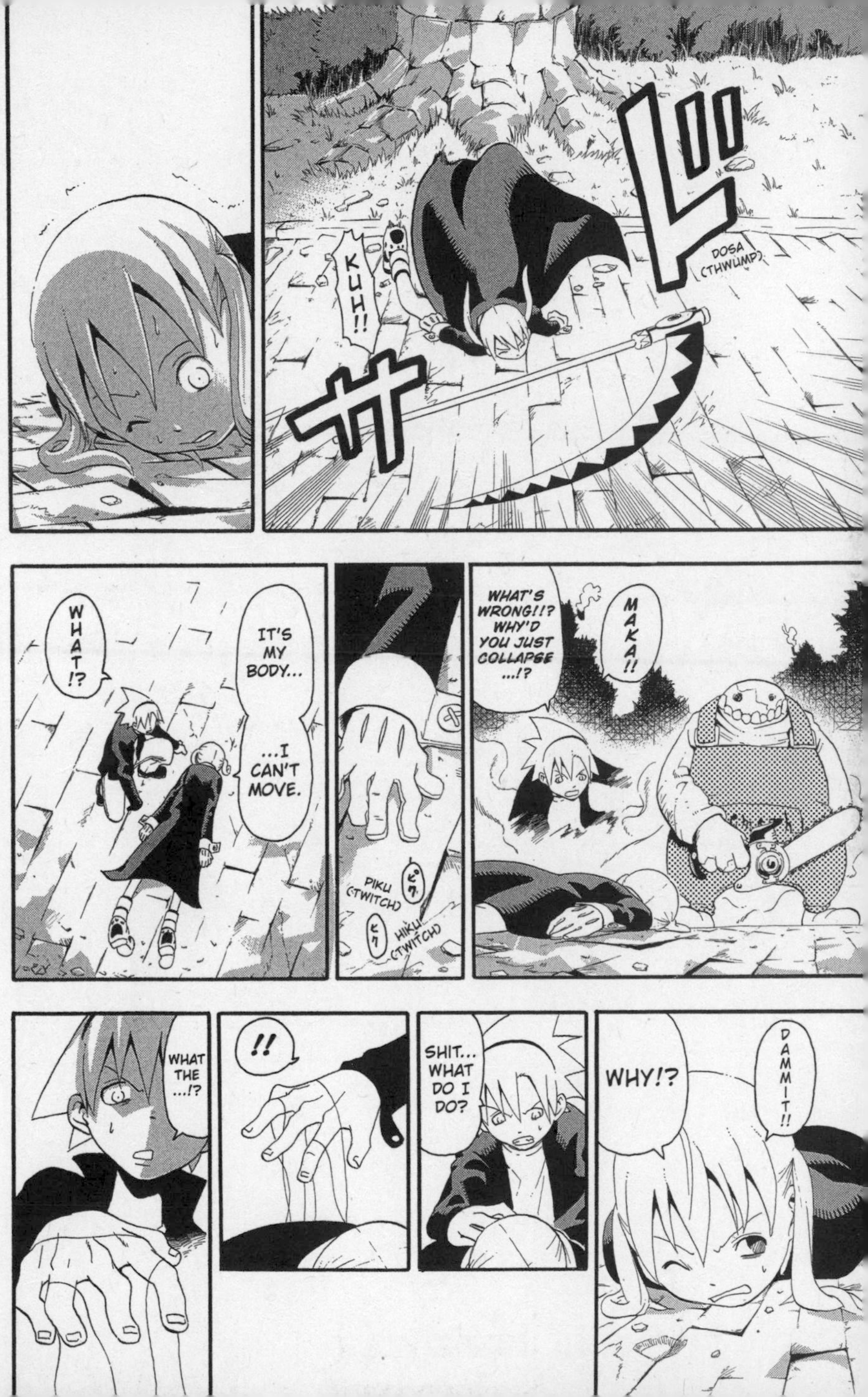
DOSA (THWUMP)
KUH!!
MAKA!!
WHAT'S WRONG!!? WHY'D YOU JUST COLLAPSE ...!?
PIKU (TWITCH)
HIKU (TWITCH)
IT'S MY BODY...
...I CAN'T MOVE.
WHAT!?
DAMMIT!!
WHY!?
SHIT... WHAT DO I DO?
!!
WHAT THE ...!?

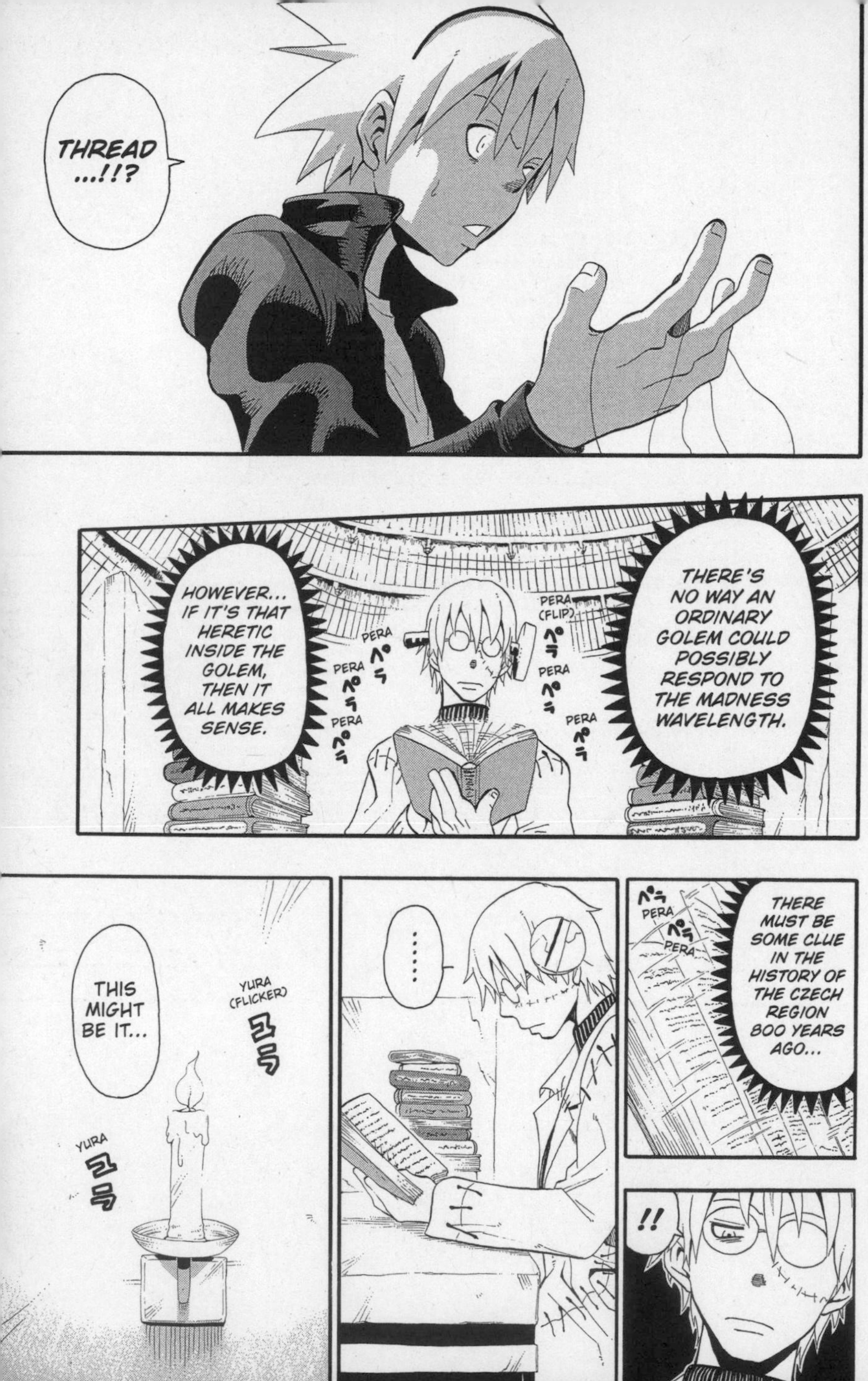
THREAD ...!!?
THERE'S NO WAY AN ORDINARY GOLEM COULD POSSIBLY RESPOND TO THE MADNESS WAVELENGTH.
PERA (FLIP) ペラ
PERA ペラ
PERA ペラ
HOWEVER... IF IT'S THAT HERETIC INSIDE THE GOLEM, THEN IT ALL MAKES SENSE.
PERA ペラ
PERA ペラ
PERA ペラ
ペラ PERA
ペラ PERA
THERE MUST BE SOME CLUE IN THE HISTORY OF THE CZECH REGION 800 YEARS AGO...
!!
......
YURA (FLICKER) ユラ
THIS MIGHT BE IT...
YURA ユラ

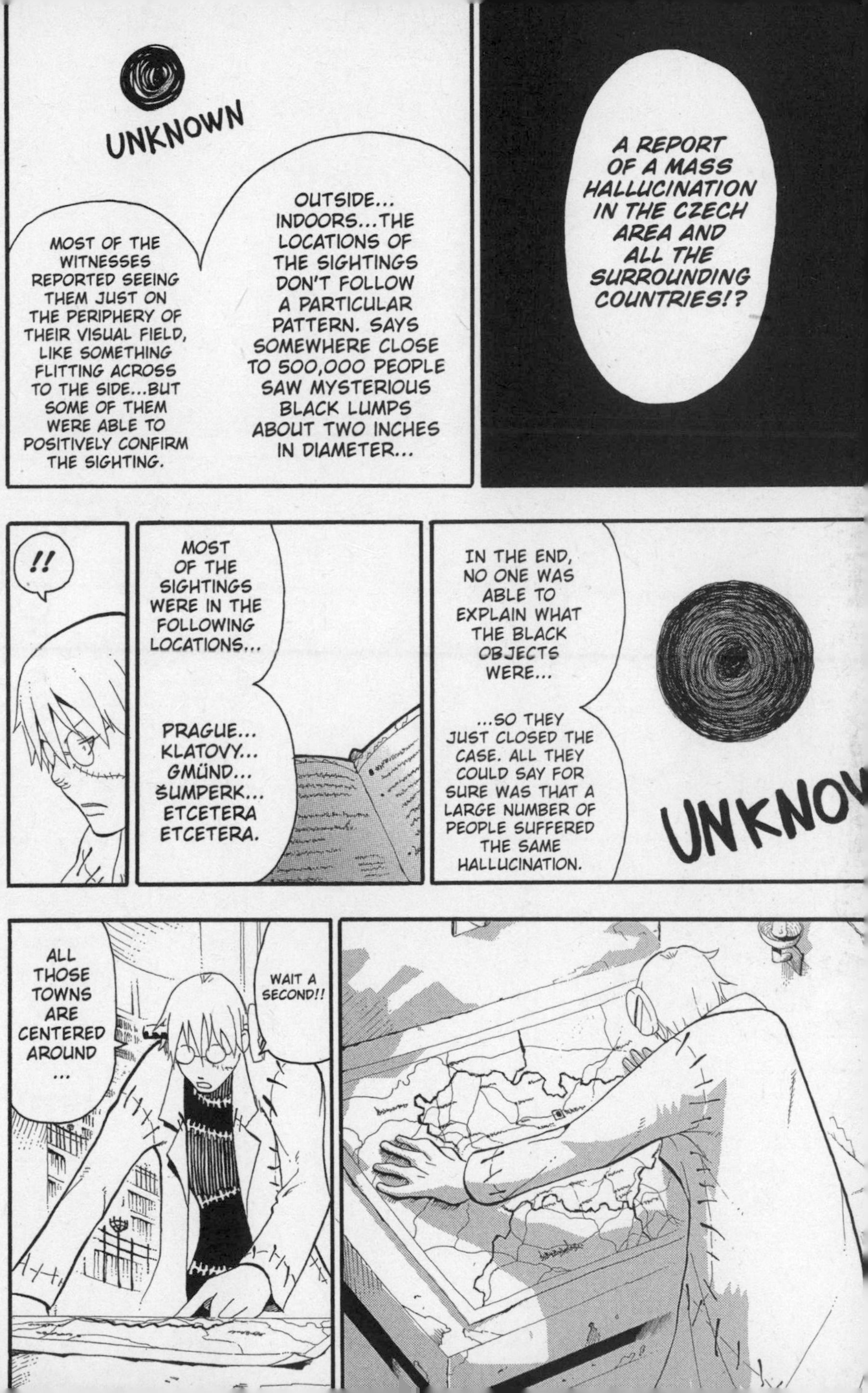
A REPORT OF A MASS HALLUCINATION IN THE CZECH AREA AND ALL THE SURROUNDING COUNTRIES!?
UNKNOWN
OUTSIDE... INDOORS...THE LOCATIONS OF THE SIGHTINGS DON'T FOLLOW A PARTICULAR PATTERN. SAYS SOMEWHERE CLOSE TO 500,000 PEOPLE SAW MYSTERIOUS BLACK LUMPS ABOUT TWO INCHES IN DIAMETER...
MOST OF THE WITNESSES REPORTED SEEING THEM JUST ON THE PERIPHERY OF THEIR VISUAL FIELD, LIKE SOMETHING FLITTING ACROSS TO THE SIDE...BUT SOME OF THEM WERE ABLE TO POSITIVELY CONFIRM THE SIGHTING.
IN THE END, NO ONE WAS ABLE TO EXPLAIN WHAT THE BLACK OBJECTS WERE...
...SO THEY JUST CLOSED THE CASE. ALL THEY COULD SAY FOR SURE WAS THAT A LARGE NUMBER OF PEOPLE SUFFERED THE SAME HALLUCINATION.
UNKNOW
MOST OF THE SIGHTINGS WERE IN THE FOLLOWING LOCATIONS...
PRAGUE... KLATOVY... GMÜND... ŠUMPERK... ETCETERA ETCETERA.
!!
WAIT A SECOND!!
ALL THOSE TOWNS ARE CENTERED AROUND ...

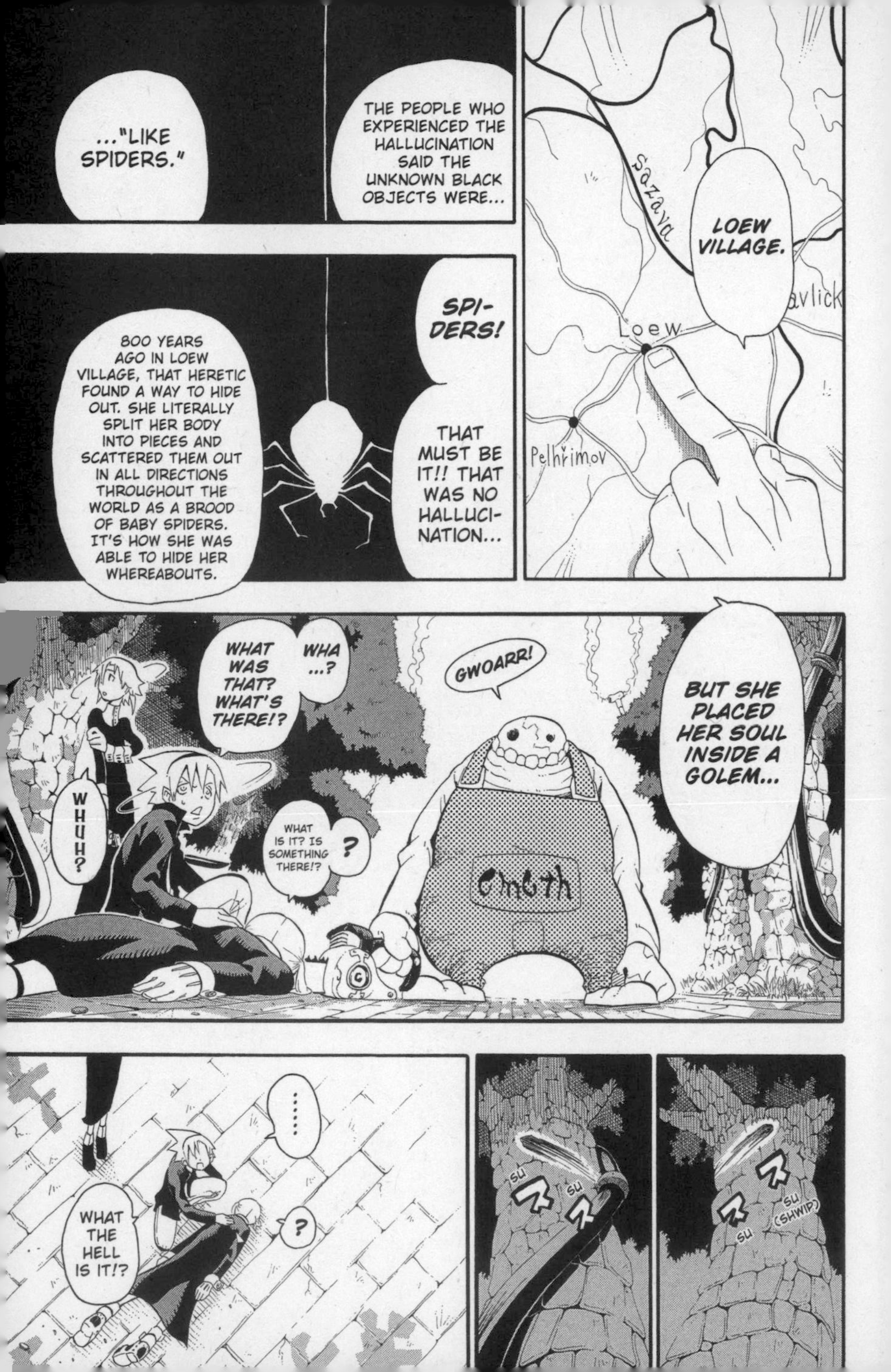
LOEW VILLAGE.
Sazava
Loew
avlick
Pelhrimov
THE PEOPLE WHO EXPERIENCED THE HALLUCINATION SAID THE UNKNOWN BLACK OBJECTS WERE...
..."LIKE SPIDERS."
SPI-DERS!
THAT MUST BE IT!! THAT WAS NO HALLUCI-NATION...
800 YEARS AGO IN LOEW VILLAGE, THAT HERETIC FOUND A WAY TO HIDE OUT. SHE LITERALLY SPLIT HER BODY INTO PIECES AND SCATTERED THEM OUT IN ALL DIRECTIONS THROUGHOUT THE WORLD AS A BROOD OF BABY SPIDERS. IT'S HOW SHE WAS ABLE TO HIDE HER WHEREABOUTS.
BUT SHE PLACED HER SOUL INSIDE A GOLEM...
GWOARR!
WHA ...?
WHAT WAS THAT? WHAT'S THERE!?
?
WHAT IS IT? IS SOMETHING THERE!?
WHUH?
SU
SU (SHWIP)
SU
SU
......
?
WHAT THE HELL IS IT!?

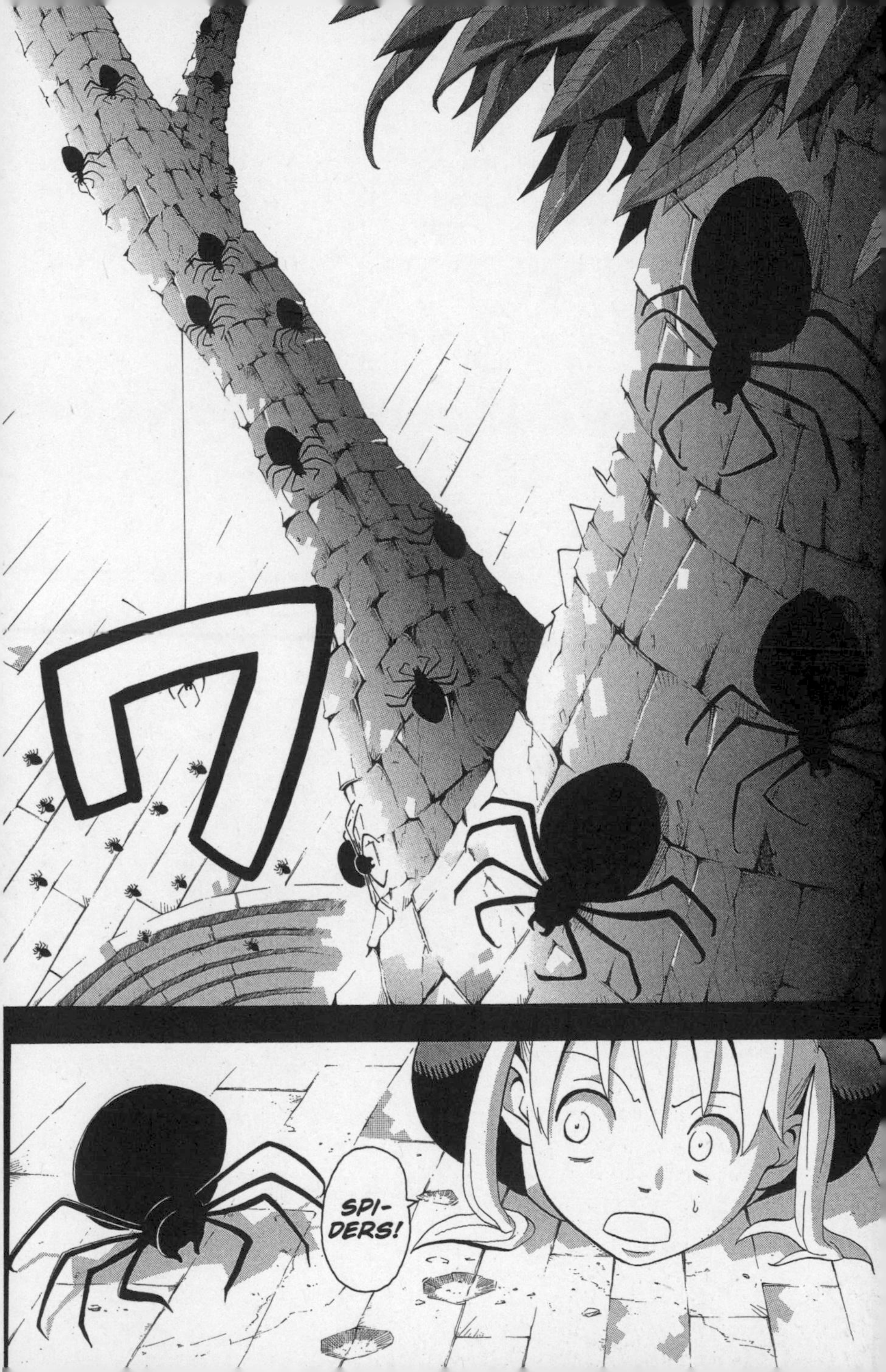
SPI-DERS!

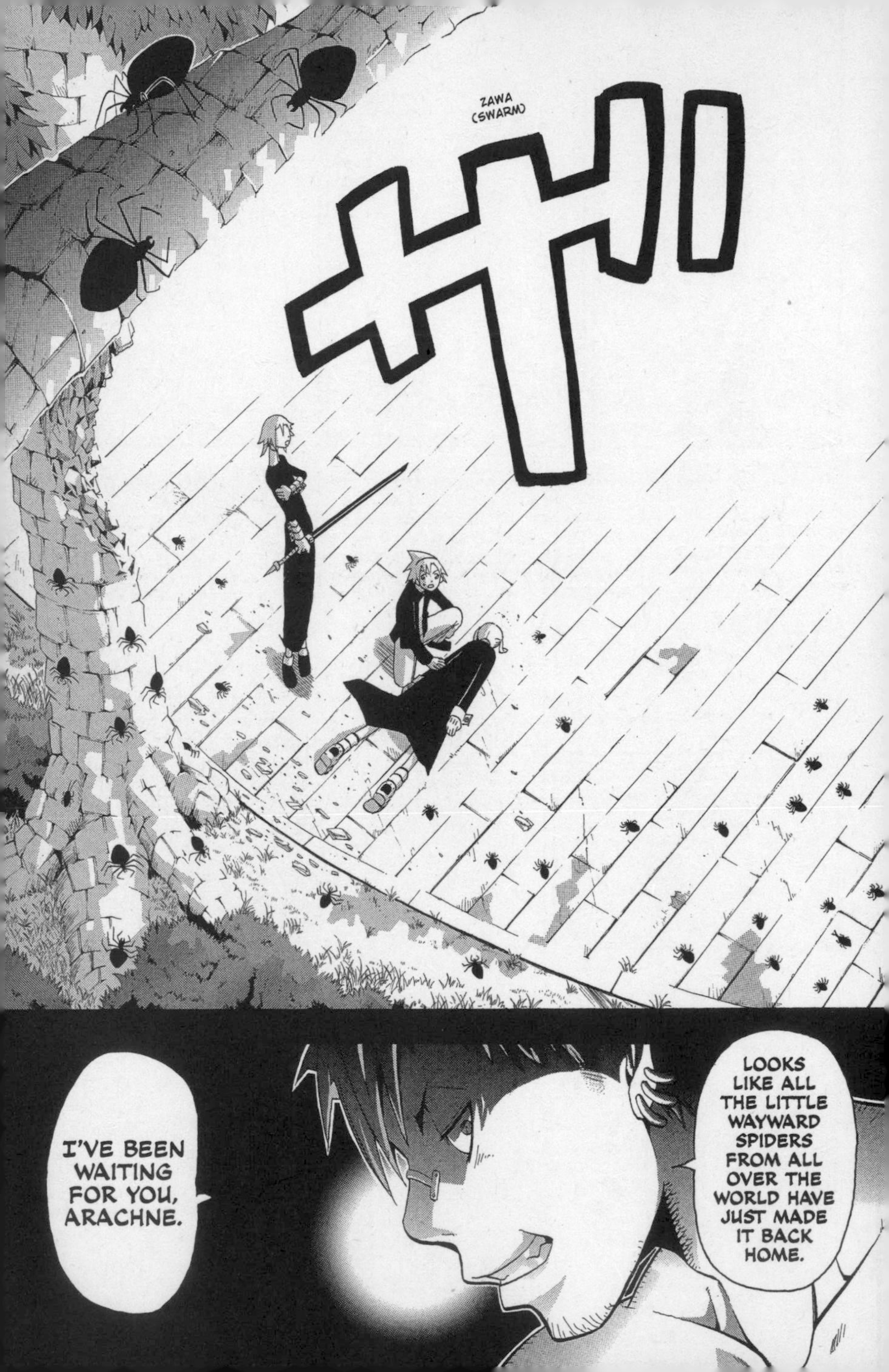
ZAWA (SWARM)
LOOKS LIKE ALL THE LITTLE WAYWARD SPIDERS FROM ALL OVER THE WORLD HAVE JUST MADE IT BACK HOME.
I'VE BEEN WAITING FOR YOU, ARACHNE.

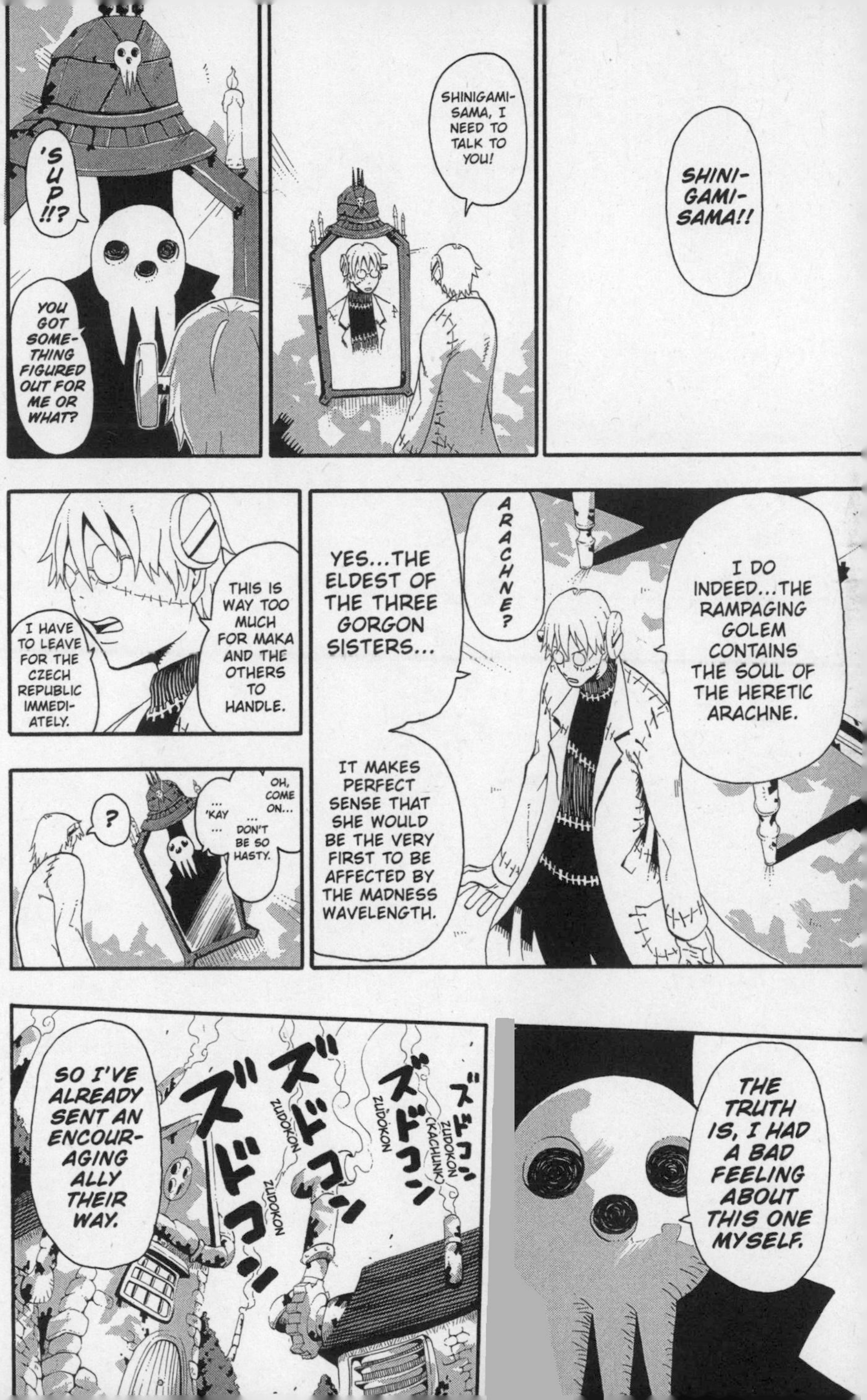
SHINI-GAMI-SAMA!!
SHINIGAMI-SAMA, I NEED TO TALK TO YOU!
'SUP!!?
YOU GOT SOMETHING FIGURED OUT FOR ME OR WHAT?
I DO INDEED...THE RAMPAGING GOLEM CONTAINS THE SOUL OF THE HERETIC ARACHNE.
ARACHNE?
YES...THE ELDEST OF THE THREE GORGON SISTERS...
IT MAKES PERFECT SENSE THAT SHE WOULD BE THE VERY FIRST TO BE AFFECTED BY THE MADNESS WAVELENGTH.
THIS IS WAY TOO MUCH FOR MAKA AND THE OTHERS TO HANDLE.
I HAVE TO LEAVE FOR THE CZECH REPUBLIC IMMEDIATELY.
OH, COME ON... ...DON'T BE SO HASTY.
...'KAY...
?
THE TRUTH IS, I HAD A BAD FEELING ABOUT THIS ONE MYSELF.
ズドコン ZUDOKON (KACHUNK)
ズドコン ZUDOKON
ズドコン ZUDOKON
ズドコン ZUDOKON
SO I'VE ALREADY SENT AN ENCOURAGING ALLY THEIR WAY.

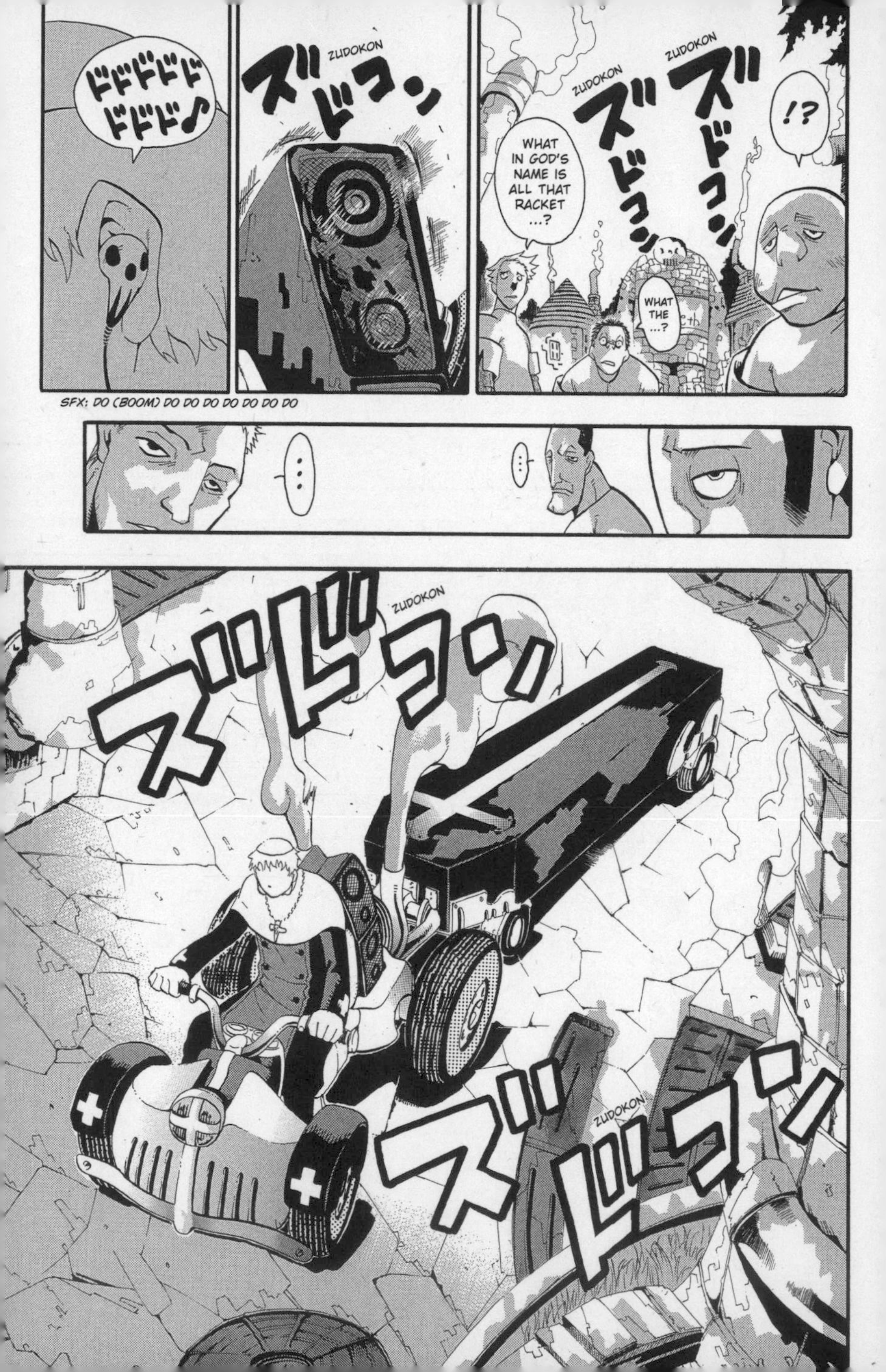
!?
ズドコン
ZUDOKON
ズドコン
ZUDOKON
WHAT IN GOD'S NAME IS ALL THAT RACKET ...?
WHAT THE ...?
ズドコン
ZUDOKON
ドドドドド ドドド♪
SFX: DO (BOOM) DO DO DO DO DO DO DO
...
...
ズドコン
ZUDOKON
ズドコン
ZUDOKON

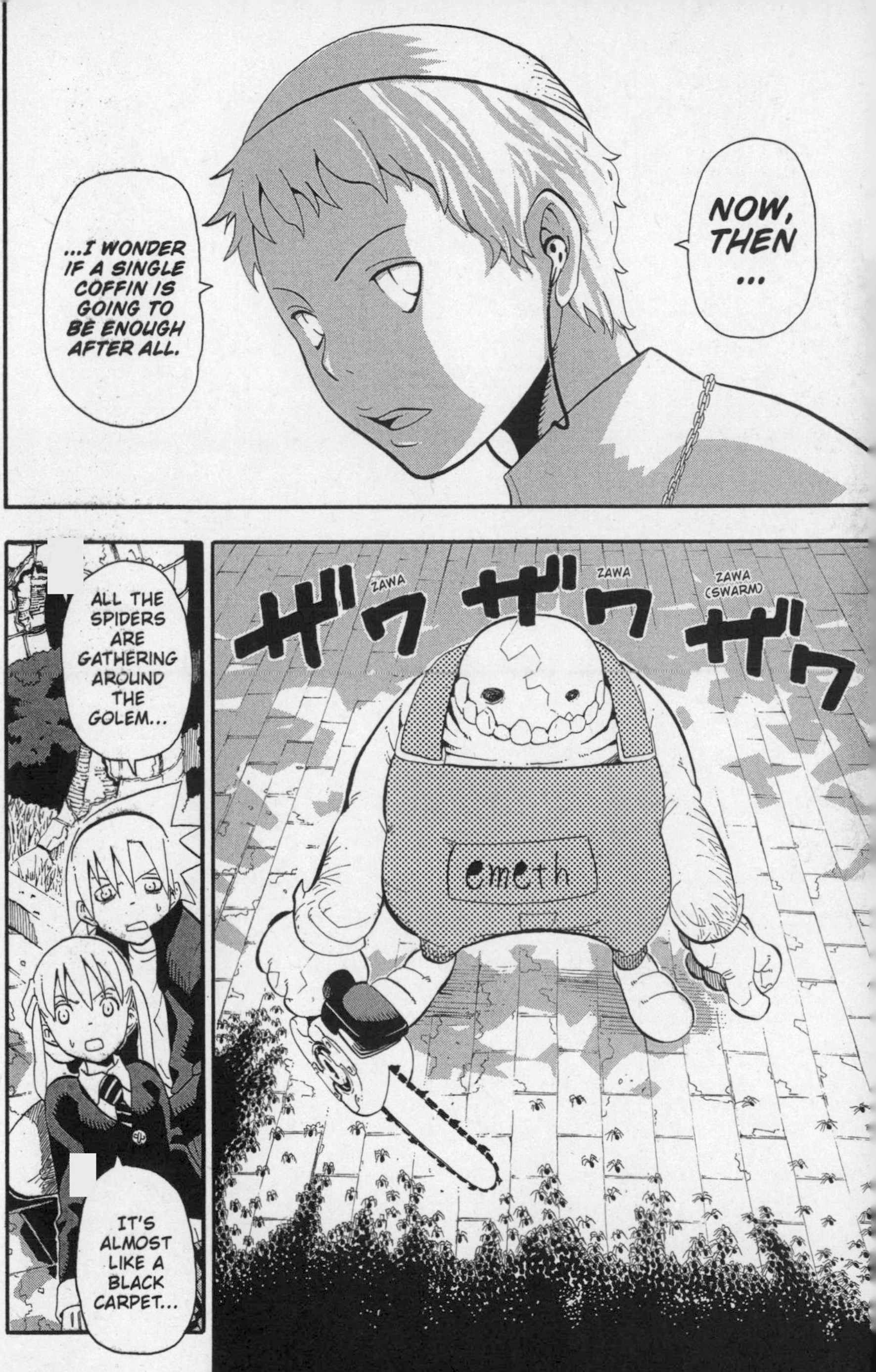
NOW, THEN ...
...I WONDER IF A SINGLE COFFIN IS GOING TO BE ENOUGH AFTER ALL.
ZAWA (SWARM)
ZAWA
ZAWA
ザワ ザワ ザワ
emeth
ALL THE SPIDERS ARE GATHERING AROUND THE GOLEM...
IT'S ALMOST LIKE A BLACK CARPET...

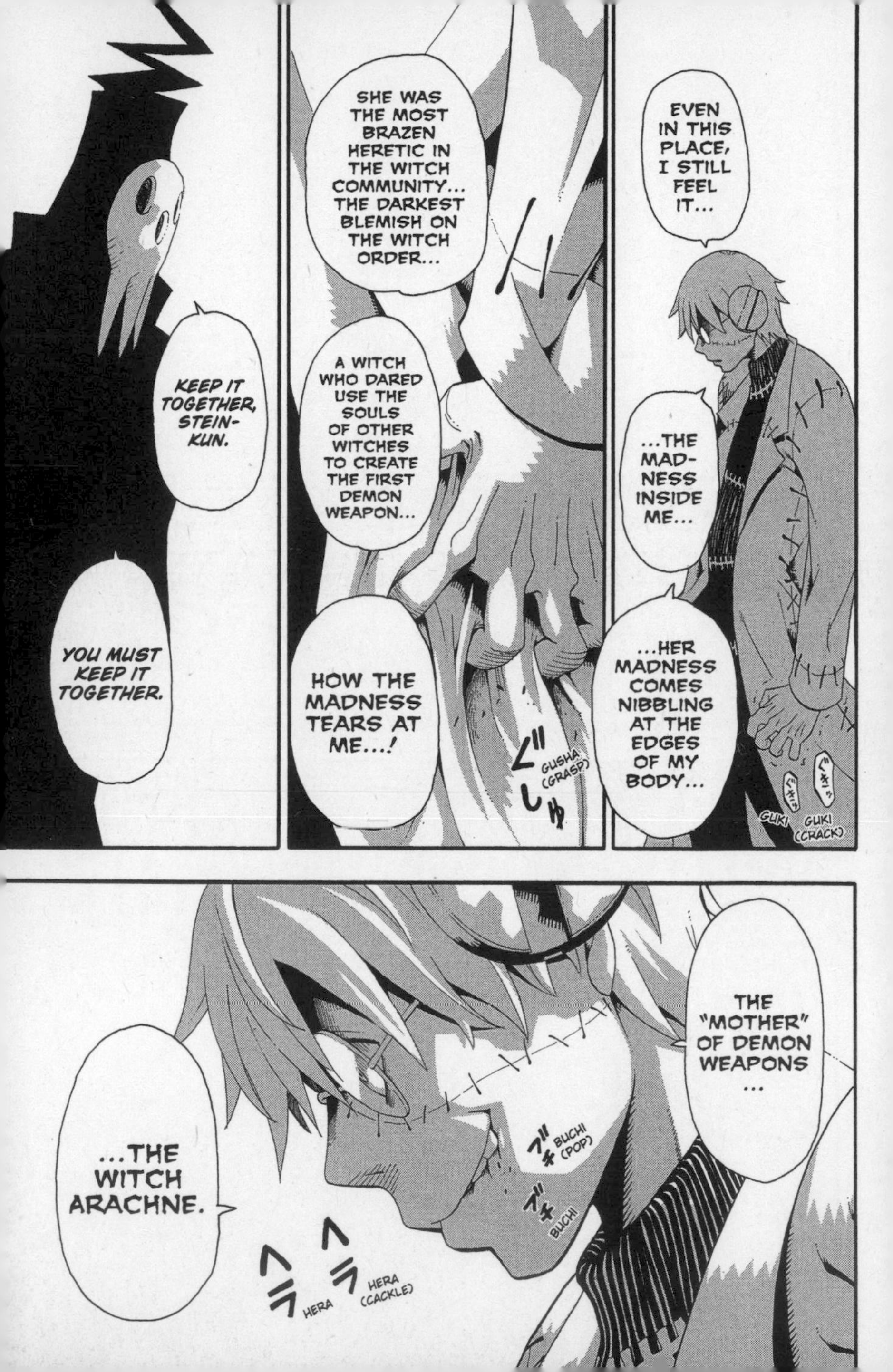
EVEN IN THIS PLACE, I STILL FEEL IT...
...THE MADNESS INSIDE ME...
...HER MADNESS COMES NIBBLING AT THE EDGES OF MY BODY...
GUKI GUKI (CRACK)
SHE WAS THE MOST BRAZEN HERETIC IN THE WITCH COMMUNITY... THE DARKEST BLEMISH ON THE WITCH ORDER...
A WITCH WHO DARED USE THE SOULS OF OTHER WITCHES TO CREATE THE FIRST DEMON WEAPON...
HOW THE MADNESS TEARS AT ME...!
GUSHA (GRASP)
KEEP IT TOGETHER, STEIN-KUN.
YOU MUST KEEP IT TOGETHER.
THE "MOTHER" OF DEMON WEAPONS...
BUCHI (POP)
BUCHI
...THE WITCH ARACHNE.
HERA HERA (CACKLE)

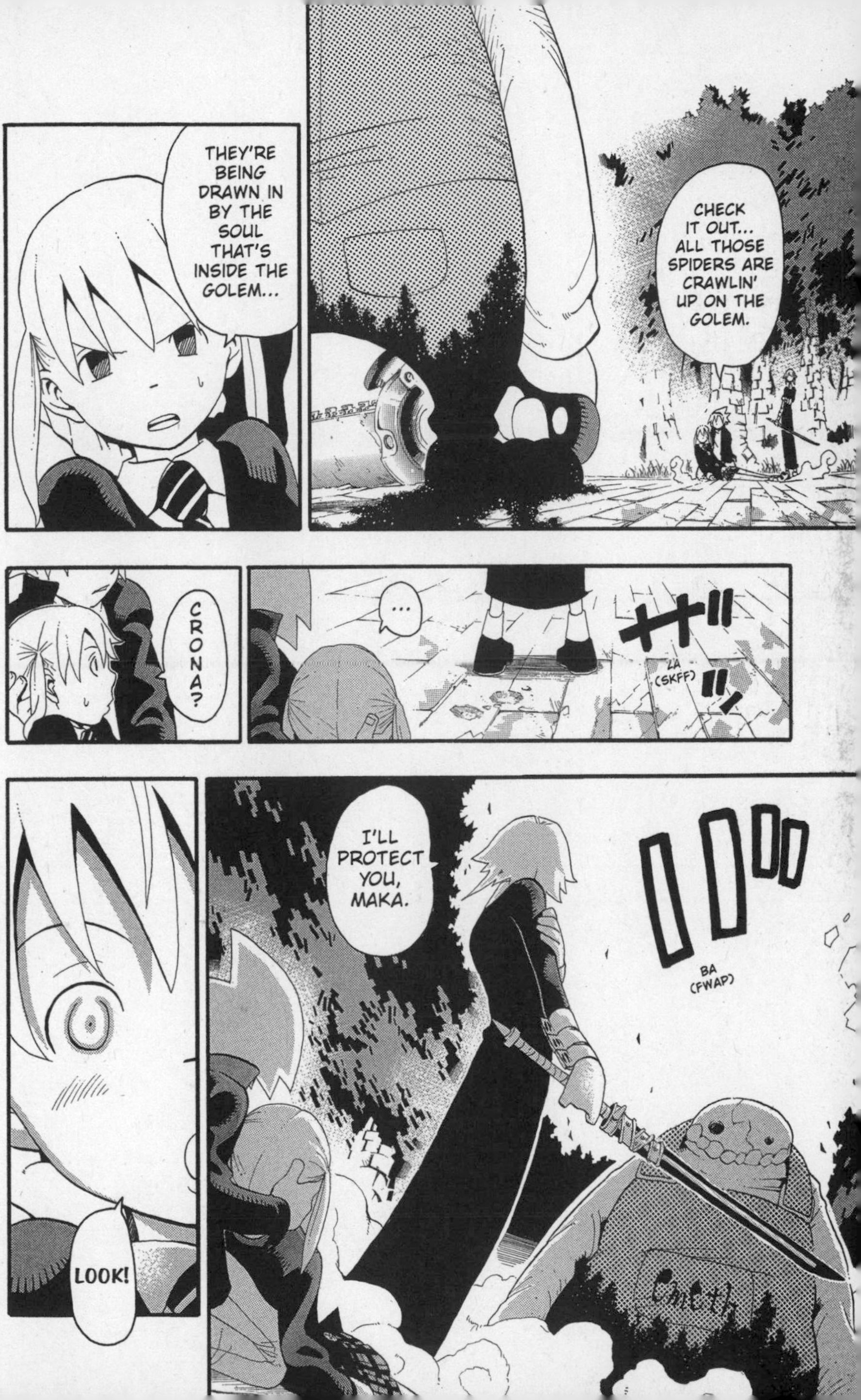
CHECK IT OUT... ALL THOSE SPIDERS ARE CRAWLIN' UP ON THE GOLEM.
THEY'RE BEING DRAWN IN BY THE SOUL THAT'S INSIDE THE GOLEM...
ZA (SKFF)
...
CRONA?
BA (FWAP)
I'LL PROTECT YOU, MAKA.
LOOK!

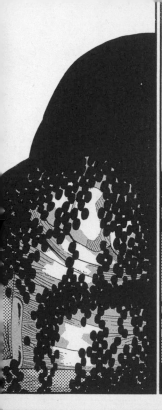
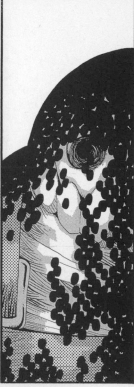
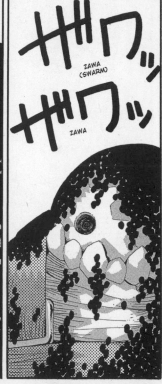

ザワッ
ZAWA
(SWARM)

ザワッ
ZAWA

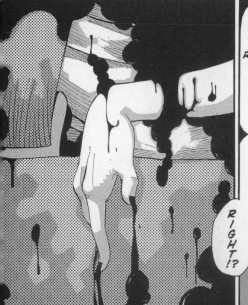
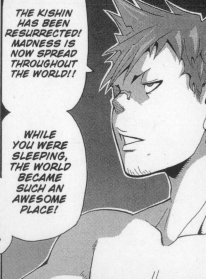

THE KISHIN HAS BEEN RESURRECTED! MADNESS IS NOW SPREAD THROUGHOUT THE WORLD!!

WHILE YOU WERE SLEEPING, THE WORLD BECAME SUCH AN AWESOME PLACE!

RIGHT!?

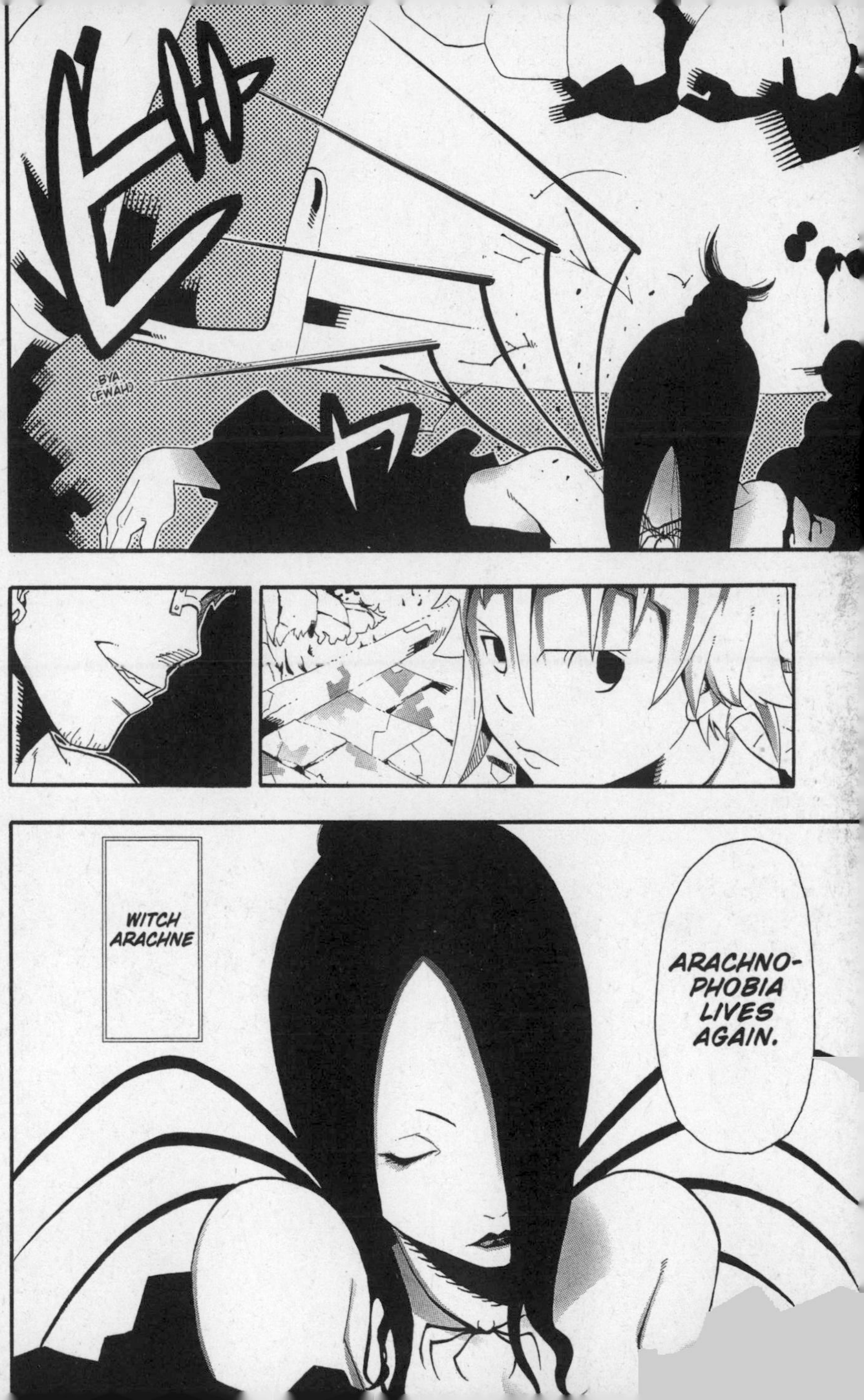
BYA (FWAH)
ARACHNO-PHOBIA LIVES AGAIN.
WITCH ARACHNE

SOUL EATER

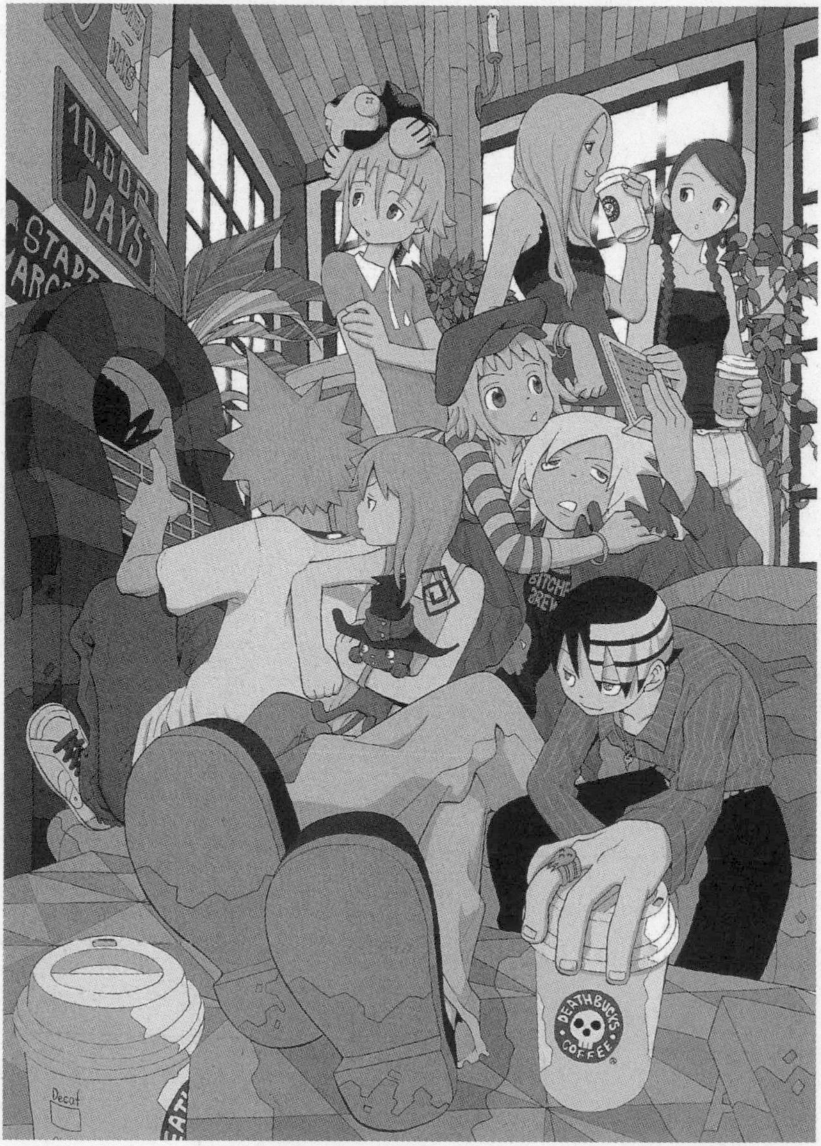
DAYS
DEATHBUCKS COFFEE
Decaf

CHAPTER 26: THE TRIAL ENROLLMENT (PART 3)

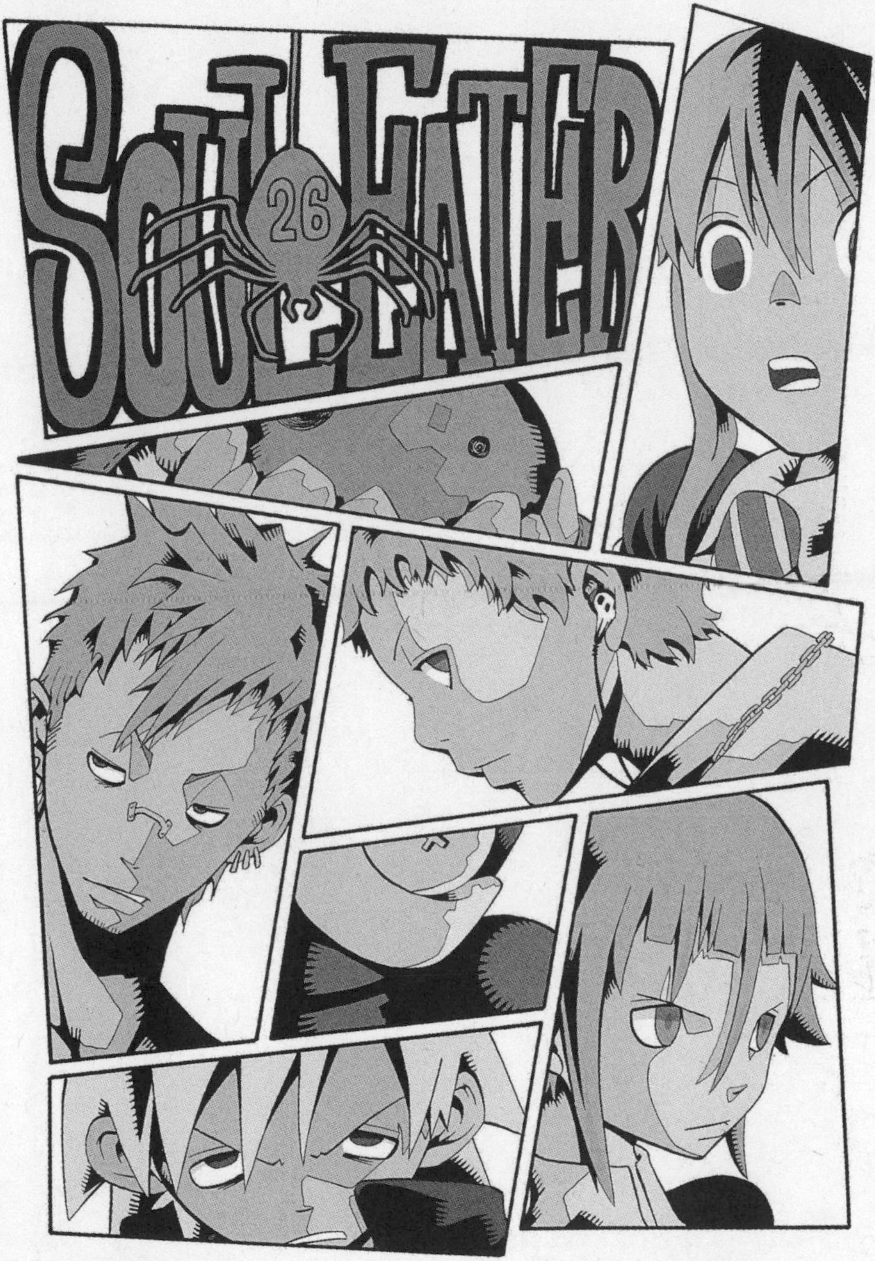
SOUL EATER
26

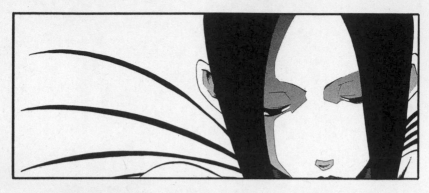

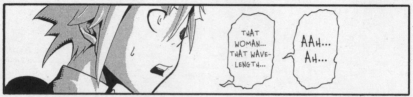

THAT WOMAN... THAT WAVE-LENGTH...

AAH... AH...

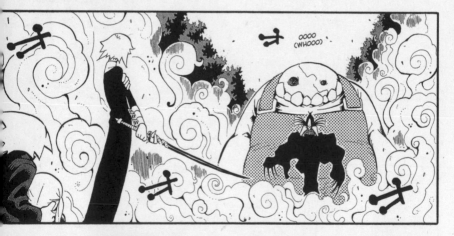

OOOO (WHOOO)

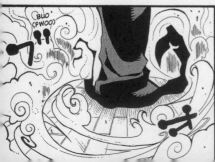

BUO (FWOO)

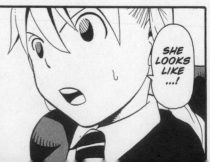

SHE LOOKS ...!

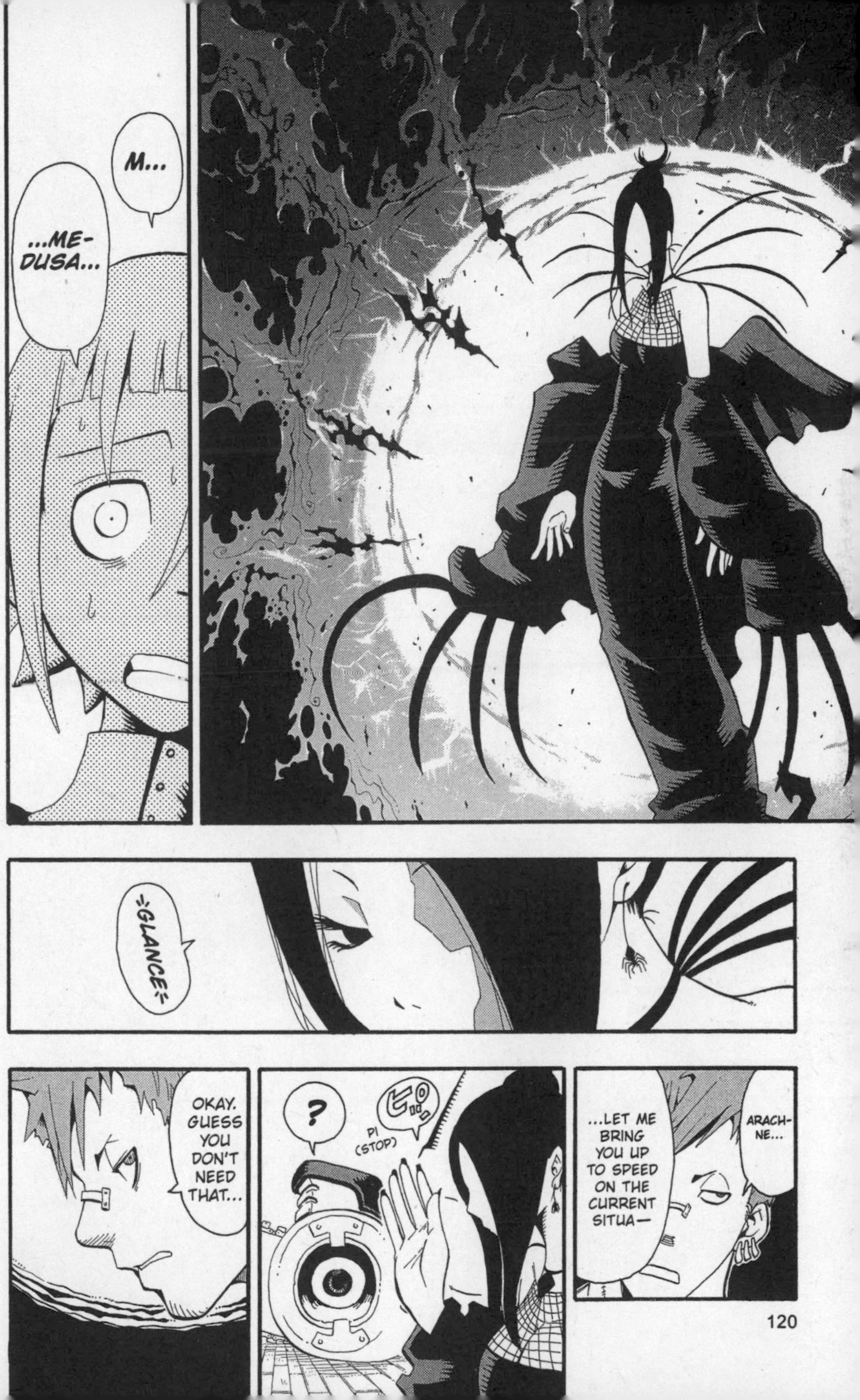
M...
...ME-DUSA...
GLANCE
ARACH-NE...
...LET ME BRING YOU UP TO SPEED ON THE CURRENT SITUA—
?
PI (STOP)
OKAY. GUESS YOU DON'T NEED THAT...

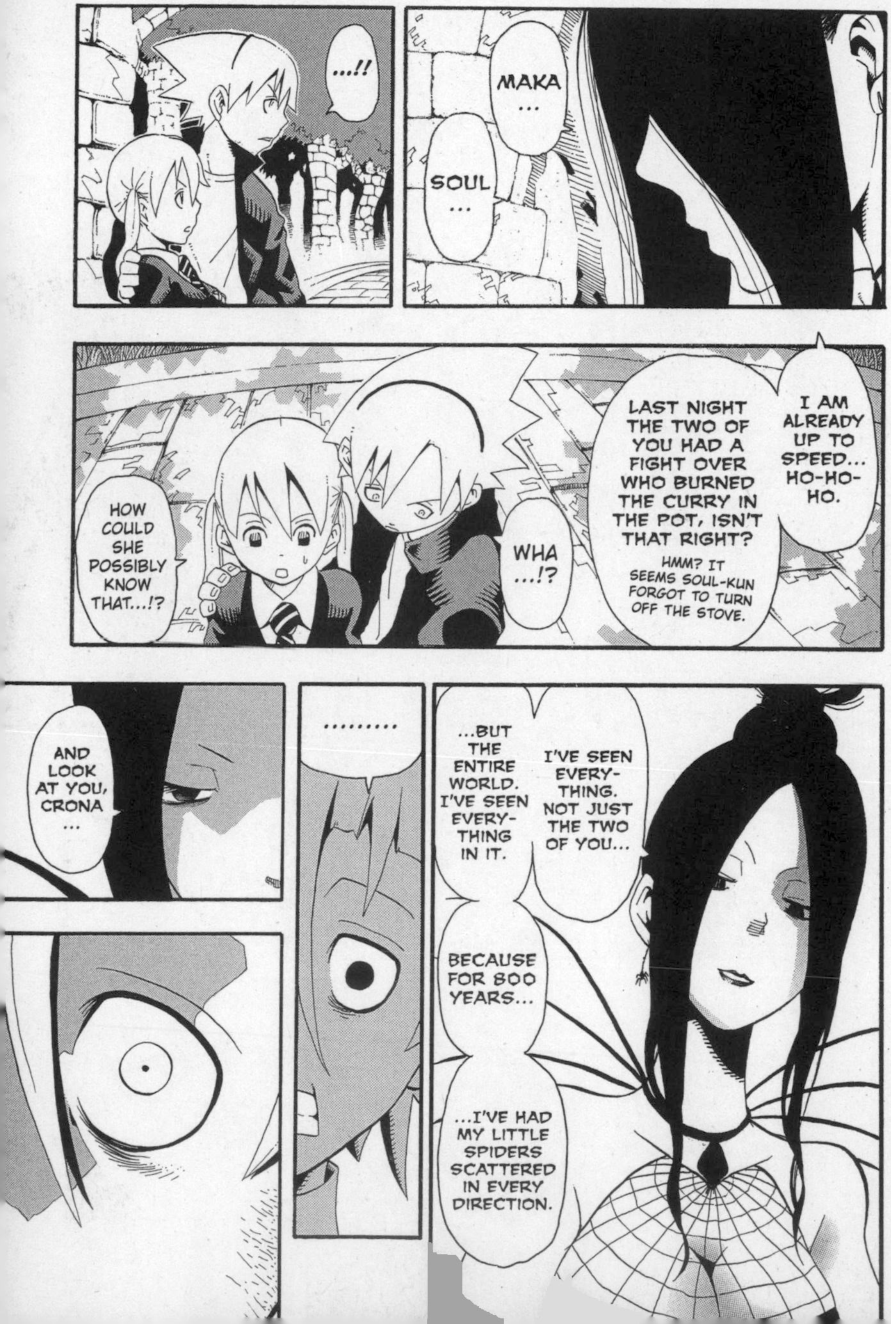
MAKA ...
SOUL ...
...!!
I AM ALREADY UP TO SPEED... HO-HO-HO.
LAST NIGHT THE TWO OF YOU HAD A FIGHT OVER WHO BURNED THE CURRY IN THE POT, ISN'T THAT RIGHT?
HMM? IT SEEMS SOUL-KUN FORGOT TO TURN OFF THE STOVE.
WHA ...!?
HOW COULD SHE POSSIBLY KNOW THAT...!?
I'VE SEEN EVERYTHING. NOT JUST THE TWO OF YOU...
...BUT THE ENTIRE WORLD. I'VE SEEN EVERYTHING IN IT.
BECAUSE FOR 800 YEARS...
...I'VE HAD MY LITTLE SPIDERS SCATTERED IN EVERY DIRECTION.
....
AND LOOK AT YOU, CRONA ...

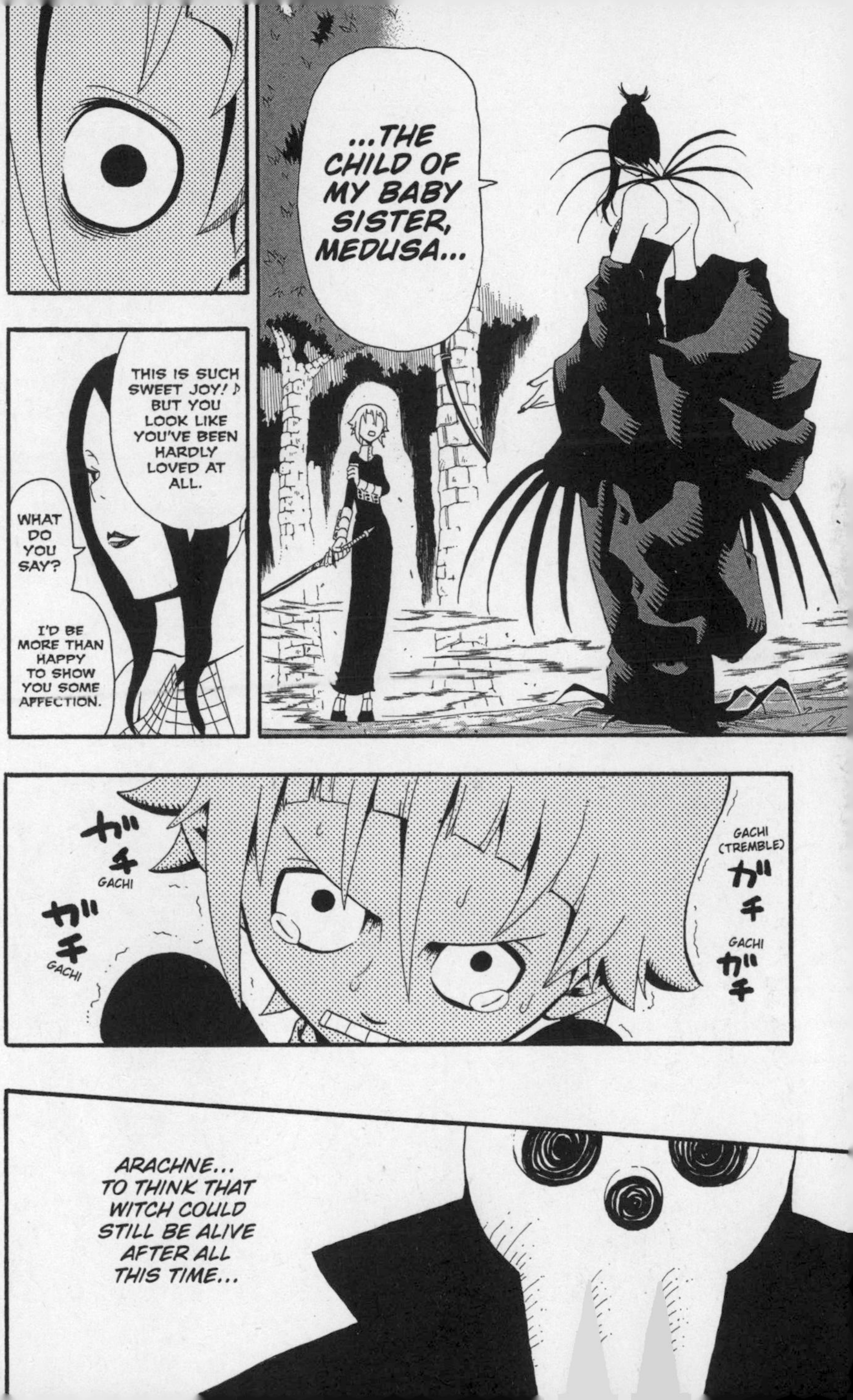
...THE CHILD OF MY BABY SISTER, MEDUSA...
THIS IS SUCH SWEET JOY! ♪ BUT YOU LOOK LIKE YOU'VE BEEN HARDLY LOVED AT ALL.
WHAT DO YOU SAY?
I'D BE MORE THAN HAPPY TO SHOW YOU SOME AFFECTION.
ガチ
GACHI (TREMBLE)
ガチ
GACHI
ガチ
GACHI
ガチ
GACHI
ARACHNE... TO THINK THAT WITCH COULD STILL BE ALIVE AFTER ALL THIS TIME...

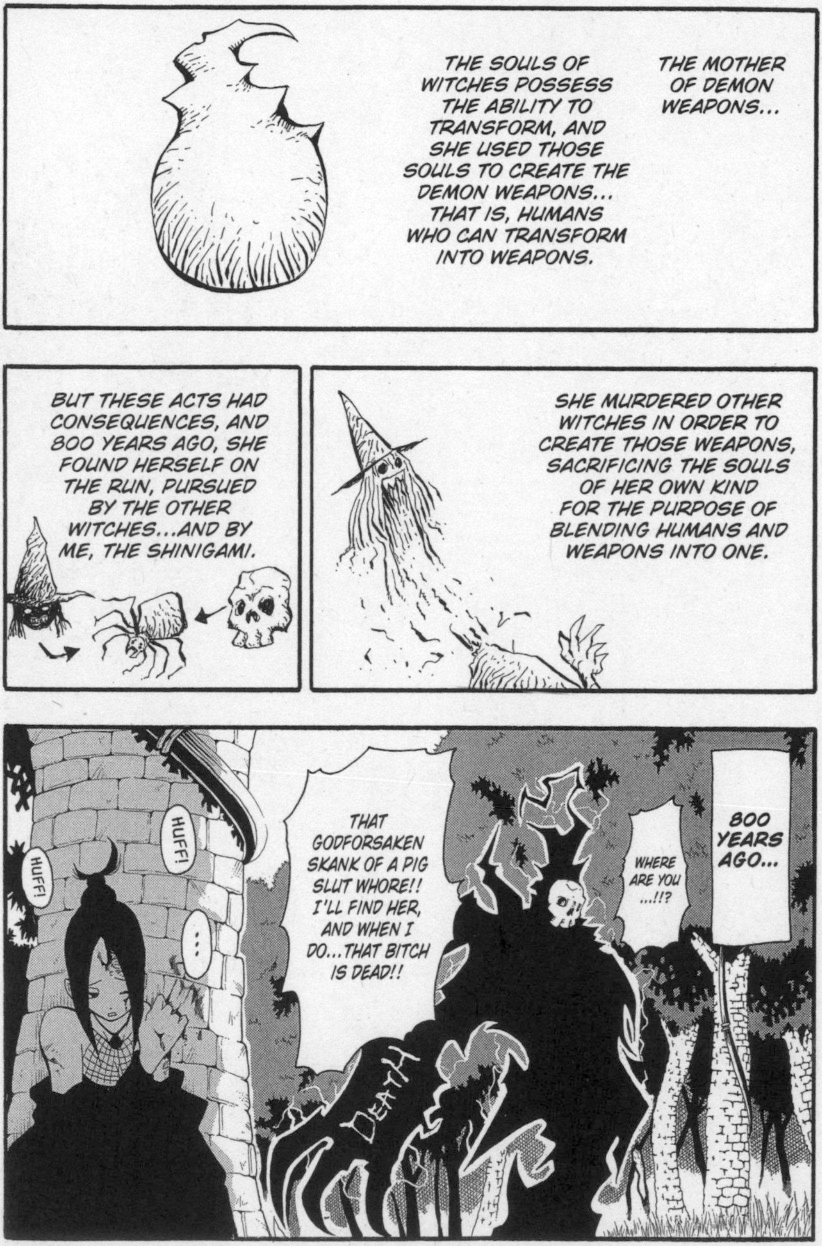
THE MOTHER OF DEMON WEAPONS...
THE SOULS OF WITCHES POSSESS THE ABILITY TO TRANSFORM, AND SHE USED THOSE SOULS TO CREATE THE DEMON WEAPONS... THAT IS, HUMANS WHO CAN TRANSFORM INTO WEAPONS.
SHE MURDERED OTHER WITCHES IN ORDER TO CREATE THOSE WEAPONS, SACRIFICING THE SOULS OF HER OWN KIND FOR THE PURPOSE OF BLENDING HUMANS AND WEAPONS INTO ONE.
BUT THESE ACTS HAD CONSEQUENCES, AND 800 YEARS AGO, SHE FOUND HERSELF ON THE RUN, PURSUED BY THE OTHER WITCHES...AND BY ME, THE SHINIGAMI.
800 YEARS AGO...
WHERE ARE YOU ...!!?
THAT GODFORSAKEN SKANK OF A PIG SLUT WHORE!! I'LL FIND HER, AND WHEN I DO...THAT BITCH IS DEAD!!
DEATH
HUFF!
HUFF!
...

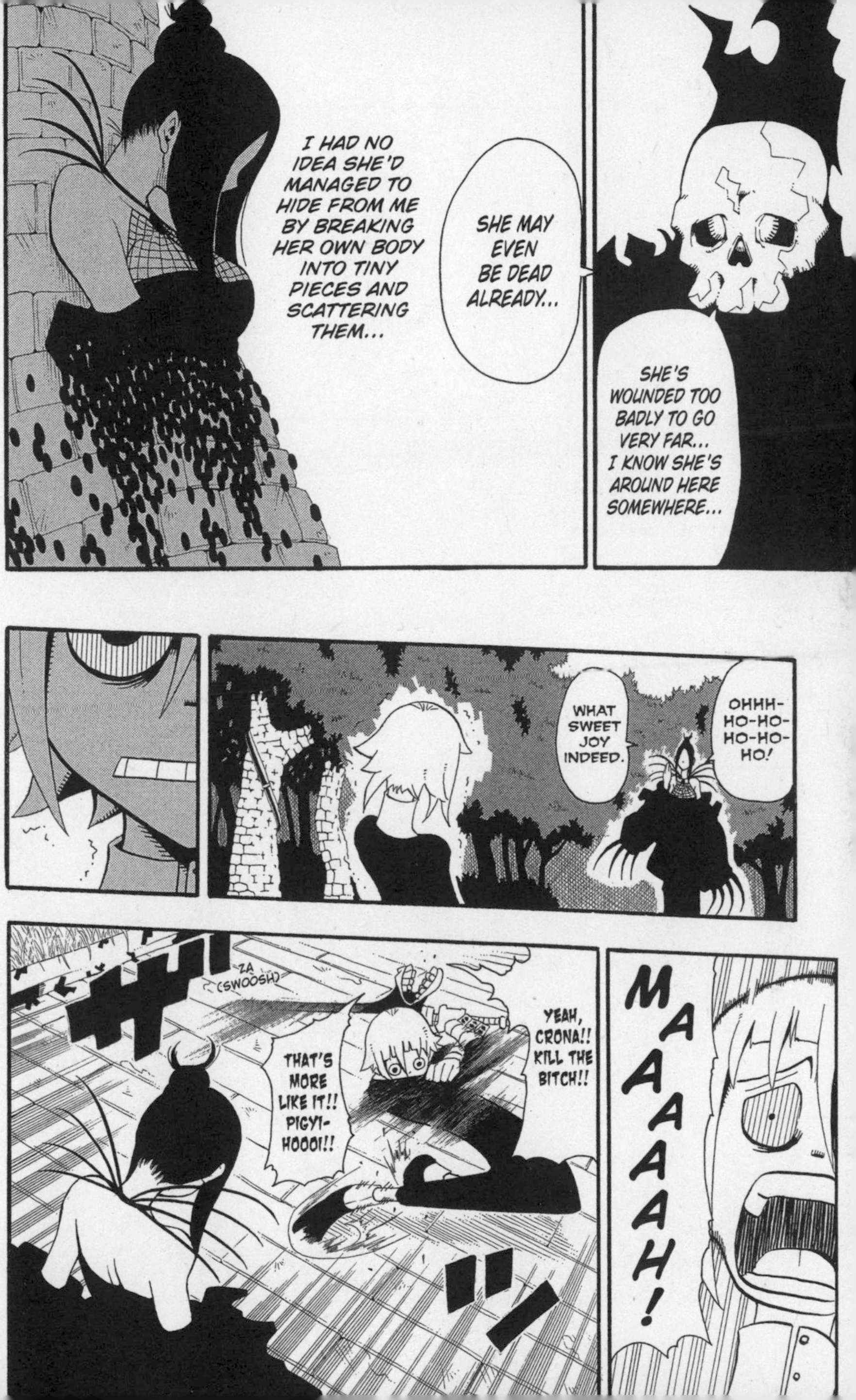
SHE'S WOUNDED TOO BADLY TO GO VERY FAR... I KNOW SHE'S AROUND HERE SOMEWHERE...
SHE MAY EVEN BE DEAD ALREADY...
I HAD NO IDEA SHE'D MANAGED TO HIDE FROM ME BY BREAKING HER OWN BODY INTO TINY PIECES AND SCATTERING THEM...
OHHH-HO-HO-HO-HO-HO!
WHAT SWEET JOY INDEED.
MAAAAAH!
YEAH, CRONA!! KILL THE BITCH!!
THAT'S MORE LIKE IT!! PIGYI-HOOOI!!
ZA (SWOOSH)

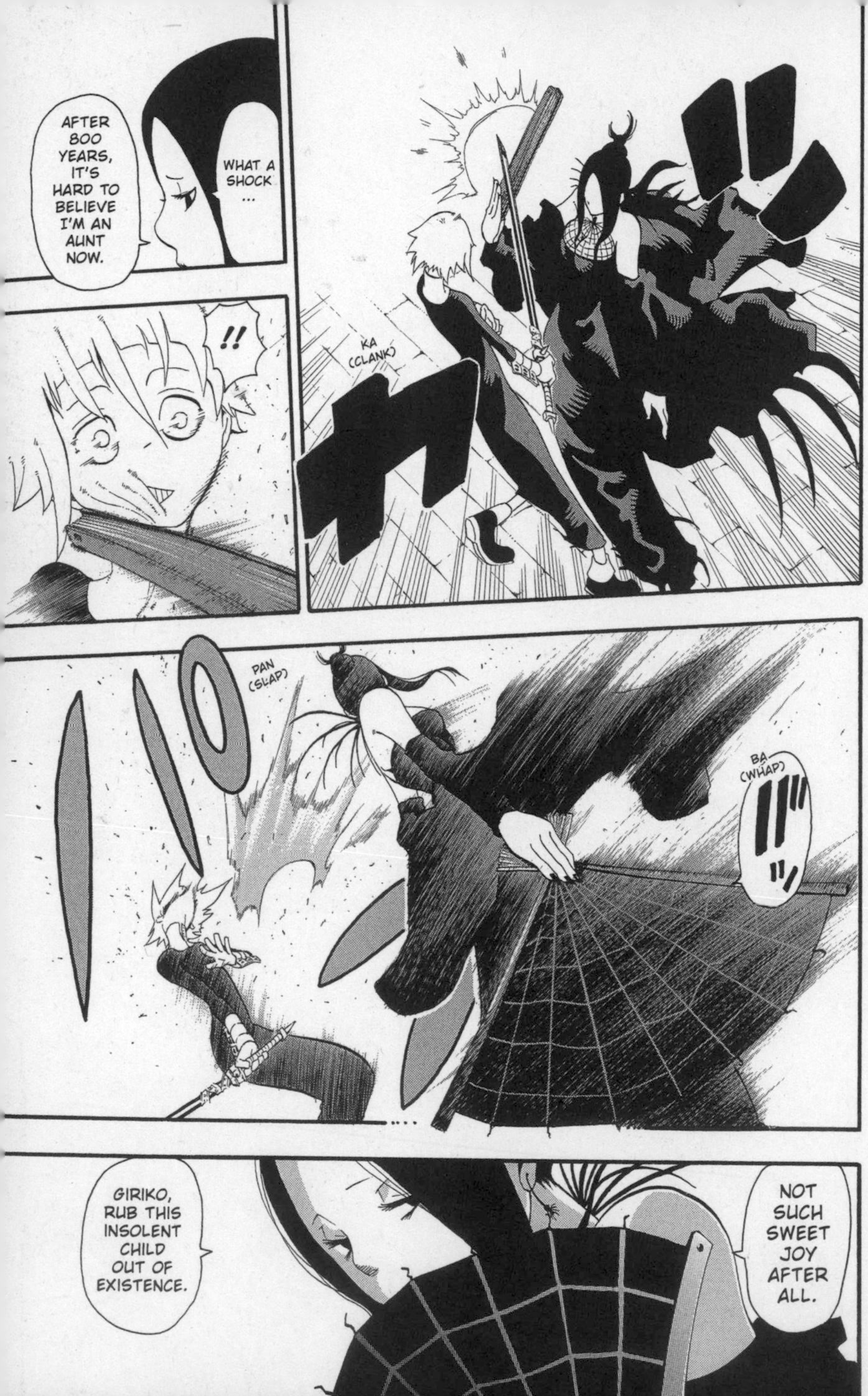
KA (CLANK)
WHAT A SHOCK ...
AFTER 800 YEARS, IT'S HARD TO BELIEVE I'M AN AUNT NOW.
!!
BA (WHAP)
PAN (SLAP)
.....
NOT SUCH SWEET JOY AFTER ALL.
GIRIKO, RUB THIS INSOLENT CHILD OUT OF EXISTENCE.

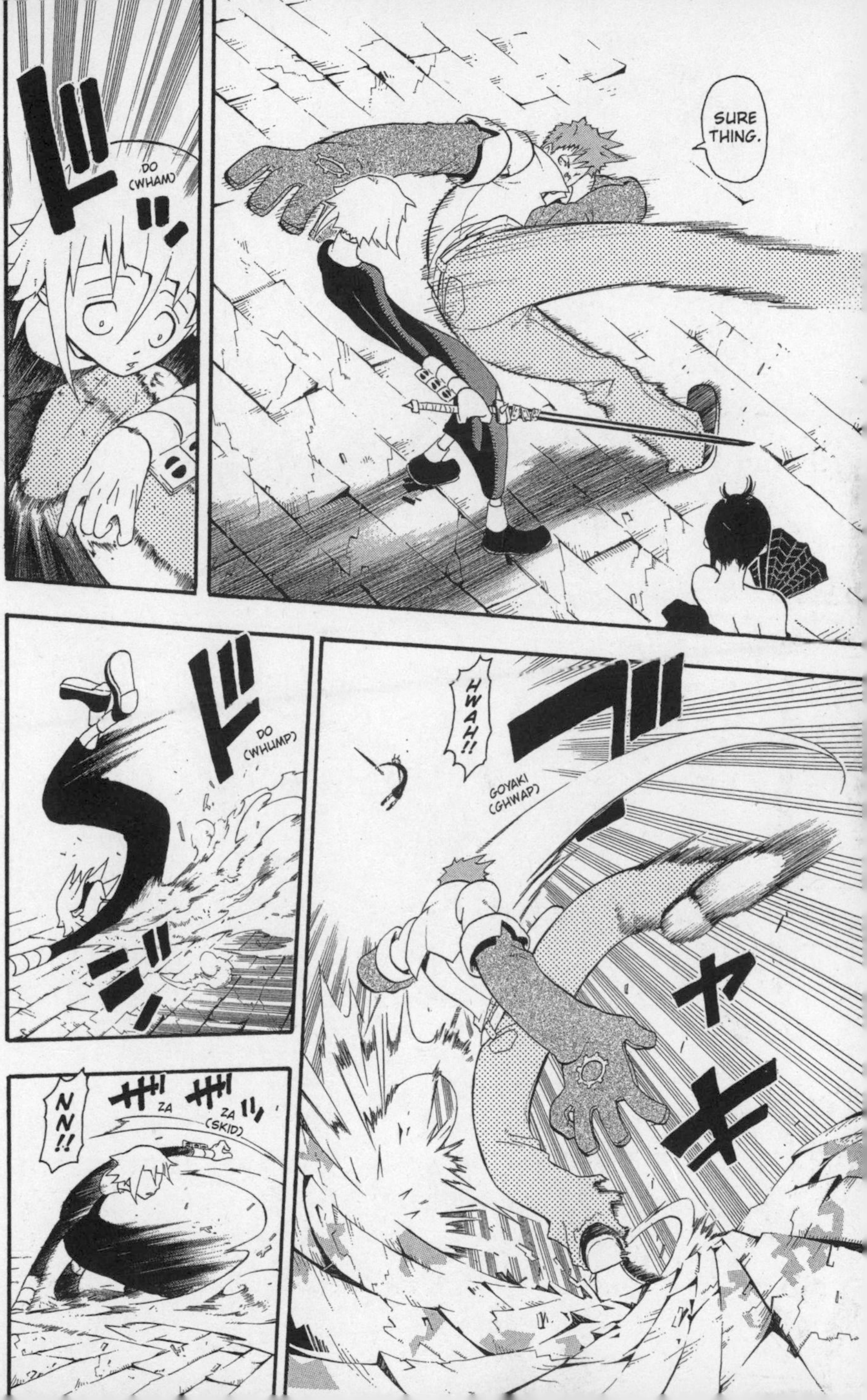

SURE THING.
DO (WHAM)
HWAH!!
GOYAKI (GHWAP)
DO (WHUMP)
NN!!
ZA ZA (SKID)

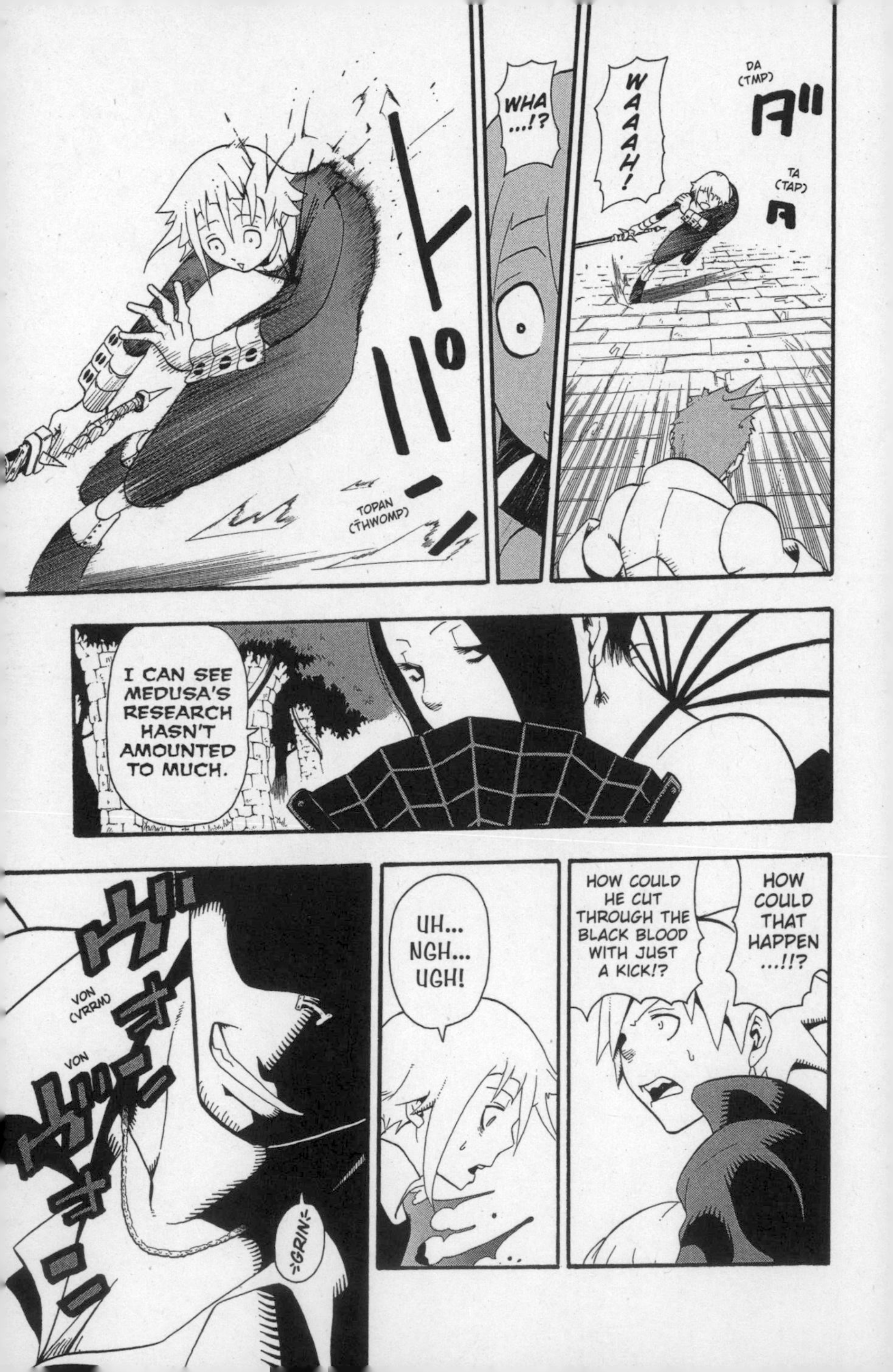
DA (TMP)
WAAAAH!
TA (TAP)
WHA ...!?
TOPAN (THWOMP)
I CAN SEE MEDUSA'S RESEARCH HASN'T AMOUNTED TO MUCH.
HOW COULD THAT HAPPEN ...!!?
HOW COULD HE CUT THROUGH THE BLACK BLOOD WITH JUST A KICK!?
UH... NGH... UGH!
VON (VRRM)
VON
GRIN

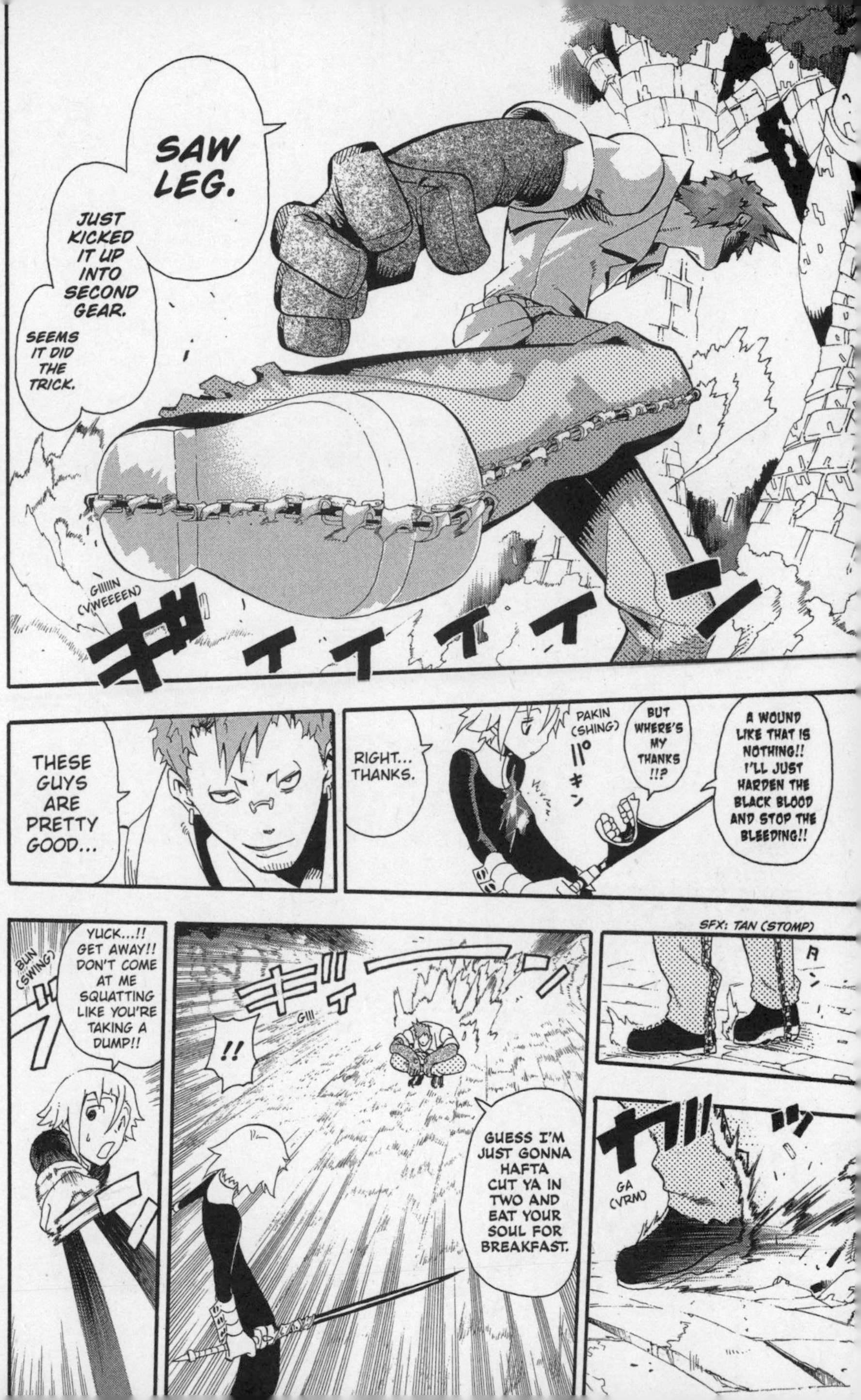
SAW LEG.
JUST KICKED IT UP INTO SECOND GEAR.
SEEMS IT DID THE TRICK.
GIIIIN (VWEEEEN)
A WOUND LIKE THAT IS NOTHING!! I'LL JUST HARDEN THE BLACK BLOOD AND STOP THE BLEEDING!!
BUT WHERE'S MY THANKS!!?
PAKIN (SHING)
RIGHT... THANKS.
THESE GUYS ARE PRETTY GOOD...
SFX: TAN (STOMP)
GA (VRM)
GIII
!!
GUESS I'M JUST GONNA HAFTA CUT YA IN TWO AND EAT YOUR SOUL FOR BREAKFAST.
BUN (SWING)
YUCK...!! GET AWAY!! DON'T COME AT ME SQUATTING LIKE YOU'RE TAKING A DUMP!!

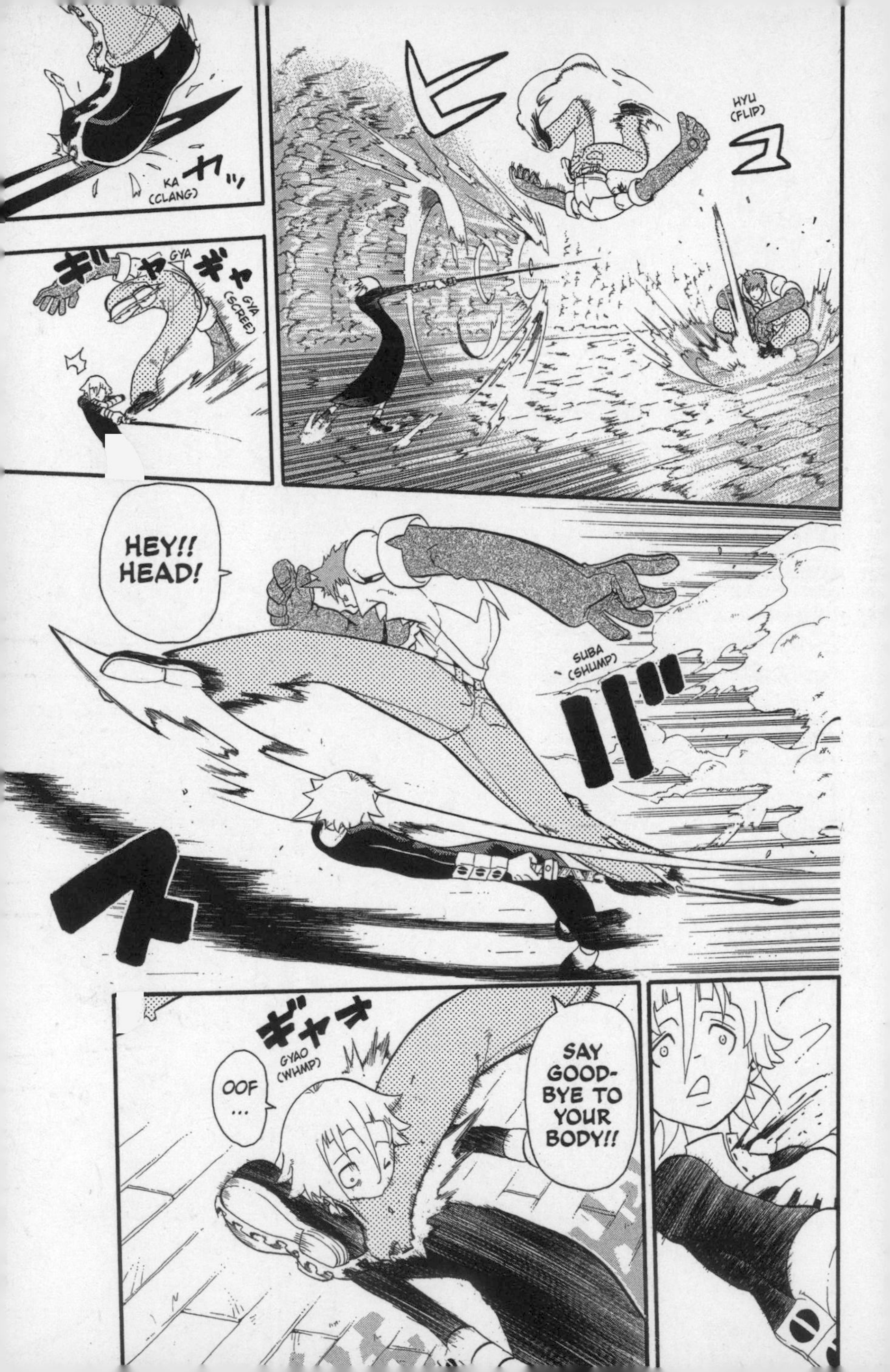

HYU (FLIP)
KA (CLANG)
GYA GYA (SCREE)
HEY!! HEAD!
SUBA (SHUMP)
SAY GOOD-BYE TO YOUR BODY!!
GYAO (WHMP)
OOF …

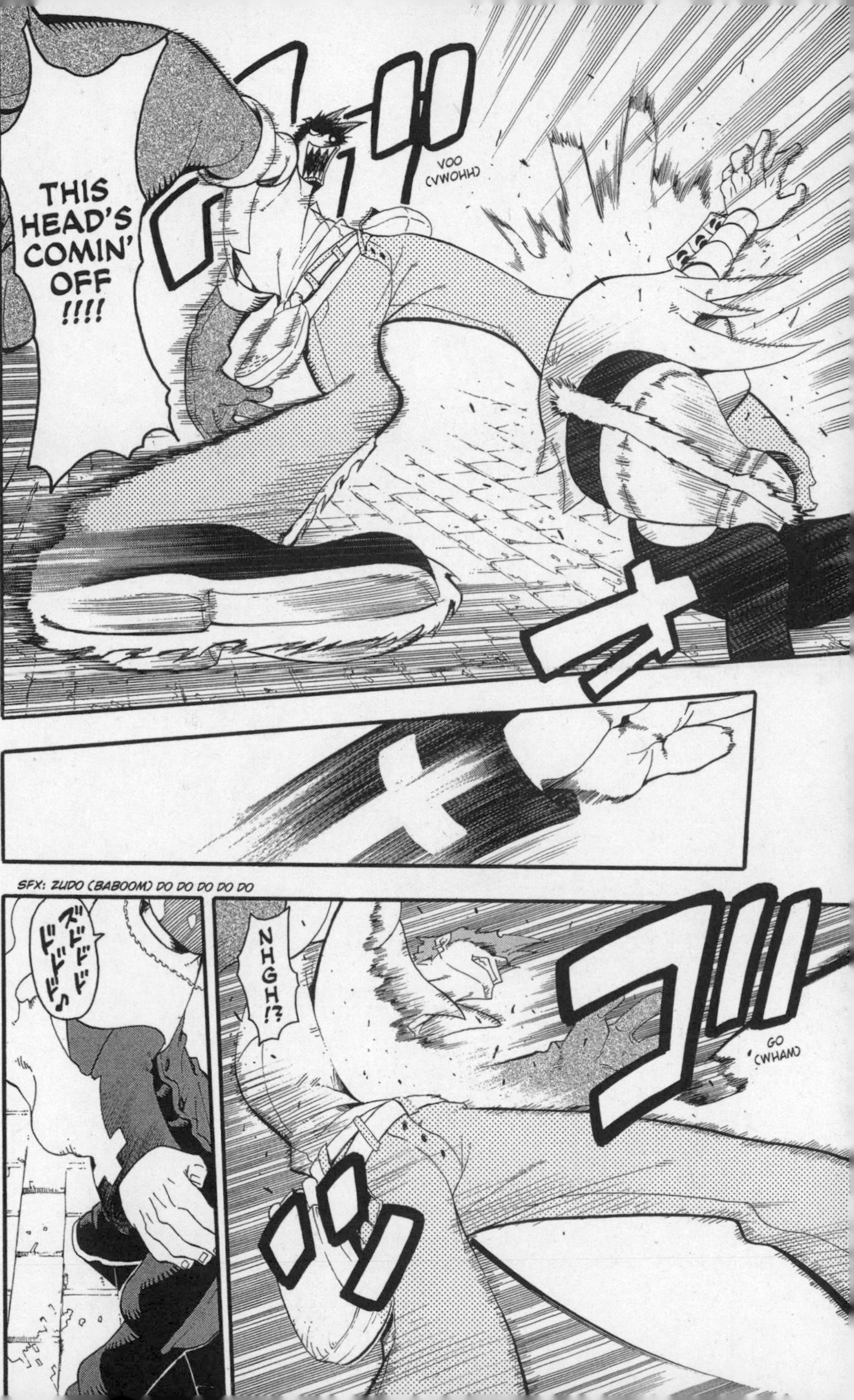
VOO (VWOHH)
THIS HEAD'S COMIN' OFF!!!!
SFX: ZUDO (BABOOM) DO DO DO DO DO
GO (WHAM)
NHGH!?
ズドドドドドド♪

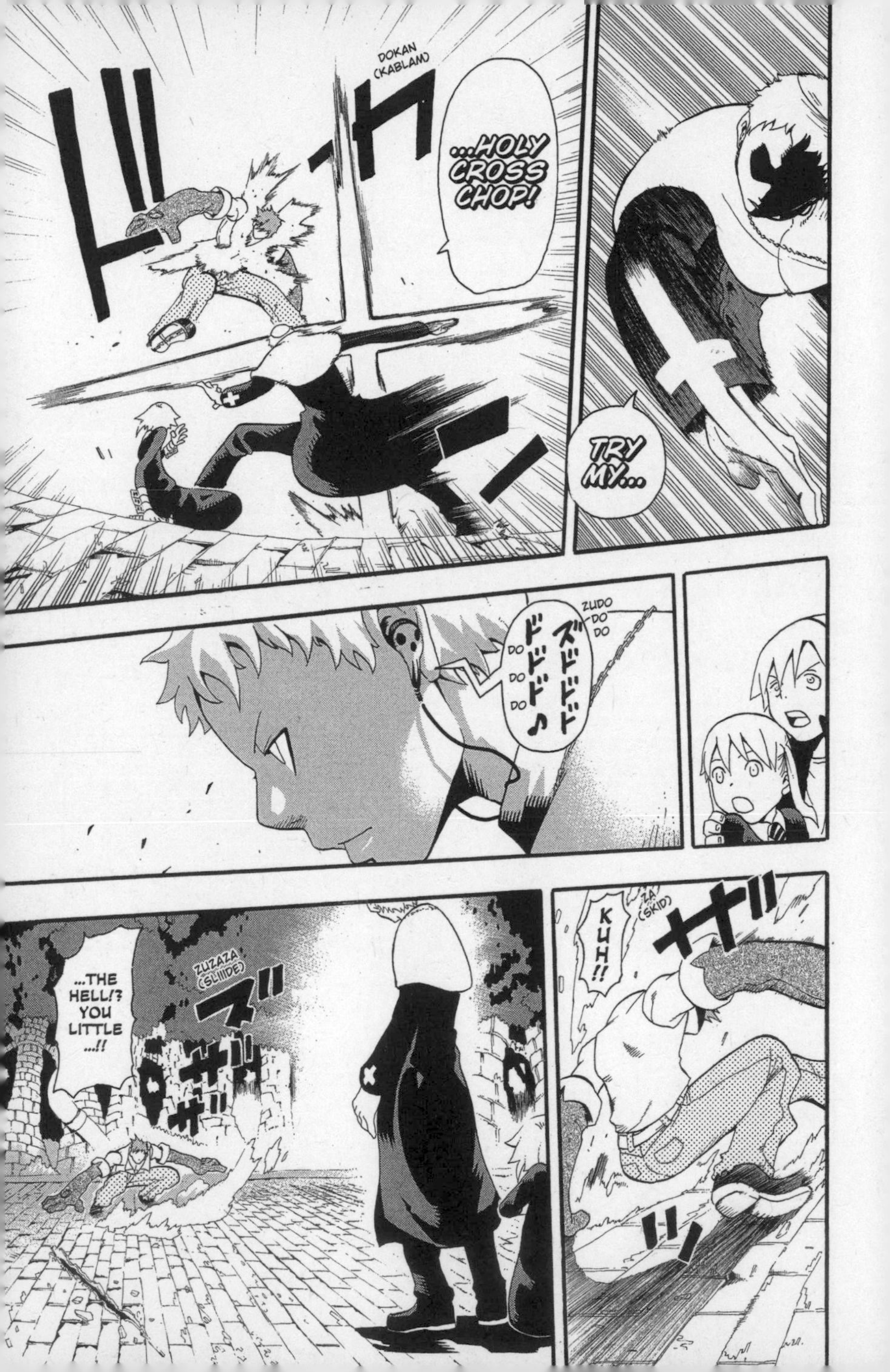
TRY MY...
DOKAN (KABLAM)
...HOLY CROSS CHOP!
ZUDO DO DO
DO DO DO
ズドドド
ドドド♪
ZA (SKID)
KUH!!
ZUZAZA (SLIIIDE)
...THE HELL!? YOU LITTLE ...!!

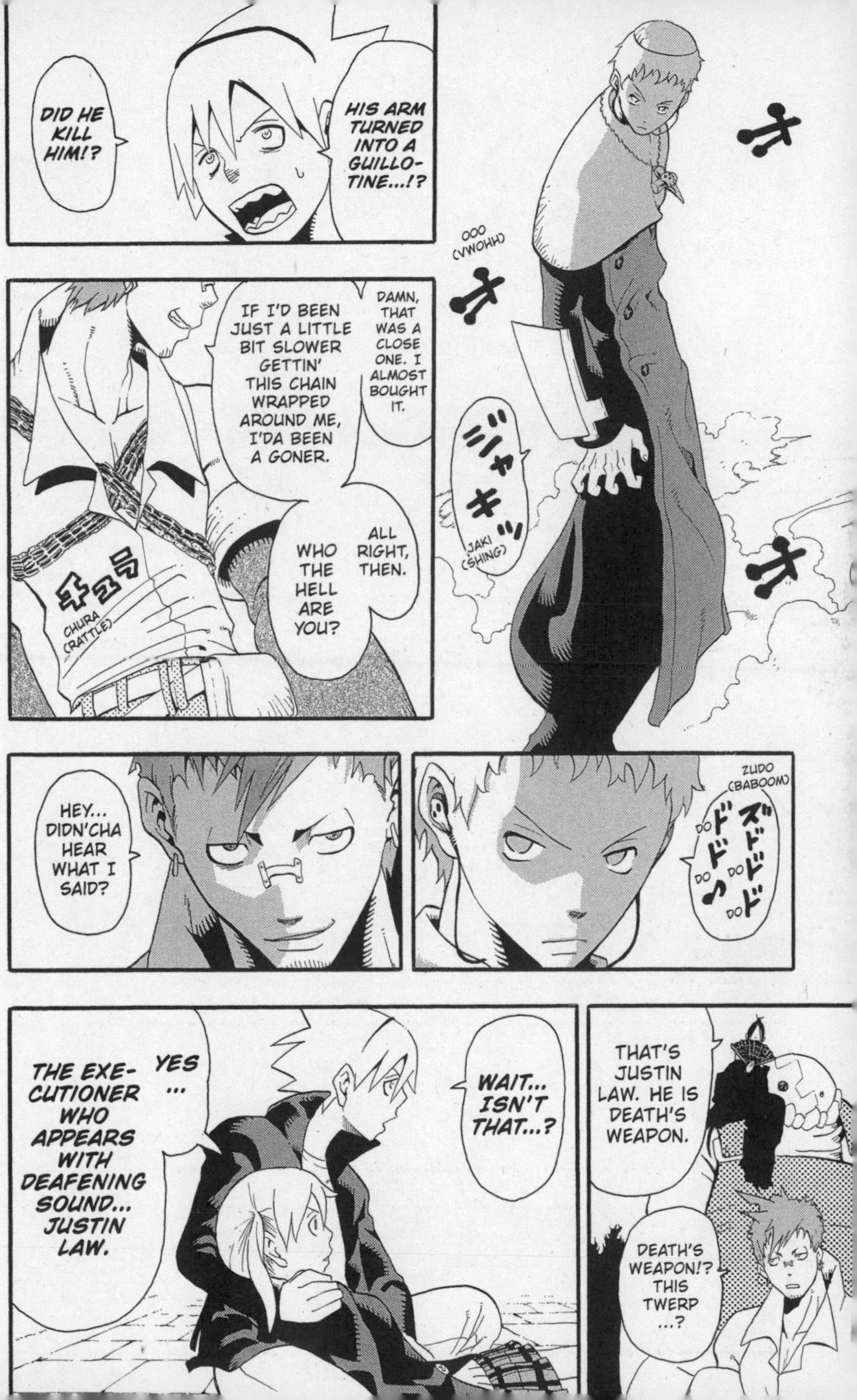

オ
オ
OOO (VWOHH)
オ
ジャキッ
JAKI (SHING)
HIS ARM TURNED INTO A GUILLO-TINE...!?
DID HE KILL HIM!?
DAMN, THAT WAS A CLOSE ONE. I ALMOST BOUGHT IT.
IF I'D BEEN JUST A LITTLE BIT SLOWER GETTIN' THIS CHAIN WRAPPED AROUND ME, I'DA BEEN A GONER.
ALL RIGHT, THEN.
WHO THE HELL ARE YOU?
CHURA (RATTLE)
ZUDO (BABOOM)
ズドドド ドド♪
DO DO DO DO DO
HEY... DIDN'CHA HEAR WHAT I SAID?
THAT'S JUSTIN LAW. HE IS DEATH'S WEAPON.
DEATH'S WEAPON!? THIS TWERP ...?
WAIT... ISN'T THAT...?
YES ...
THE EXE-CUTIONER WHO APPEARS WITH DEAFENING SOUND... JUSTIN LAW.

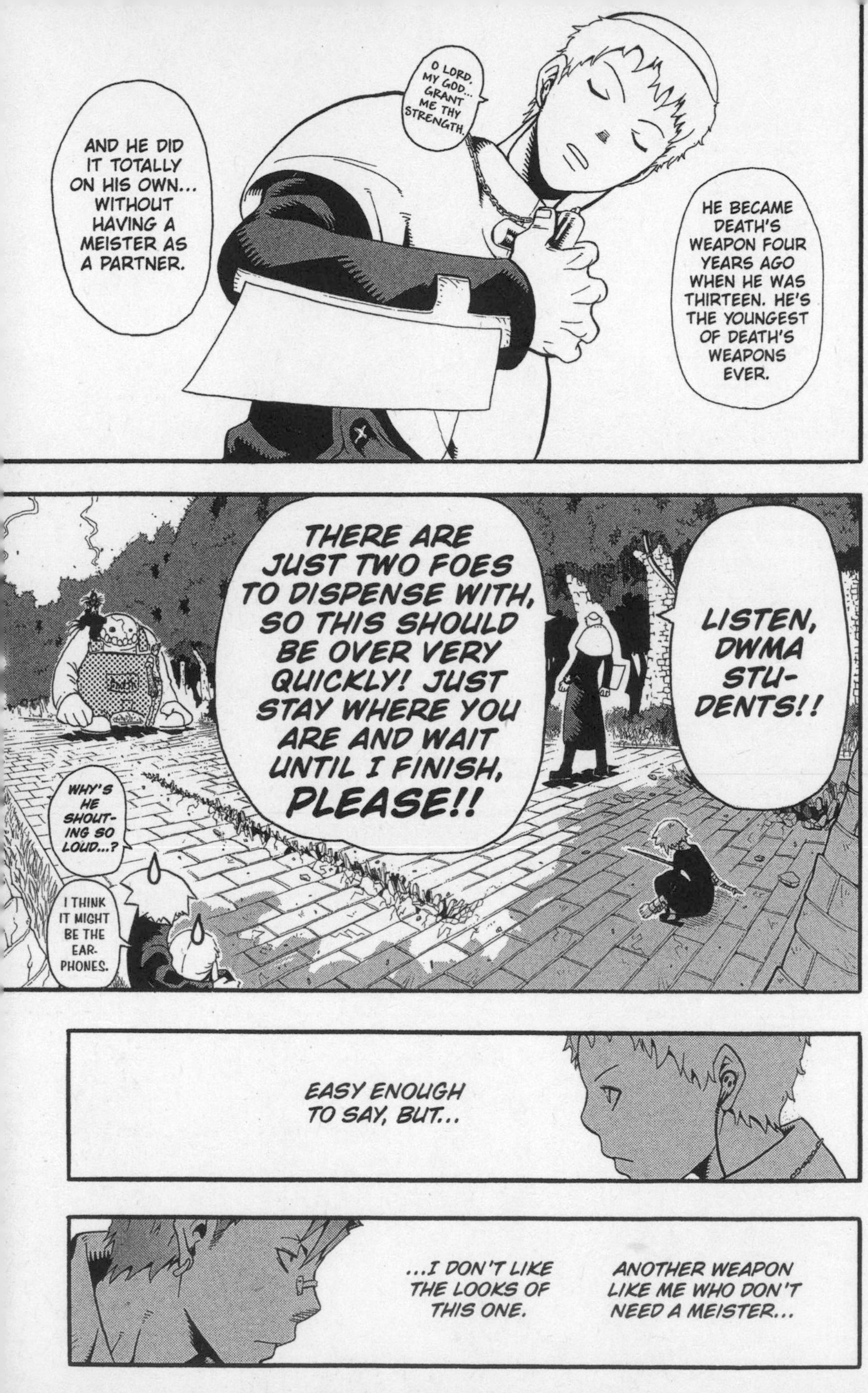
O LORD, MY GOD... GRANT ME THY STRENGTH.
HE BECAME DEATH'S WEAPON FOUR YEARS AGO WHEN HE WAS THIRTEEN. HE'S THE YOUNGEST OF DEATH'S WEAPONS EVER.
AND HE DID IT TOTALLY ON HIS OWN... WITHOUT HAVING A MEISTER AS A PARTNER.
LISTEN, DWMA STU-DENTS!!
THERE ARE JUST TWO FOES TO DISPENSE WITH, SO THIS SHOULD BE OVER VERY QUICKLY! JUST STAY WHERE YOU ARE AND WAIT UNTIL I FINISH, PLEASE!!
WHY'S HE SHOUT-ING SO LOUD...?
I THINK IT MIGHT BE THE EAR-PHONES.
EASY ENOUGH TO SAY, BUT...
ANOTHER WEAPON LIKE ME WHO DON'T NEED A MEISTER...
...I DON'T LIKE THE LOOKS OF THIS ONE.

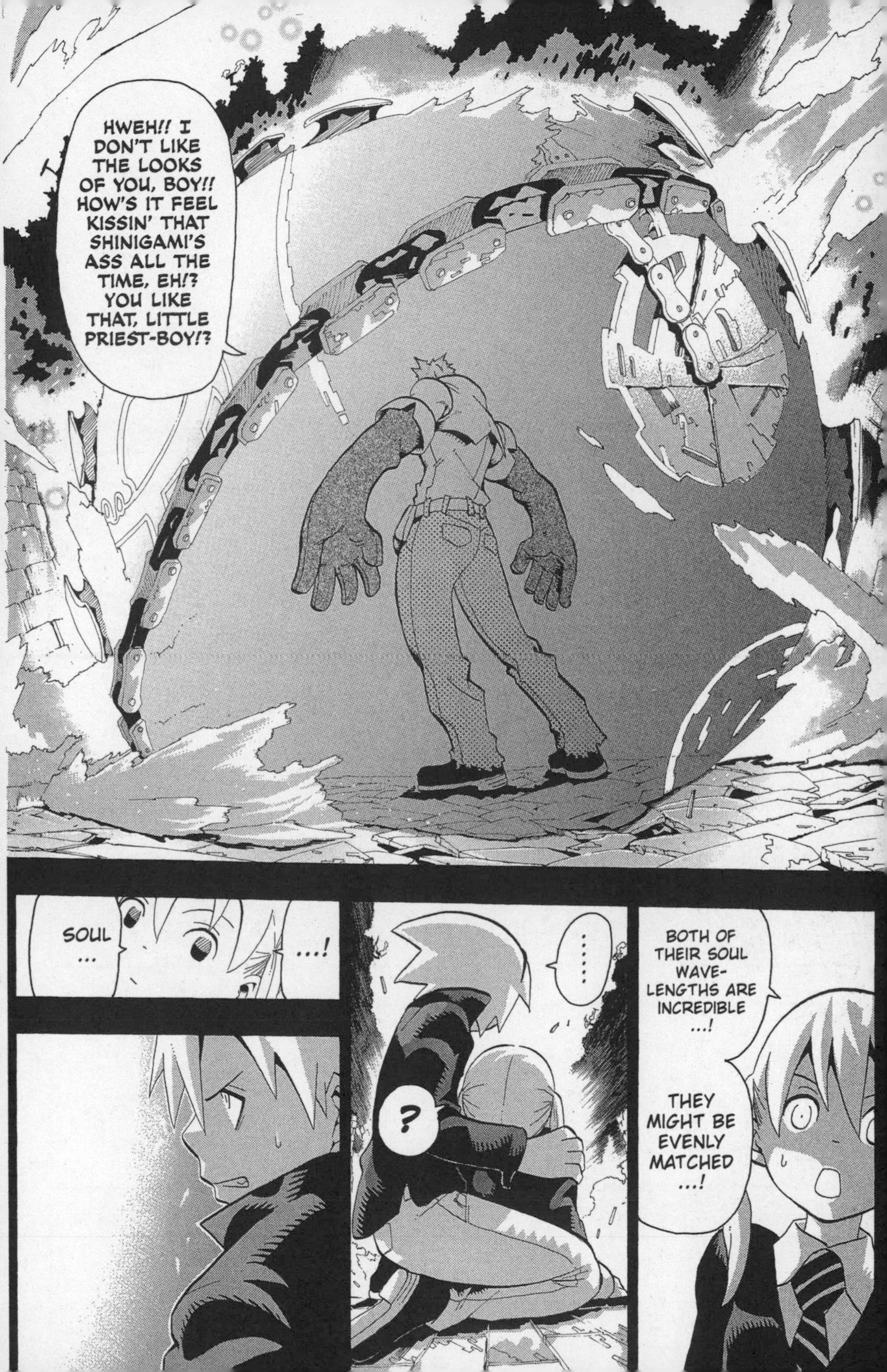
HWEH!! I DON'T LIKE THE LOOKS OF YOU, BOY!! HOW'S IT FEEL KISSIN' THAT SHINIGAMI'S ASS ALL THE TIME, EH!? YOU LIKE THAT, LITTLE PRIEST-BOY!?
BOTH OF THEIR SOUL WAVE-LENGTHS ARE INCREDIBLE ...!
THEY MIGHT BE EVENLY MATCHED ...!
......
?
...!
SOUL ...

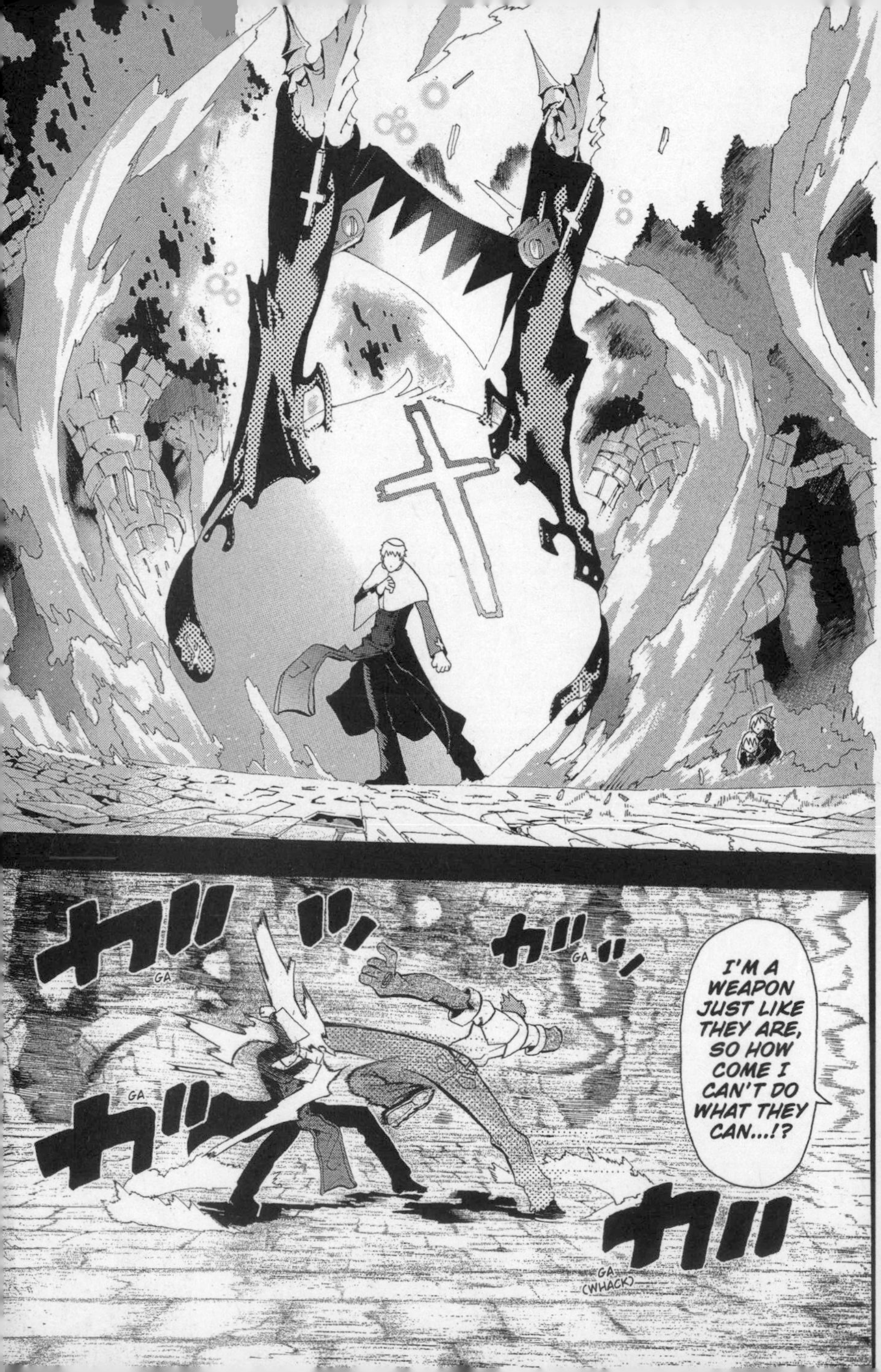

I'M A WEAPON JUST LIKE THEY ARE, SO HOW COME I CAN'T DO WHAT THEY CAN...!?
ガッ
GA
ガッ
GA
ガッ
GA
ガッ
GA
(WHACK)

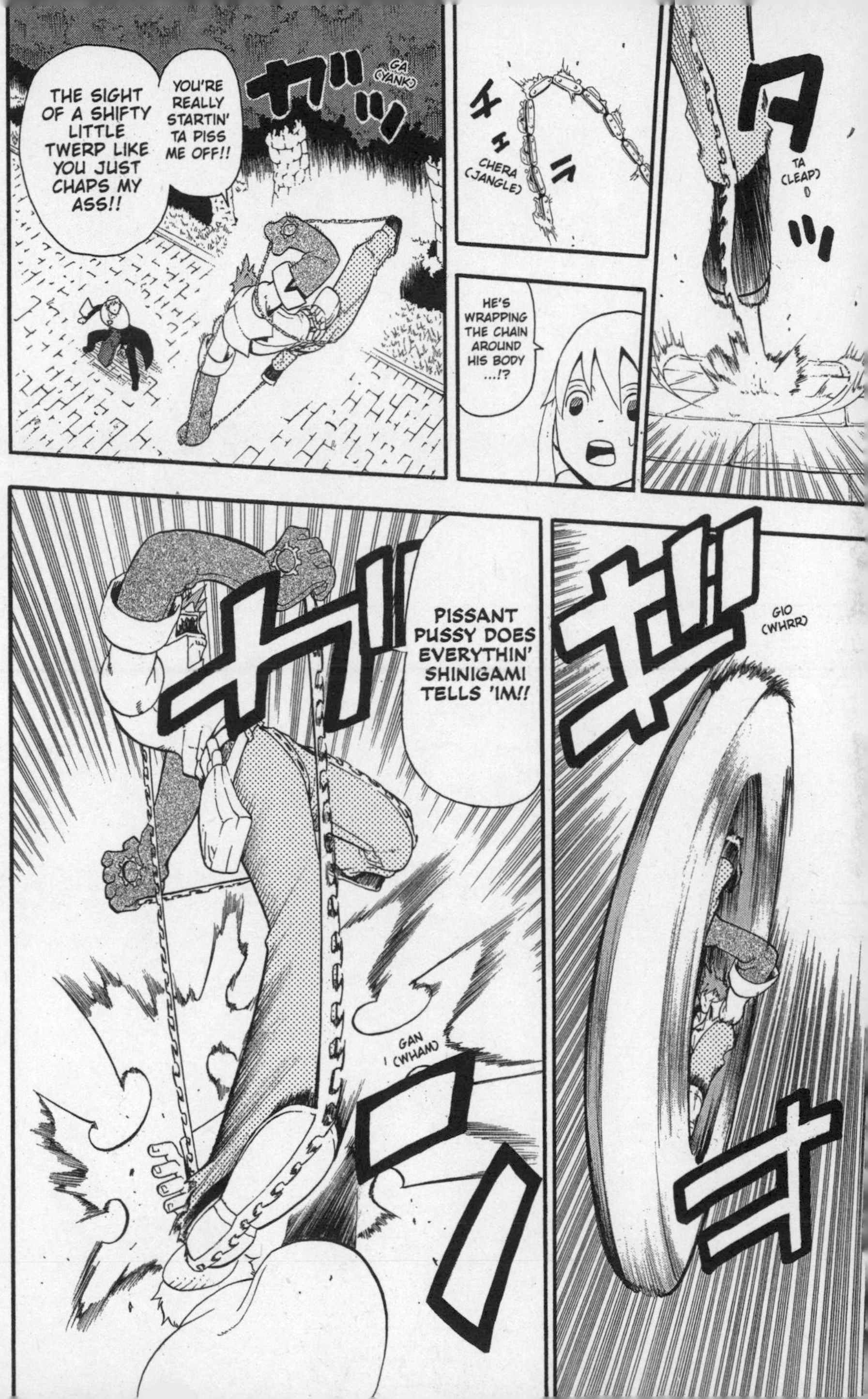
TA (LEAP)
CHERA (JANGLE)
HE'S WRAPPING THE CHAIN AROUND HIS BODY ...!?
YOU'RE REALLY STARTIN' TA PISS ME OFF!!
THE SIGHT OF A SHIFTY LITTLE TWERP LIKE YOU JUST CHAPS MY ASS!!
GA (YANK)
GIO (WHRR)
PISSANT PUSSY DOES EVERYTHIN' SHINIGAMI TELLS 'IM!!
GAN (WHAM)

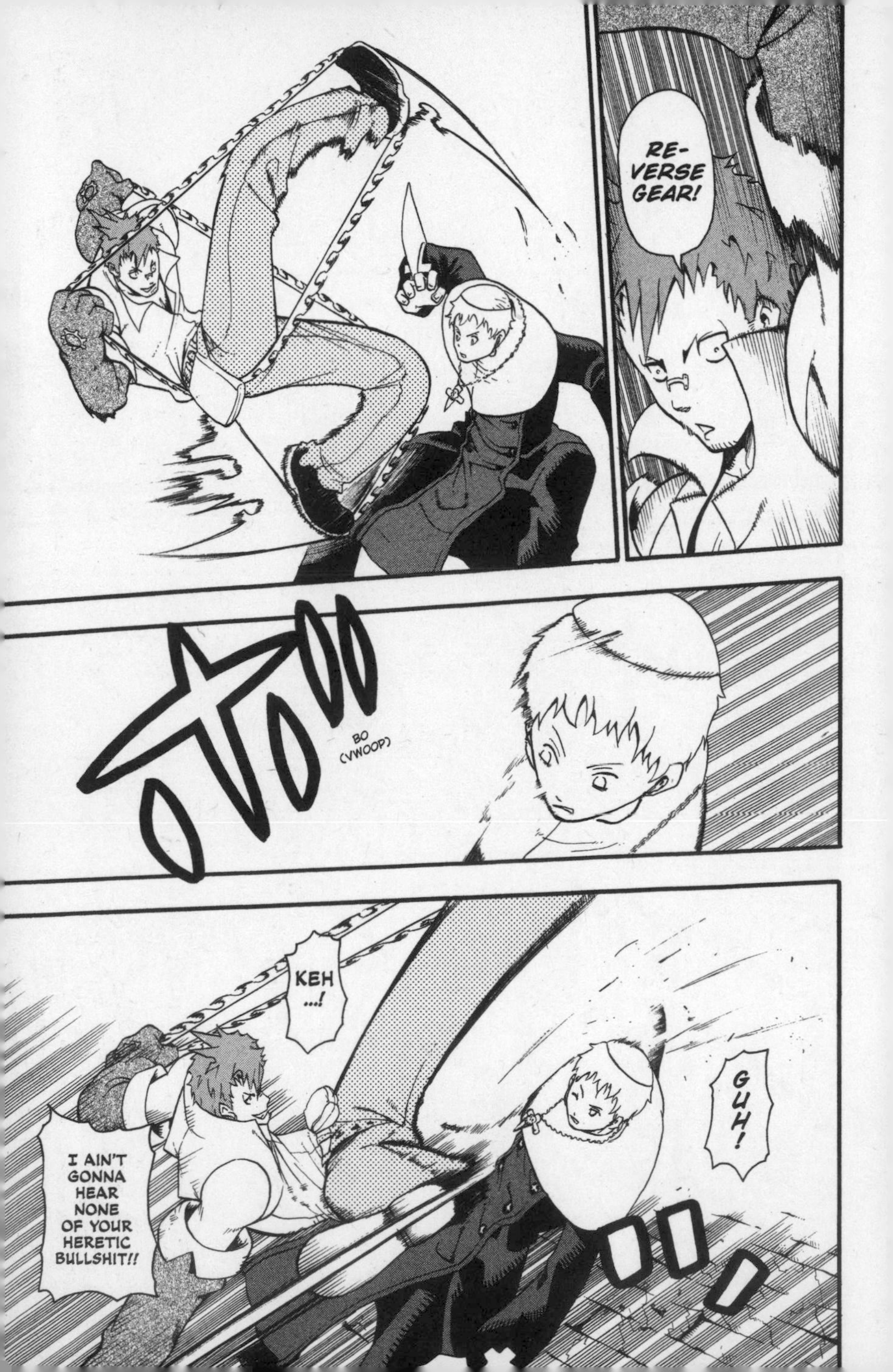

RE-VERSE GEAR!
BO (VWOOP)
GUH!
KEH ...!
I AIN'T GONNA HEAR NONE OF YOUR HERETIC BULLSHIT!!

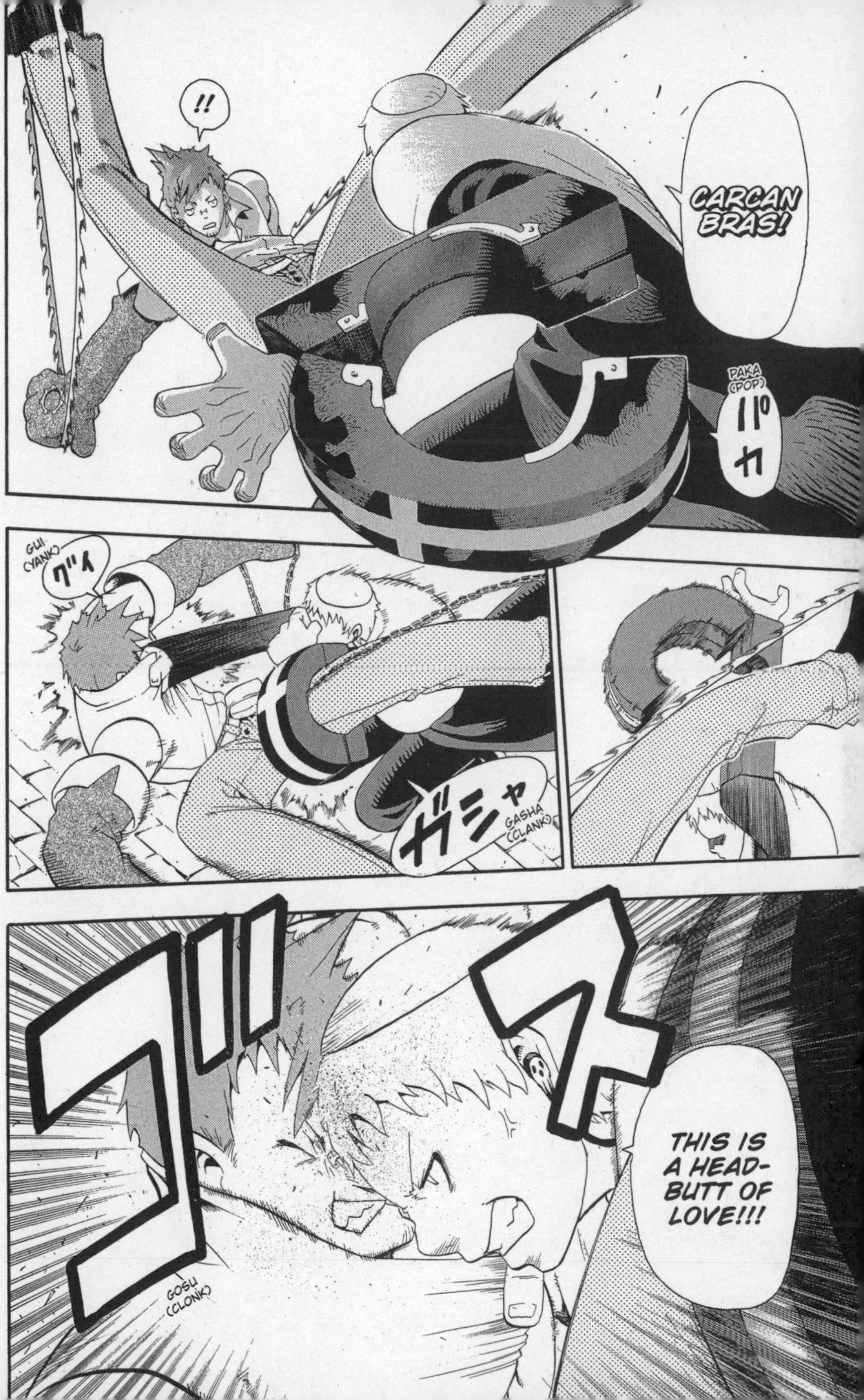
CARCAN BRAS!
PAKA (POP)
パカ
!!
GUI (YANK)
グイ
GASHA (CLANK)
ガシャ
THIS IS A HEAD-BUTT OF LOVE!!!
ゴス
GOSU (CLONK)

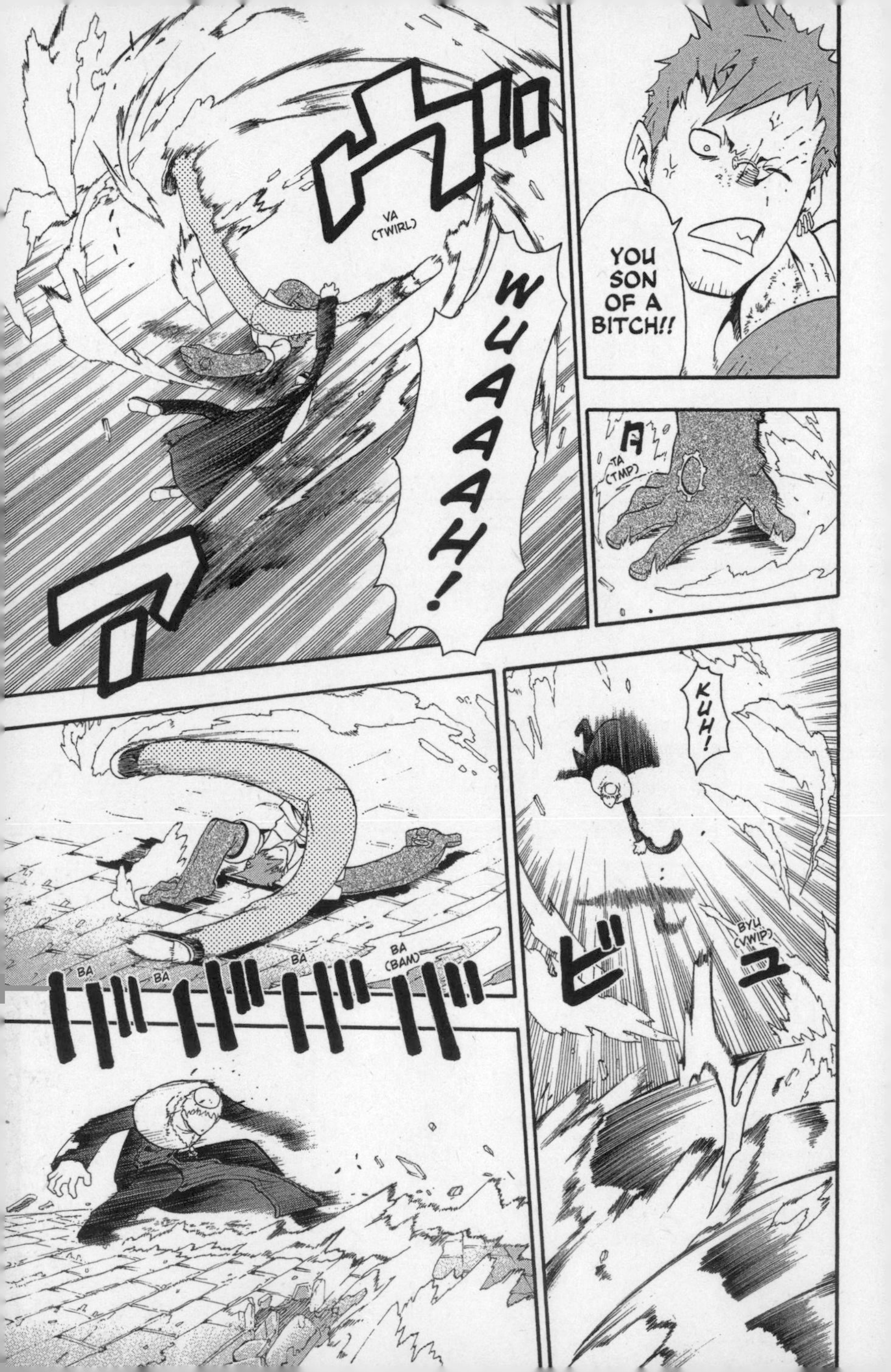
YOU SON OF A BITCH!!
TA (TMP)
VA (TWIRL)
WUAAAAH!
KUH!
BYU (VWIP)
BA BA BA BA (BAM)

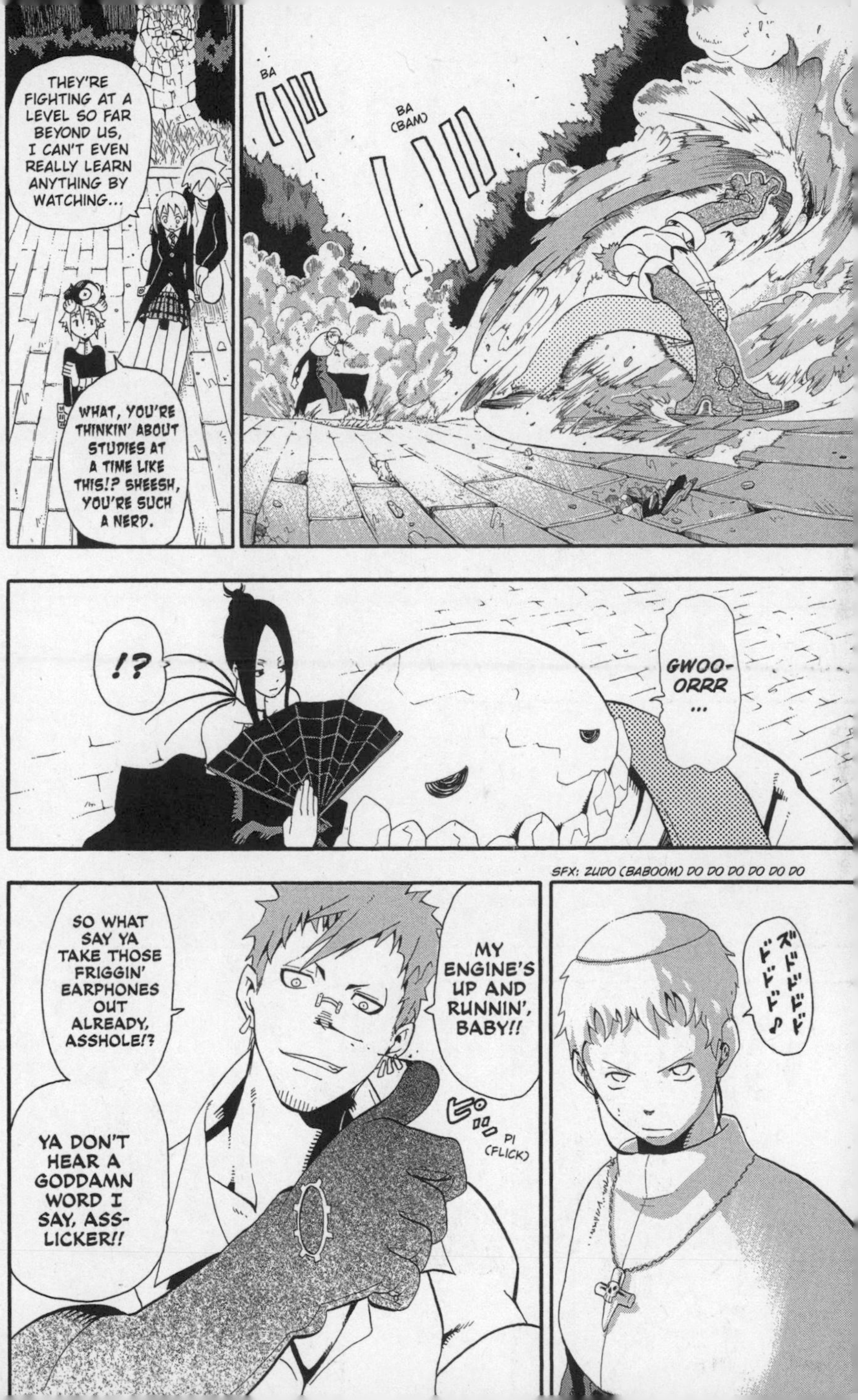
BA
BA (BAM)
THEY'RE FIGHTING AT A LEVEL SO FAR BEYOND US, I CAN'T EVEN REALLY LEARN ANYTHING BY WATCHING...
WHAT, YOU'RE THINKIN' ABOUT STUDIES AT A TIME LIKE THIS!? SHEESH, YOU'RE SUCH A NERD.
GWOO-ORRR ...
!?
SFX: ZUDO (BABOOM) DO DO DO DO DO DO
ズドドド ドドドド♪
MY ENGINE'S UP AND RUNNIN', BABY!!
PI (FLICK)
SO WHAT SAY YA TAKE THOSE FRIGGIN' EARPHONES OUT ALREADY, ASSHOLE!?
YA DON'T HEAR A GODDAMN WORD I SAY, ASS-LICKER!!

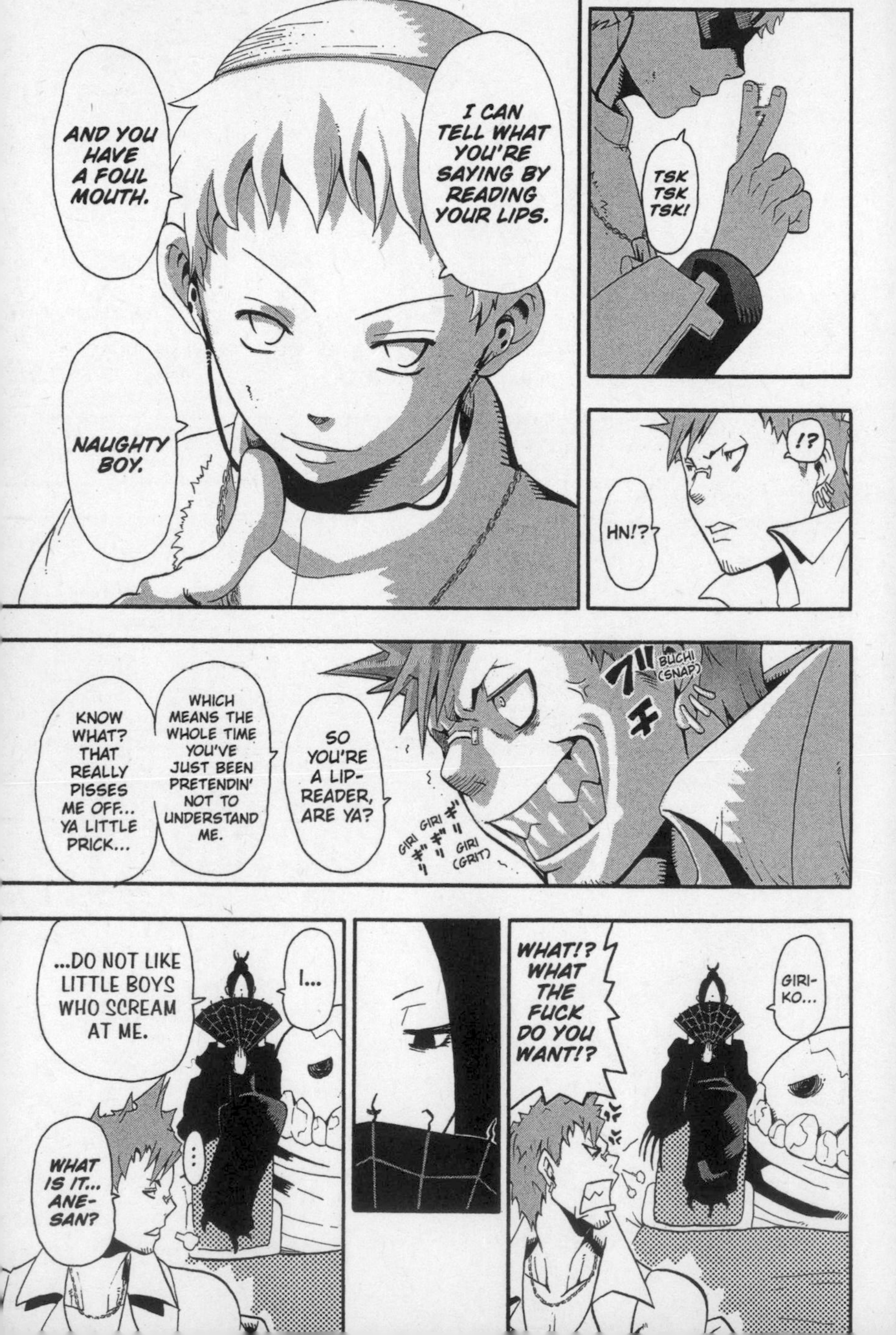
TSK TSK TSK!
!?
HN!?
I CAN TELL WHAT YOU'RE SAYING BY READING YOUR LIPS.
AND YOU HAVE A FOUL MOUTH.
NAUGHTY BOY.
BUCHI (SNAP)
SO YOU'RE A LIP-READER, ARE YA?
WHICH MEANS THE WHOLE TIME YOU'VE JUST BEEN PRETENDIN' NOT TO UNDERSTAND ME.
KNOW WHAT? THAT REALLY PISSES ME OFF... YA LITTLE PRICK...
GIRI GIRI GIRI (GRIT)
GIRI-KO...
WHAT!? WHAT THE FUCK DO YOU WANT!?
I...
...DO NOT LIKE LITTLE BOYS WHO SCREAM AT ME.
...
WHAT IS IT... ANE-SAN?

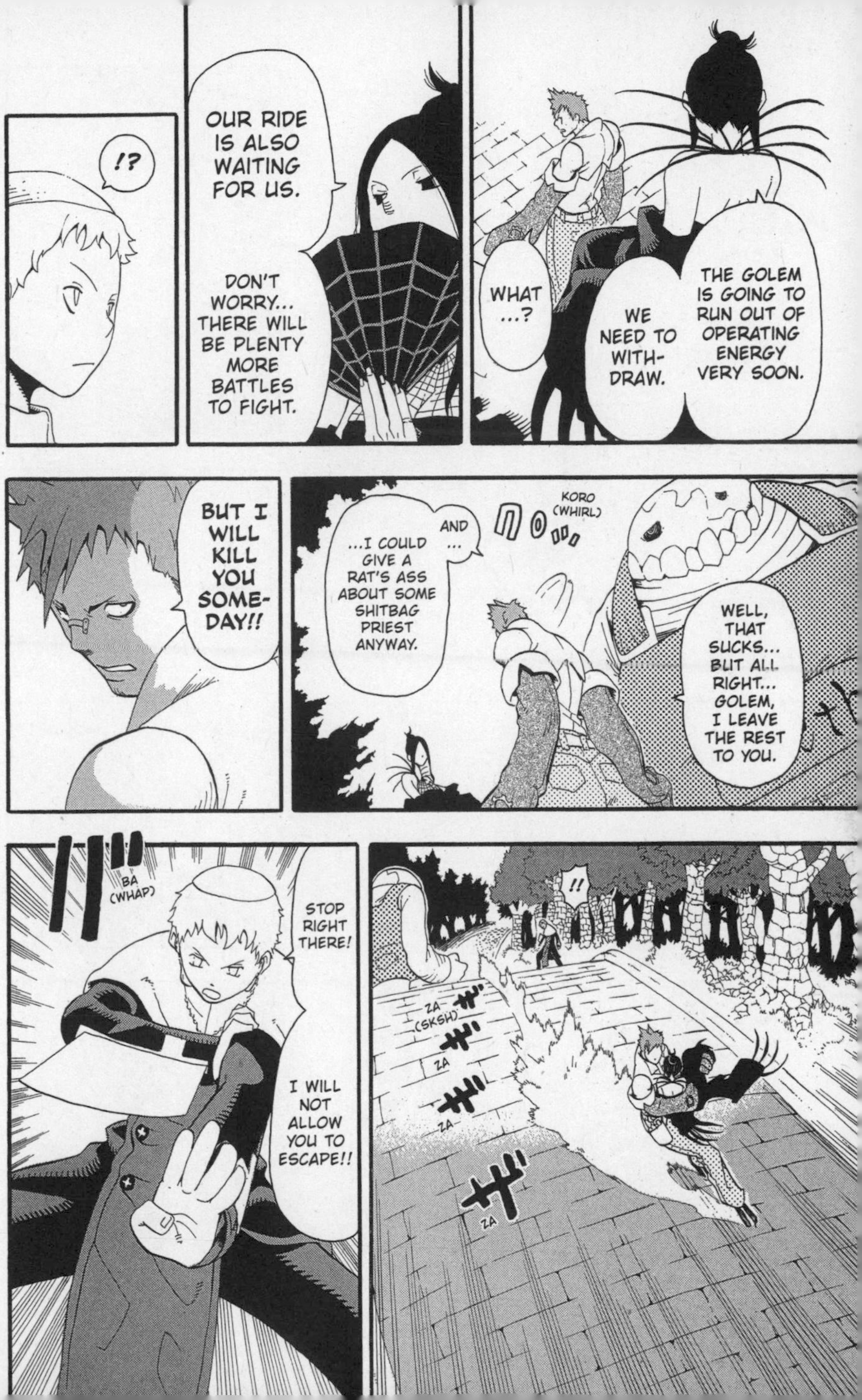
THE GOLEM IS GOING TO RUN OUT OF OPERATING ENERGY VERY SOON.
WE NEED TO WITH-DRAW.
WHAT ...?
OUR RIDE IS ALSO WAITING FOR US.
DON'T WORRY... THERE WILL BE PLENTY MORE BATTLES TO FIGHT.
!?
KORO (WHIRL)
WELL, THAT SUCKS... BUT ALL RIGHT... GOLEM, I LEAVE THE REST TO YOU.
AND ...
...I COULD GIVE A RAT'S ASS ABOUT SOME SHITBAG PRIEST ANYWAY.
BUT I WILL KILL YOU SOME-DAY!!
!!
ZA (SKSH)
ZA
ZA
ZA
BA (WHAP)
STOP RIGHT THERE!
I WILL NOT ALLOW YOU TO ESCAPE!!

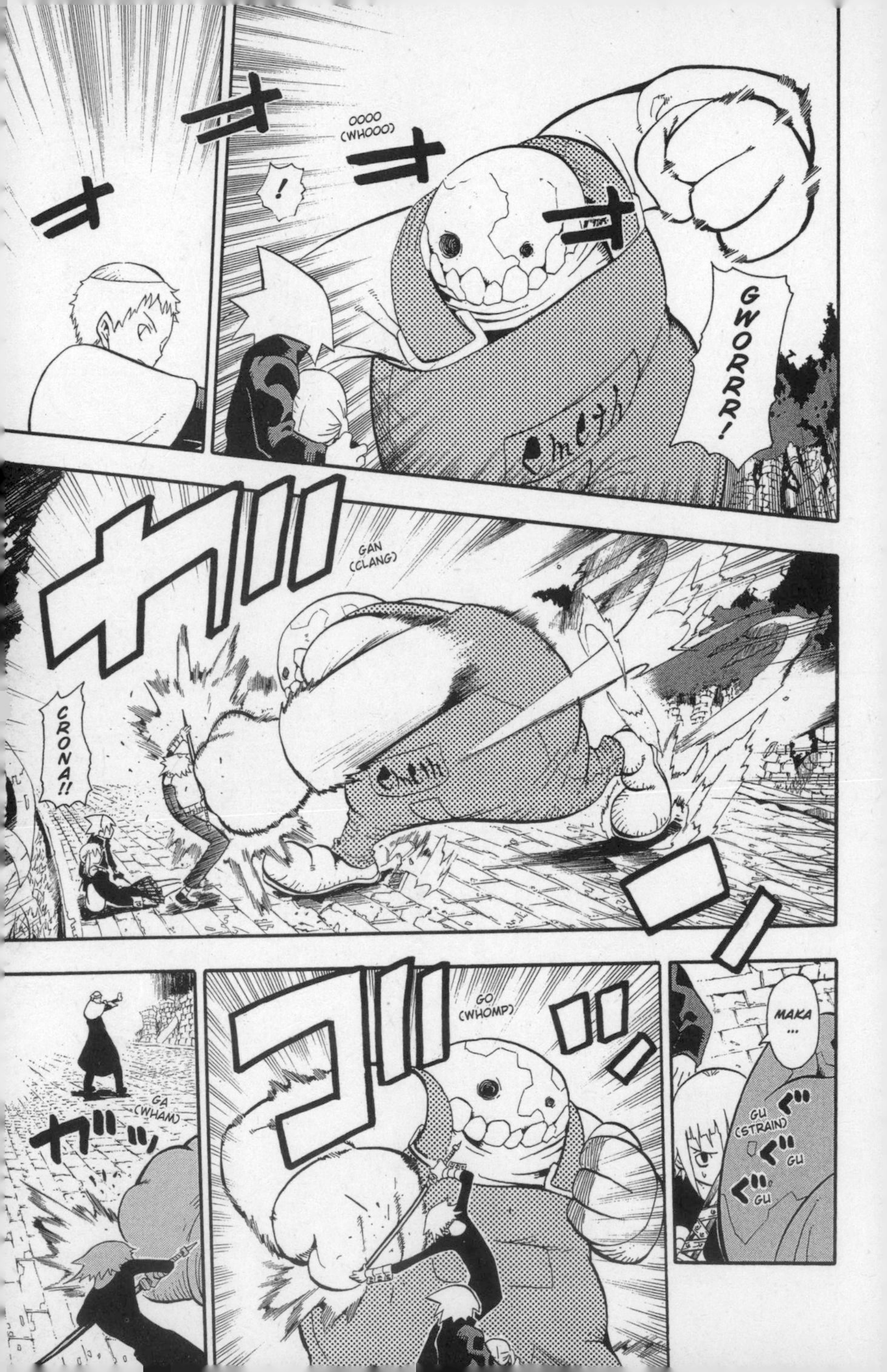
OOOO (WHOOO)
!
GWORRR!
GAN (CLANG)
CRONA!!
MAKA ...
GU (STRAIN)
GU
GU
GO (WHOMP)
GA (WHAM)

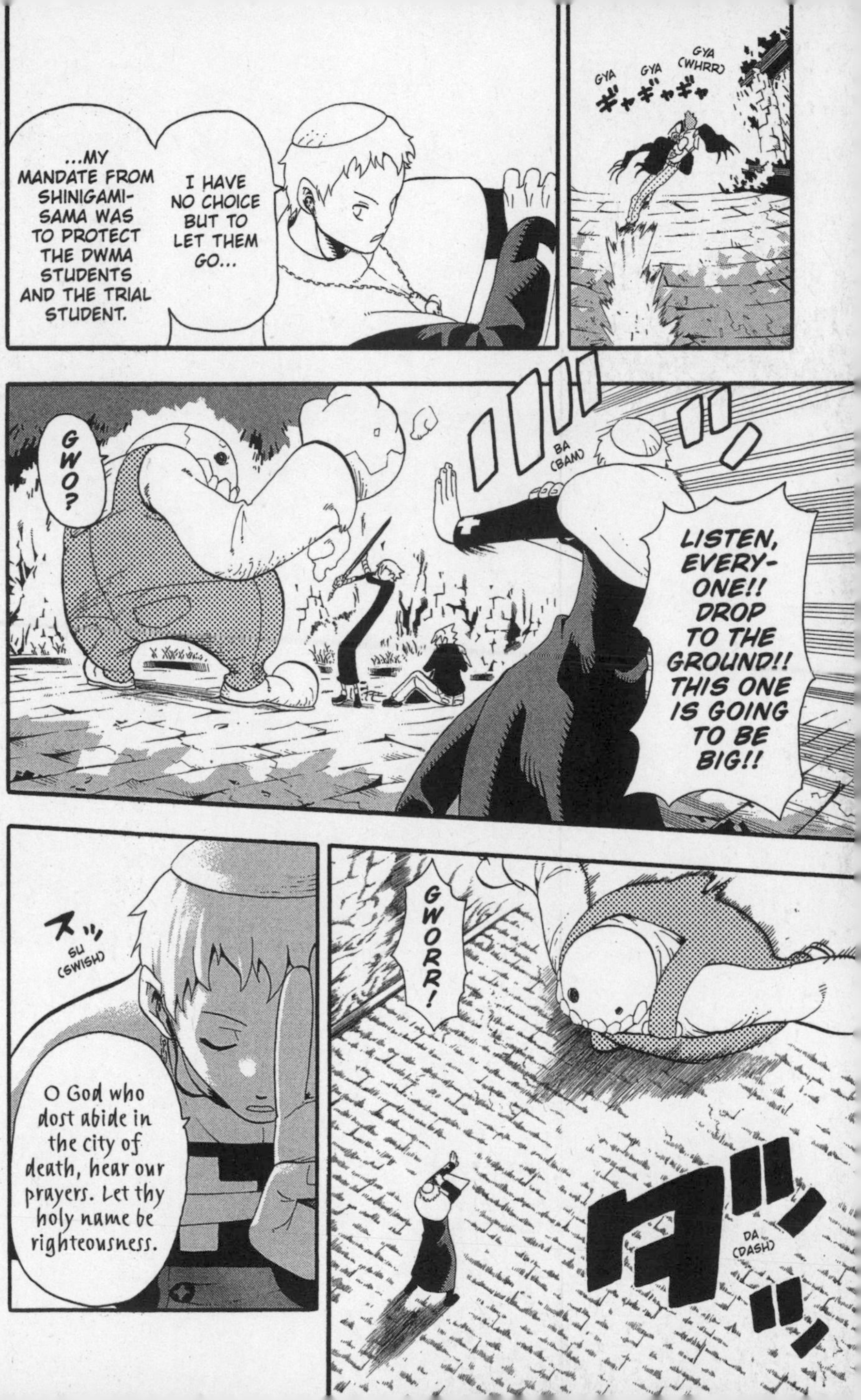

GYA GYA GYA (WHRR)
ギャギャギャ
I HAVE NO CHOICE BUT TO LET THEM GO...
...MY MANDATE FROM SHINIGAMI-SAMA WAS TO PROTECT THE DWMA STUDENTS AND THE TRIAL STUDENT.
BA (BAM)
LISTEN, EVERYONE!! DROP TO THE GROUND!! THIS ONE IS GOING TO BE BIG!!
GWO?
GWORR!
DA (DASH)
スッ
SU (SWISH)
O God who dost abide in the city of death, hear our prayers. Let thy holy name be righteousness.

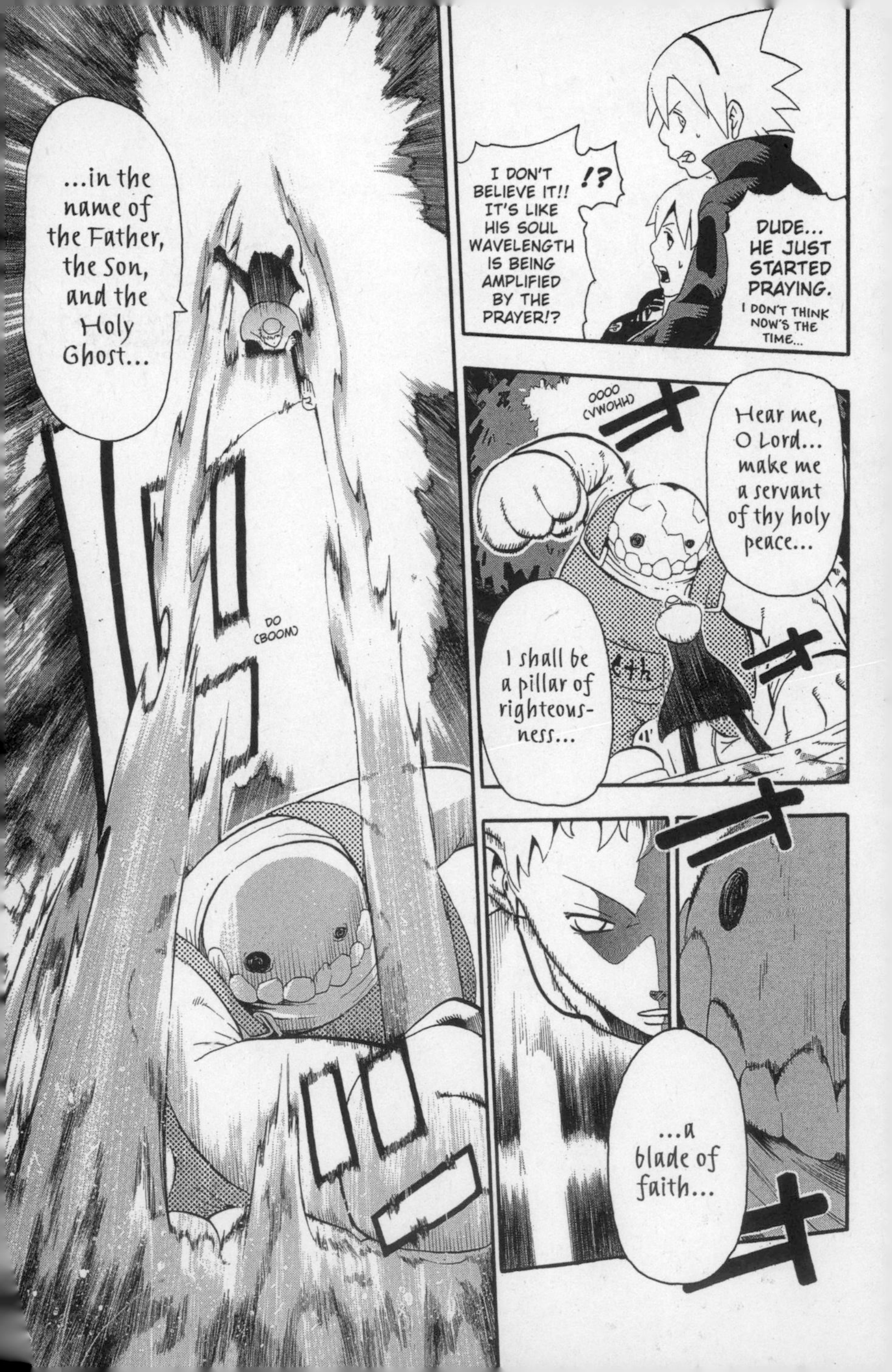

!?
DUDE... HE JUST STARTED PRAYING.
I DON'T THINK NOW'S THE TIME...
I DON'T BELIEVE IT!! IT'S LIKE HIS SOUL WAVELENGTH IS BEING AMPLIFIED BY THE PRAYER!?
OOOO (VWOHH)
Hear me, O Lord... make me a servant of thy holy peace...
I shall be a pillar of righteous-ness...
...a blade of faith...
...in the name of the Father, the Son, and the Holy Ghost...
DO (BOOM)

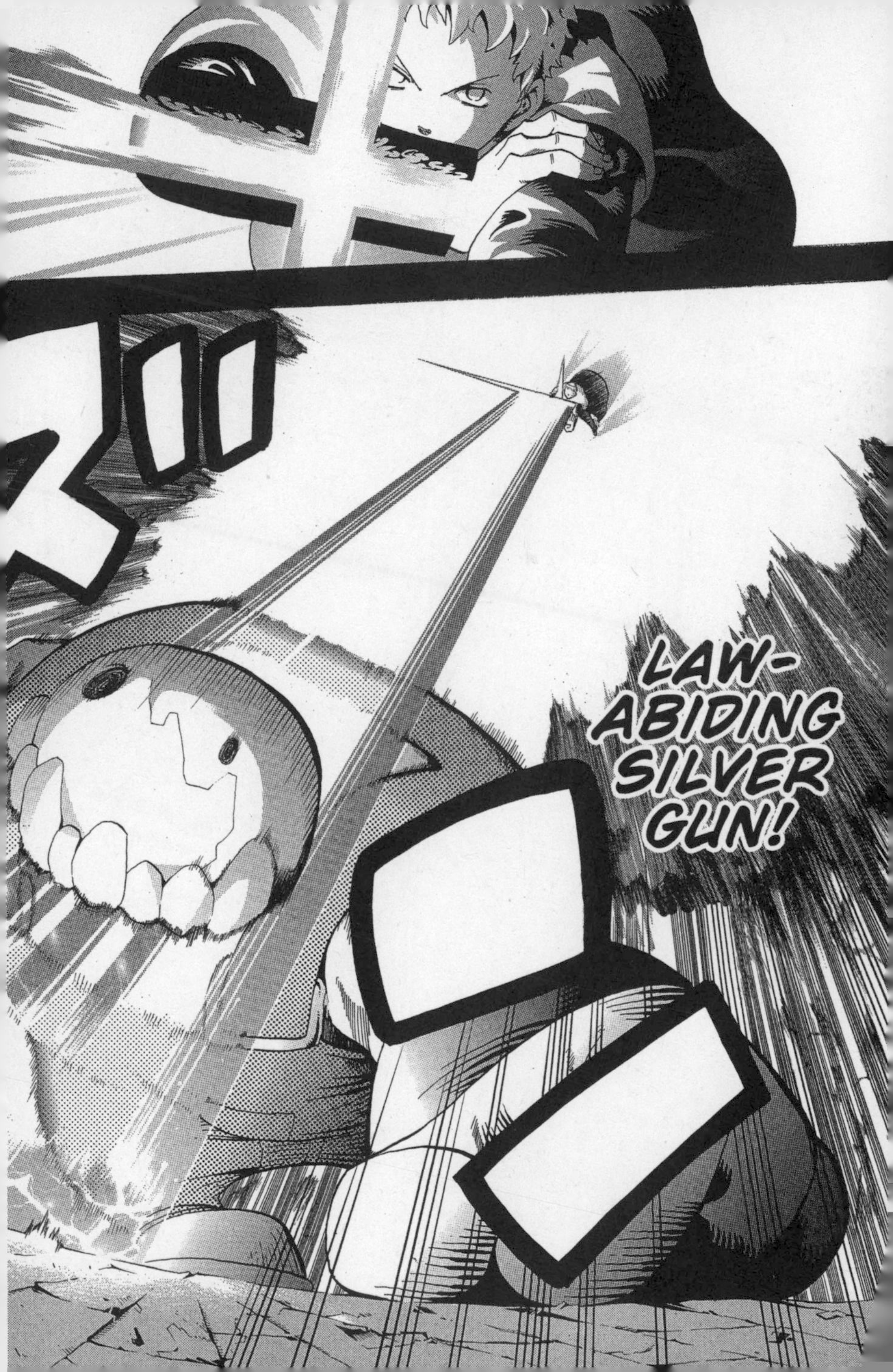
LAW-ABIDING SILVER GUN!

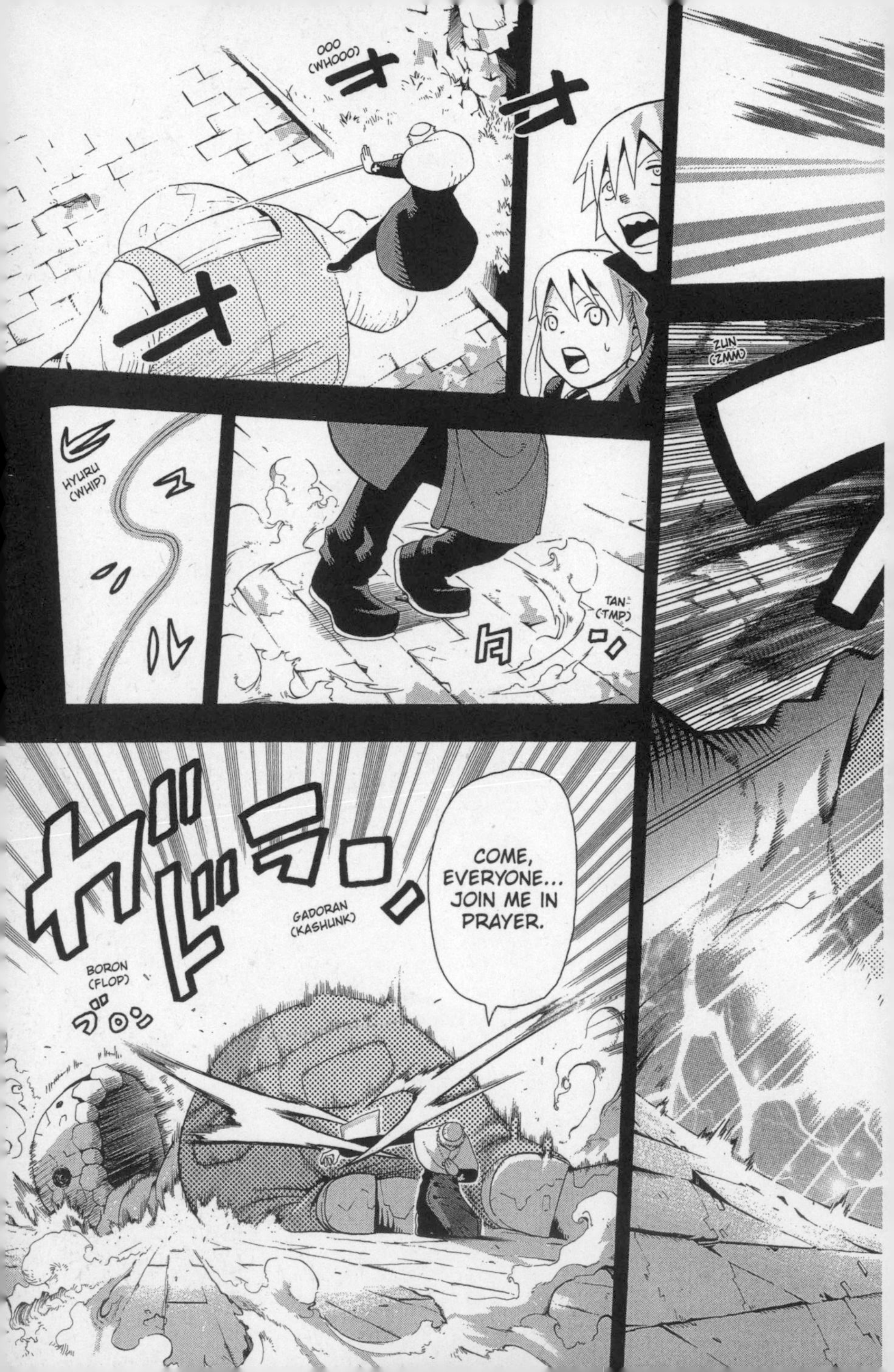
ZUN
(ZMM)
OOO
(WHOOO)
TAN
(TMP)
HYURU
(WHIP)
COME, EVERYONE... JOIN ME IN PRAYER.
GADORAN
(KASHUNK)
BORON
(FLOP)

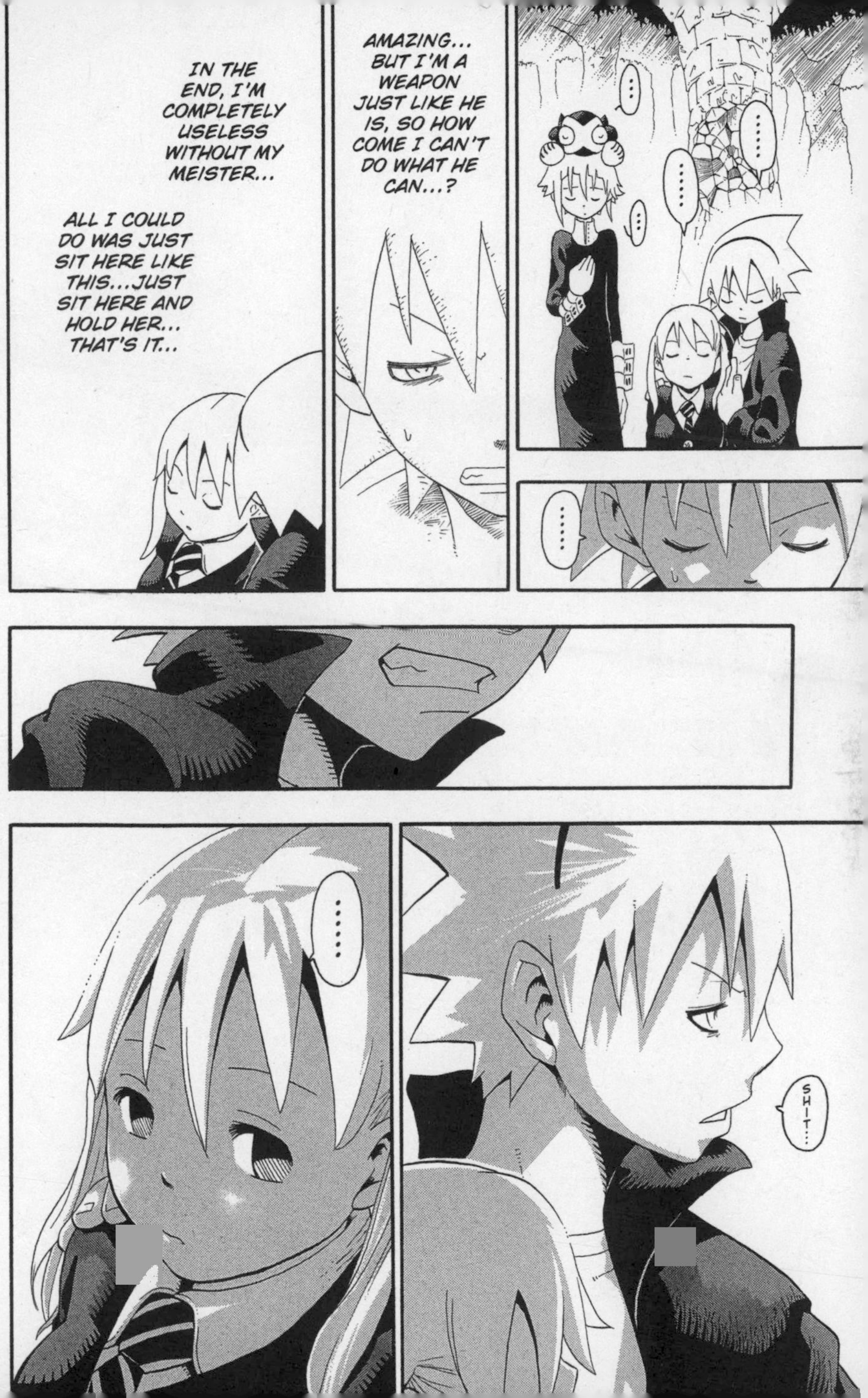
......
......
......
...
......
AMAZING... BUT I'M A WEAPON JUST LIKE HE IS, SO HOW COME I CAN'T DO WHAT HE CAN...?
IN THE END, I'M COMPLETELY USELESS WITHOUT MY MEISTER...
ALL I COULD DO WAS JUST SIT HERE LIKE THIS...JUST SIT HERE AND HOLD HER... THAT'S IT...
SHIT...
......

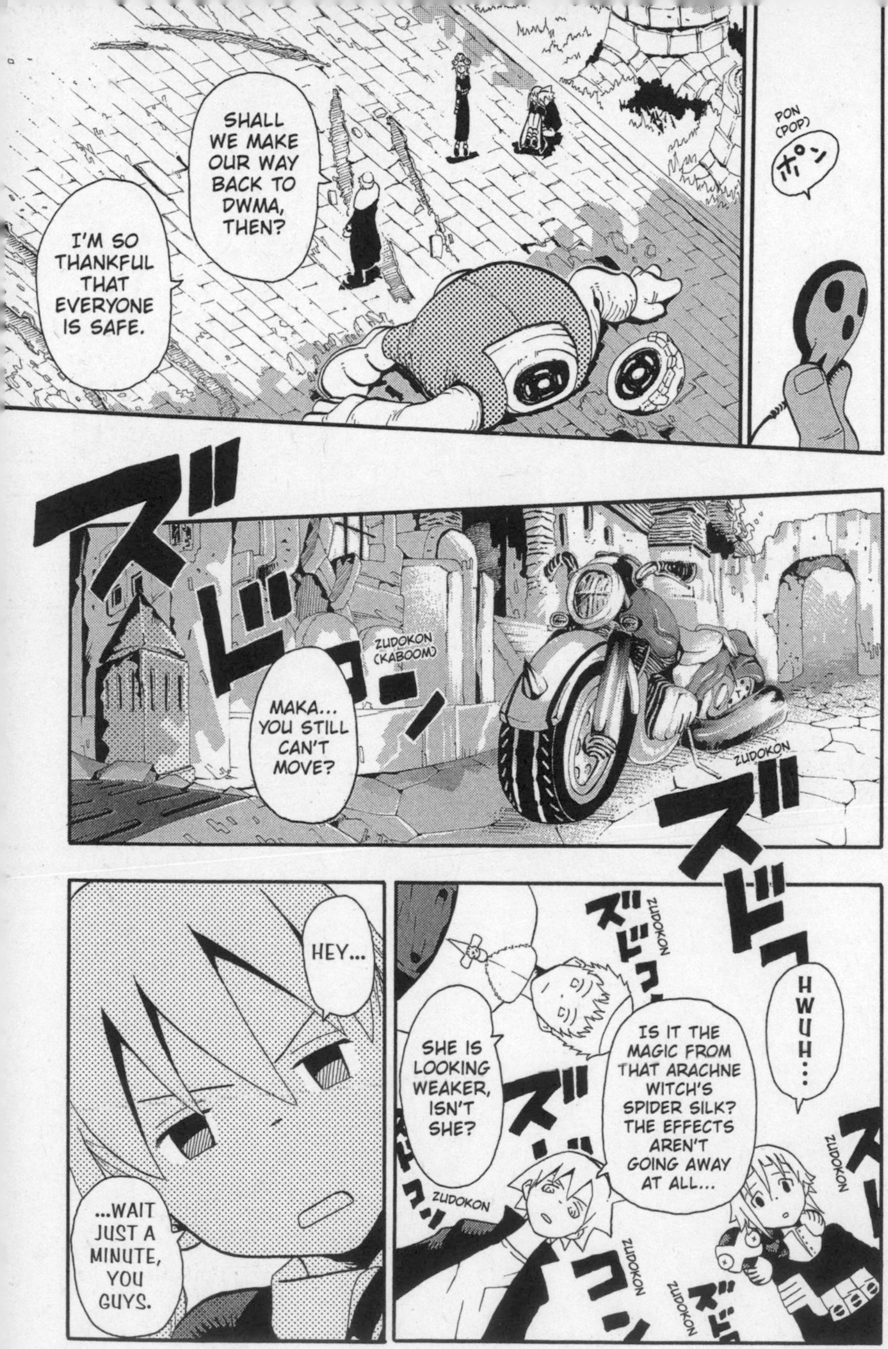
PON (POP)
ポン
SHALL WE MAKE OUR WAY BACK TO DWMA, THEN?
I'M SO THANKFUL THAT EVERYONE IS SAFE.
ZUDOKON (KABOOM)
MAKA... YOU STILL CAN'T MOVE?
ZUDOKON
HWUH...
IS IT THE MAGIC FROM THAT ARACHNE WITCH'S SPIDER SILK? THE EFFECTS AREN'T GOING AWAY AT ALL...
SHE IS LOOKING WEAKER, ISN'T SHE?
ZUDOKON
ZUDOKON
ZUDOKON
ZUDOKON
ZUDOKON
HEY...
...WAIT JUST A MINUTE, YOU GUYS.

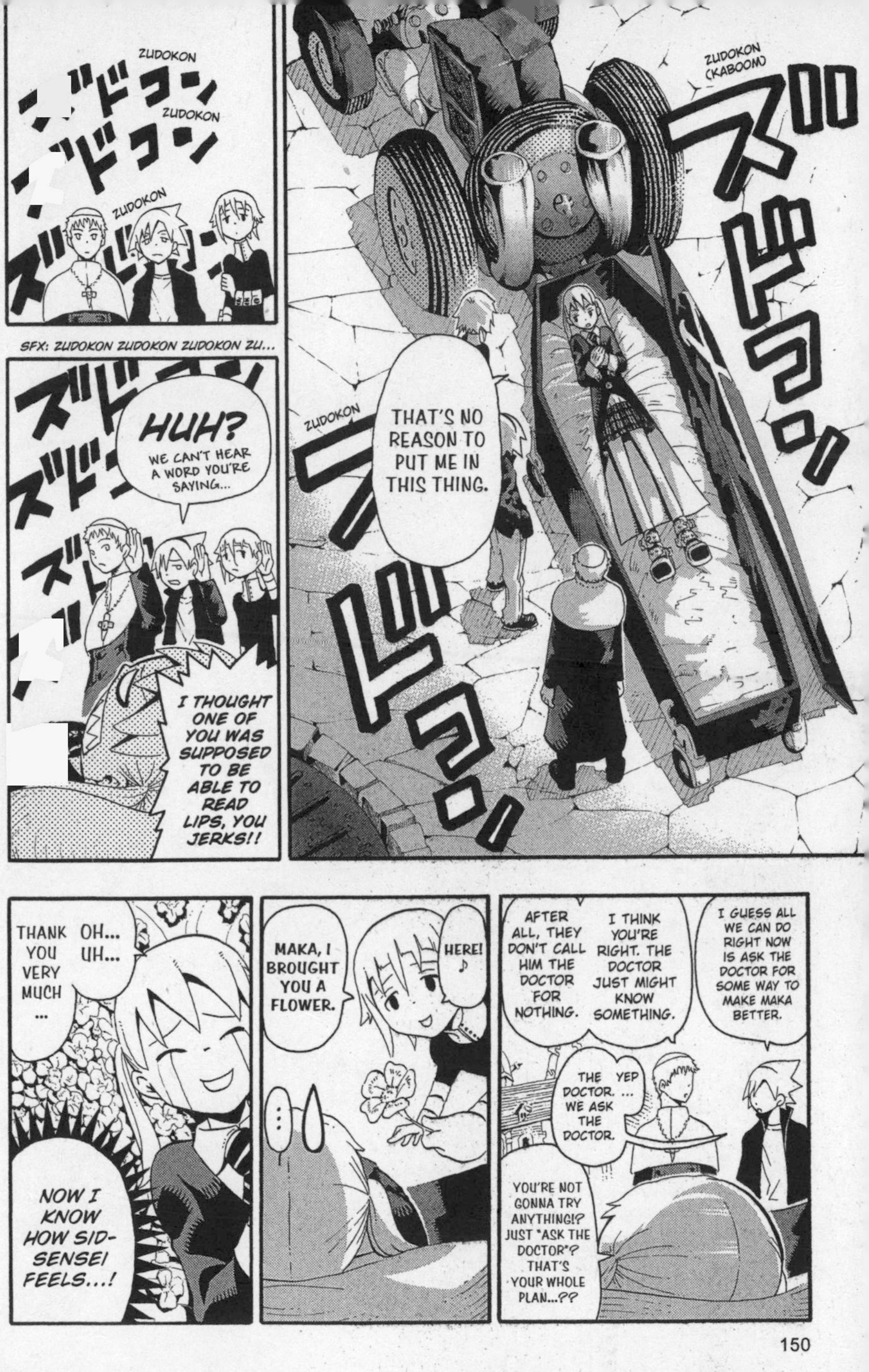
ZUDOKON (KABOOM)
ZUDOKON
THAT'S NO REASON TO PUT ME IN THIS THING.
ZUDOKON
ZUDOKON
ZUDOKON
SFX: ZUDOKON ZUDOKON ZUDOKON ZU...
HUH? WE CAN'T HEAR A WORD YOU'RE SAYING...
I THOUGHT ONE OF YOU WAS SUPPOSED TO BE ABLE TO READ LIPS, YOU JERKS!!
I GUESS ALL WE CAN DO RIGHT NOW IS ASK THE DOCTOR FOR SOME WAY TO MAKE MAKA BETTER.
I THINK YOU'RE RIGHT. THE DOCTOR JUST MIGHT KNOW SOMETHING.
AFTER ALL, THEY DON'T CALL HIM THE DOCTOR FOR NOTHING.
YEP...
THE DOCTOR. WE ASK THE DOCTOR.
YOU'RE NOT GONNA TRY ANYTHING!? JUST "ASK THE DOCTOR"? THAT'S YOUR WHOLE PLAN...??
HERE! ♪
MAKA, I BROUGHT YOU A FLOWER.
...
OH... UH...
THANK YOU VERY MUCH ...
NOW I KNOW HOW SID-SENSEI FEELS...!

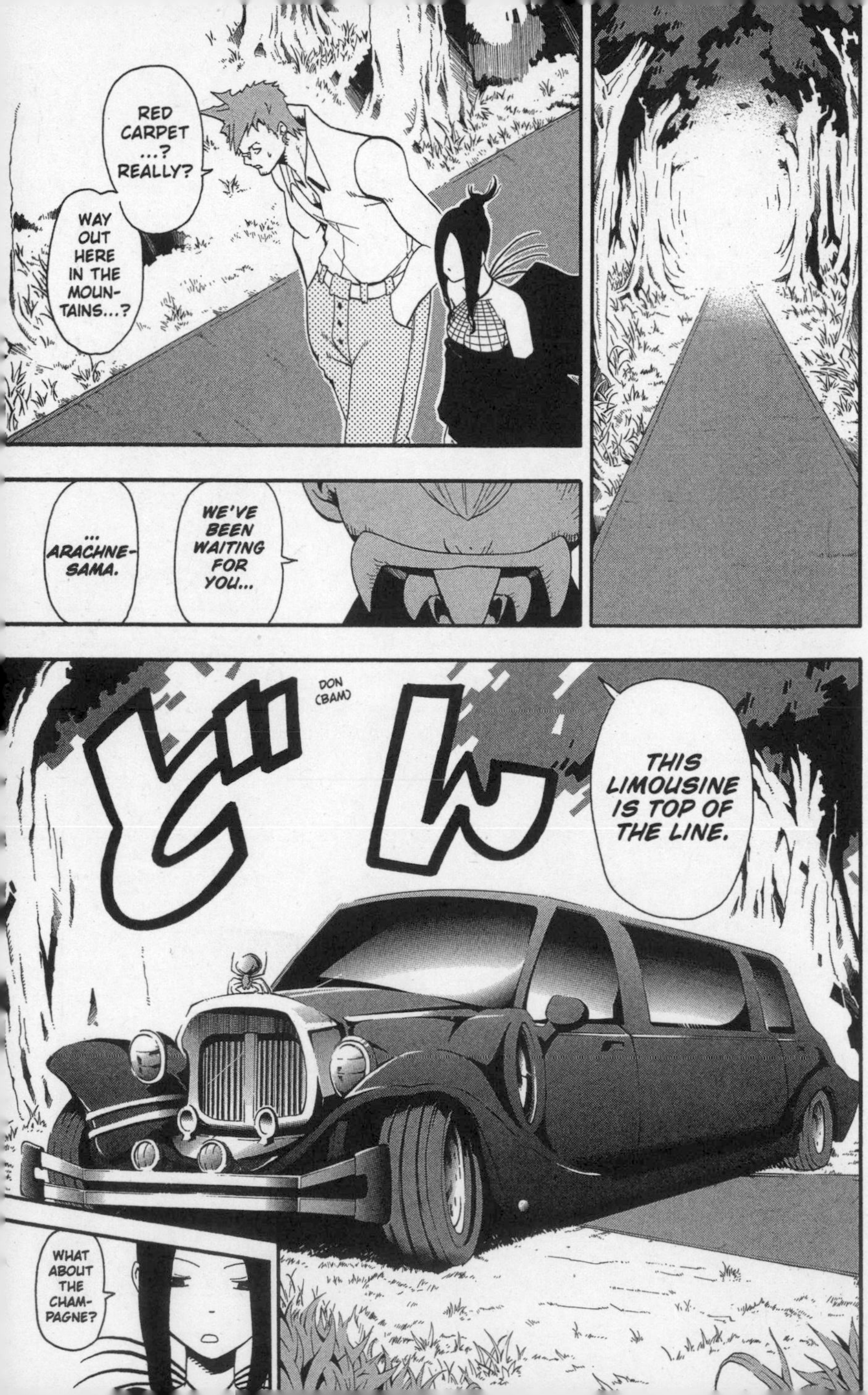
RED CARPET ...? REALLY?
WAY OUT HERE IN THE MOUN-TAINS...?
WE'VE BEEN WAITING FOR YOU...
... ARACHNE-SAMA.
THIS LIMOUSINE IS TOP OF THE LINE.
DON (BAM)
WHAT ABOUT THE CHAM-PAGNE?

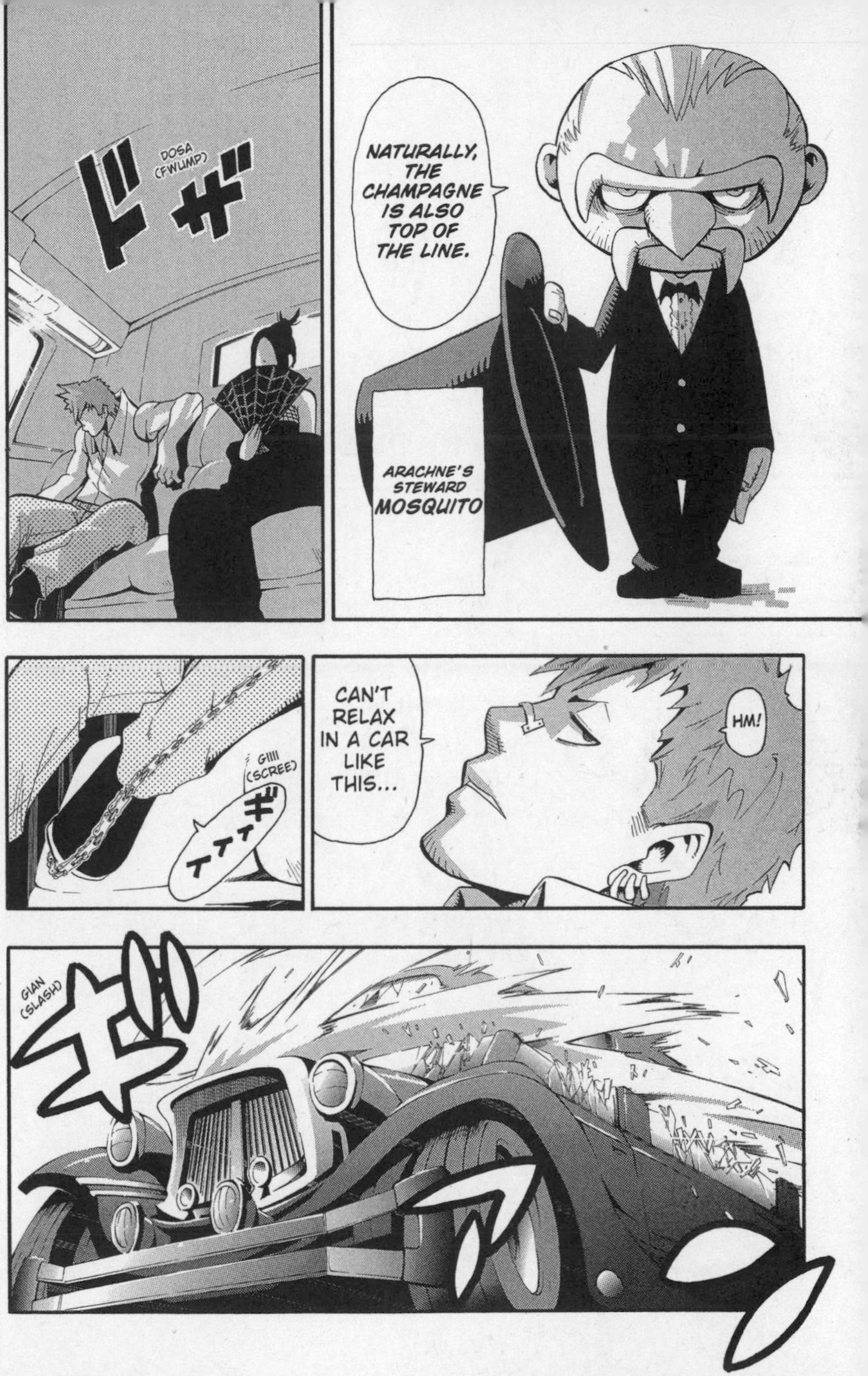
NATURALLY, THE CHAMPAGNE IS ALSO TOP OF THE LINE.
ARACHNE'S STEWARD MOSQUITO
DOSA (FWUMP)
HM!
CAN'T RELAX IN A CAR LIKE THIS...
GIIII (SCREE)
ギィィ
GIAN (SLASH)

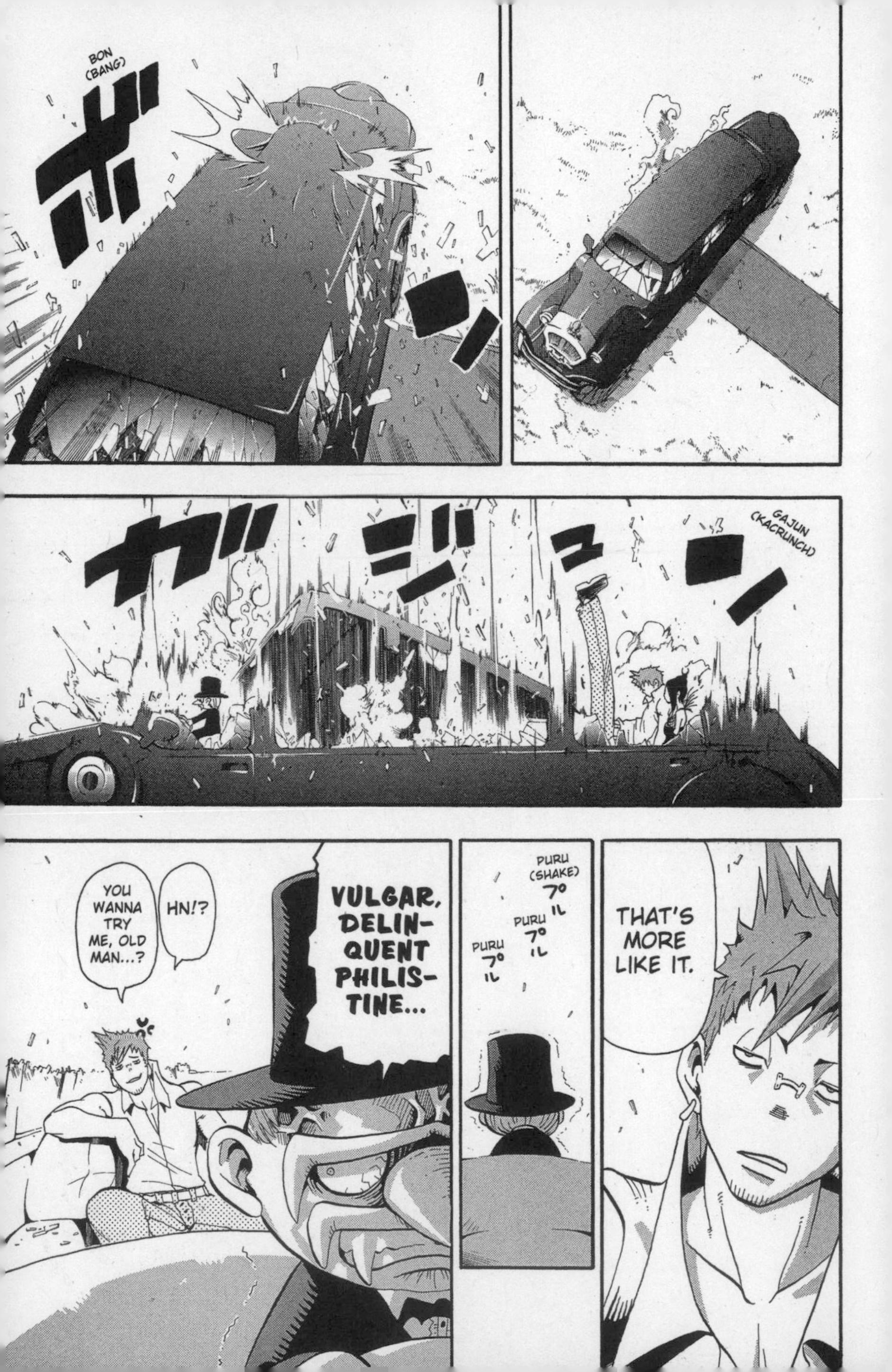
BON (BANG)
GAJUN (KACRUNCH)
THAT'S MORE LIKE IT.
PURU (SHAKE)
PURU
PURU
VULGAR, DELIN-QUENT PHILIS-TINE...
HN!?
YOU WANNA TRY ME, OLD MAN...?

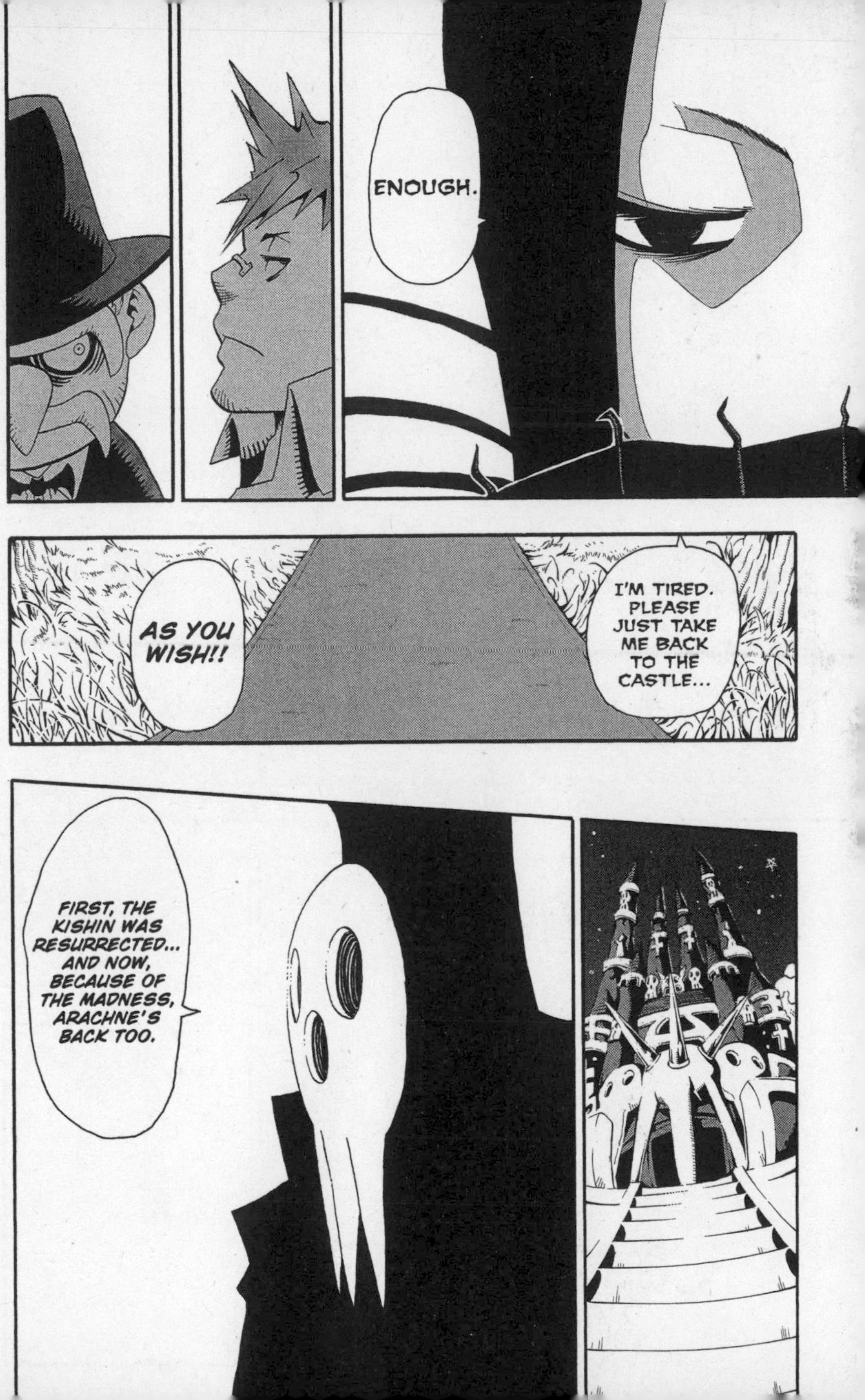
ENOUGH.
I'M TIRED. PLEASE JUST TAKE ME BACK TO THE CASTLE...
AS YOU WISH!!
FIRST, THE KISHIN WAS RESURRECTED... AND NOW, BECAUSE OF THE MADNESS, ARACHNE'S BACK TOO.

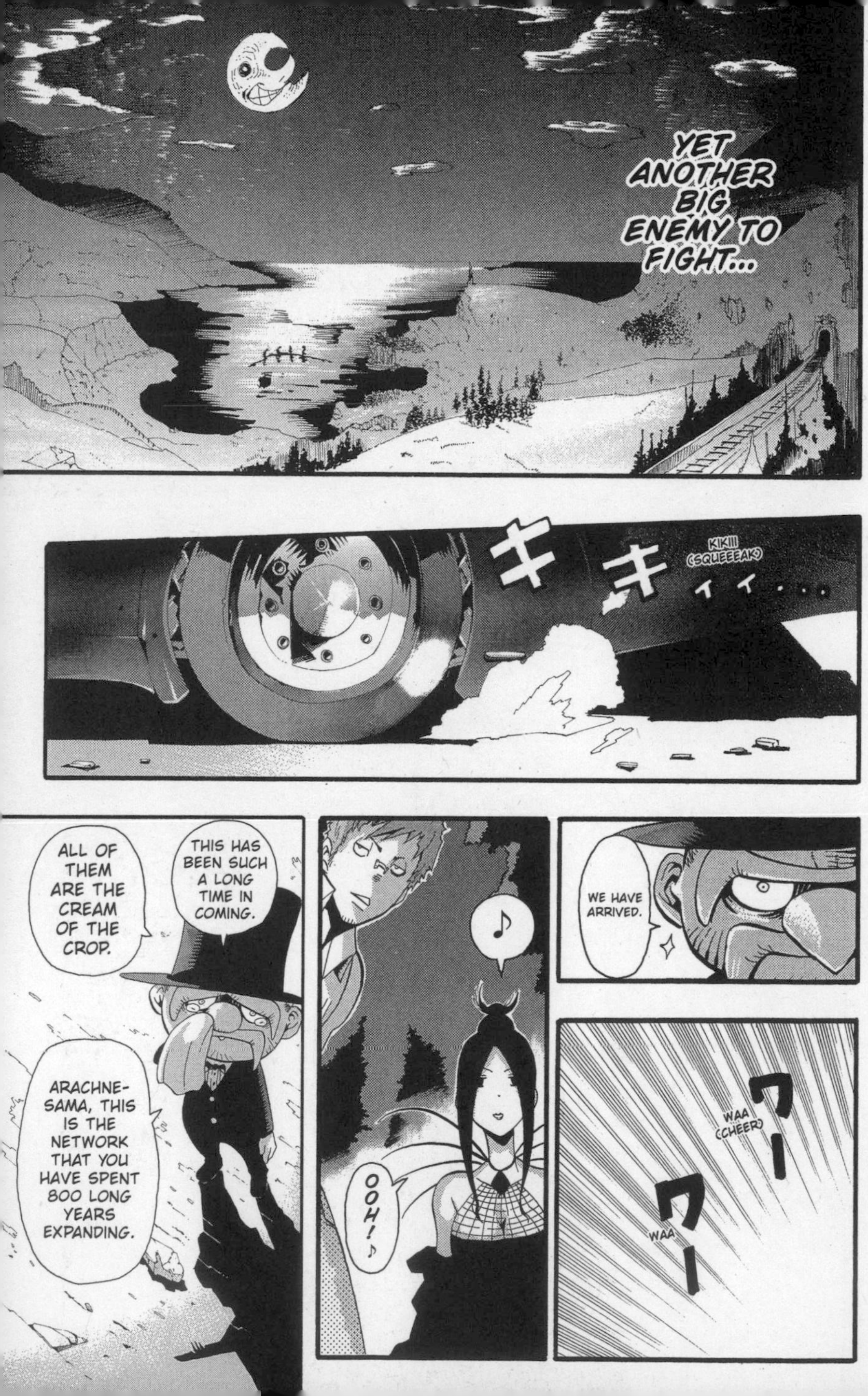
YET ANOTHER BIG ENEMY TO FIGHT...
キキィ...
KIKIII (SQUEEEAK)
WE HAVE ARRIVED.
ワー
WAA (CHEER)
ワー
WAA
♪
OOH! ♪
THIS HAS BEEN SUCH A LONG TIME IN COMING.
ALL OF THEM ARE THE CREAM OF THE CROP.
ARACHNE-SAMA, THIS IS THE NETWORK THAT YOU HAVE SPENT 800 LONG YEARS EXPANDING.

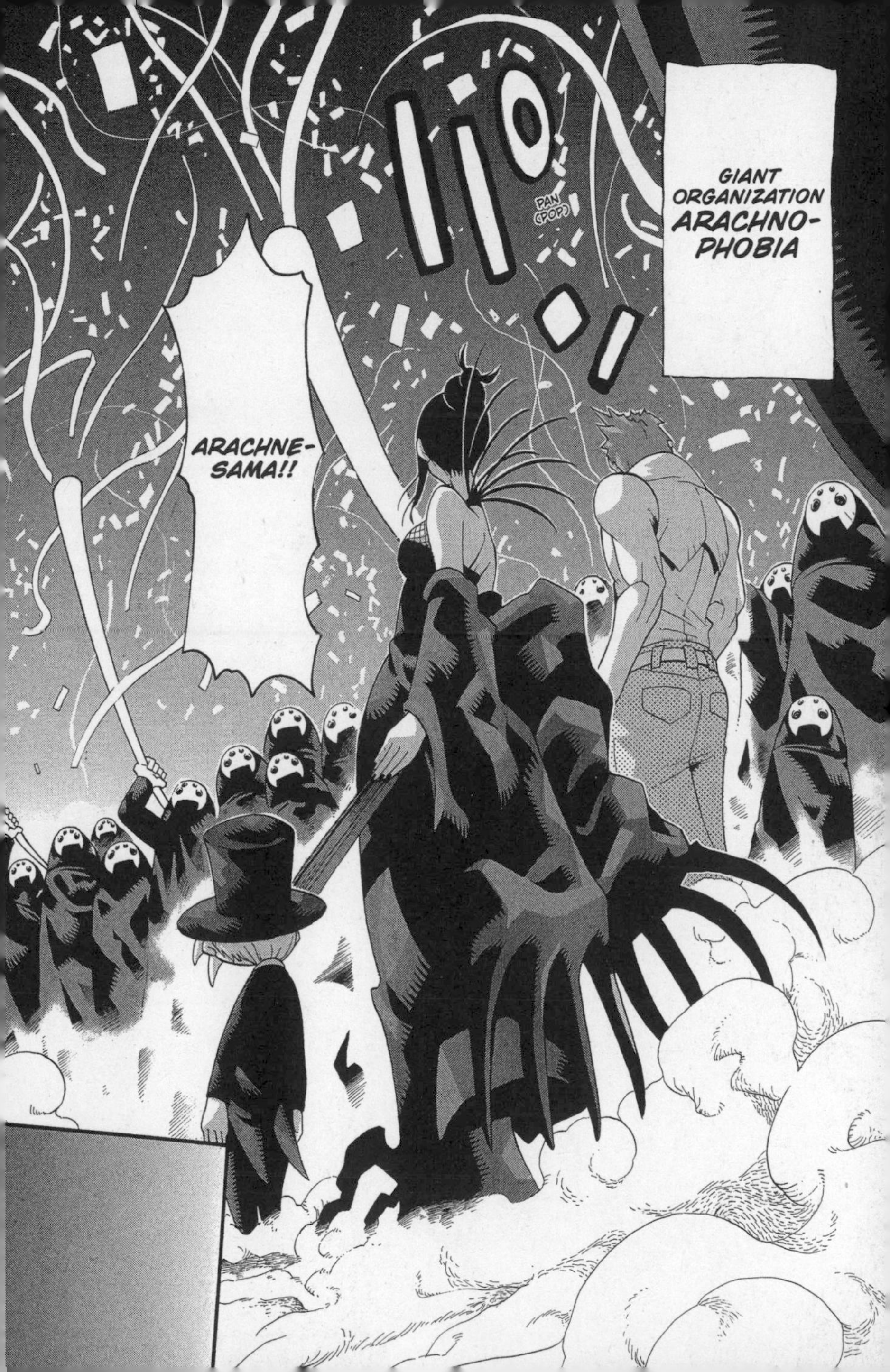
GIANT ORGANIZATION ARACHNOPHOBIA
PAN (POP)
ARACHNE-SAMA!!

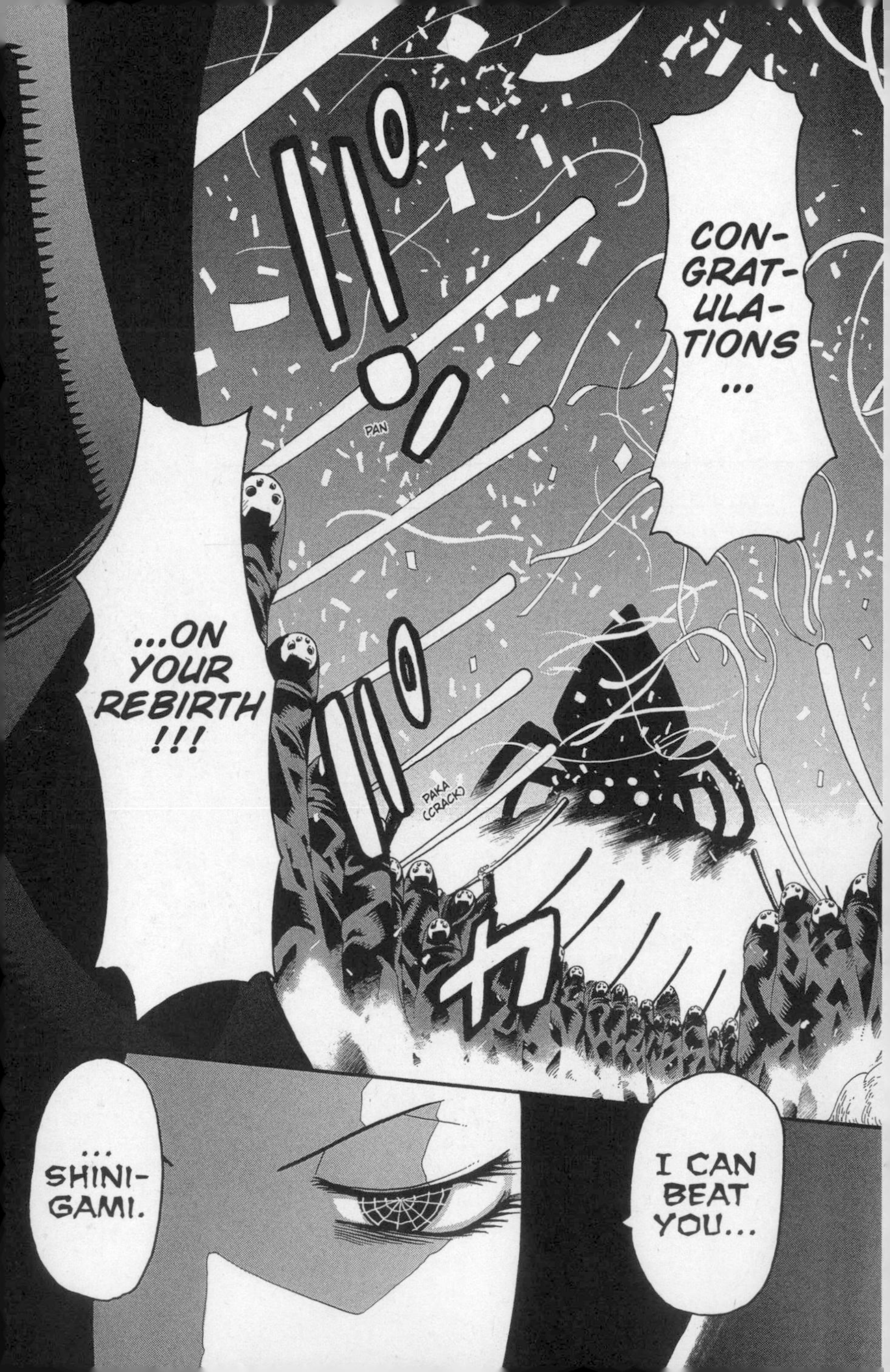
CON-GRAT-ULA-TIONS...
PAN
...ON YOUR REBIRTH!!!
PAKA (CRACK)
I CAN BEAT YOU...
...SHINI-GAMI.

SOUL EATER

SOUL EATER

CHAPTER 27: THE BODYGUARD (PART 1)

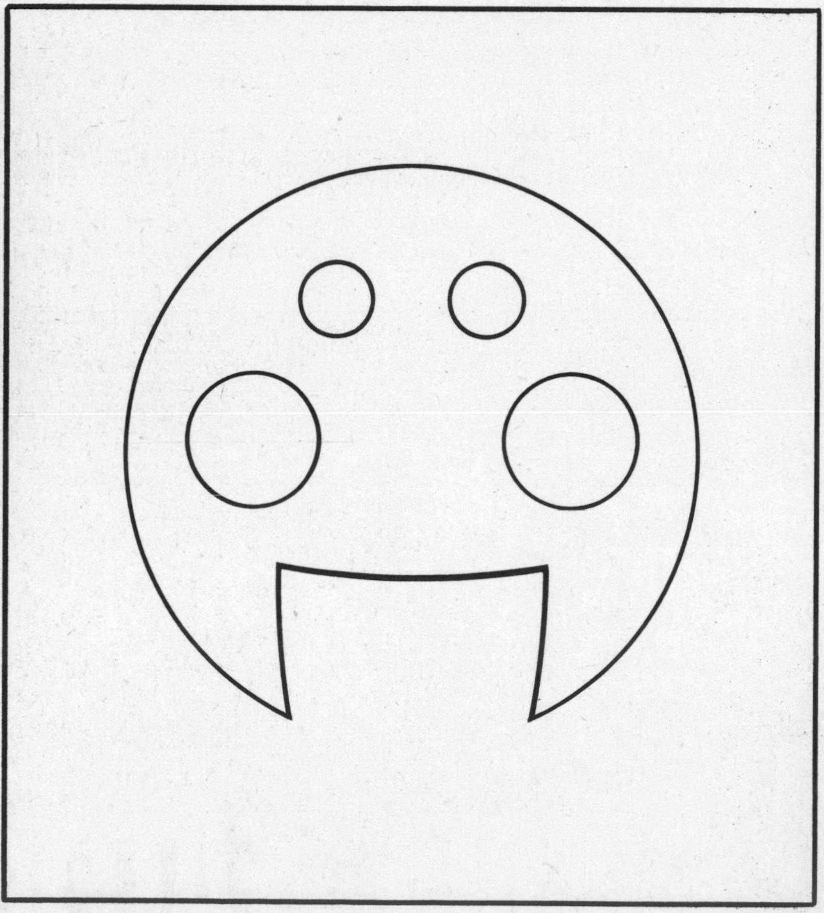

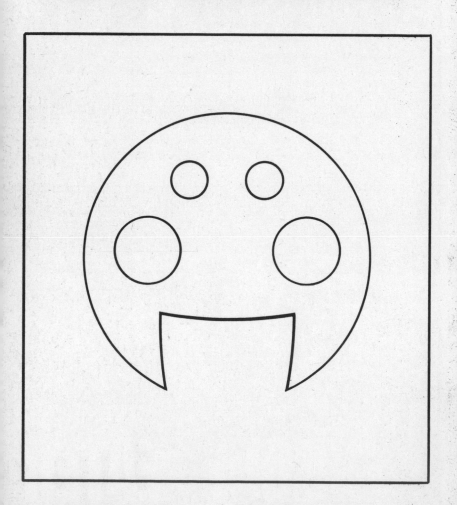

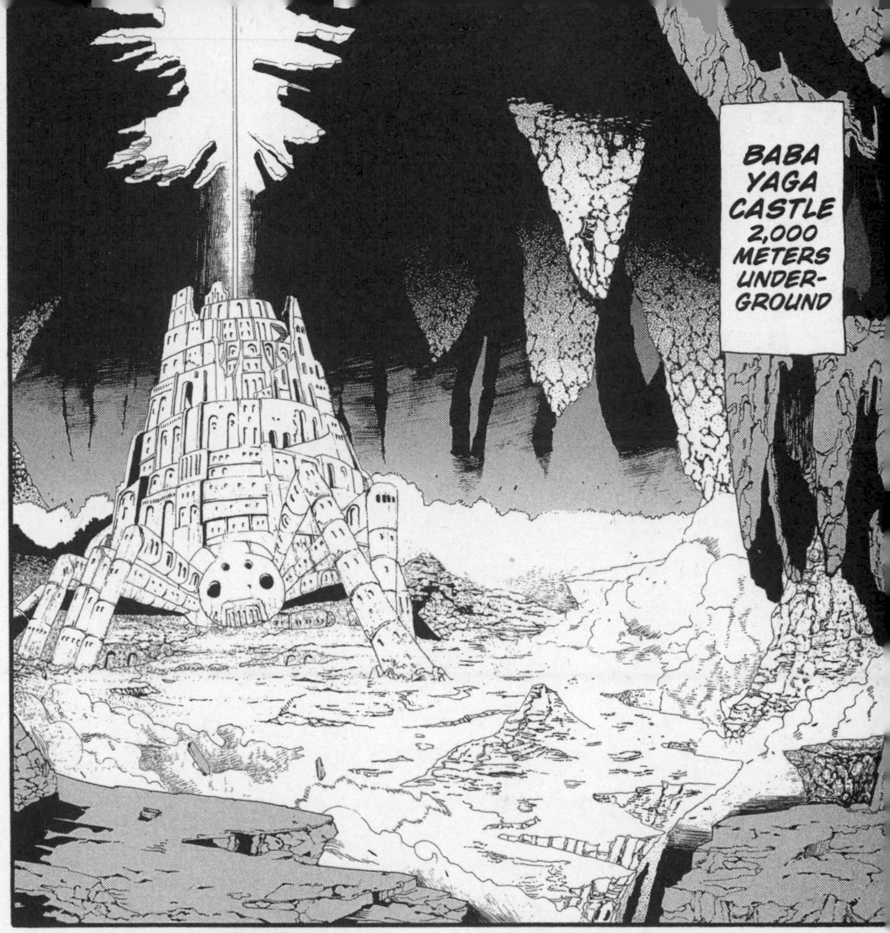
BABA YAGA CASTLE 2,000 METERS UNDER-GROUND
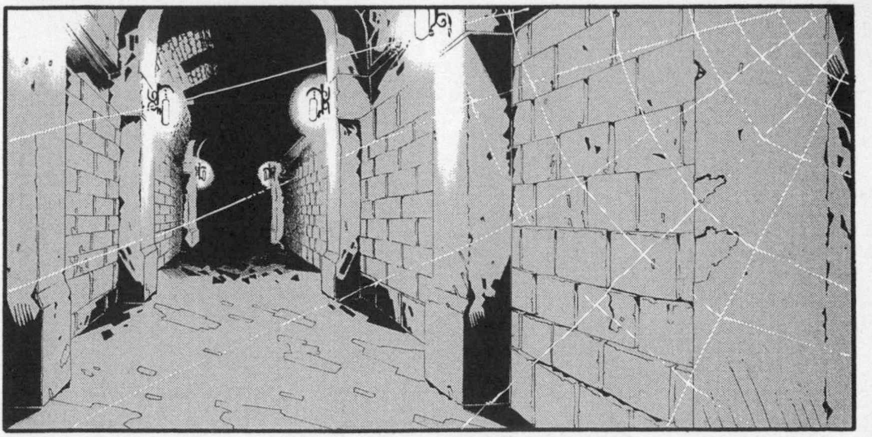

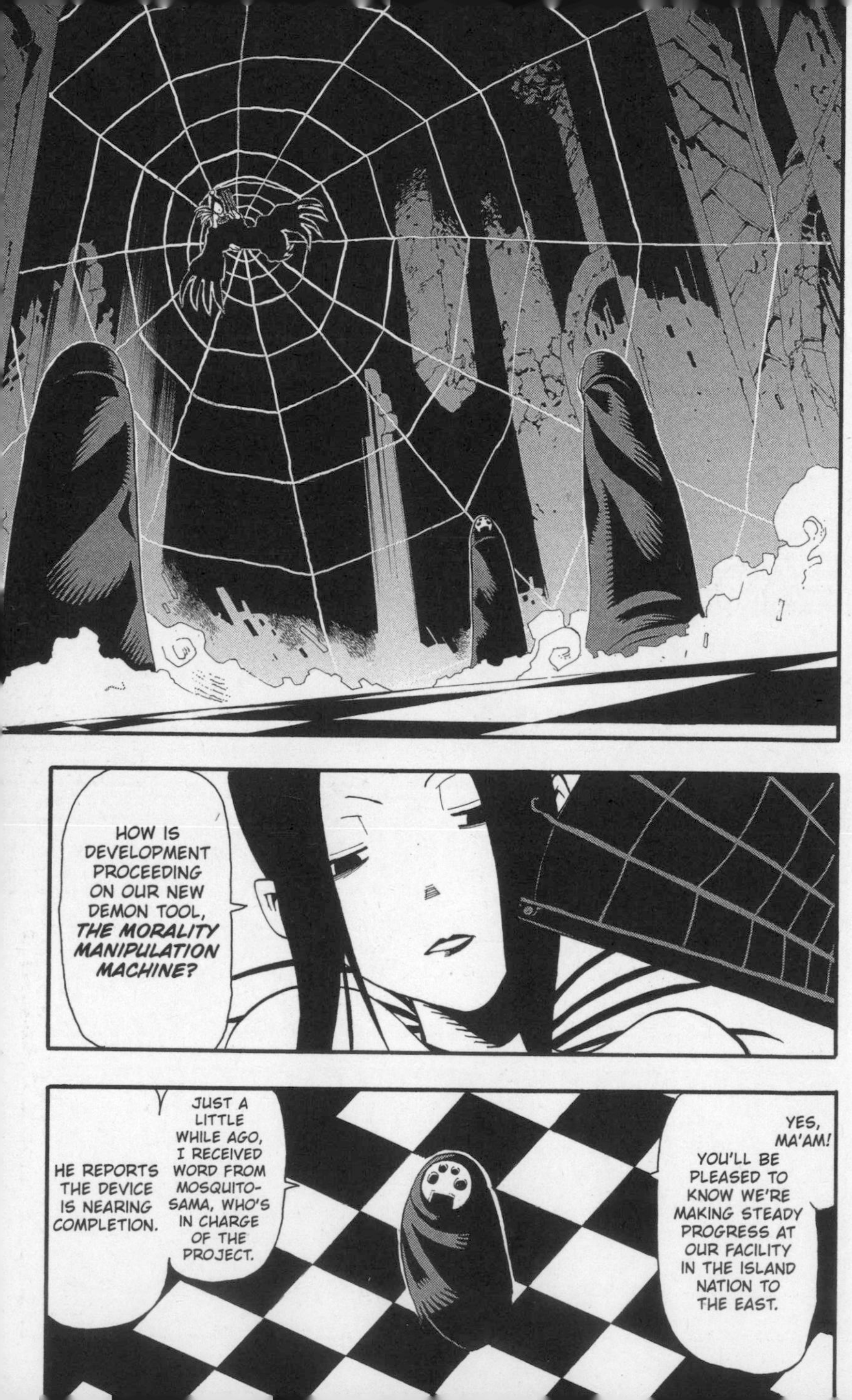
HOW IS DEVELOPMENT PROCEEDING ON OUR NEW DEMON TOOL, ***THE MORALITY MANIPULATION MACHINE?***
YES, MA'AM! YOU'LL BE PLEASED TO KNOW WE'RE MAKING STEADY PROGRESS AT OUR FACILITY IN THE ISLAND NATION TO THE EAST.
JUST A LITTLE WHILE AGO, I RECEIVED WORD FROM MOSQUITO-SAMA, WHO'S IN CHARGE OF THE PROJECT.
HE REPORTS THE DEVICE IS NEARING COMPLETION.

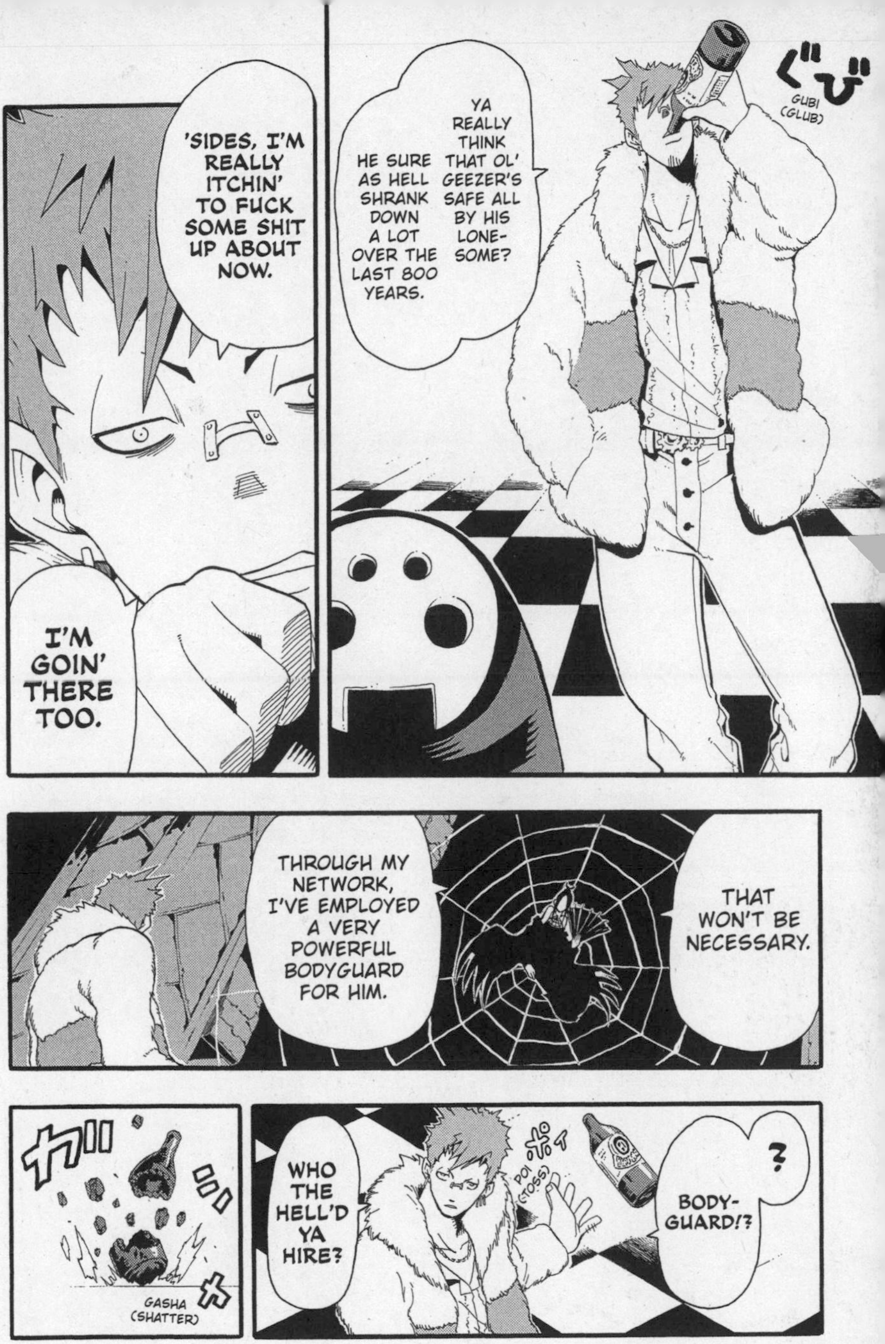
ぐび
GUBI (GLUB)
YA REALLY THINK THAT OL' GEEZER'S SAFE ALL BY HIS LONE-SOME?
HE SURE AS HELL SHRANK DOWN A LOT OVER THE LAST 800 YEARS.
'SIDES, I'M REALLY ITCHIN' TO FUCK SOME SHIT UP ABOUT NOW.
I'M GOIN' THERE TOO.
THAT WON'T BE NECESSARY.
THROUGH MY NETWORK, I'VE EMPLOYED A VERY POWERFUL BODYGUARD FOR HIM.
?
BODY-GUARD!?
ポイ
POI (TOSS)
WHO THE HELL'D YA HIRE?
GASHA (SHATTER)

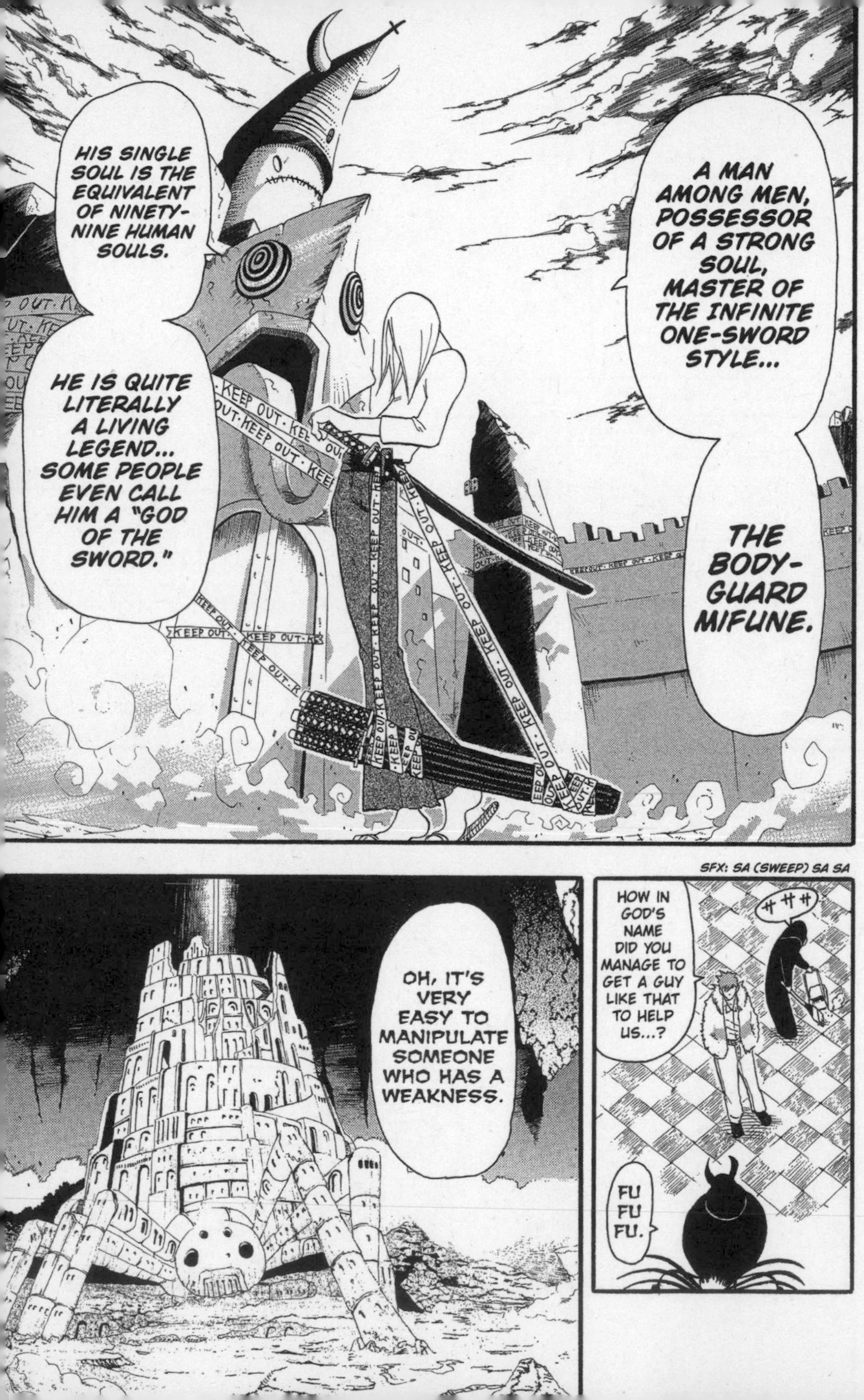
A MAN AMONG MEN, POSSESSOR OF A STRONG SOUL, MASTER OF THE INFINITE ONE-SWORD STYLE...
THE BODY-GUARD MIFUNE.
HIS SINGLE SOUL IS THE EQUIVALENT OF NINETY-NINE HUMAN SOULS.
HE IS QUITE LITERALLY A LIVING LEGEND... SOME PEOPLE EVEN CALL HIM A "GOD OF THE SWORD."
SFX: SA (SWEEP) SA SA
HOW IN GOD'S NAME DID YOU MANAGE TO GET A GUY LIKE THAT TO HELP US...?
FU FU FU.
OH, IT'S VERY EASY TO MANIPULATE SOMEONE WHO HAS A WEAKNESS.

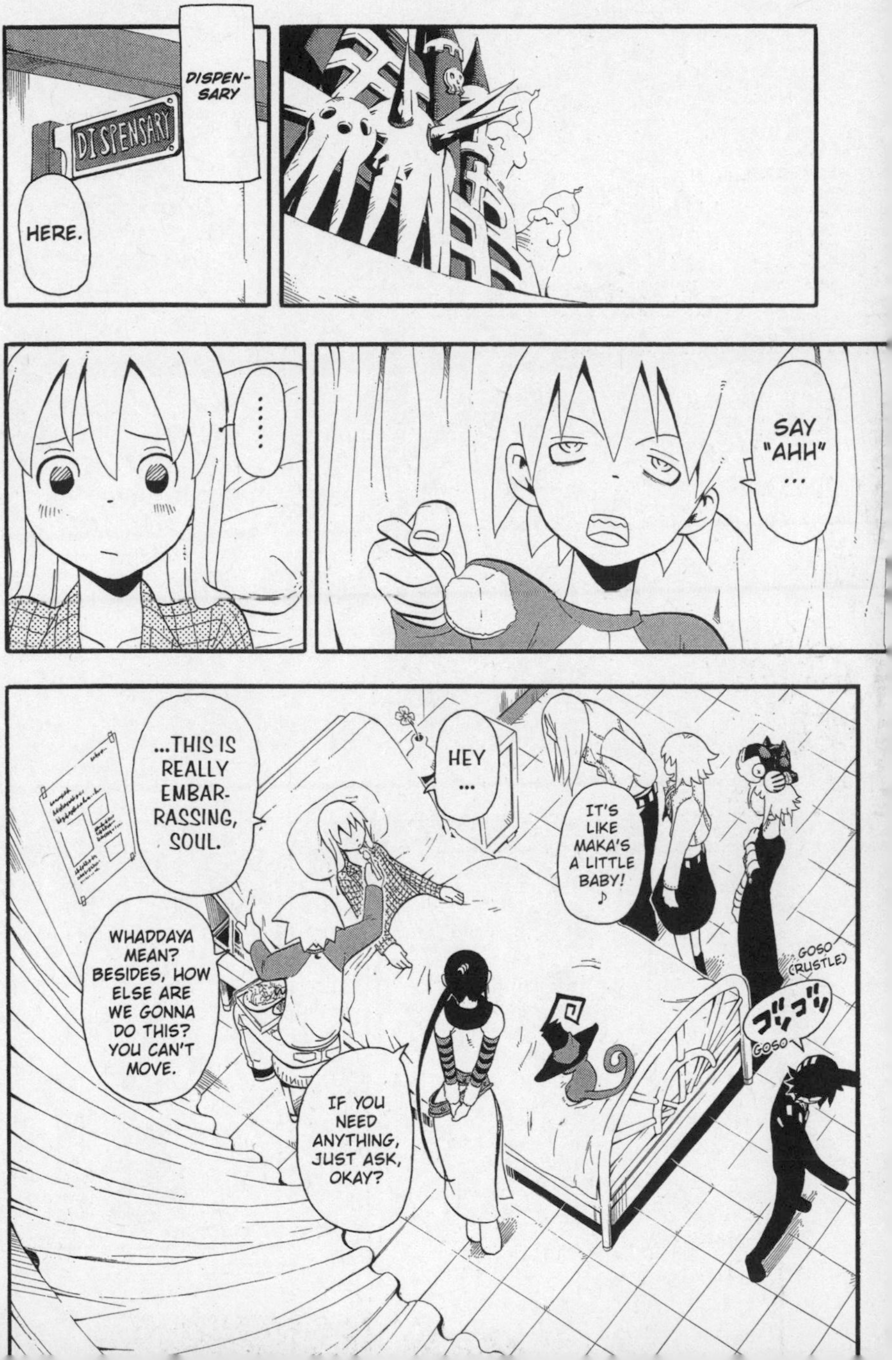
DISPEN-SARY
DISPENSARY
HERE.
SAY "AHH" ...
......
HEY ...
IT'S LIKE MAKA'S A LITTLE BABY! ♪
...THIS IS REALLY EMBARRASSING, SOUL.
GOSO (RUSTLE)
GOSO
WHADDAYA MEAN? BESIDES, HOW ELSE ARE WE GONNA DO THIS? YOU CAN'T MOVE.
IF YOU NEED ANYTHING, JUST ASK, OKAY?

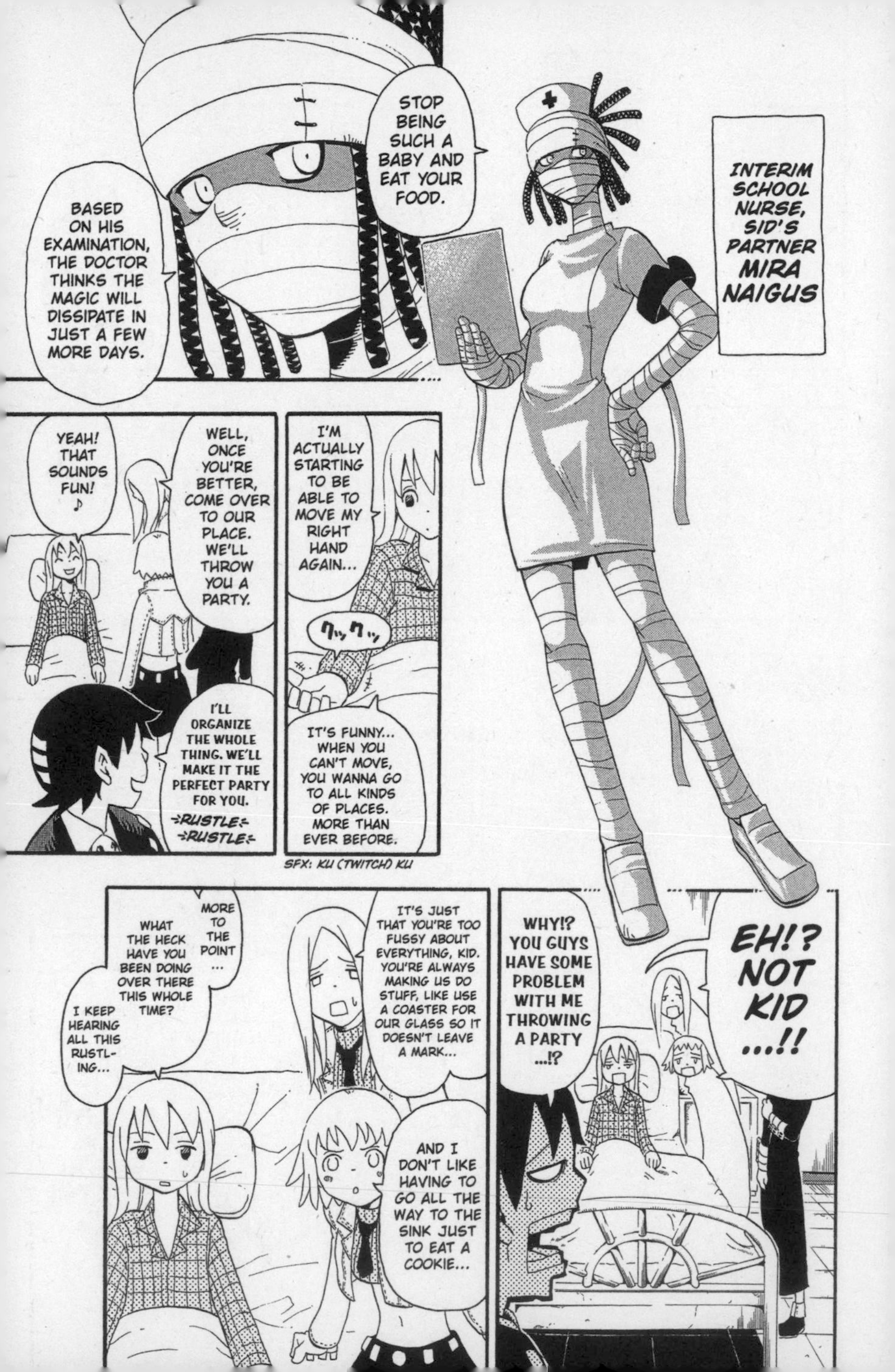
INTERIM SCHOOL NURSE, SID'S PARTNER MIRA NAIGUS
STOP BEING SUCH A BABY AND EAT YOUR FOOD.
BASED ON HIS EXAMINATION, THE DOCTOR THINKS THE MAGIC WILL DISSIPATE IN JUST A FEW MORE DAYS.
.....
I'M ACTUALLY STARTING TO BE ABLE TO MOVE MY RIGHT HAND AGAIN...
クッ, クッ
IT'S FUNNY... WHEN YOU CAN'T MOVE, YOU WANNA GO TO ALL KINDS OF PLACES. MORE THAN EVER BEFORE.
WELL, ONCE YOU'RE BETTER, COME OVER TO OUR PLACE. WE'LL THROW YOU A PARTY.
YEAH! THAT SOUNDS FUN! ♪
I'LL ORGANIZE THE WHOLE THING. WE'LL MAKE IT THE PERFECT PARTY FOR YOU.
RUSTLE RUSTLE
SFX: KU (TWITCH) KU
EH!? NOT KID ...!!
WHY!? YOU GUYS HAVE SOME PROBLEM WITH ME THROWING A PARTY ...!?
IT'S JUST THAT YOU'RE TOO FUSSY ABOUT EVERYTHING, KID. YOU'RE ALWAYS MAKING US DO STUFF, LIKE USE A COASTER FOR OUR GLASS SO IT DOESN'T LEAVE A MARK...
AND I DON'T LIKE HAVING TO GO ALL THE WAY TO THE SINK JUST TO EAT A COOKIE...
MORE TO THE POINT ...
WHAT THE HECK HAVE YOU BEEN DOING OVER THERE THIS WHOLE TIME?
I KEEP HEARING ALL THIS RUSTL-ING...

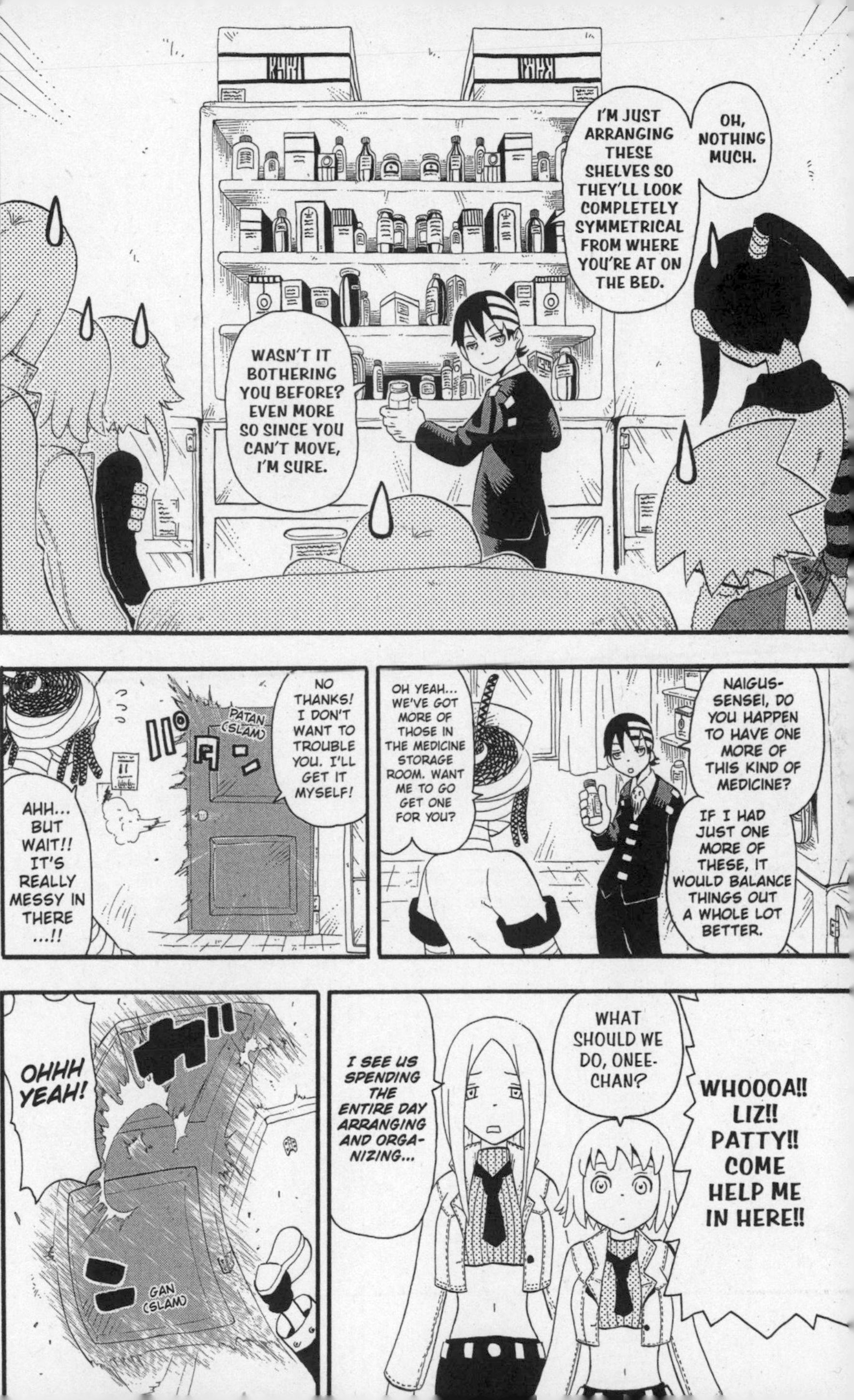
OH, NOTHING MUCH.
I'M JUST ARRANGING THESE SHELVES SO THEY'LL LOOK COMPLETELY SYMMETRICAL FROM WHERE YOU'RE AT ON THE BED.
WASN'T IT BOTHERING YOU BEFORE? EVEN MORE SO SINCE YOU CAN'T MOVE, I'M SURE.
NAIGUS-SENSEI, DO YOU HAPPEN TO HAVE ONE MORE OF THIS KIND OF MEDICINE?
IF I HAD JUST ONE MORE OF THESE, IT WOULD BALANCE THINGS OUT A WHOLE LOT BETTER.
OH YEAH... WE'VE GOT MORE OF THOSE IN THE MEDICINE STORAGE ROOM. WANT ME TO GO GET ONE FOR YOU?
NO THANKS! I DON'T WANT TO TROUBLE YOU. I'LL GET IT MYSELF!
PATAN (SLAM)
AHH... BUT WAIT!! IT'S REALLY MESSY IN THERE ...!!
WHOOOA!! LIZ!! PATTY!! COME HELP ME IN HERE!!
WHAT SHOULD WE DO, ONEE-CHAN?
I SEE US SPENDING THE ENTIRE DAY ARRANGING AND ORGA-NIZING...
OHHH YEAH!
GAN (SLAM)

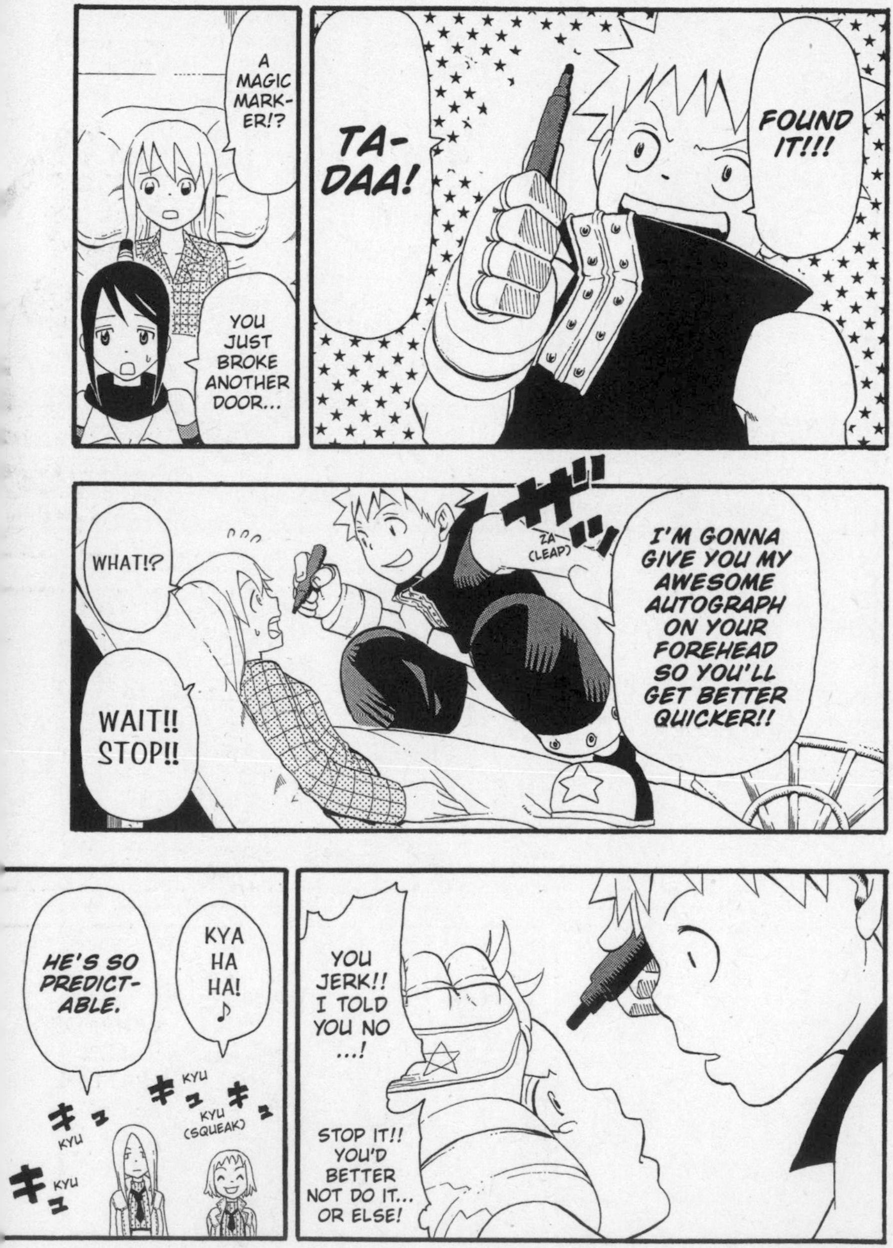
FOUND IT!!!
TA-DAA!
A MAGIC MARKER!?
YOU JUST BROKE ANOTHER DOOR...
ZA (LEAP)
I'M GONNA GIVE YOU MY AWESOME AUTOGRAPH ON YOUR FOREHEAD SO YOU'LL GET BETTER QUICKER!!
WHAT!?
WAIT!! STOP!!
YOU JERK!! I TOLD YOU NO ...!
STOP IT!! YOU'D BETTER NOT DO IT... OR ELSE!
KYA HA HA! ♪
HE'S SO PREDICT-ABLE.
KYU
KYU (SQUEAK)
KYU
KYU

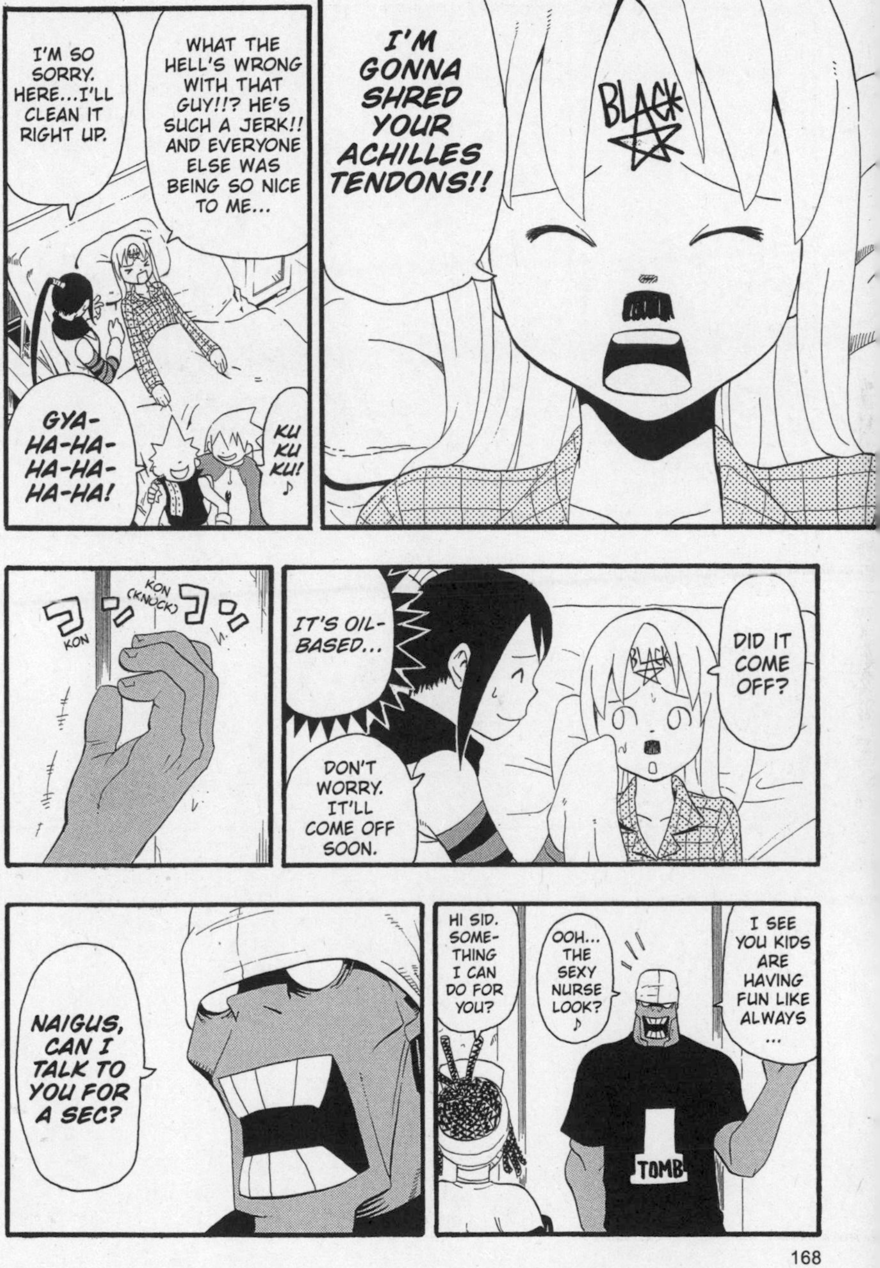
I'M GONNA SHRED YOUR ACHILLES TENDONS!!
BLACK☆
WHAT THE HELL'S WRONG WITH THAT GUY!!? HE'S SUCH A JERK!! AND EVERYONE ELSE WAS BEING SO NICE TO ME...
I'M SO SORRY. HERE...I'LL CLEAN IT RIGHT UP.
KU KU KU! ♪
GYA-HA-HA-HA-HA-HA-HA!
DID IT COME OFF?
BLACK☆
IT'S OIL-BASED...
DON'T WORRY. IT'LL COME OFF SOON.
KON (KNOCK)
KON
I SEE YOU KIDS ARE HAVING FUN LIKE ALWAYS ...
OOH... THE SEXY NURSE LOOK? ♪
HI SID. SOMETHING I CAN DO FOR YOU?
TOMB
NAIGUS, CAN I TALK TO YOU FOR A SEC?

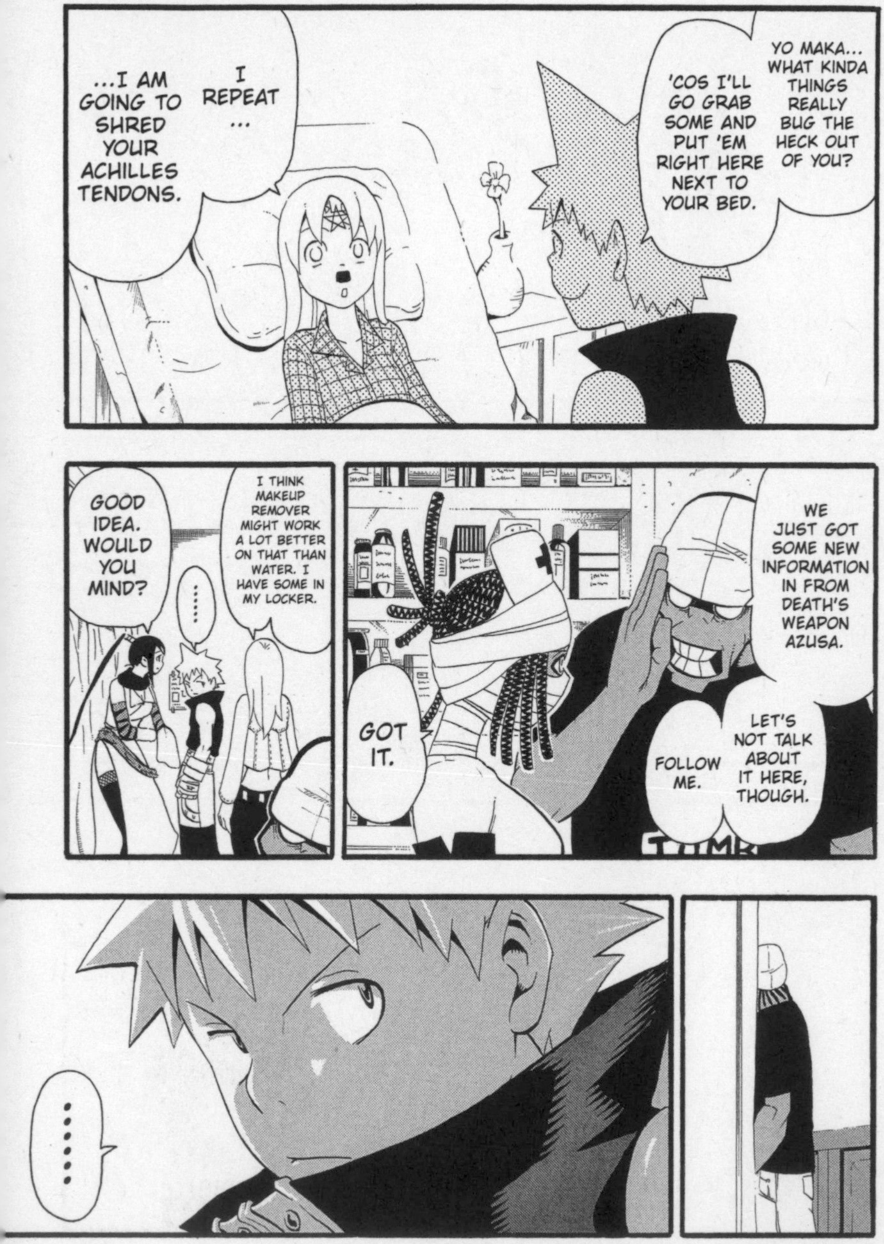
YO MAKA... WHAT KINDA THINGS REALLY BUG THE HECK OUT OF YOU?
'COS I'LL GO GRAB SOME AND PUT 'EM RIGHT HERE NEXT TO YOUR BED.
I REPEAT ...
...I AM GOING TO SHRED YOUR ACHILLES TENDONS.
WE JUST GOT SOME NEW INFORMATION IN FROM DEATH'S WEAPON AZUSA.
LET'S NOT TALK ABOUT IT HERE, THOUGH.
FOLLOW ME.
GOT IT.
I THINK MAKEUP REMOVER MIGHT WORK A LOT BETTER ON THAT THAN WATER. I HAVE SOME IN MY LOCKER.
......
GOOD IDEA. WOULD YOU MIND?
......

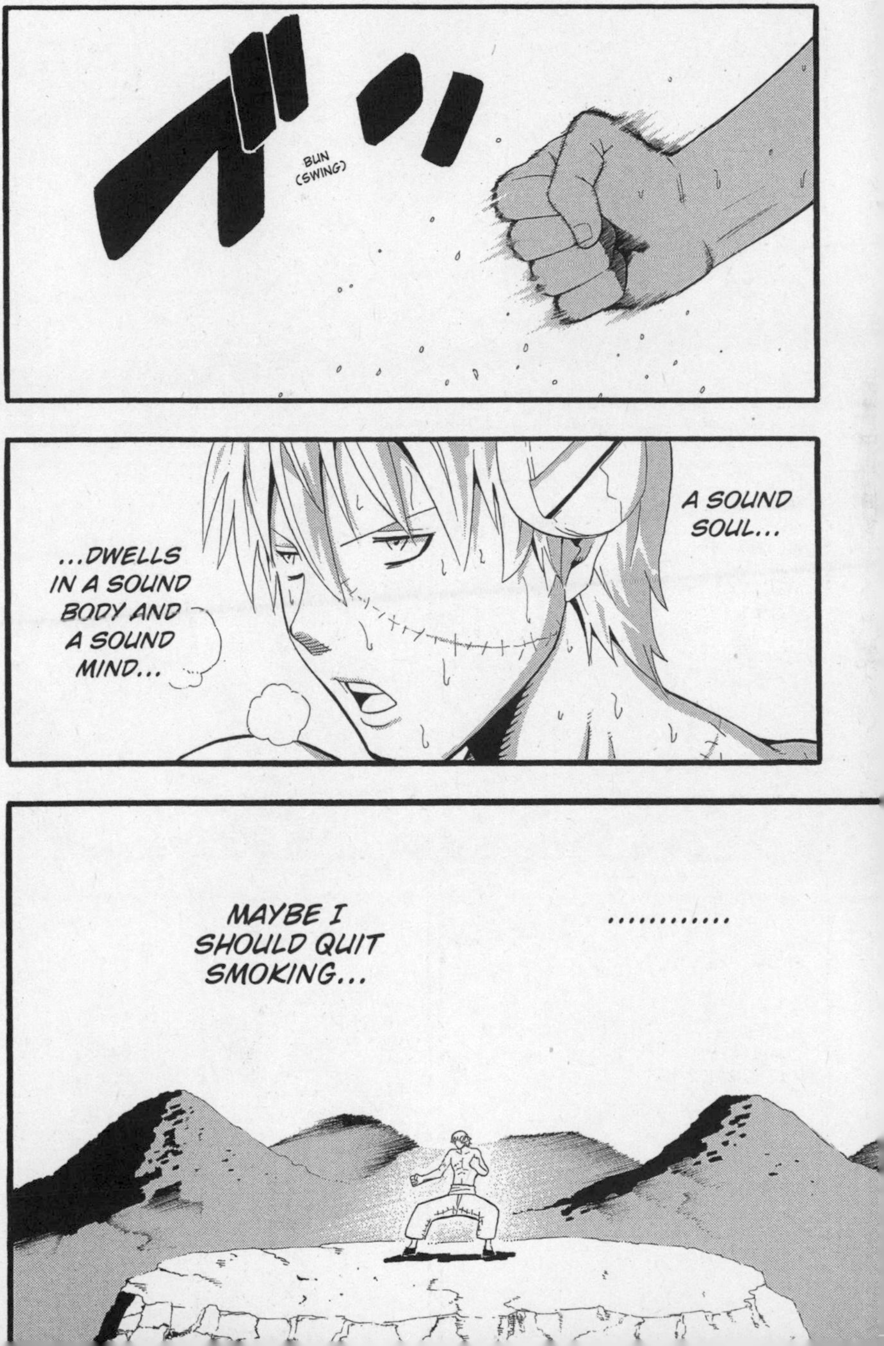
BUN (SWING)
A SOUND SOUL...
...DWELLS IN A SOUND BODY AND A SOUND MIND...
....
MAYBE I SHOULD QUIT SMOKING...

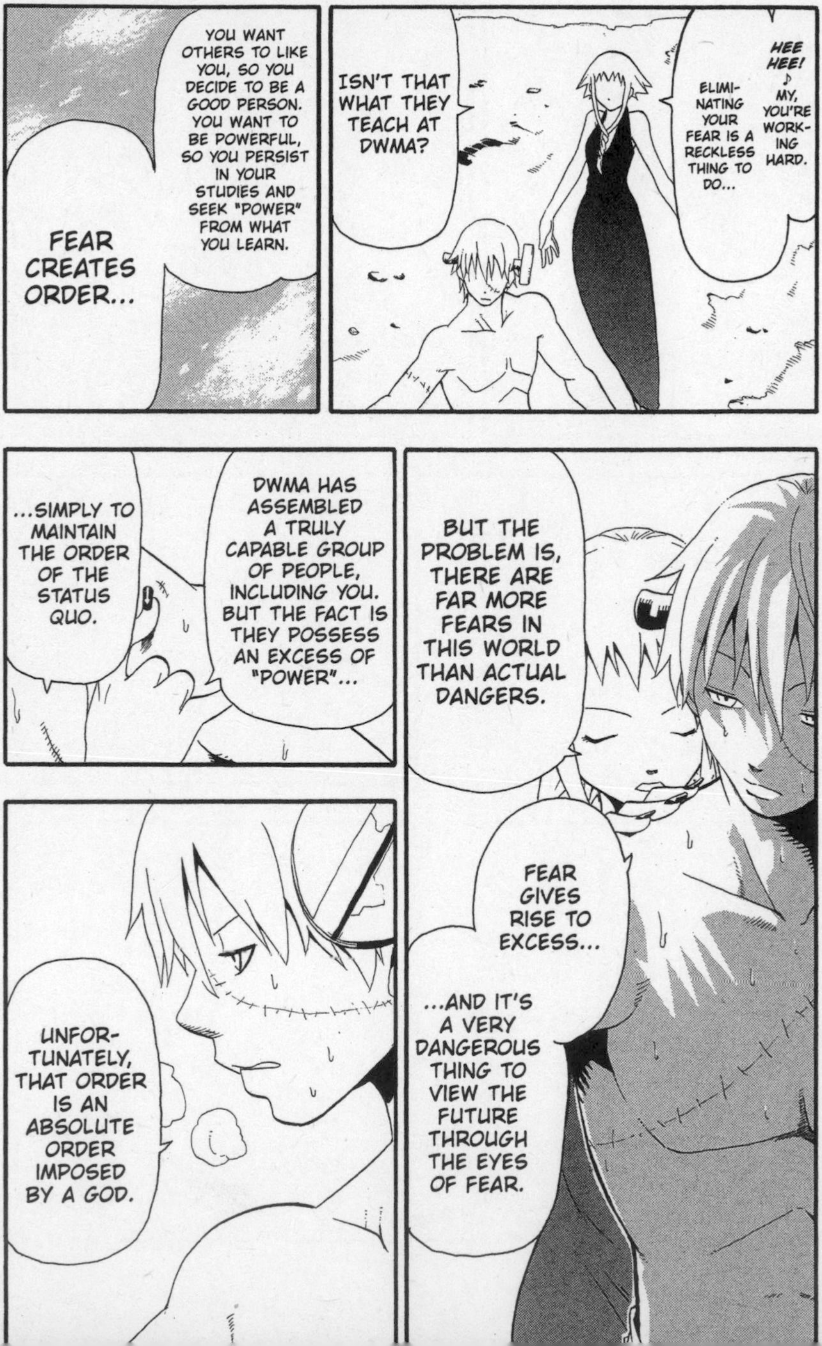
HEE HEE! ♪ MY, YOU'RE WORKING HARD.
ELIMINATING YOUR FEAR IS A RECKLESS THING TO DO...
ISN'T THAT WHAT THEY TEACH AT DWMA?
YOU WANT OTHERS TO LIKE YOU, SO YOU DECIDE TO BE A GOOD PERSON. YOU WANT TO BE POWERFUL, SO YOU PERSIST IN YOUR STUDIES AND SEEK "POWER" FROM WHAT YOU LEARN.
FEAR CREATES ORDER...
BUT THE PROBLEM IS, THERE ARE FAR MORE FEARS IN THIS WORLD THAN ACTUAL DANGERS.
FEAR GIVES RISE TO EXCESS...
...AND IT'S A VERY DANGEROUS THING TO VIEW THE FUTURE THROUGH THE EYES OF FEAR.
DWMA HAS ASSEMBLED A TRULY CAPABLE GROUP OF PEOPLE, INCLUDING YOU. BUT THE FACT IS THEY POSSESS AN EXCESS OF "POWER"...
...SIMPLY TO MAINTAIN THE ORDER OF THE STATUS QUO.
UNFORTUNATELY, THAT ORDER IS AN ABSOLUTE ORDER IMPOSED BY A GOD.

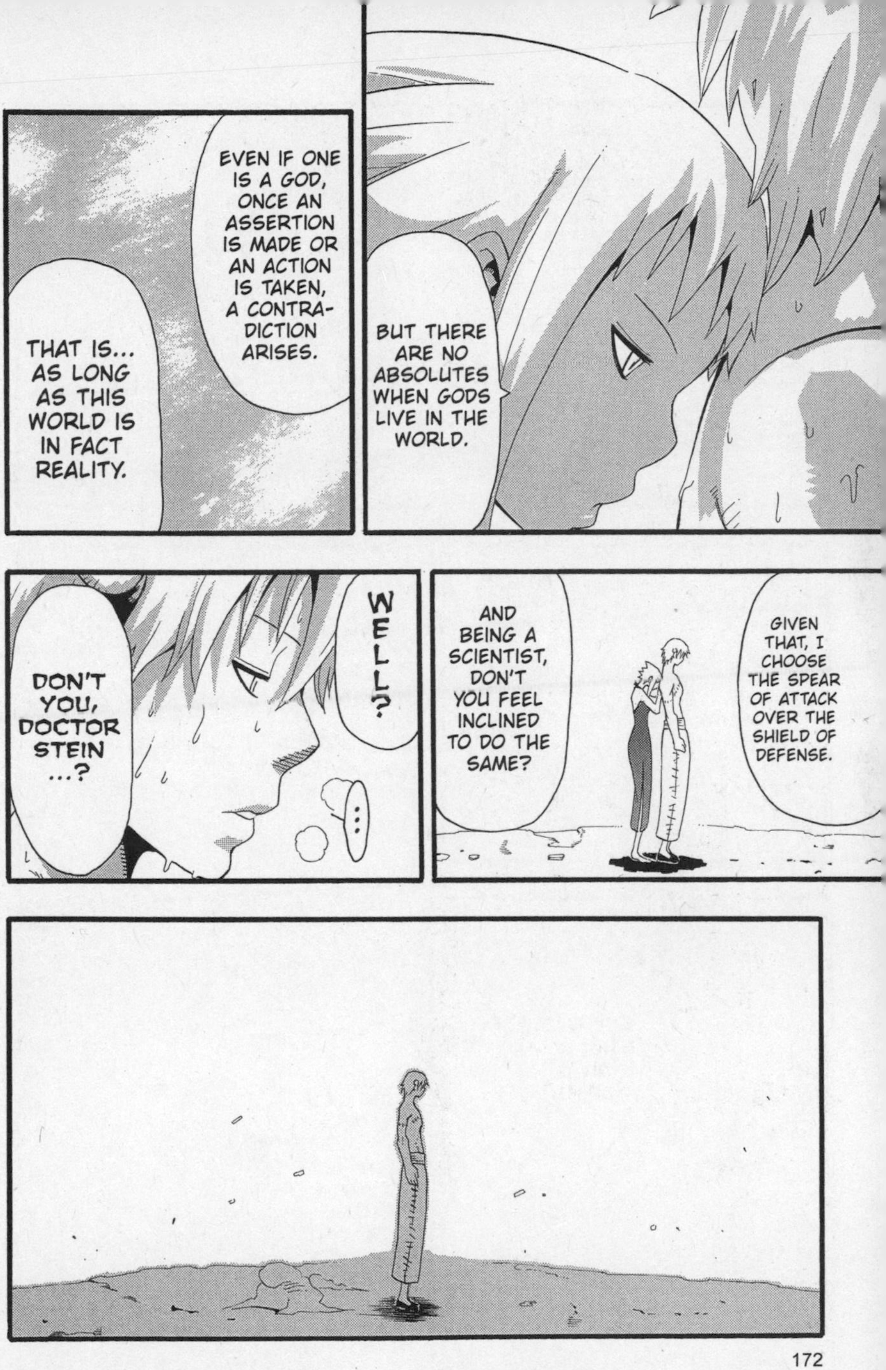
BUT THERE ARE NO ABSOLUTES WHEN GODS LIVE IN THE WORLD.
EVEN IF ONE IS A GOD, ONCE AN ASSERTION IS MADE OR AN ACTION IS TAKEN, A CONTRA-DICTION ARISES.
THAT IS... AS LONG AS THIS WORLD IS IN FACT REALITY.
GIVEN THAT, I CHOOSE THE SPEAR OF ATTACK OVER THE SHIELD OF DEFENSE.
AND BEING A SCIENTIST, DON'T YOU FEEL INCLINED TO DO THE SAME?
WELL?
...
DON'T YOU, DOCTOR STEIN ...?

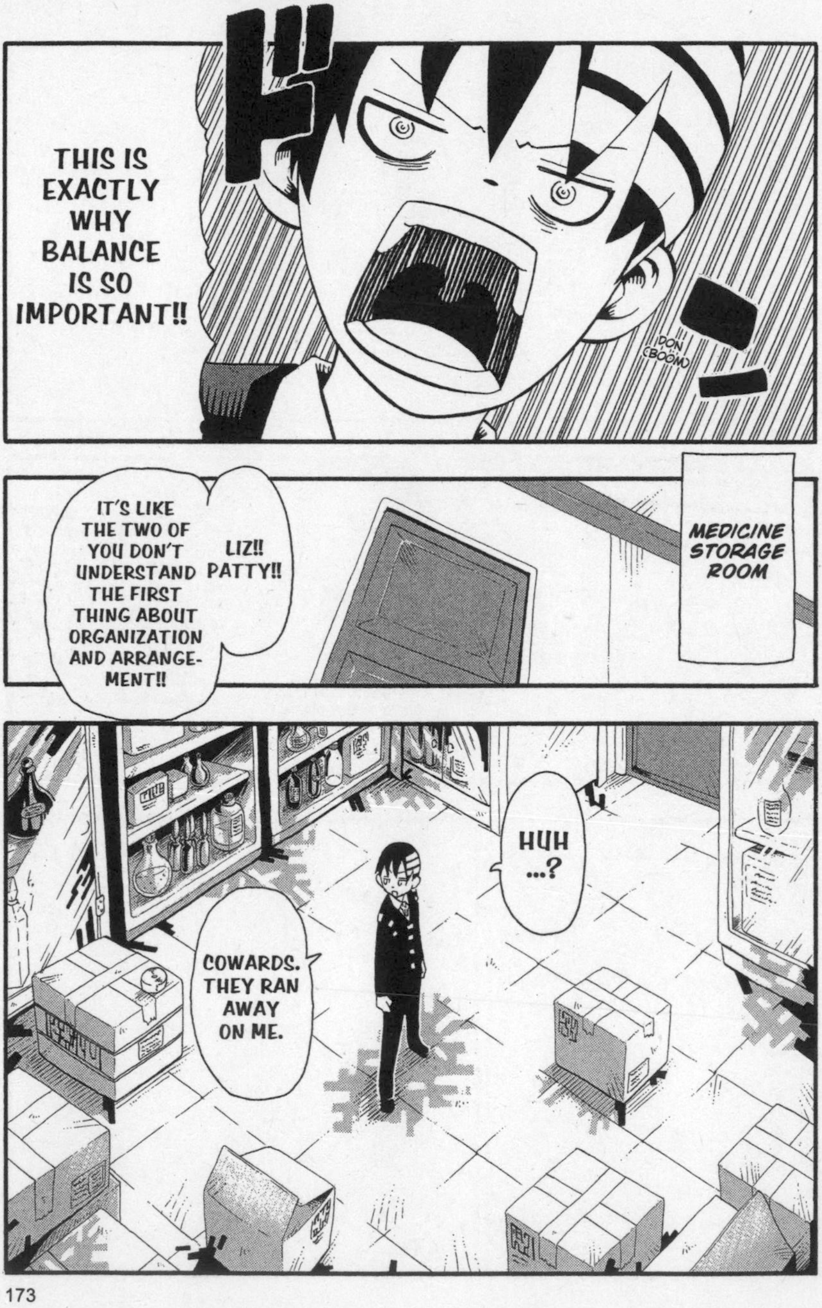
THIS IS EXACTLY WHY BALANCE IS SO IMPORTANT!!
DON (BOOM)
MEDICINE STORAGE ROOM
LIZ!! PATTY!!
IT'S LIKE THE TWO OF YOU DON'T UNDERSTAND THE FIRST THING ABOUT ORGANIZATION AND ARRANGE-MENT!!
HUH ...?
COWARDS. THEY RAN AWAY ON ME.

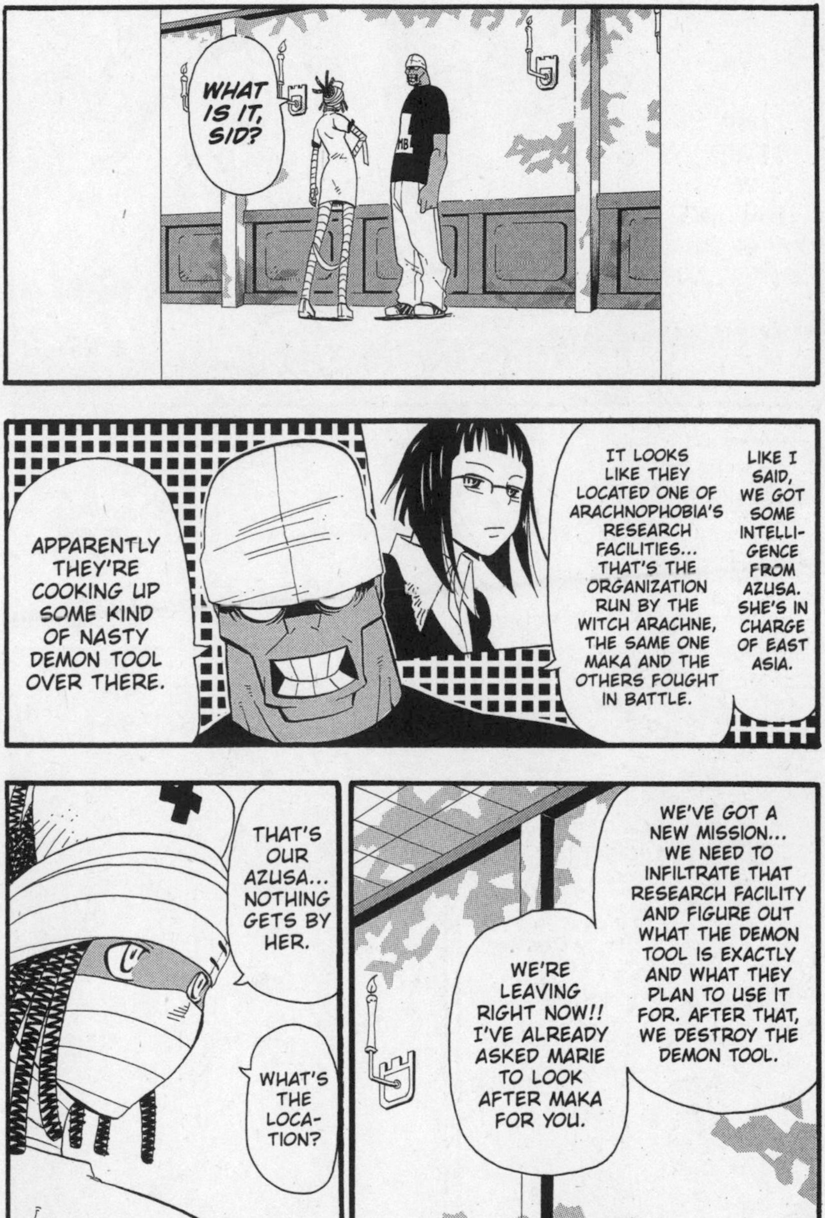
WHAT IS IT, SID?
LIKE I SAID, WE GOT SOME INTELLIGENCE FROM AZUSA. SHE'S IN CHARGE OF EAST ASIA.
IT LOOKS LIKE THEY LOCATED ONE OF ARACHNOPHOBIA'S RESEARCH FACILITIES... THAT'S THE ORGANIZATION RUN BY THE WITCH ARACHNE, THE SAME ONE MAKA AND THE OTHERS FOUGHT IN BATTLE.
APPARENTLY THEY'RE COOKING UP SOME KIND OF NASTY DEMON TOOL OVER THERE.
WE'VE GOT A NEW MISSION... WE NEED TO INFILTRATE THAT RESEARCH FACILITY AND FIGURE OUT WHAT THE DEMON TOOL IS EXACTLY AND WHAT THEY PLAN TO USE IT FOR. AFTER THAT, WE DESTROY THE DEMON TOOL.
WE'RE LEAVING RIGHT NOW!! I'VE ALREADY ASKED MARIE TO LOOK AFTER MAKA FOR YOU.
THAT'S OUR AZUSA... NOTHING GETS BY HER.
WHAT'S THE LOCATION?

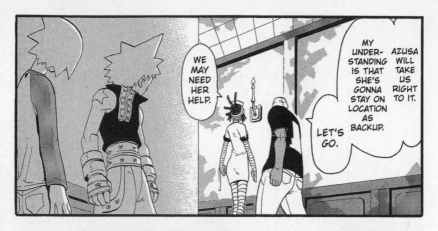

AZUSA WILL TAKE US RIGHT TO IT.
MY UNDERSTANDING IS THAT SHE'S GONNA STAY ON LOCATION AS BACKUP.
LET'S GO.
WE MAY NEED HER HELP.
SOUL... GO GET TSUBAKI FOR ME.
!!
BLACK☆STAR, WHAT'S GOING...
I'M GONNA FOLLOW SID AND MIRA TO THAT RESEARCH FACILITY. THEN I'M GONNA BLOW IT TO SMITHEREENS.
THAT'S CRAZY! YOU CAN'T DO THAT! I SAW THAT WITCH WITH MY OWN EYES, MAN.
...AND SHE AIN'T YOUR AVERAGE WITCH.

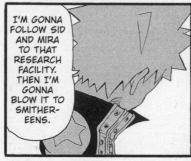

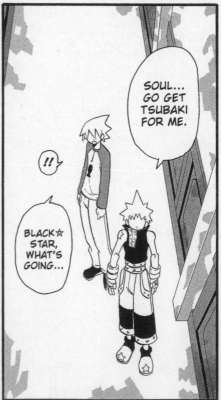

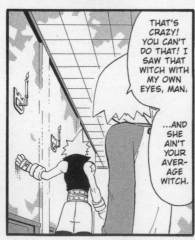

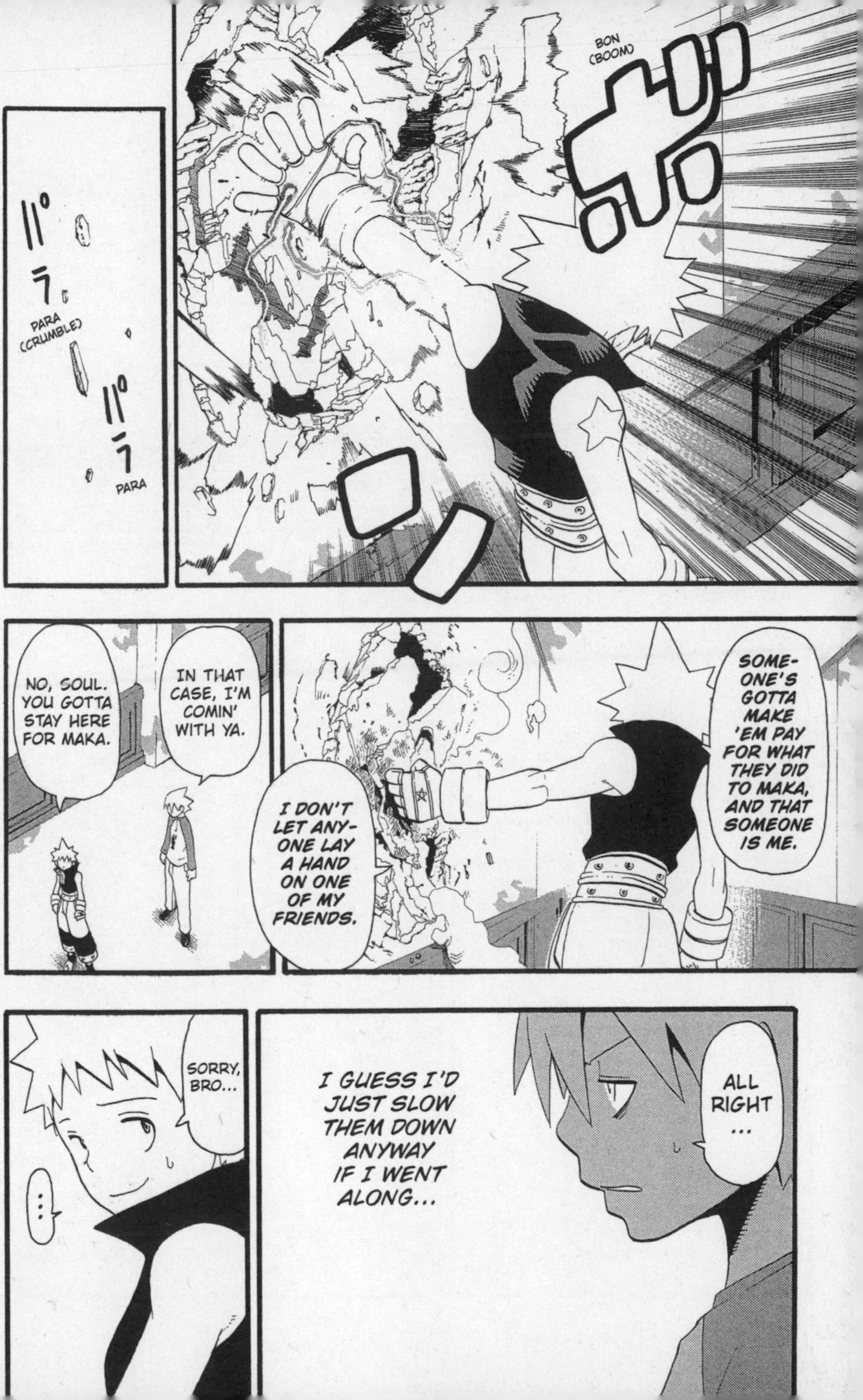

BON
(BOOM)
PARA
(CRUMBLE)
PARA
SOME-ONE'S GOTTA MAKE 'EM PAY FOR WHAT THEY DID TO MAKA, AND THAT SOMEONE IS ME.
I DON'T LET ANY-ONE LAY A HAND ON ONE OF MY FRIENDS.
IN THAT CASE, I'M COMIN' WITH YA.
NO, SOUL. YOU GOTTA STAY HERE FOR MAKA.
ALL RIGHT ...
I GUESS I'D JUST SLOW THEM DOWN ANYWAY IF I WENT ALONG...
SORRY, BRO...
...

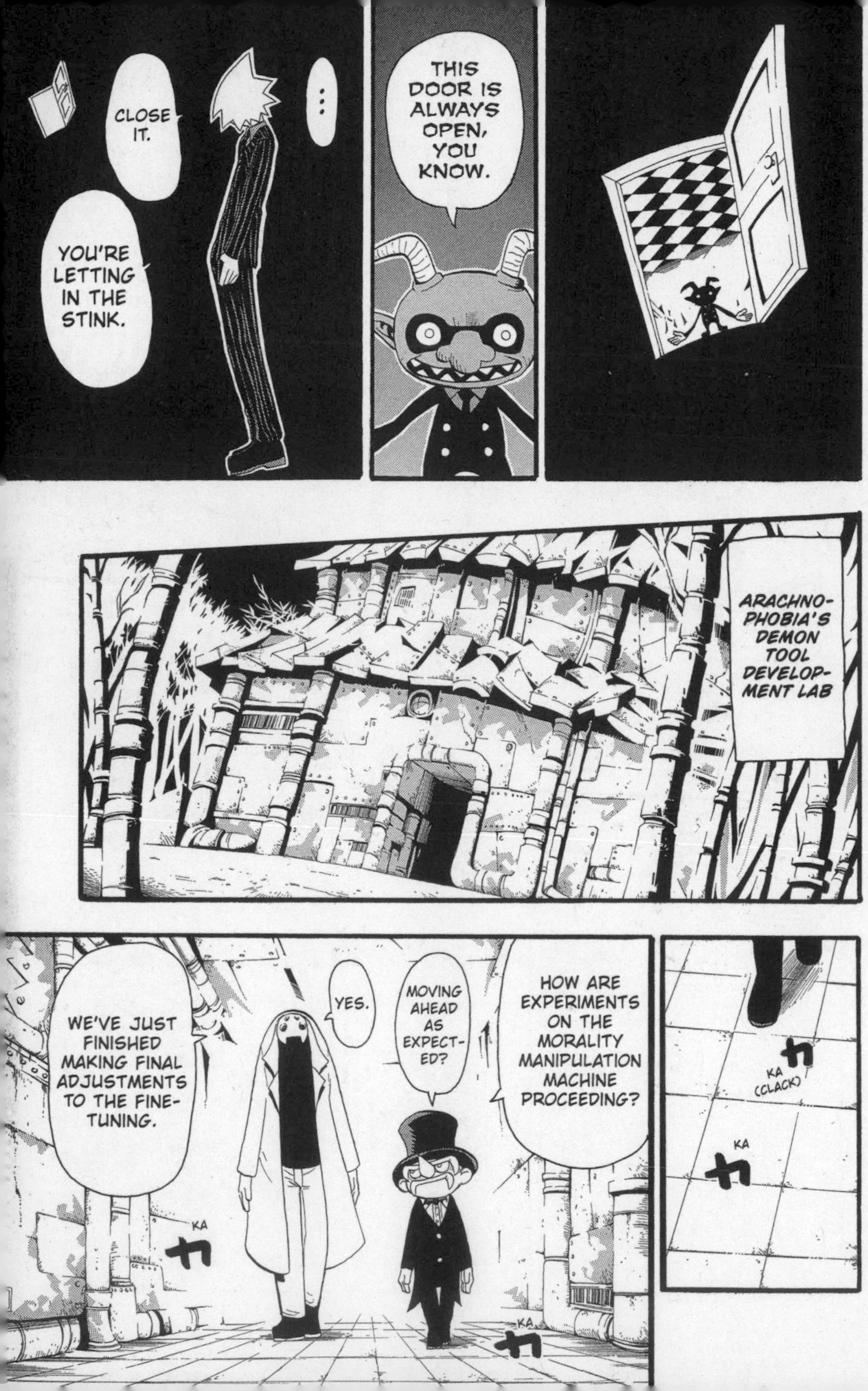
THIS DOOR IS ALWAYS OPEN, YOU KNOW.
...
CLOSE IT.
YOU'RE LETTING IN THE STINK.
ARACHNOPHOBIA'S DEMON TOOL DEVELOPMENT LAB
KA (CLACK)
KA
HOW ARE EXPERIMENTS ON THE MORALITY MANIPULATION MACHINE PROCEEDING?
MOVING AHEAD AS EXPECTED?
YES.
WE'VE JUST FINISHED MAKING FINAL ADJUSTMENTS TO THE FINE-TUNING.
KA
KA

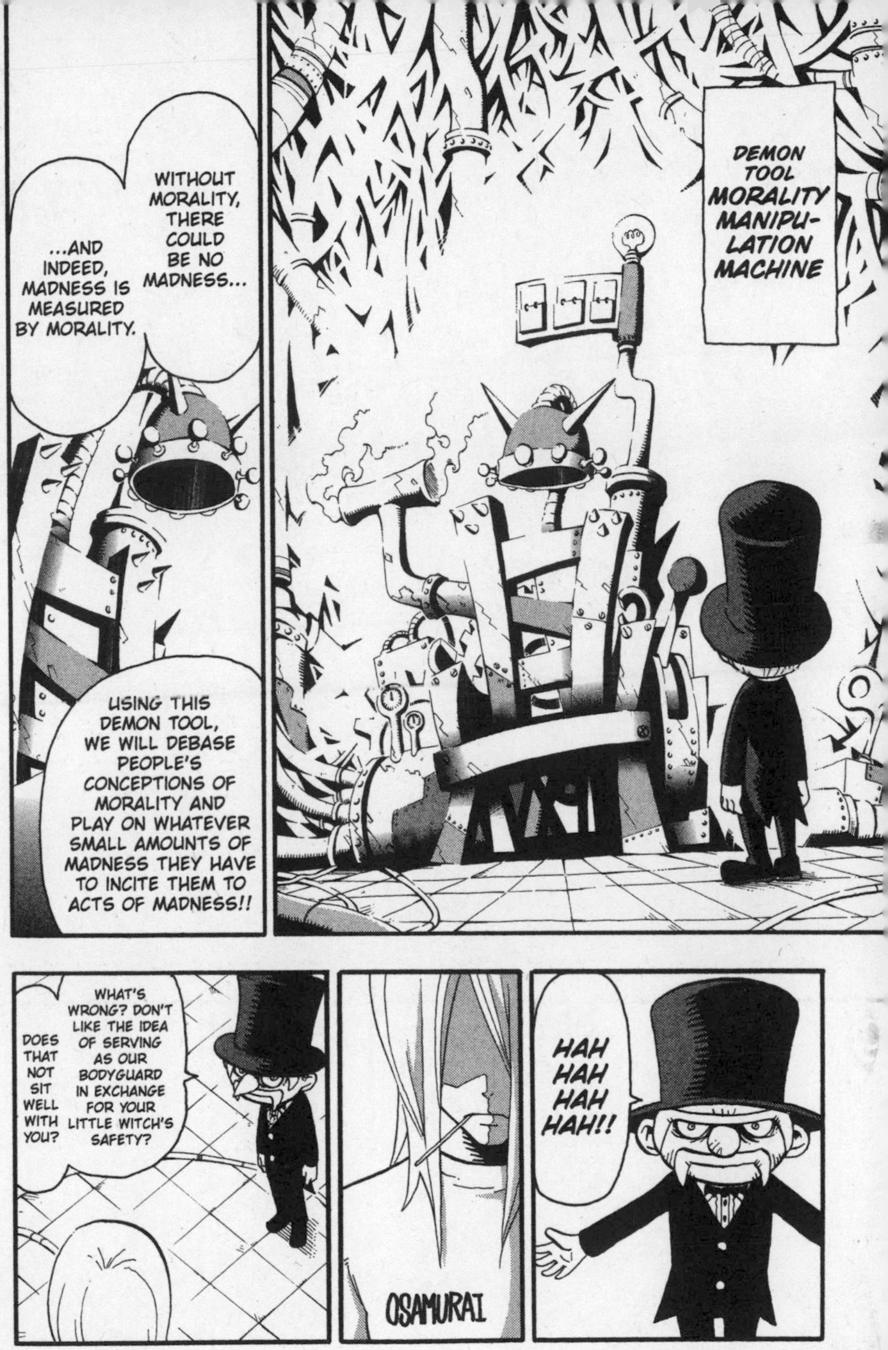
DEMON TOOL MORALITY MANIPU-LATION MACHINE
WITHOUT MORALITY, THERE COULD BE NO MADNESS...
...AND INDEED, MADNESS IS MEASURED BY MORALITY.
USING THIS DEMON TOOL, WE WILL DEBASE PEOPLE'S CONCEPTIONS OF MORALITY AND PLAY ON WHATEVER SMALL AMOUNTS OF MADNESS THEY HAVE TO INCITE THEM TO ACTS OF MADNESS!!
HAH HAH HAH HAH!!
OSAMURAI
WHAT'S WRONG? DON'T LIKE THE IDEA OF SERVING AS OUR BODYGUARD IN EXCHANGE FOR YOUR LITTLE WITCH'S SAFETY?
DOES THAT NOT SIT WELL WITH YOU?

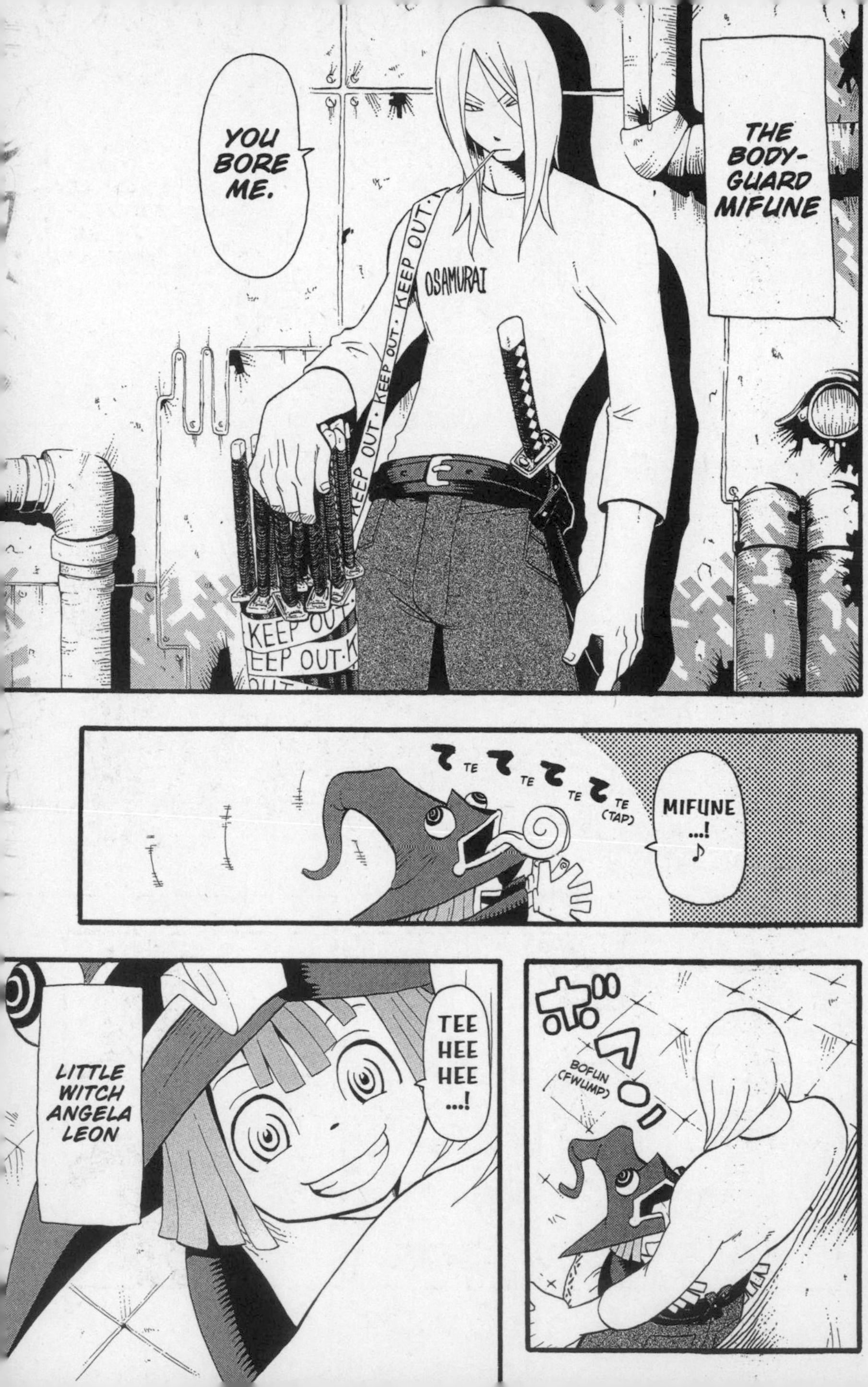
THE BODY-GUARD MIFUNE
YOU BORE ME.
OSAMURAI
KEEP OUT · KEEP OUT · KEEP OUT
KEEP OUT
KEEP OUT
TE TE TE TE (TAP)
MIFUNE ...! ♪
BOFUN (FWUMP)
TEE HEE HEE ...!
LITTLE WITCH ANGELA LEON

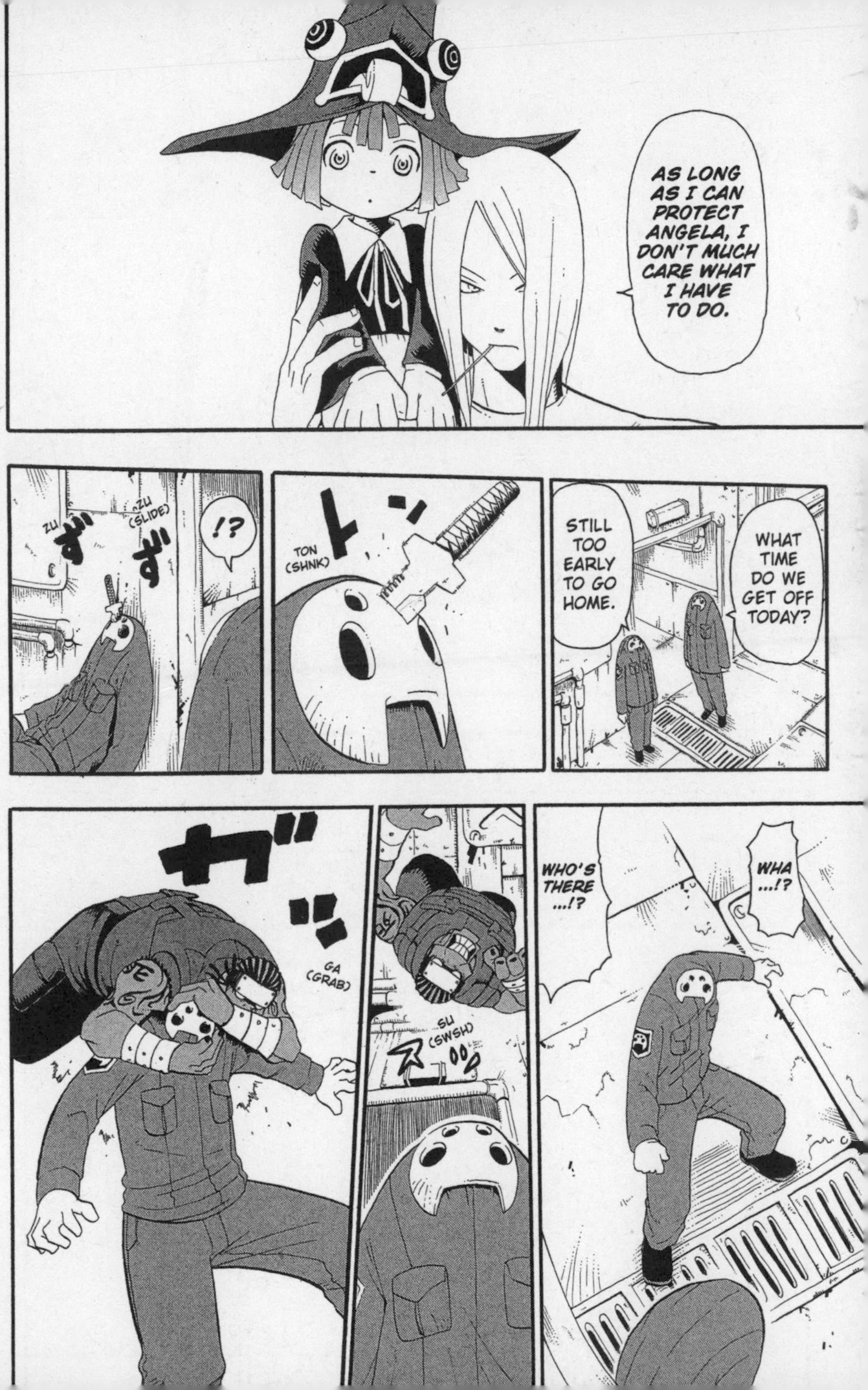
AS LONG AS I CAN PROTECT ANGELA, I DON'T MUCH CARE WHAT I HAVE TO DO.
WHAT TIME DO WE GET OFF TODAY?
STILL TOO EARLY TO GO HOME.
TON (SHNK)
!?
ZU (SLIDE)
ZU
WHA ...!?
WHO'S THERE ...!?
SU (SWSH)
GA (GRAB)

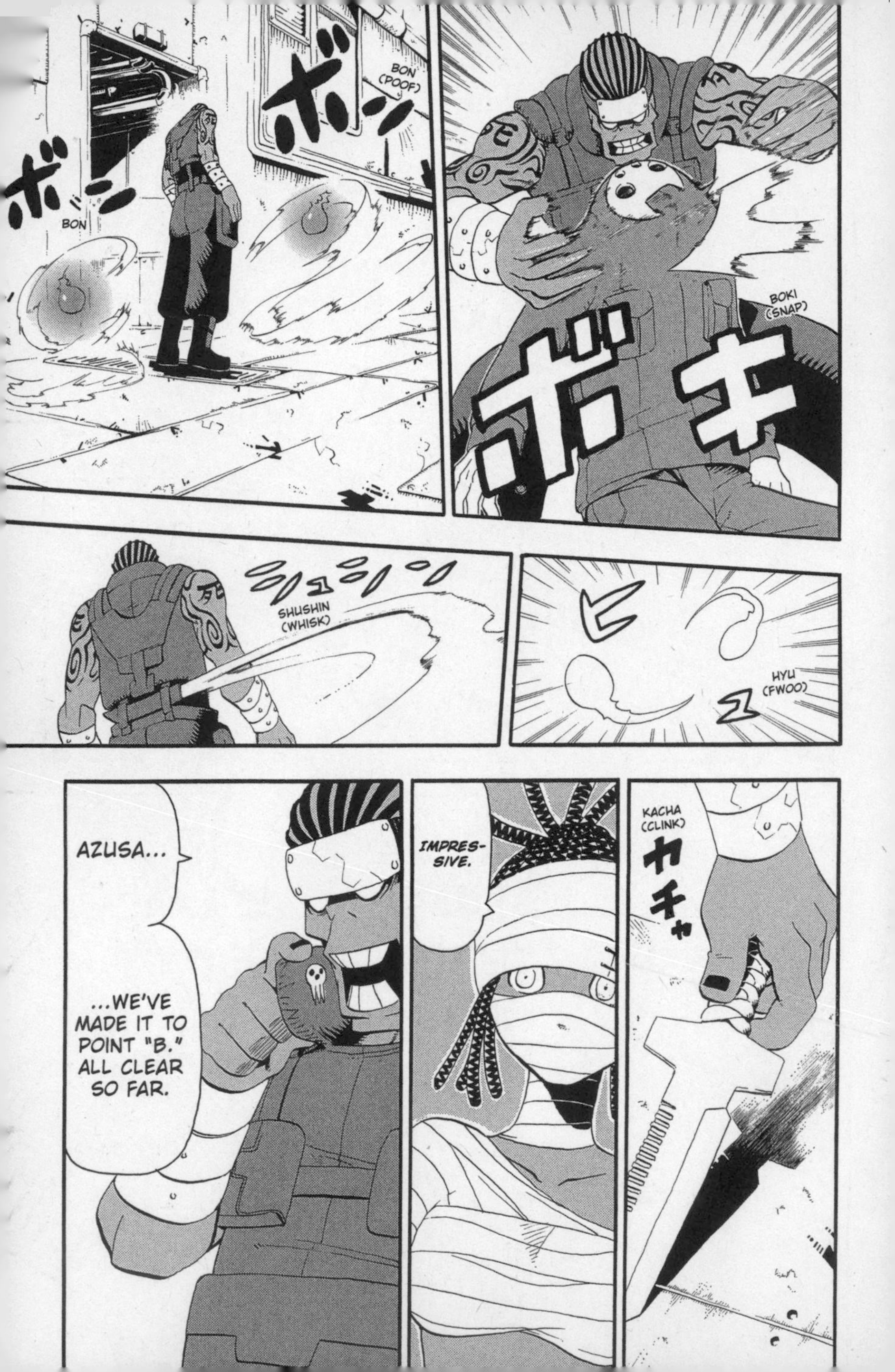
BOKI (SNAP)
ボキ
BON (POOF)
ボン
BON
ボン
HYU (FWOO)
ヒュ
SHUSHIN (WHISK)
シュシーン
KACHA (CLINK)
カチャ
IMPRES-SIVE.
AZUSA...
...WE'VE MADE IT TO POINT "B." ALL CLEAR SO FAR.

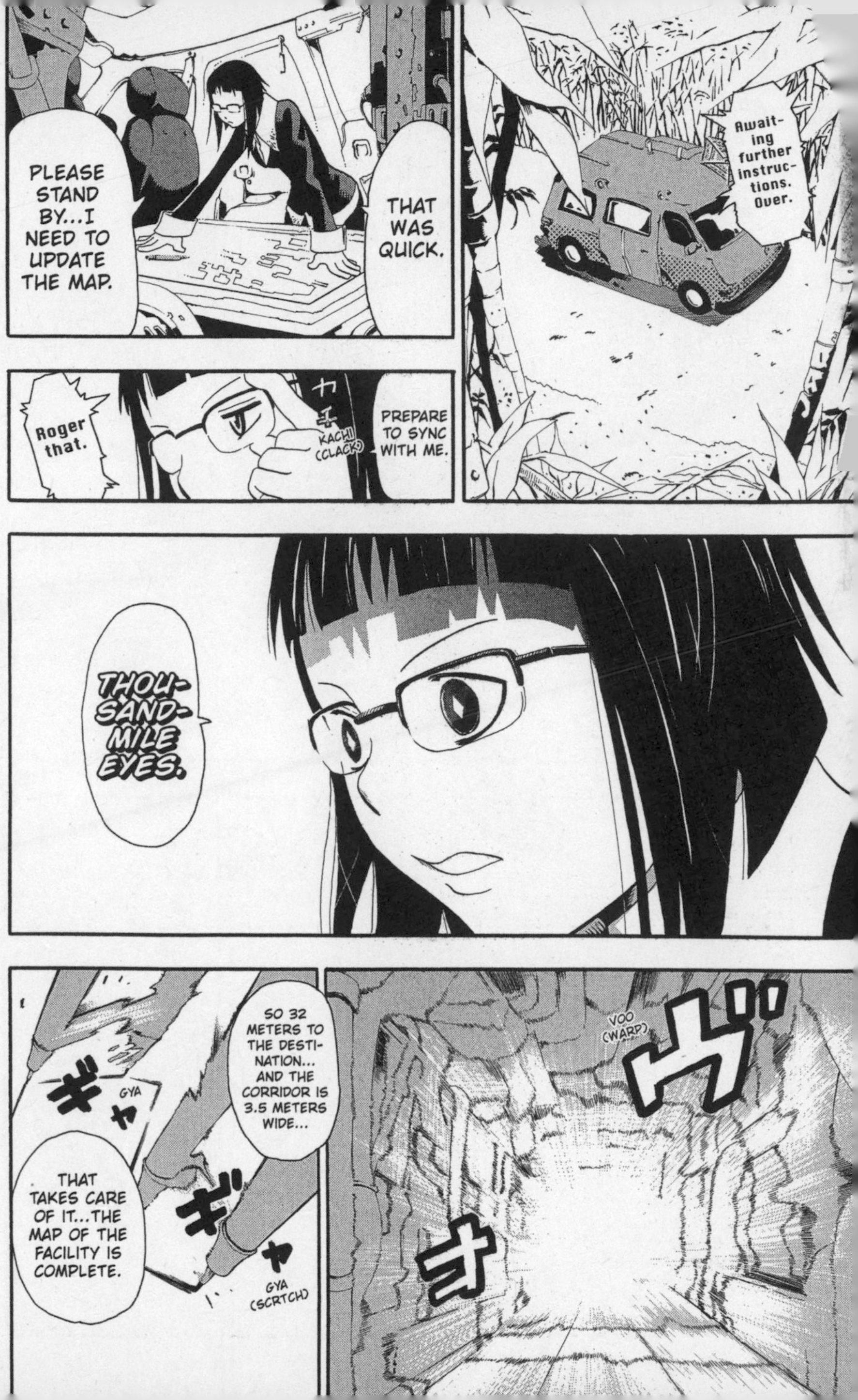
Await-ing further instruc-tions. Over.
THAT WAS QUICK.
PLEASE STAND BY...I NEED TO UPDATE THE MAP.
PREPARE TO SYNC WITH ME.
KACHI (CLACK)
Roger that.
THOU-SAND-MILE EYES.
VOO (WARP)
SO 32 METERS TO THE DESTI-NATION... AND THE CORRIDOR IS 3.5 METERS WIDE...
GYA
THAT TAKES CARE OF IT...THE MAP OF THE FACILITY IS COMPLETE.
GYA (SCRTCH)

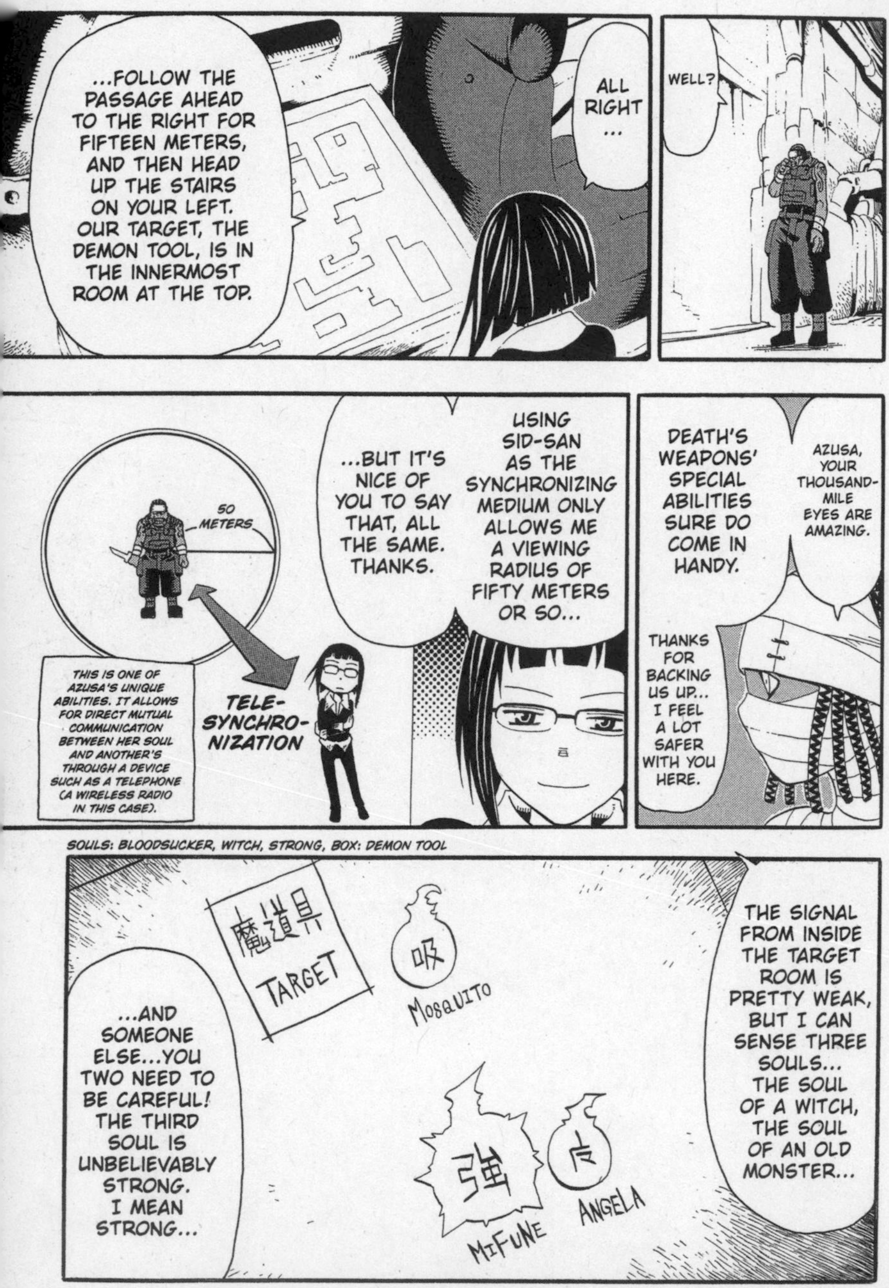
WELL?
ALL RIGHT...
...FOLLOW THE PASSAGE AHEAD TO THE RIGHT FOR FIFTEEN METERS, AND THEN HEAD UP THE STAIRS ON YOUR LEFT. OUR TARGET, THE DEMON TOOL, IS IN THE INNERMOST ROOM AT THE TOP.
AZUSA, YOUR THOUSAND-MILE EYES ARE AMAZING.
DEATH'S WEAPONS' SPECIAL ABILITIES SURE DO COME IN HANDY.
THANKS FOR BACKING US UP... I FEEL A LOT SAFER WITH YOU HERE.
USING SID-SAN AS THE SYNCHRONIZING MEDIUM ONLY ALLOWS ME A VIEWING RADIUS OF FIFTY METERS OR SO...
...BUT IT'S NICE OF YOU TO SAY THAT, ALL THE SAME. THANKS.
50 METERS
TELE-SYNCHRO-NIZATION
THIS IS ONE OF AZUSA'S UNIQUE ABILITIES. IT ALLOWS FOR DIRECT MUTUAL COMMUNICATION BETWEEN HER SOUL AND ANOTHER'S THROUGH A DEVICE SUCH AS A TELEPHONE (A WIRELESS RADIO IN THIS CASE).
SOULS: BLOODSUCKER, WITCH, STRONG, BOX: DEMON TOOL
THE SIGNAL FROM INSIDE THE TARGET ROOM IS PRETTY WEAK, BUT I CAN SENSE THREE SOULS... THE SOUL OF A WITCH, THE SOUL OF AN OLD MONSTER...
魔道具
TARGET
吸
MOSQUITO
疒
ANGELA
強
MIFUNE
...AND SOMEONE ELSE...YOU TWO NEED TO BE CAREFUL! THE THIRD SOUL IS UNBELIEVABLY STRONG. I MEAN STRONG...

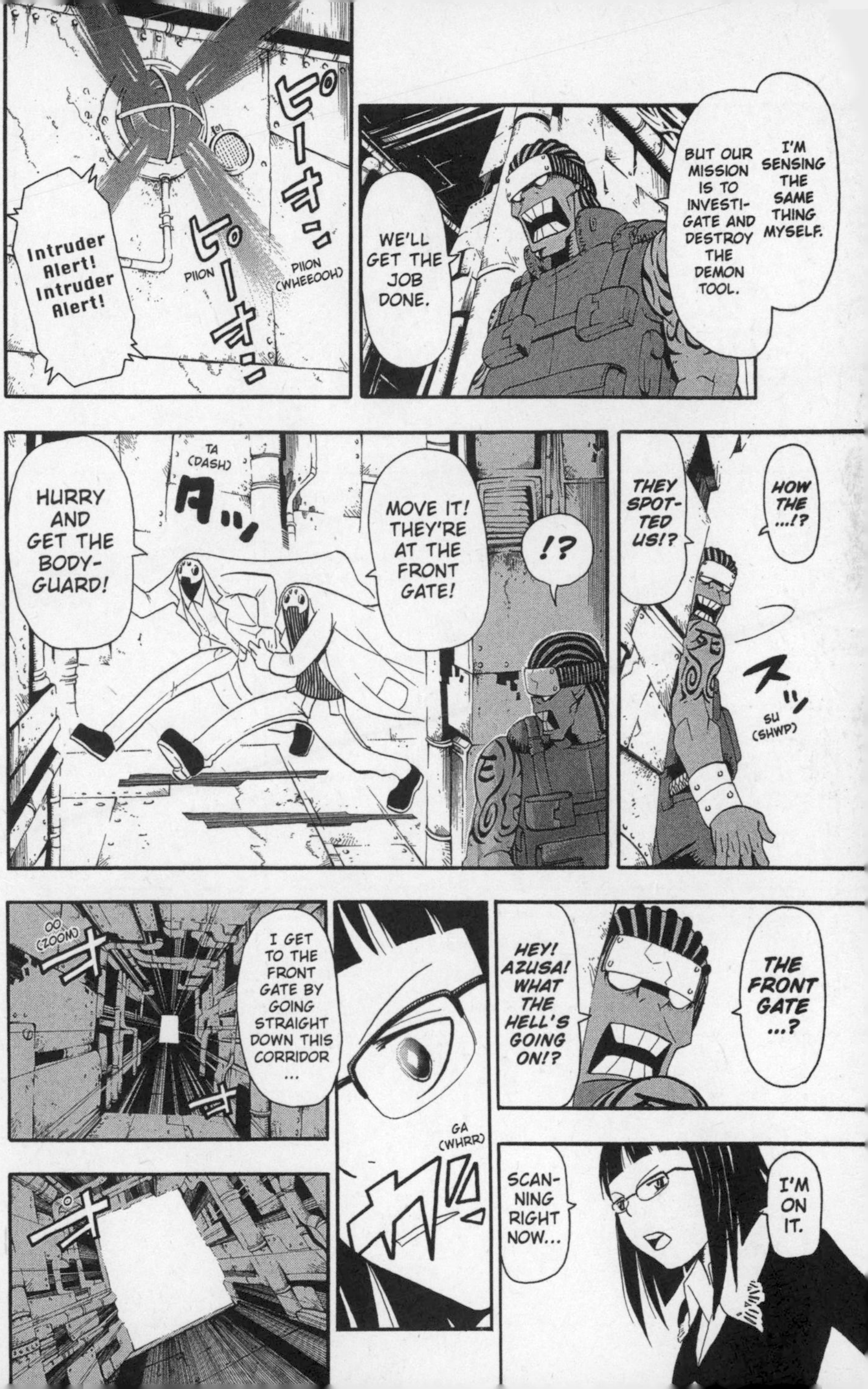
I'M SENSING THE SAME THING MYSELF.
BUT OUR MISSION IS TO INVESTI-GATE AND DESTROY THE DEMON TOOL.
WE'LL GET THE JOB DONE.
PIION (WHEEOOH)
PIION
Intruder Alert! Intruder Alert!
HOW THE ...!?
THEY SPOT-TED US!?
SU (SHWP)
!?
MOVE IT! THEY'RE AT THE FRONT GATE!
TA (DASH)
HURRY AND GET THE BODY-GUARD!
THE FRONT GATE ...?
HEY! AZUSA! WHAT THE HELL'S GOING ON!?
I GET TO THE FRONT GATE BY GOING STRAIGHT DOWN THIS CORRIDOR ...
OO (ZOOM)
I'M ON IT.
SCAN-NING RIGHT NOW...
GA (WHRR)

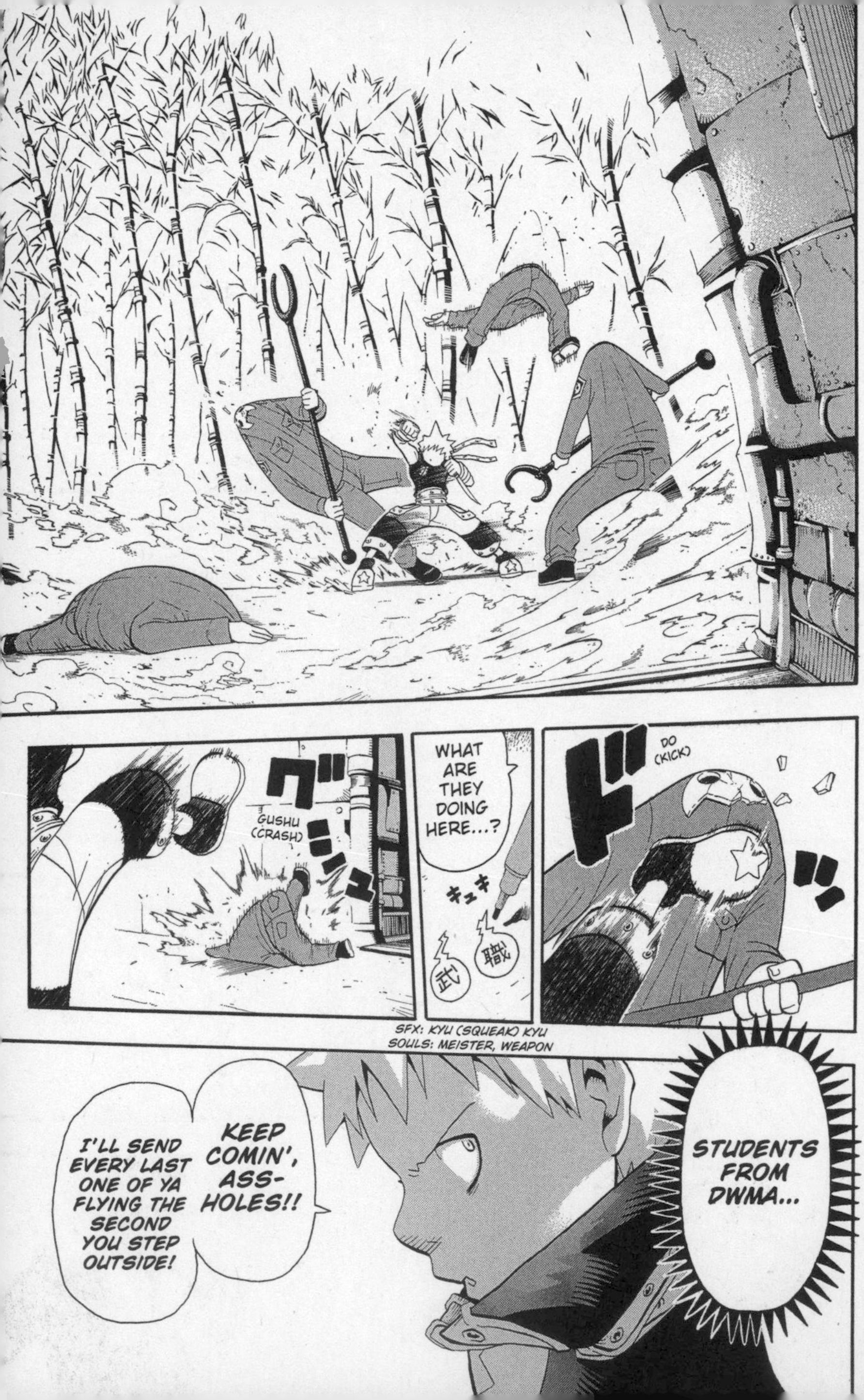
ドッ
DO (KICK)
WHAT ARE THEY DOING HERE...?
キュキ
職
武
グシュ
GUSHU (CRASH)
SFX: KYU (SQUEAK) KYU
SOULS: MEISTER, WEAPON
STUDENTS FROM DWMA...
KEEP COMIN', ASS-HOLES!!
I'LL SEND EVERY LAST ONE OF YA FLYING THE SECOND YOU STEP OUTSIDE!

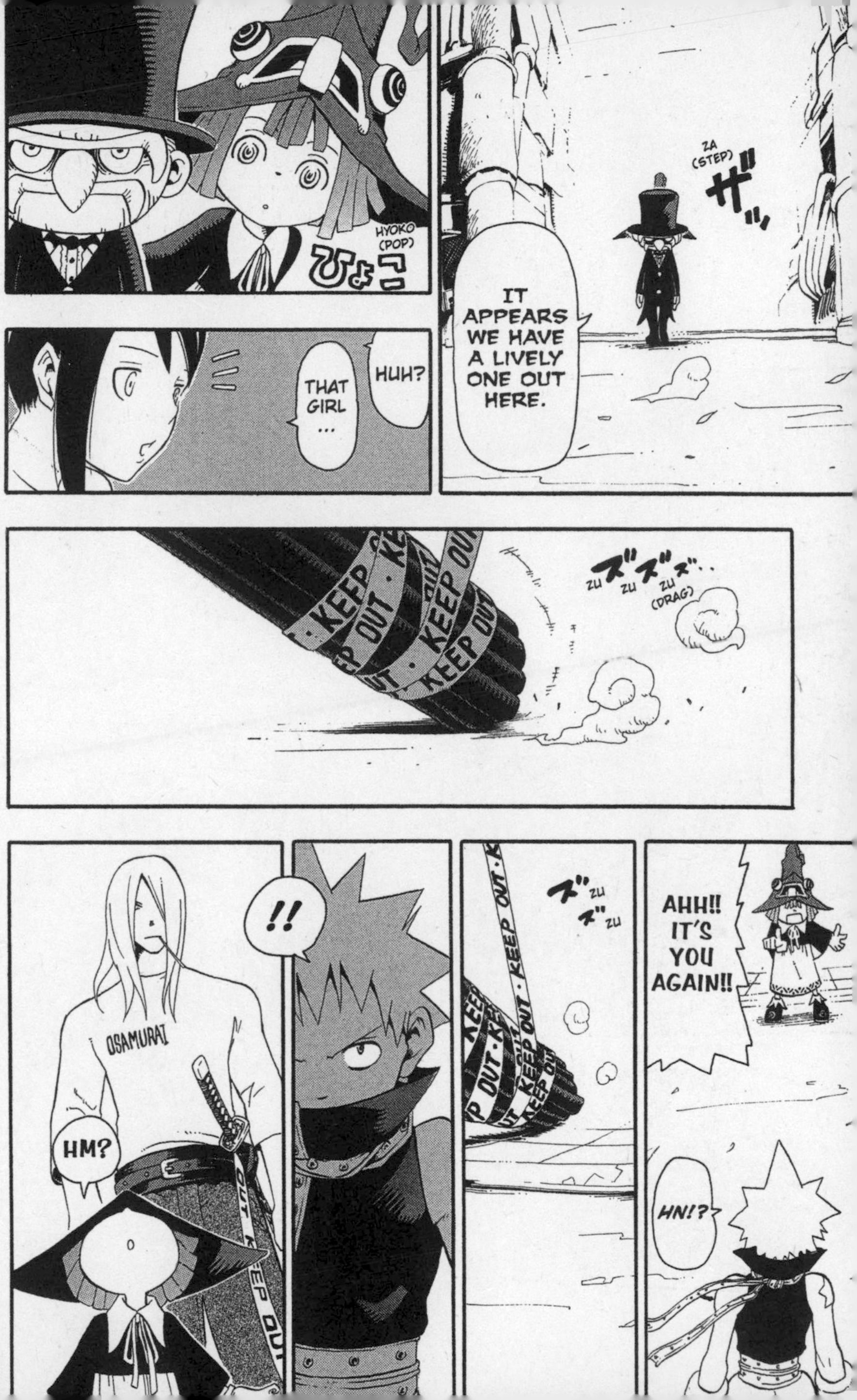
ZA
(STEP)
IT APPEARS WE HAVE A LIVELY ONE OUT HERE.
HYOKO
(POP)
HUH?
THAT GIRL ...
ZU ZU ZU
(DRAG)
AHH!! IT'S YOU AGAIN!!
HN!?
ZU ZU
!!
OSAMURAI
HM?

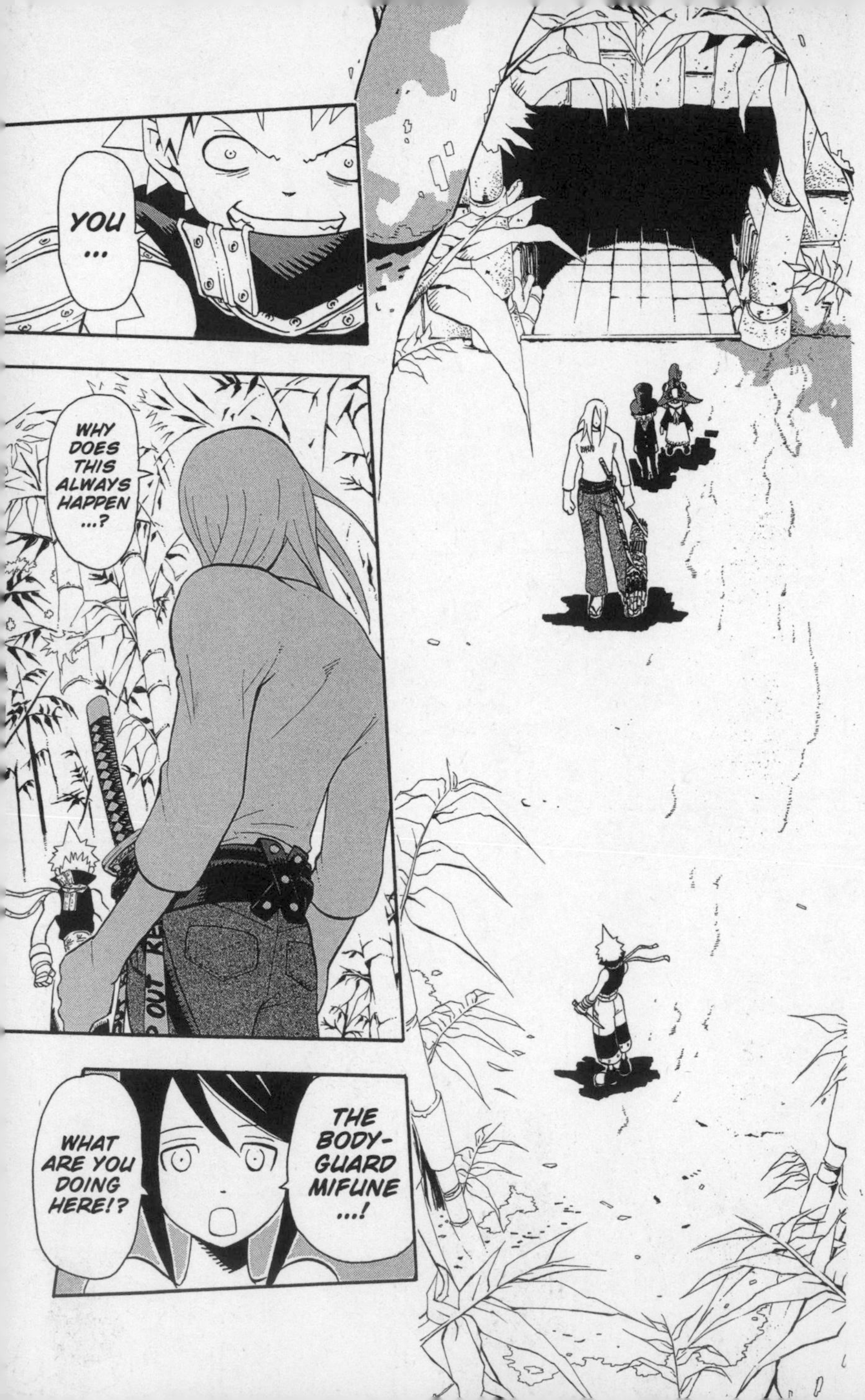
YOU ...
WHY DOES THIS ALWAYS HAPPEN ...?
THE BODY-GUARD MIFUNE ...!
WHAT ARE YOU DOING HERE!?

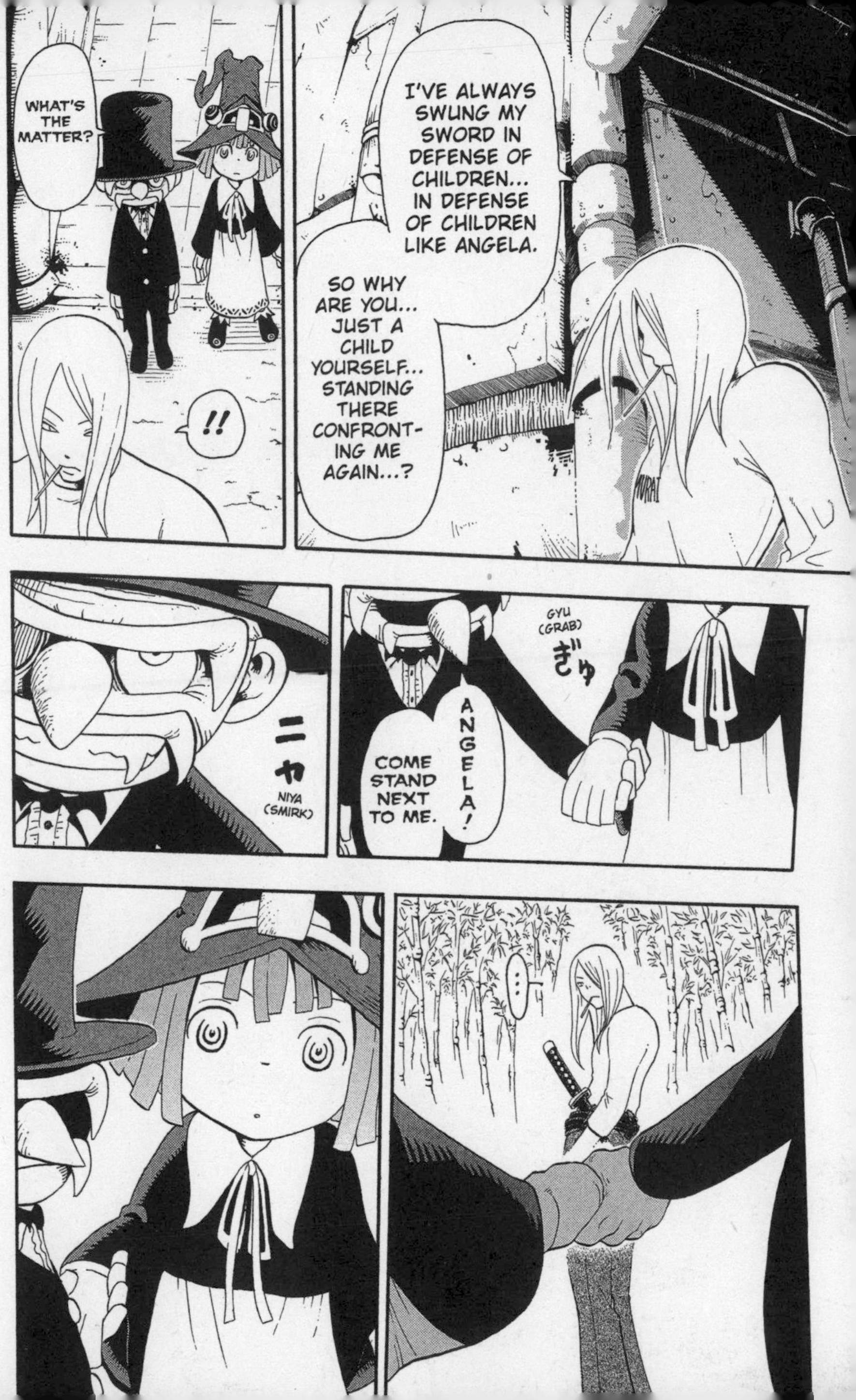
I'VE ALWAYS SWUNG MY SWORD IN DEFENSE OF CHILDREN... IN DEFENSE OF CHILDREN LIKE ANGELA.
SO WHY ARE YOU... JUST A CHILD YOURSELF... STANDING THERE CONFRONTING ME AGAIN...?
WHAT'S THE MATTER?
!!
GYU (GRAB)
ぎゅ
ANGELA!
COME STAND NEXT TO ME.
ニヤ
NIYA (SMIRK)
...

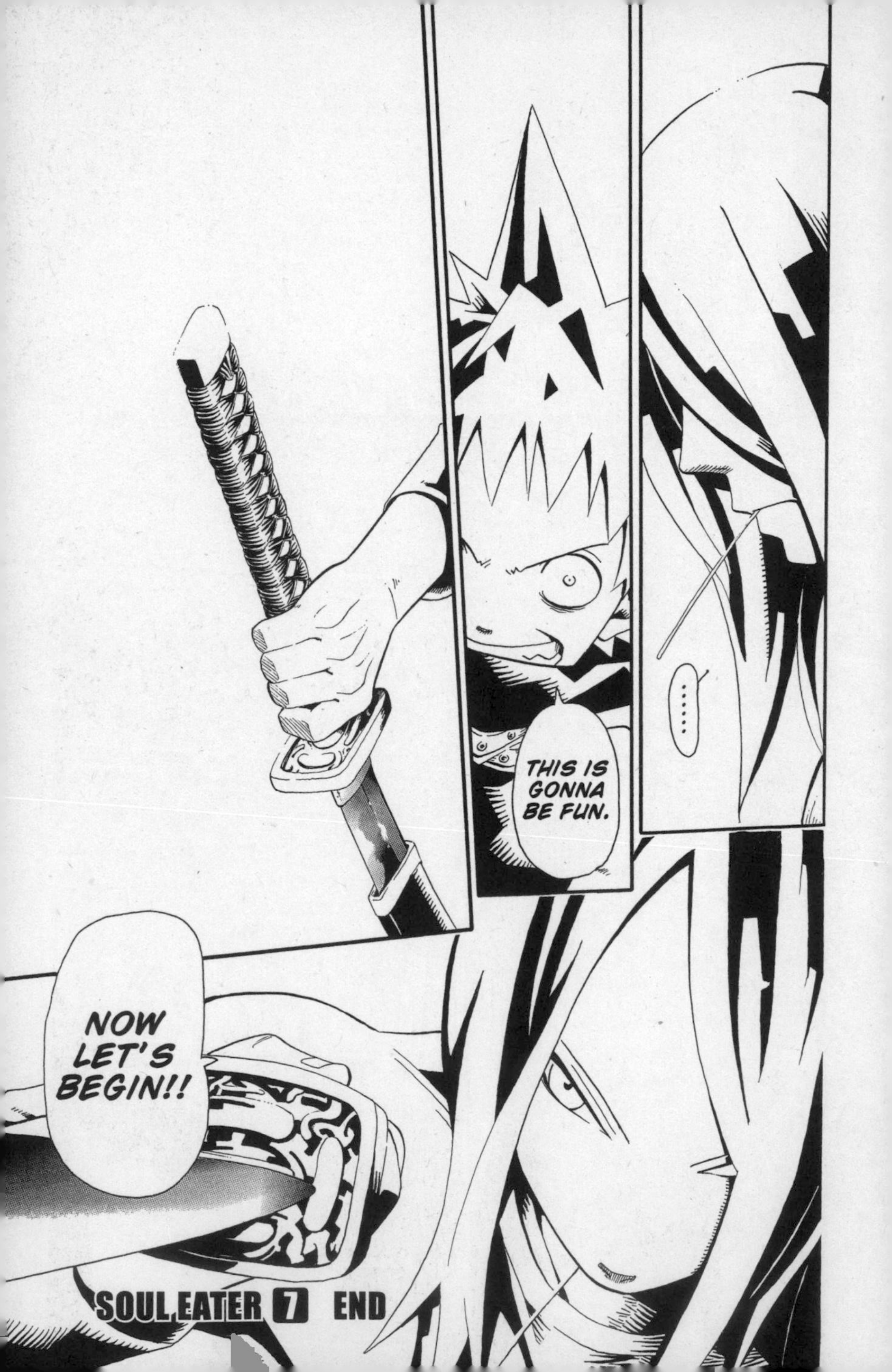
……
THIS IS GONNA BE FUN.
NOW LET'S BEGIN!!

SOUL EATER 7 END

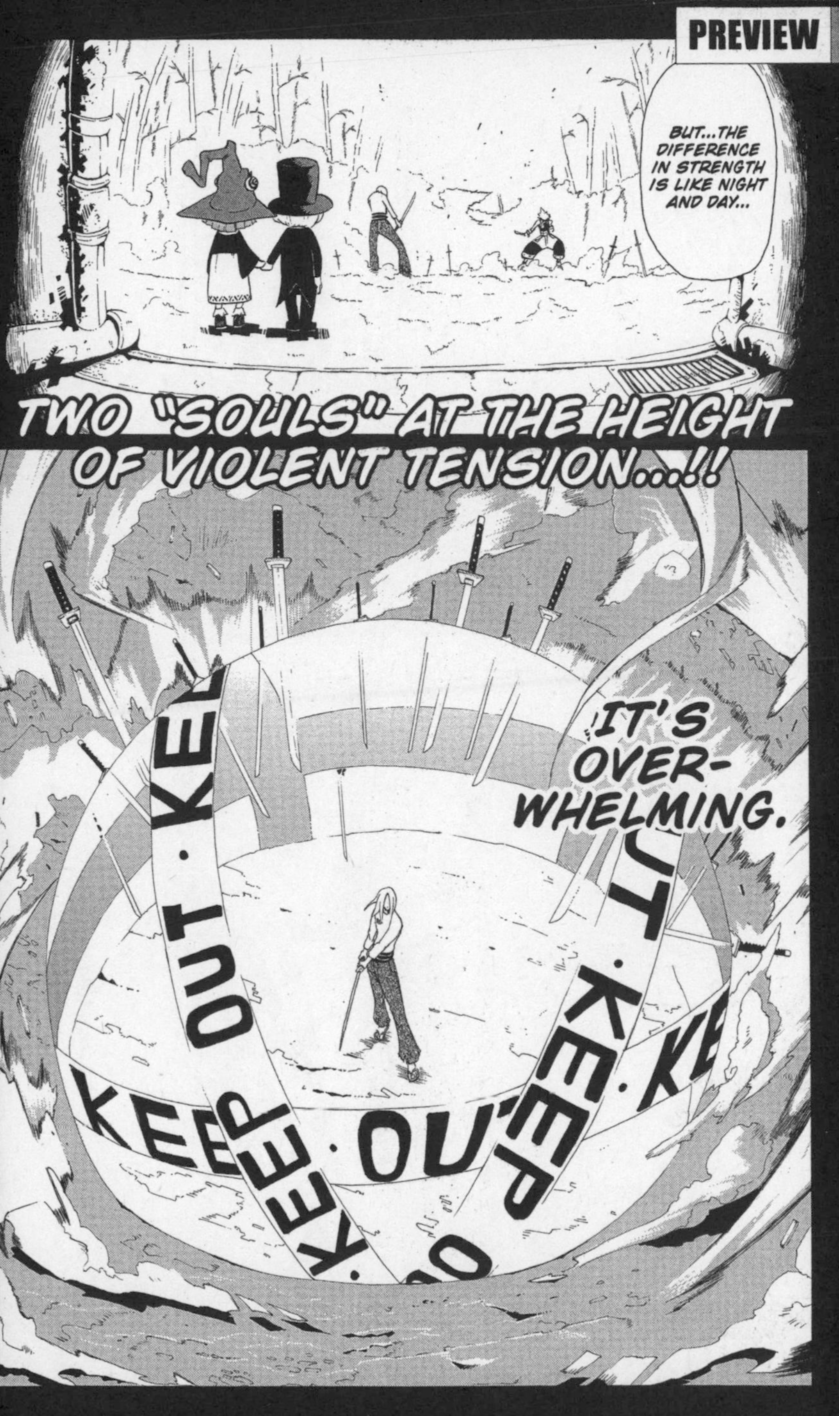
PREVIEW
BUT...THE DIFFERENCE IN STRENGTH IS LIKE NIGHT AND DAY...
TWO "SOULS" AT THE HEIGHT OF VIOLENT TENSION...!!
IT'S OVER-WHELMING.
KEEP OUT · KEEP · OUT · KEEP

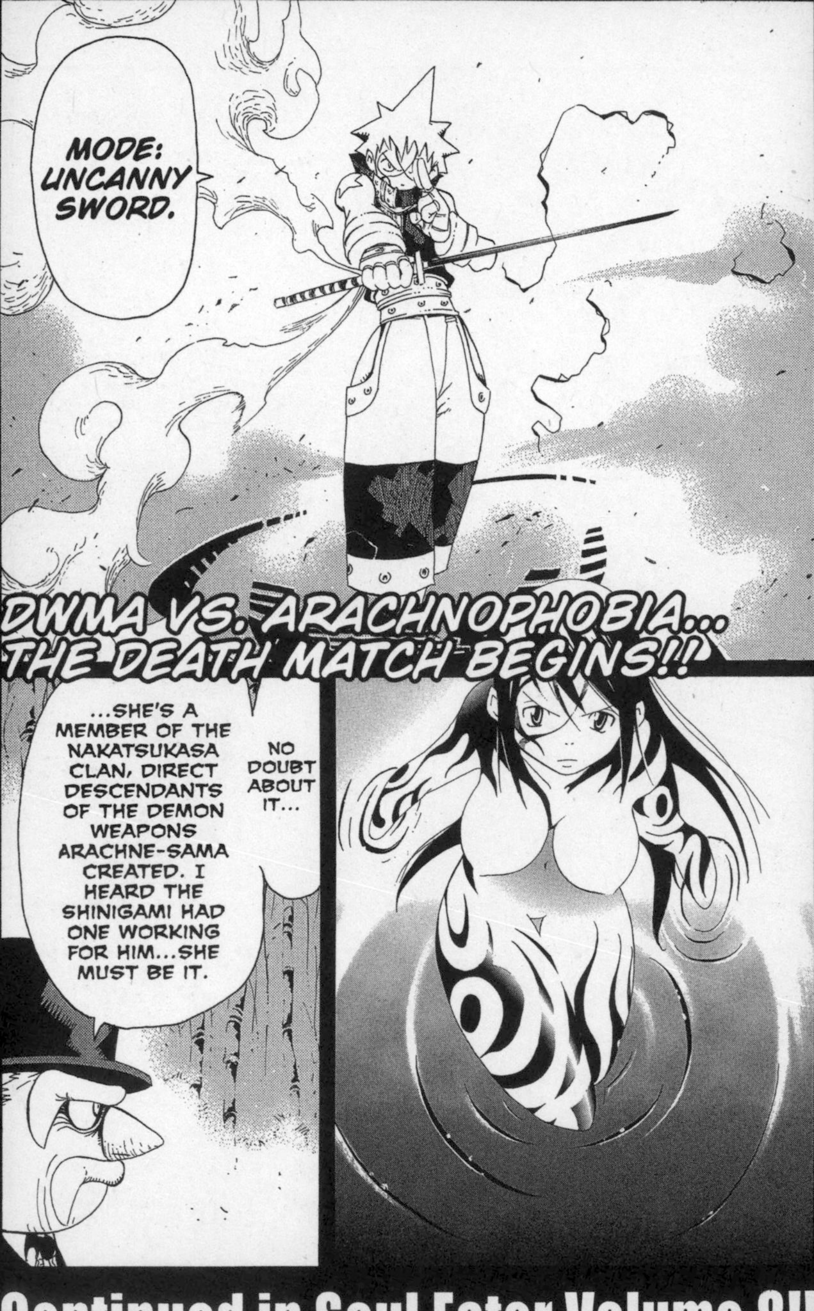
MODE: UNCANNY SWORD.
DWMA VS. ARACHNOPHOBIA... THE DEATH MATCH BEGINS!!
NO DOUBT ABOUT IT...
...SHE'S A MEMBER OF THE NAKATSUKASA CLAN, DIRECT DESCENDANTS OF THE DEMON WEAPONS ARACHNE-SAMA CREATED. I HEARD THE SHINIGAMI HAD ONE WORKING FOR HIM...SHE MUST BE IT.

Continued in Soul Eater Volume 8!!

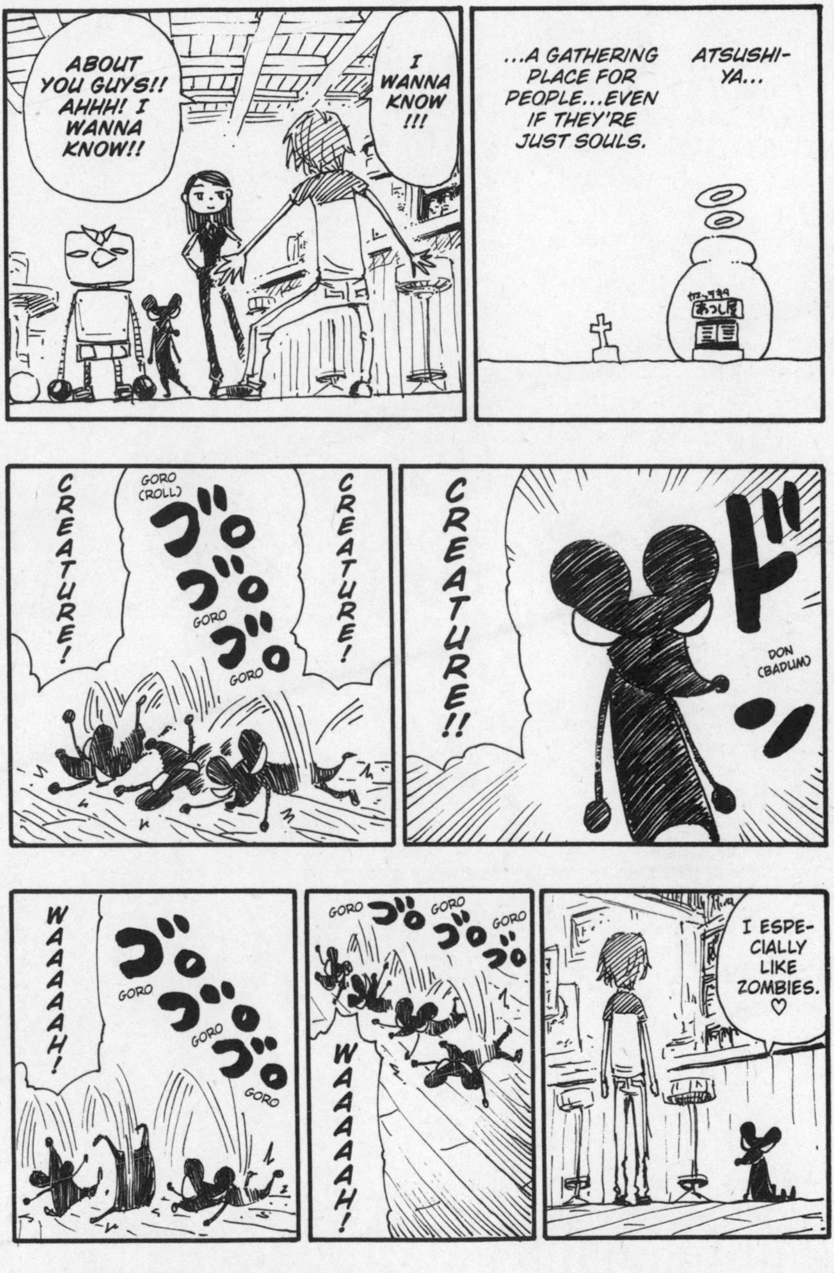
ATSUSHI-YA...
...A GATHERING PLACE FOR PEOPLE...EVEN IF THEY'RE JUST SOULS.
あつし屋
I WANNA KNOW!!!
ABOUT YOU GUYS!! AHHH! I WANNA KNOW!!
CREATURE!!
ドン
DON (BADUM)
CREATURE!
ゴロゴロゴロ
GORO (ROLL)
GORO
GORO
CREATURE!
I ESPECIALLY LIKE ZOMBIES. ♡
ゴロゴロゴ
GORO
GORO
GORO
WAAAAAAH!
WAAAAAAH!
ゴロゴロゴロ
GORO
GORO
GORO

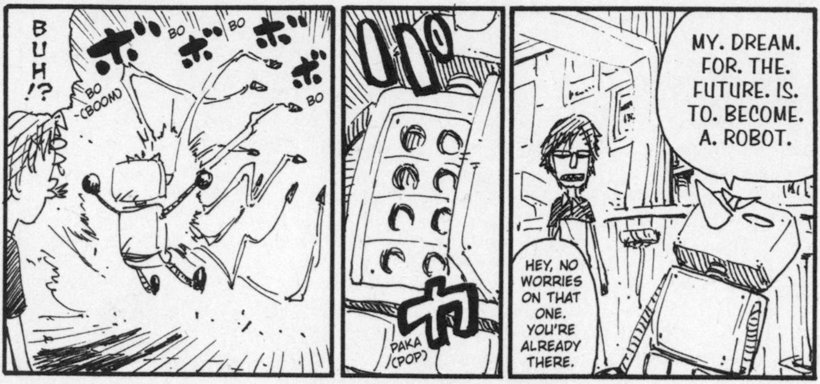
MY. DREAM. FOR. THE. FUTURE. IS. TO. BECOME. A. ROBOT.
HEY, NO WORRIES ON THAT ONE. YOU'RE ALREADY THERE.
PAKA (POP)
BO BO
BO
BO (BOOM)
BUH!?

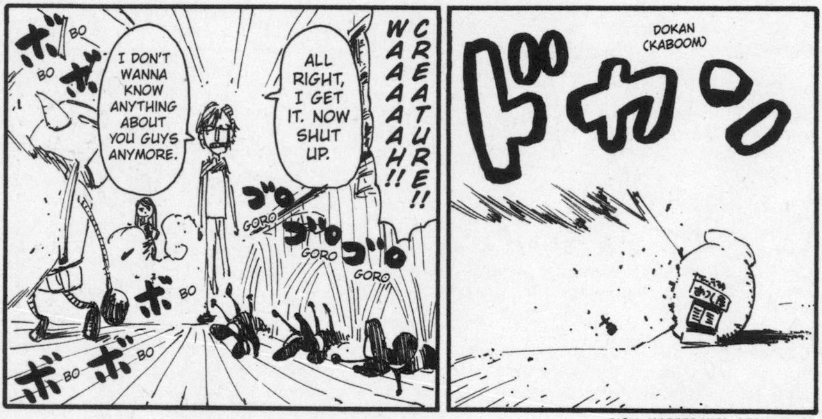
DOKAN (KABOOM)
CREATURE!!
WAAAAAAAH!!
ALL RIGHT, I GET IT. NOW SHUT UP.
I DON'T WANNA KNOW ANYTHING ABOUT YOU GUYS ANYMORE.
GORO
GORO
GORO
BO
BO
BO
BO BO

SIGN: KAETTE KITA, ATSUSHI-YA

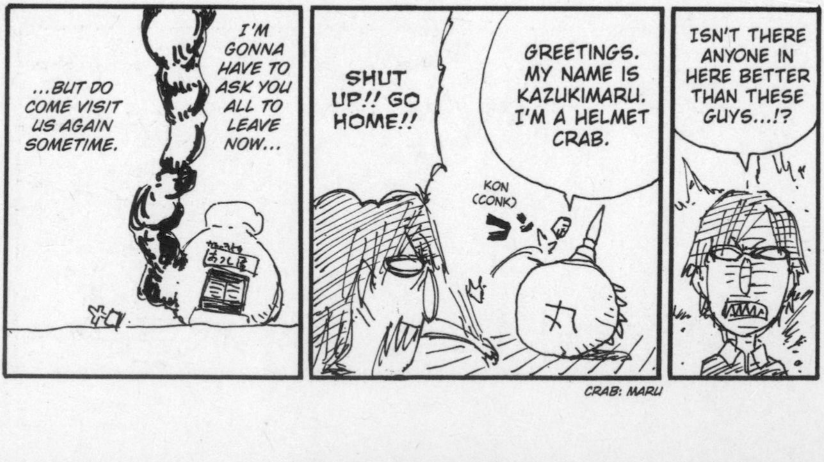
ISN'T THERE ANYONE IN HERE BETTER THAN THESE GUYS...!?
GREETINGS. MY NAME IS KAZUKIMARU. I'M A HELMET CRAB.
KON (CONK)
SHUT UP!! GO HOME!!
I'M GONNA HAVE TO ASK YOU ALL TO LEAVE NOW...
...BUT DO COME VISIT US AGAIN SOMETIME.

CRAB: MARU

Translation Notes

Common Honorifics

no honorific: Indicates familiarity or closeness; if used without permission or reason, addressing someone in this manner would constitute an insult.

-san: The Japanese equivalent of Mr./Mrs./Miss. If a situation calls for politeness, this is the fail-safe honorific.

-sama: Conveys great respect; may also indicate that the social status of the speaker is lower than that of the addressee.

-kun: Used most often when referring to boys, this indicates affection or familiarity. Occasionally used by older men among their peers, but it may also be used by anyone referring to a person of lower standing.

-chan: An affectionate honorific indicating familiarity used mostly in reference to girls; also used in reference to cute persons or animals of either gender.

-senpai: A suffix used to address upperclassmen or more experienced coworkers.

-sensei: A respectful term for teachers, artists, or high-level professionals.

Page 9
Marie Mjolnir is named after Thor's hammer from Norse mythology. The hammer was one of the most powerful weapons in the world, capable of crushing almost anything.

Azusa's name is a pun on *azusa yumi* "birchwood bow." In ancient Japan, bows were commonly made out of the wood of the Japanese cherry birch, so much so that the phrase *azusa yumi* came to be used as a stock phrase in poetry for conjuring up images of pulling and twanging.

Page 55
Rather than **Roomsy Korneikov**, Crona actually calls the room corners "*Heya no Sumisu*," a mixture of *heya no sumi* (room corner) and the Japanese pronunciation of the name "Smith." The joke makes very little sense in translation, so I adapted it by playing off the name of the Russian composer, Rimsky-Korsakov.

Page 66
According to Jewish legend, a **golem** is a dumb servant/protector made of mud or rocks that is magically animated by writing an inscription in Hebrew either somewhere on its body (usually the forehead) or on a piece of paper, which is then fed to the golem. The Hebrew word "*emet*" ("truth" in Hebrew, written as "emeth" here) is a typical activation word because when the first letter, *aleph*, is rubbed out, the word becomes "*met*" (death), which stops the golem dead in its tracks.

Page 68
The name of **Loew Village** comes from the famous legend of a 16th-century rabbi from Prague named Judah Loew ben Bezalel, who fashioned a golem from the mud of the Vltava river to protect a Jewish ghetto from the attacks of the anti-Semitic forces of the Holy Roman Empire.

Page 107
The name **Arachne** comes from the Greek word "*arachne*," meaning "spider." According to legend, the first spider was originally a human woman (named Arachne) who was such a skilled weaver that she boasted she could weave better than Athena (goddess of crafts, among other things). After a weaving contest that didn't end in her favor, Athena flew into a rage and turned Arachne into a spider.

Page 139
Justin's **Carcan Bras** attack comes from the French words "*carcan*" ("iron collar," e.g., a pillory) and "*bras*" ("arm.") As you can see from the art, his arm turns into an iron collar.

Page 141
Here Giriko uses **ane-san** (literally "big sister") to address Arachne. Both *ane-san* and the more standard *onee-san* are commonly used to address an older sister or older sister figure, but the *ane* variant also carries the nuance that the woman being addressed is tough or formidable in some way. It's also considerably less polite than *onee-san*.

Page 160
Baba Yaga Castle, Arachnophobia's base of operations, comes from the Slavic stories of the *baba yaga* (witchy old hag), a witch-like character that plays many roles in folklore.

Page 165
Mira Naigus's first name comes from the Japanese word for "mummy," and her last name is a pun on the Japanese pronunciation of the English word "knives" (*naibusu → naigusu*).

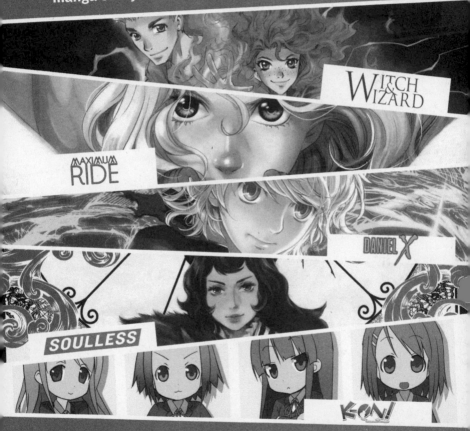
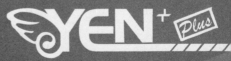

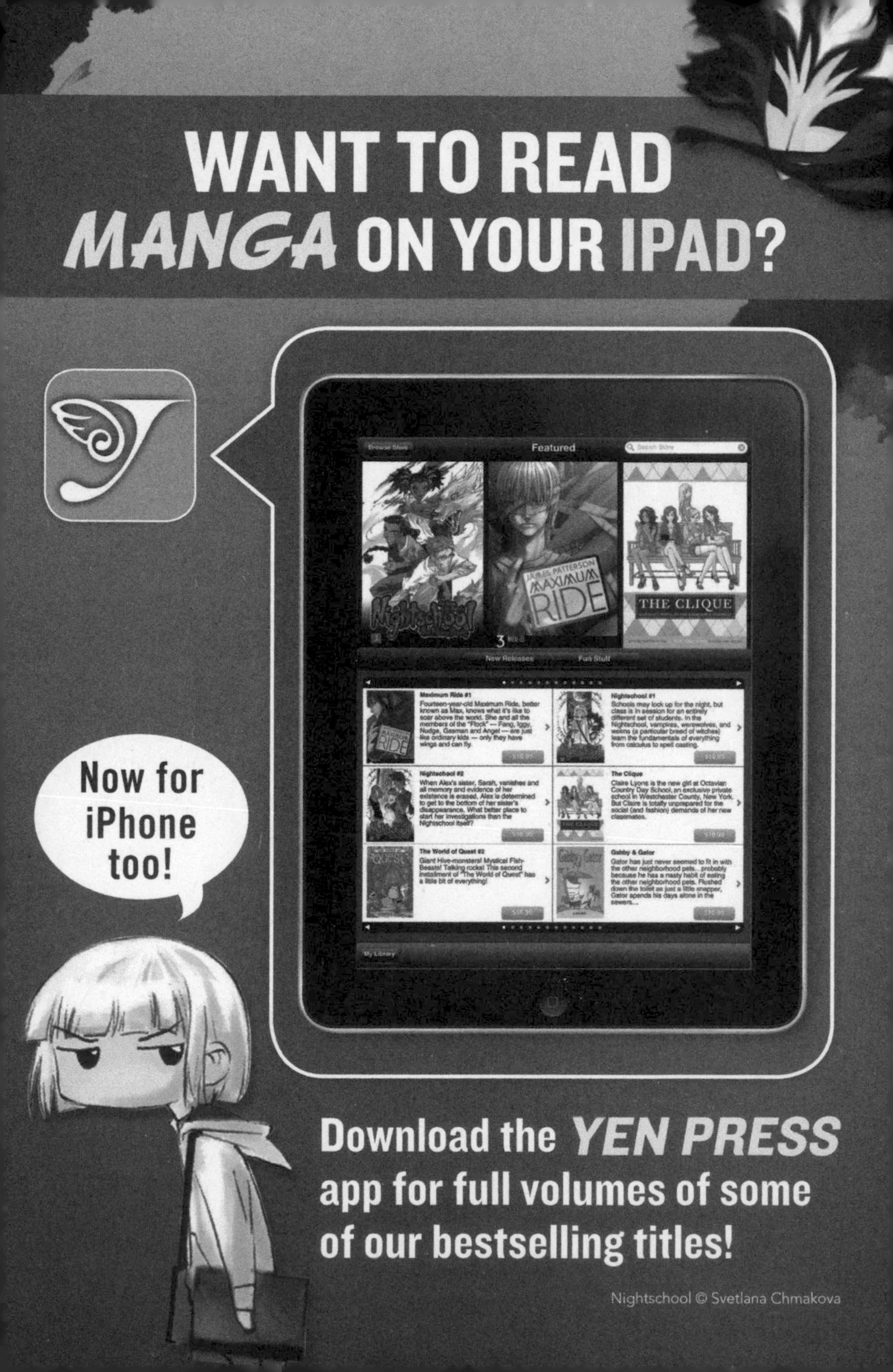
WANT TO READ
MANGA ON YOUR IPAD?
Featured
JAMES PATTERSON MAXIMUM RIDE
THE CLIQUE
New Releases
Fun Stuff
Now for iPhone too!
Download the YEN PRESS app for full volumes of some of our bestselling titles!
Nightschool © Svetlana Chmakova

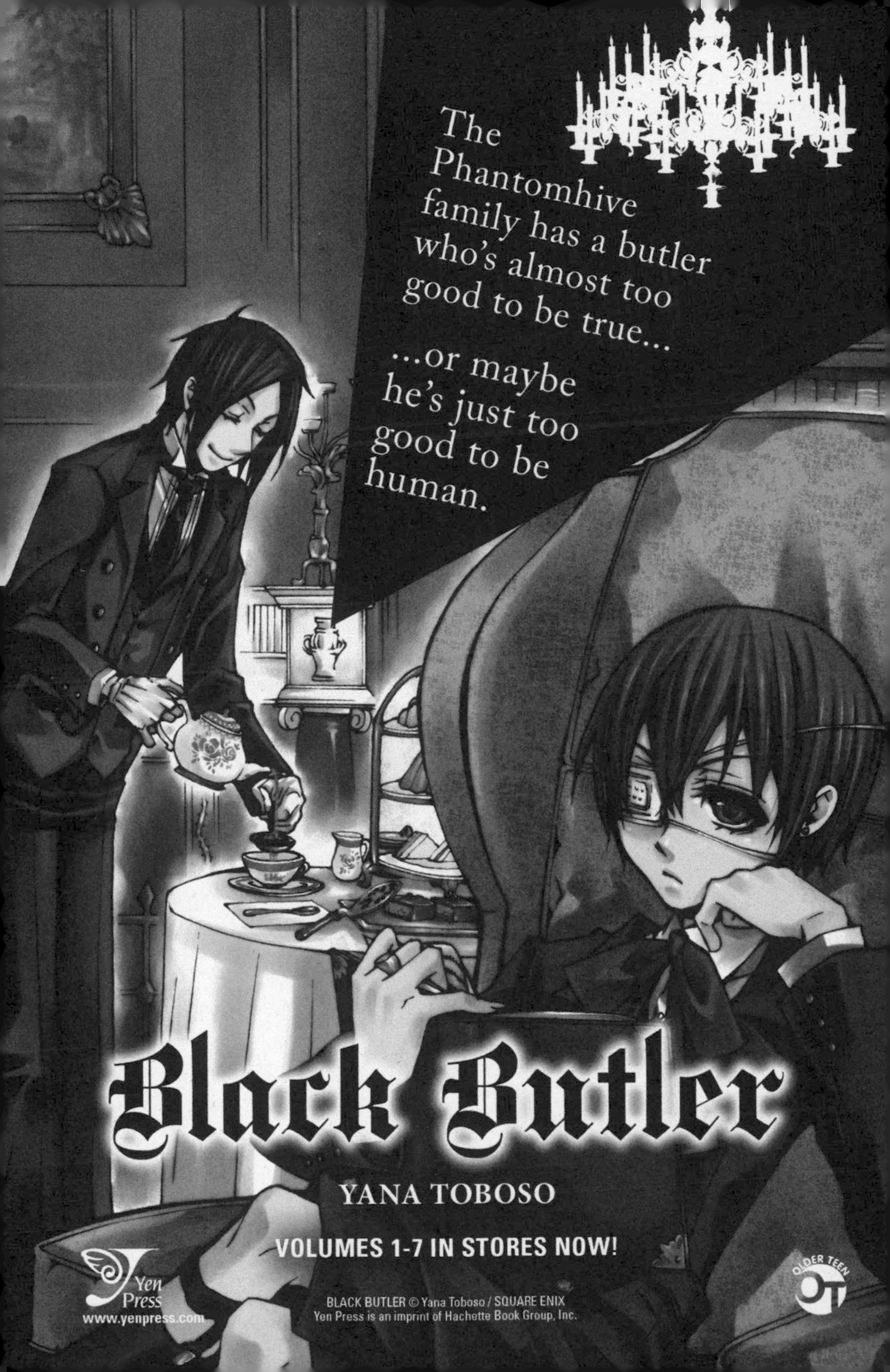

The Phantomhive family has a butler who's almost too good to be true...
...or maybe he's just too good to be human.
Black Butler
YANA TOBOSO
VOLUMES 1-7 IN STORES NOW!
Yen Press
www.yenpress.com
BLACK BUTLER © Yana Toboso / SQUARE ENIX
Yen Press is an imprint of Hachette Book Group, Inc.
OLDER TEEN
OT

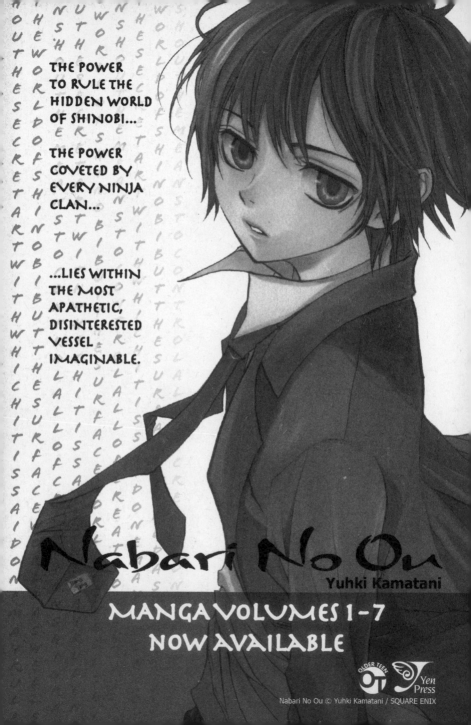

THE POWER
TO RULE THE
HIDDEN WORLD
OF SHINOBI...

THE POWER
COVETED BY
EVERY NINJA
CLAN...

...LIES WITHIN
THE MOST
APATHETIC,
DISINTERESTED
VESSEL
IMAGINABLE.

Nabari No Ou
Yuhki Kamatani

MANGA VOLUMES 1-7
NOW AVAILABLE

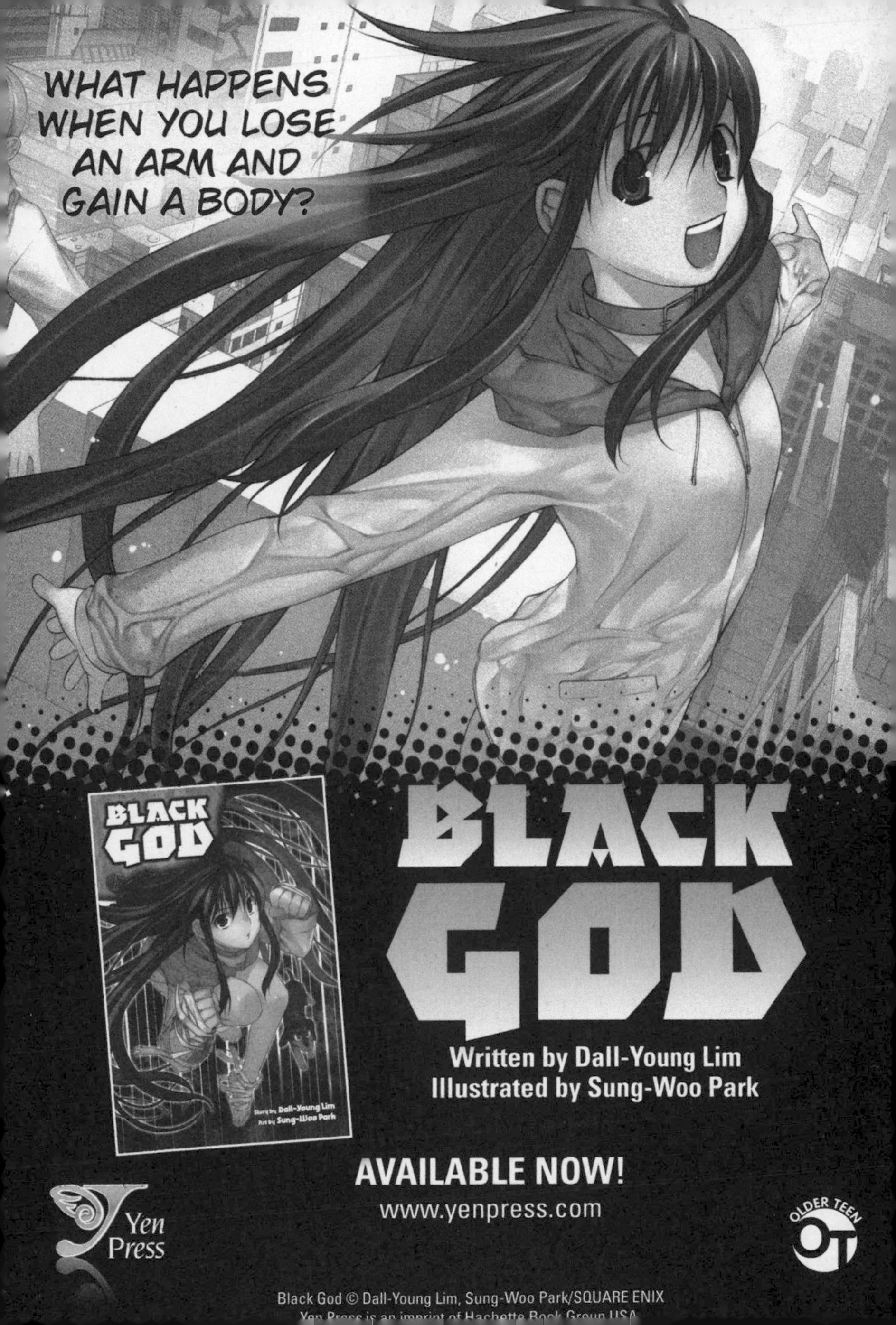
WHAT HAPPENS WHEN YOU LOSE AN ARM AND GAIN A BODY?
BLACK GOD
BLACK GOD
Story by Dall-Young Lim
Art by Sung-Woo Park
BLACK GOD
Written by Dall-Young Lim
Illustrated by Sung-Woo Park
AVAILABLE NOW!
www.yenpress.com
Yen Press
OLDER TEEN
OT
Black God © Dall-Young Lim, Sung-Woo Park/SQUARE ENIX
Yen Press is an imprint of Hachette Book Group USA

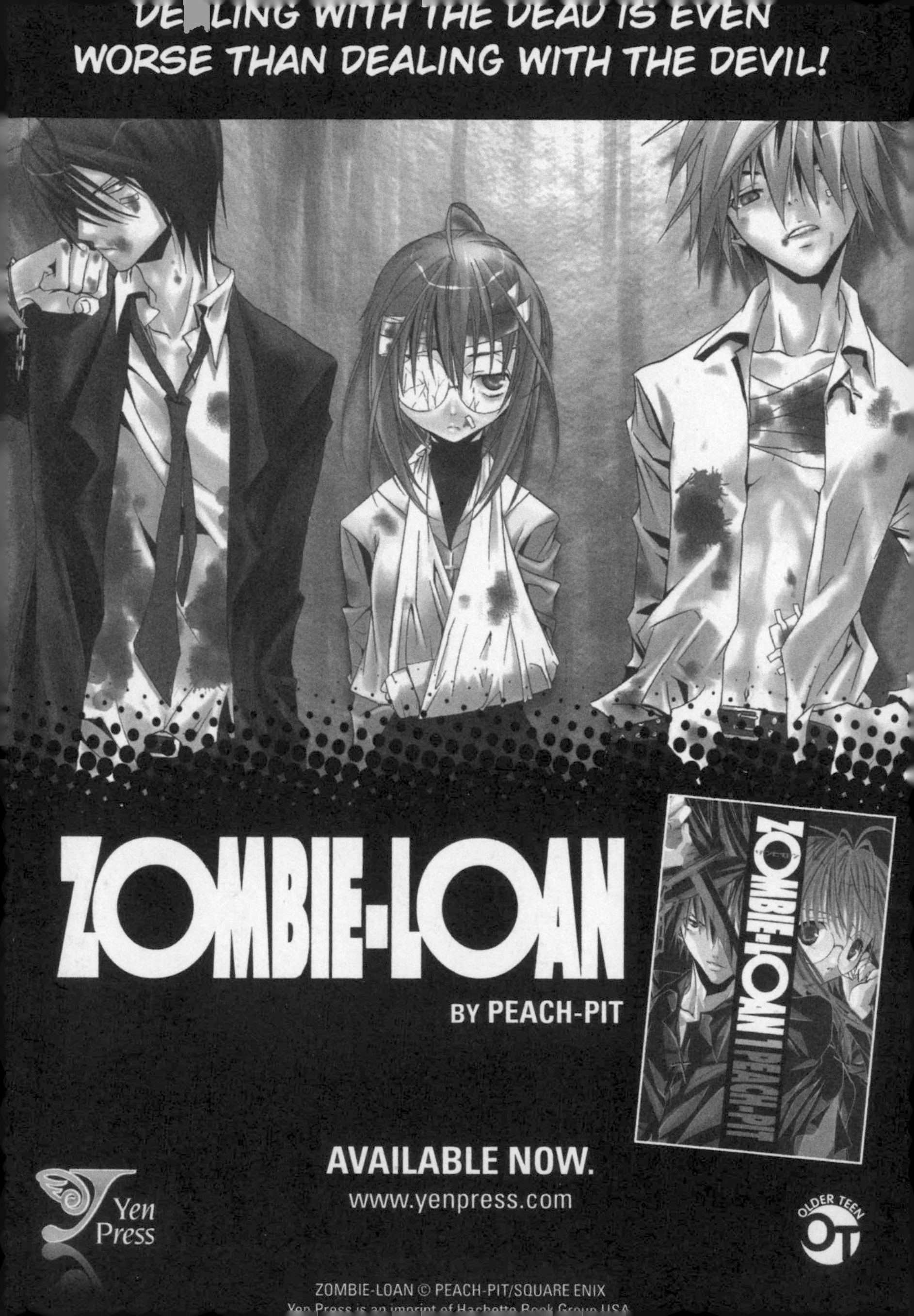
DEALING WITH THE DEAD IS EVEN
WORSE THAN DEALING WITH THE DEVIL!
ZOMBIE-LOAN
BY PEACH-PIT
ZOMBIE-LOAN 1 PEACH-PIT
AVAILABLE NOW.
www.yenpress.com
Yen Press
OLDER TEEN
OT
ZOMBIE-LOAN © PEACH-PIT/SQUARE ENIX
Yen Press is an imprint of Hachette Book Group USA

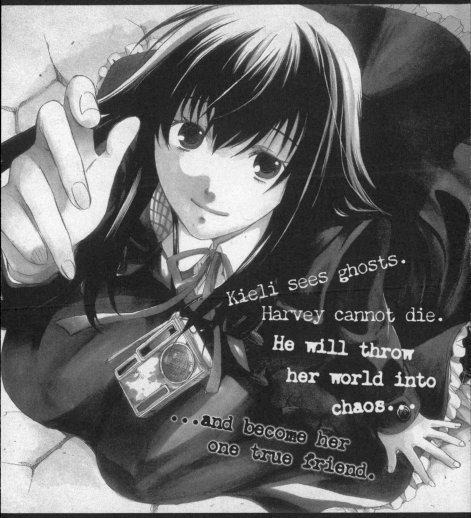
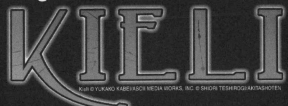

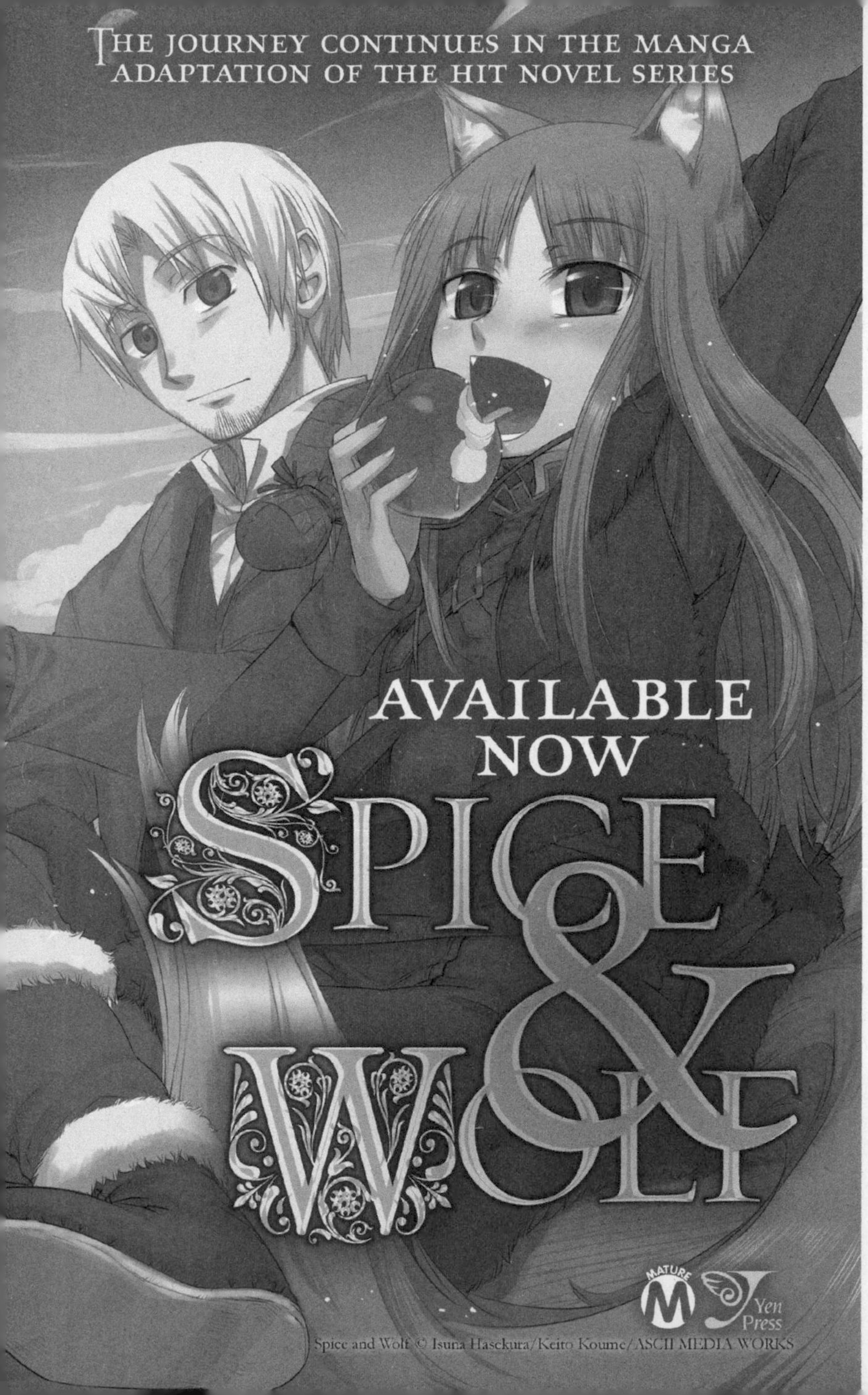
THE JOURNEY CONTINUES IN THE MANGA
ADAPTATION OF THE HIT NOVEL SERIES
AVAILABLE
NOW
SPICE & WOLF
MATURE
M
Yen
Press
Spice and Wolf © Isuna Hasekura/Keito Koume/ASCII MEDIA WORKS

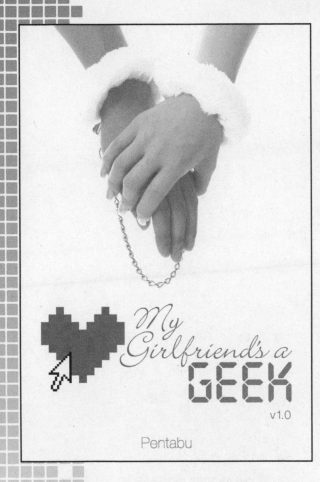

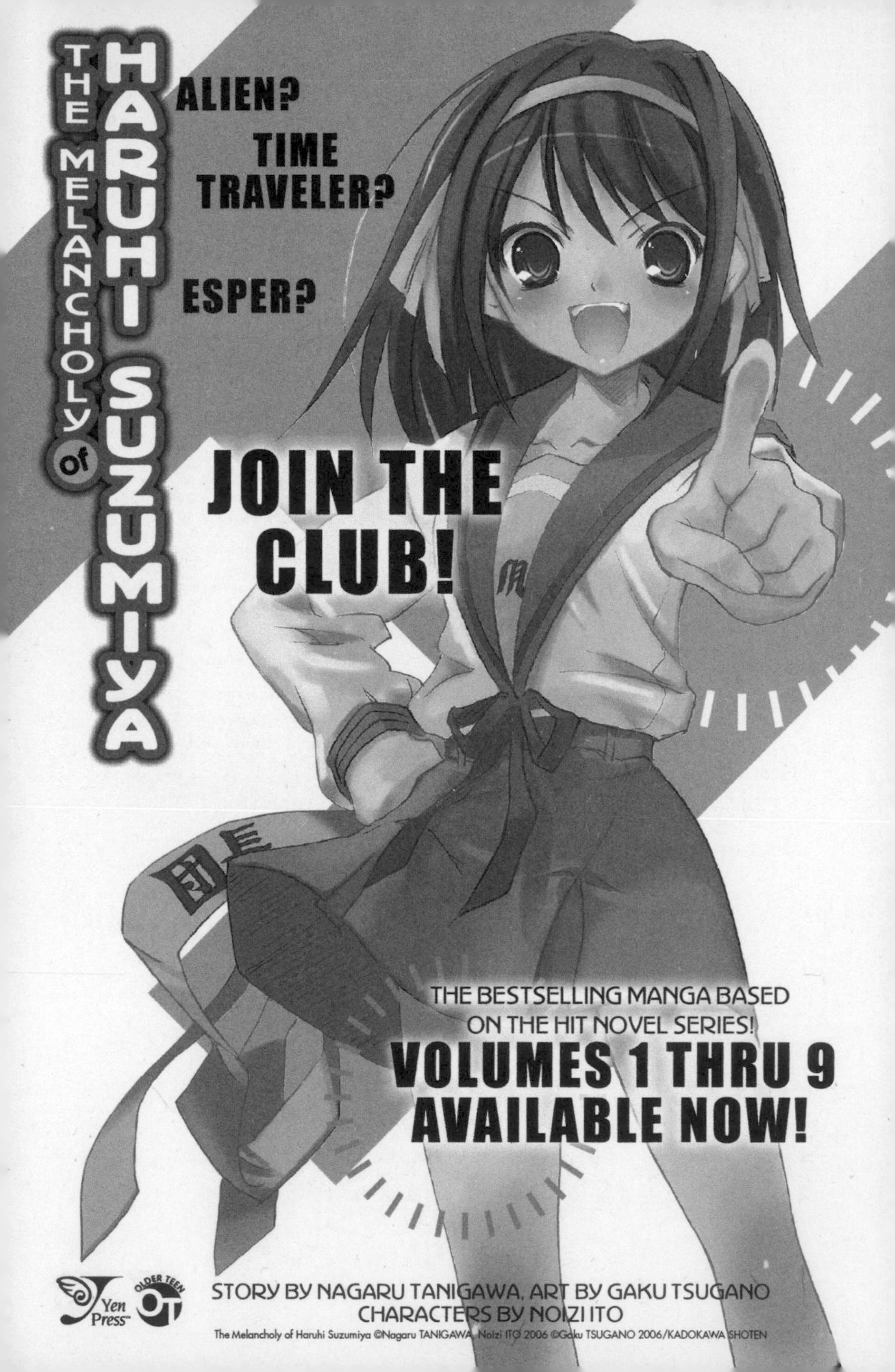

THE MELANCHOLY of HARUHI SUZUMIYA
ALIEN?
TIME TRAVELER?
ESPER?
JOIN THE CLUB!
THE BESTSELLING MANGA BASED ON THE HIT NOVEL SERIES!
VOLUMES 1 THRU 9 AVAILABLE NOW!
Yen Press
OLDER TEEN OT
STORY BY NAGARU TANIGAWA, ART BY GAKU TSUGANO
CHARACTERS BY NOIZI ITO
The Melancholy of Haruhi Suzumiya ©Nagaru TANIGAWA, Noizi ITO 2006 ©Gaku TSUGANO 2006/KADOKAWA SHOTEN

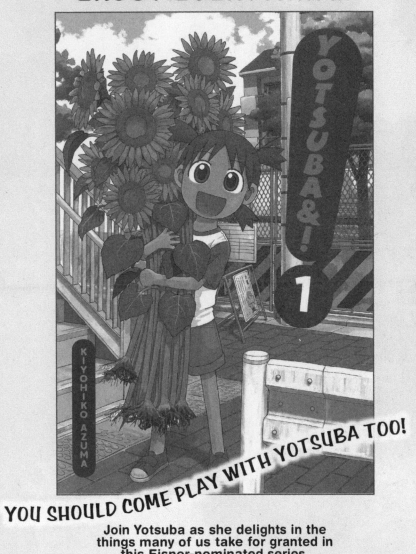

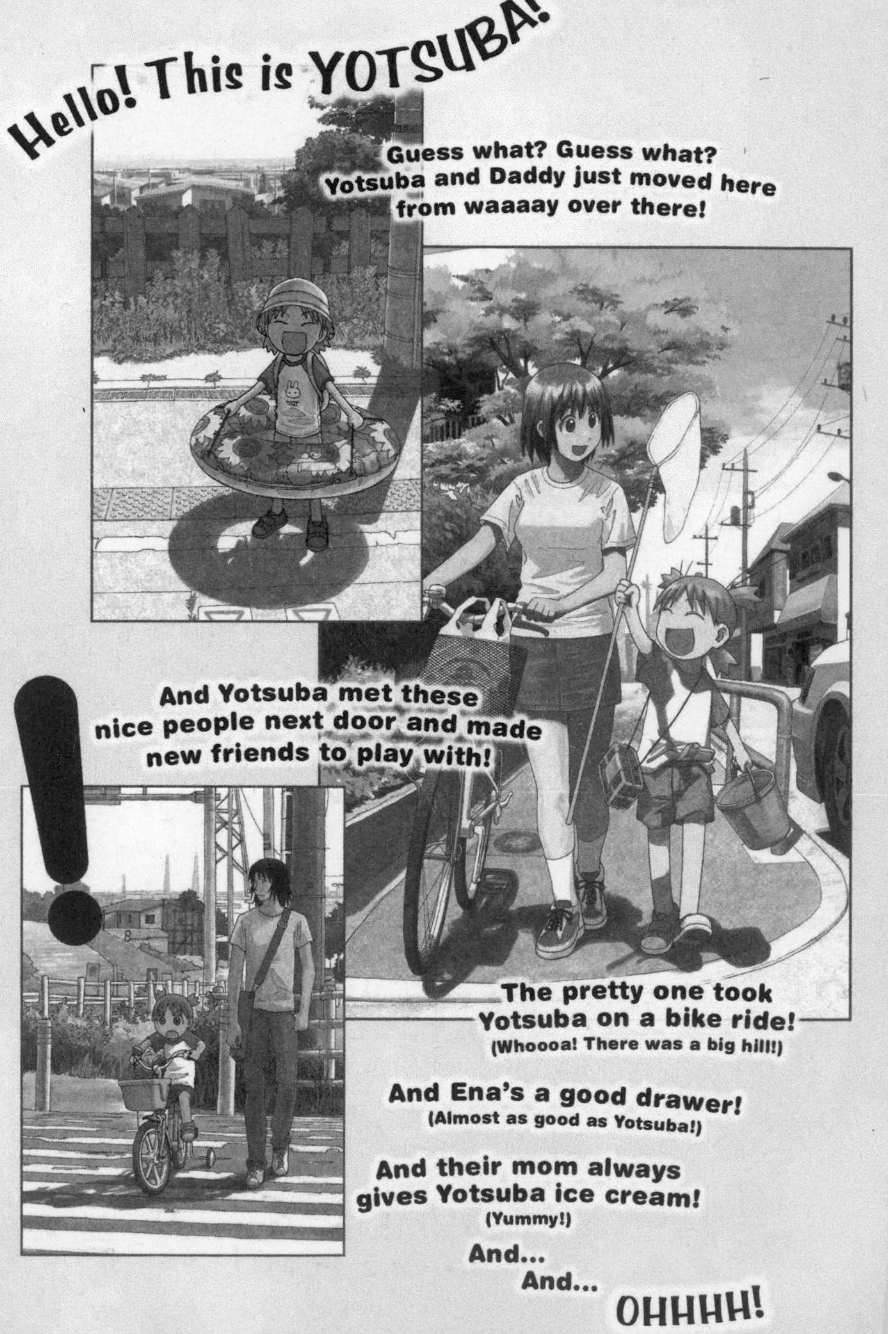

Hello! This is YOTSUBA!

Guess what? Guess what? Yotsuba and Daddy just moved here from waaaay over there!

And Yotsuba met these nice people next door and made new friends to play with!

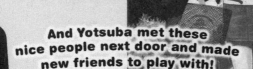

The pretty one took Yotsuba on a bike ride!
(Whoooa! There was a big hill!!)

And Ena's a good drawer!
(Almost as good as Yotsuba!)

And their mom always gives Yotsuba ice cream!
(Yummy!)

And...
And...
OHHHH!

SOUL EATER ⑦

ATSUSHI OHKUBO

Translation: Jack Wiedrick

Lettering: Alexis Eckerman

SOUL EATER Vol. 7 © 2006 Atsushi Ohkubo / SQUARE ENIX. All rights reserved. First published in Japan in 2006 by SQUARE ENIX CO., LTD. English translation rights arranged with SQUARE ENIX CO., LTD. and Hachette Book Group through Tuttle-Mori Agency, Inc.

Translation © 2011 by SQUARE ENIX CO., LTD.

Yen Press
Hachette Book Group
1290 Avenue of the Americas, New York, NY 10104

www.HachetteBookGroup.com
www.YenPress.com

Yen Press is an imprint of Hachette Book Group, Inc. The Yen Press name and logo are trademarks of Hachette Book Group, Inc.

First Yen Press Edition: October 2011

ISBN: 978-0-316-07110-9

10 9

BVG

Printed in the United States of America

D0557220